Goethe: Musical Poet, Musical Catalyst

Goethe: Musical Poet, Musical Catalyst

Proceedings of the Conference hosted by the
Department of Music
National University of Ireland
Maynooth
26 & 27 March 2004

Edited by Lorraine Byrne

Carysfort Press

A Carysfort Press Book in association with Peter Lang
Goethe: Musical Poet, Musical Catalyst Edited
by Lorraine Byrne

First published in Ireland in 2004 as a paperback original by
Carysfort Press, 58 Woodfield, Scholarstown Road,
Dublin 16, Ireland

ISBN 978-1-78997-105-7
© 2004
Copyright remains with the authors

Typeset by Carysfort Press
Cover design by Brian O'Connor

Caution: All rights reserved. No part of this book may be printed or reproduced or utilized in any form or by any electronic, mechanical, or other means, now known or hereafter invented including photocopying and recording, or in any information storage or retrieval system without permission in writing from the publishers.

Für Dan
Ein Lehrer, der die Welt eines großen Dichters erschließen kann,
verleiht ein Geschenk auf Lebenszeit.

Contents

Contributors	x
Editorial Note and Acknowledgements	xvii
List of Abbreviations	xxiii
List of Figures	xxiv
List of Illustrations	xxv
List of Musical Quotations	xxvi
List of Tables	xxvii
Message from Dr Gottfried Haas, Ambassador of the Federal Republic of Germany	xxix
Micheal O'Siadhail, 'Hopscotch' and 'Caprice'	xxxi

Preface 1
Susan Youens

A: Goethe's Musical Aesthetics

1 | Goethe's Presence in the Vienna Music Scene of his Era 7
Otto Biba

2 | Goethe and Zelter: An Exchange of Musical Letters 41
Lorraine Byrne

B: Goethe and Beethoven

3 | Göthe and Beethowen: Men of Genius between Distance and Affinity 69
Claus Canisius

4 | 'Ich denke dein': Beethoven's Retelling of Goethe's Poetry 100
Amanda Glauert

5 | *Fidelio* and *Faust* in the German 'Wende' of 1989/90 126
Moray McGowan

C: Goethe as Musical Catalyst

6 | Goethe and the Czechs 159
Jan Smaczny

7 | Bettina von Arnim, Goethe and the Boundaries of Creativity 185
Briony Williams

8 | *Blumengruß und Blumenglöckchen*: Goethe's Influence on Anton Webern 203
Gareth Cox

D: Musical and Philosophical Reflections
of *Wilhelm Meisters Lehrjahre*

9 | 'Thealogy': Gods, Goddesses, and *Wilhelm Meisters Lehrjahre* 225
Nicholas Boyle

10 | Schumann's *Requiem für Mignon* and the Concept of Music as Literature 242
Julian Horton

11 | Mignon's Exequies and Aesthetic Reflections of the Liturgy in Music 272
Adolf Nowak

12 | Mignon und der Harfner 294
Seóirse Bodley

Appendices
Appendix 1 | Conference Programme *346*
Appendix 2 | Goethe and the Guitar *352*
Index *365*

Contributors

Otto Biba is Director of the Archives, the Library and the Collections of the Gesellschaft der Musikfreunde in Vienna. He has lectured at the University of Vienna and was Professor at the University for Music in Vienna from 1973 to 2002. He is a member of international musicological institutions (e.g. Zentralinstitut für Mozartforschung Salzburg, Joseph Haydn-Institut Köln) and member of managing and advisory committees of international publication projects (e.g. Johannes Brahms Complete Edition, München-Kiel). He has numerous publications, primarily on old-Austrian music history of the 17th to 20th century, and has prepared editions of over 120 compositions of the 18th and 19th century. He is responsible for the scientific organization of music exhibitions in Austria, Europe, USA and Japan.

Seóirse Bodley, Emeritus Professor UCD, was born in Dublin. Studies in Ireland and Germany led to a teaching appointment at the Music Department of University College Dublin, where he was awarded the degree of D.Mus.

Influences on his compositions include a range of musical styles from the European avant-garde to Irish traditional music. His works include five symphonies for full orchestra, two chamber symphonies and numerous orchestral, choral, vocal and chamber pieces. The many commissions he has received include his Third Symphony, commissioned for the opening of the National Concert Hall in Dublin, and his Fourth Symphony, commissioned by the Arturo Toscanini Symphony Orchestra of Parma, Italy. In addition to many performances in Ireland, his music has been broadcast and performed in North America, many European countries, Australia and China. Awards include the Arts Council Prize for Composition, a Travelling Studentship of the National University of Ireland, the Macauley Fellowship in Music Composition and the Marten Toonder Award. His is founder-member of Aosdána, Ireland's academy of creative artists.

Recent works include: the piano-piece *Chiaroscuro*, premiered at the AXA Dublin International Piano Competition (2000). A *Sinfonietta* commissioned and premiered by the Irish National Youth Orchestra and included in their millennium tour of Ireland and Germany ending with a performance at the Konzerthaus, Berlin (2000). The first performance of *Earlsfort Suite* for mezzo Bernadette Greevy and orchestra, National Concert Hall, 2000. More recently: *News from Donabate*, a fifty-minute work for solo piano (2001); *An Exchange of Letters* for solo piano (2002) performed by Rolf Hind in the NCH; *After Great Pain*, song-cycle (2002) performed by Aylish Kerrigan (mezzo soprano) and Gabrielle Schimmerling (piano) in Stuttgart.

Seóirse Bodley's first Goethe setting, that of *Wandrers Nachtlied*, was performed last year, leading on to his song-cycle *Mignon und der Harfner*, first performed in March 2004 at the conference, 'Goethe: Musical Poet, Musical Catalyst', NUI Maynooth. This cycle was the first of three new compositions premiered in the early months of 2004; the others are *Metamorphoses on the name Schumann* for orchestra, premiered at the National Concert Hall Dublin by the National Symphony Orchestra under Gerhardt Markson and the third string quartet *Ave atque Vale*, performed by the Vogler Quartet in Sligo.

Nicholas Boyle was born in London in 1946 and was brought up in Malvern and Worcester. He studied Modern Languages at Cambridge in Magdalene College, of which he has been a Fellow since 1968, and apart from spells working in Göttingen and Berlin he has taught German in Cambridge ever since. He was made Reader in German Literary and Intellectual History in 1993 and Professor in 2000 and from 1996 to 2001 was the Head of the Department of German. He is probably best known for his biography of Goethe, still in progress (volume 1, 1991, volume 2, 2000), which has been translated into German and has won several prizes. He is also the author of *Who Are We Now?*; *Christian Humanism and the Global Market from Hegel to Heaney*, a volume of essays on the contemporary world, and in 2002-03 delivered the Erasmus Lectures at Notre Dame University on *Sacred and Secular Scriptures: a Catholic approach to literature*, published in 2004. He is a Fellow of the British Academy and in 2000 was awarded the Goethe Medal of the Goethe Institute. In 1983 Nicholas Boyle married Rosemary Devlin, a lawyer, and they have four children.

Lorraine Byrne holds a PhD in German and Music from University College Dublin with primary degrees in Music, English and German. In February 2001 she was awarded the Goethe Prize by the English Goethe Society; in July 2001 she was awarded an IRCHSS Government of Ireland Post-Doctoral Fellowship to pursue full-time research in the Department of Germanic Studies, Trinity College Dublin; in June 2003 she was appointed Post-Doctoral Fellow in the Department of Music, NUI Maynooth and in

July 2004 she was appointed Head of the Department of Music at Mater Dei, a College of Dublin City University.

Dr Byrne's book on *Schubert's Goethe Settings* was published by Ashgate in 2003. Her piano reduction of the Schubert/Goethe *Singspiel, Claudine von Villa Bella*, was published by Carysfort Press in December 2002 and the first stage performance in English of this *Singspiel* took place in Dublin in April 2003. She is co-editor of *Goethe and Schubert: Across the Divide* (Dublin: Carysfort Press, December 2003), and is currently completing a critical translation of the discussion of music in Goethe's letters to the composer, Zelter.

Dr Byrne has lectured extensively and internationally including Rhodes College, USA (2003); English Goethe Society, King's College London (2003) and St Petersburg (2004). Her edition of *Claudine von Villa Bella* will be performed at the conference, *Schubert and the Unknown*, University of Regina, Canada in December 2004. She is keynote speaker at this conference and at the RAM Schiller Symposium in London, 2005.

Claus Canisius was born in Kolberg (Ostsee), Germany. He studied at the Staatliche Hochschule für Musik, Karlsruhe, the Royal Academy of Music in London, and at Heidelberg University (Music, Musicology, Anglistics, Psychology). He wrote his doctoral thesis at Heidelberg on Beethoven's 5th Symphony. In his professional career he has worked with Pierre Boulez in Basle. He has been a lecturer at Heidelberg University in Music and Literature, and editor of classical and contemporary music at the Südwestfunk, Baden-Baden and the Süddeutsche Rundfunk, Studio Karlsruhe. He is working at the Badisches Konservatorium für Musik, Karlsruhe and for Deutschland Radio, Berlin.

Dr Canisius's publications include: *100 Jahre Badisches Konservatorium Karlsruhe* (Karlsruhe, 1984); *Ludwig van Beethoven, Sehnsucht und Unruhe in der Musik* (München, 1992); *Goethe und die Musik, Gast in einer fremden Wohnung* (Munich, 1998); *Goethes Anverwandlungen mündlich überlieferter Poesie* (Frankfurt, Oxford 2002); 200 Broadcasting Essays: *Musik und Kommentar* (SWR, Karlsruhe).

Gareth Cox graduated from Trinity College Dublin, the Royal Irish Academy of Music, and the University of Freiburg (with a doctoral dissertation on 'Die Sätze für Soloklavier aus der Studienzeit Anton Weberns' under the supervision of Hermann Danuser). He taught for many years at the Municipal School of Music in Offenburg and is now Senior Lecturer and Head of the Department of Music at Mary Immaculate College, University of Limerick. He has recently co-edited *Irish Music in the Twentieth Century* (Four Courts Press) and *The Life and Music of Brian Boydell* (Irish Academic Press) and is a contributor to Modern Germany: An *Encyclopaedia of History, People, and Culture*; *The New Grove*; and *Die Musik in Geschichte und Gegenwart*.

John Feeley Described by the Washington Post as 'Ireland's leading classical guitarist' and by Michael Dervan in the *Irish Times* as 'a trailblazer [...] when it comes to the guitar and guitar-playing in Ireland', John Feeley enjoys a very active performance career. In addition to solo and chamber concerts he has performed widely with numerous orchestras including the American Symphony Orchestra and the National Chamber Orchestra, Washington DC. He regularly performs at many international guitar festivals.

A graduate in music from Trinity College, Dublin and Queens College of the City University, New York, he has held teaching positions at Memphis State University and the Conservatory of Music, Dublin Institute of Technology. He has won a number of prizes in international competitions, including the special Award for interpretation in the Mauro Giuliani competition in Italy. He is also highly regarded for his performances of new works by Irish composers.

Feeley's CD recordings, with K-Tel, Gael-Linn, CBA Classics, Ossian Records, Castle Communications and Blackbox Records have received international critical acclaim. He is also renowned for his guitar arrangements of Irish music, which appear on several of his many recordings. Concerts have taken him around the world and include appearances at the Sydney Opera House, the Old Opera House, Frankfurt, the L'Arena in Verona, and New York's Carnegie Hall. He has also recorded with the Chieftains and famous Spanish Soprano Montserrat Caballes.

Amanda Glauert has studied at Clare College Cambridge and Goldsmiths' College (University of London), and held lecturing posts at the music departments of Trinity College Dublin and Colchester Institute. She is now Head of Research at the RAM. Having published with CUP on the songs of *Hugo Wolf* (*Hugo Wolf and the Wagnerian Inheritance*), she is now completing a book on Beethoven's relation to Herder's aesthetics of the Lied (*Beethoven and the Lyrical Impulse*).

Julian Horton is a College Lecturer in Music at University College Dublin. He completed his doctoral research at Trinity College, Cambridge, where he also held a Research Fellowship in Musicology from 1996-2000, and has taught both at the University of Cambridge and at King's College, London.

Dr Horton's research focuses primarily on the analysis and reception of nineteenth-century music, with special interests in the music of Anton Bruckner, issues of tonal theory and the analysis of sonata forms. His book *Bruckner's Symphonies: Analysis, Reception and Cultural Politics* is forthcoming from Cambridge University Press, and the article 'Bruckner and the Symphony Orchestra' is to appear in *The Cambridge Companion to Bruckner*. Other publications include 'Postmodernism and the Critique of Musical Analysis' in *The Musical Quarterly*, 85/2 (2001) and 'Recent Developments in Bruckner Scholarship' in *Music and Letters*, 85/1 (2004).

Derek McCulloch lectured in German for thirty-six years at the University of Surrey. Simultaneously for some time he was counter-tenor lay-clerk at St George's Chapel, Windsor Castle, and was to be heard as soloist on various recordings with Roger Norrington and Helmuth Rilling, as well as with his own ensemble *Collegium Sagittarii*. Since 1985 he has directed *Café Mozart* in performances of late 18th century music on period instruments, recording for BBC Radio 4 political songs c.1800. He has also broadcast on such people as Heinrich Schütz, Johann Rosenmüller, the Bach family, the Earl of Abingdon, Emma Hamilton and Jane Austen, whose family music library he researched and catalogued in 1996 – winning in the process a Classic FM Joie de Vivre award. In retirement he continues to research, and is currently considering the music written to commemorate the death of Nelson in 1805. His main focus remains 'Haydn in England', a theme on which he has written extensively. His latest CD *Goethe & the Guitar*, recorded with *Café Mozart*, has been enthusiastically received in the early music press and by such august bodies as the Haydn, Schubert, and Spohr Societies in the UK.

Moray McGowan, born in 1950, B.A., M.A. (Newcastle-upon-Tyne), Dr. phil. (Hamburg), taught at the Universities of Siegen, Kassel, Lancaster, Hull, Strathclyde. From 1989-2000 he was Professor of German and Head of the Department of Germanic Studies, Sheffield, UK. Since September 2000 he has been Professor of German and Head of the Department of Germanic Studies, Trinity College Dublin. He is currently working on German theatre and drama and its relationship to the fall of the GDR and to German unification, on Turkish-German writing, and on ideas of Europe in German-speaking culture. Publications include: *Marieluise Fleißer* (Munich, 1987); 'German writing in the West (1945-1990)' in the *Cambridge History of German Literature* (1997); numerous essays on modern and contemporary literature and culture, including Heinrich Böll, Volker Braun, Bertolt Brecht, Hans Magnus Enzensberger, Franz Xaver Kroetz, Ulrike Meinhof, Heiner Müller, 'Neue Subjecktivität', Zafer Şenocak, Botho Strauß, metaphors in Turkish-German writing and its reception, and the theatre and drama of the 'Wende' period.

Adolf Nowak, born 1941, studied Musicology and Philosophy and completed his doctoral dissertation on Hegel's Music Aesthetics in 1969. He completed his Habilitationschrift on the problems of musical logic at the Freie Universität Berlin in

1979 and was appointed Professor of Music in the Gesamthochschule in Kassel the following year. Since 1994 he holds the chair in Musicology at the Goethe-Universität, Frankfurt am Main. His research areas include Aesthetics and Musical Theory as well as Music History in the 19th and 20th centuries.

Micheal O'Siadhail, a full-time writer, has published ten collections of poetry. He was awarded an Irish American Cultural Institute prize for poetry in 1982, the Marten Toonder prize for Literature in 1998 and was short-listed for the 2003 Wingate Jewish Quarterly Literature Prize. His poem suites, *The Naked Flame*, *Earlsfort Suite* (with Seóirse Bodley) *Summerfest* (with Colman Pearce) and *Dublin Spring* (with James Wilson) were commissioned and set to music for performance and broadcasting.

O'Siadhail's collections of poetry are *The Leap Year* (1978), *Rungs of Time* (1980), *Belonging* (1982), *Springnight* (1983), *The Image Wheel* (1985), *The Chosen Garden* (1990), *Hail! Madam Jazz: New and Selected Poems* (Bloodaxe Books, 1992), *A Fragile City* (Bloodaxe Books, 1995), *Our Double Time* (Bloodaxe Books, 1998), *Poems 1975-1995* (Bloodaxe Books, 1999) and *The Gossamer Wall* (Bloodaxe Books/Time Being Books, 2002). His work has been translated into several languages including books in German and Japanese.

Micheal O'Siadhail has given poetry readings and broadcast extensively in Ireland, Britain, Europe, North America and Japan. In 1985 he was invited to give the Vernam Hull Lecture at Harvard and the Trumbull Lecture at Yale University. He represented Ireland at the Poetry Society's European Poetry Festival in London in 1981 and at the Frankfurt Book Fair in 1997. He was writer-in-residence at the Yeats Summer School in 1991.

O'Siadhail has been a lecturer at Trinity College Dublin and a professor at the Dublin Institute for Advanced Studies. Among his many academic works are *Learning Irish* (Yale University Press 1988) and *Modern Irish* (Cambridge University Press 1989). He was a member of the Arts Council of the Republic of Ireland (1988-93) and of the Advisory Committee on Cultural Relations (1989-97), a founder member of Aosdána and a former editor of *Poetry Ireland Review*. He was the founding chairman of ILE (Ireland Literature Exchange).

Jan Smaczny took his undergraduate degree and doctorate at Magdalen College, Oxford. He also studied in Prague at the Charles University as a British Council scholar. He has lectured at the universities of Oxford (where he was college lecturer at St Peter's), the University of Birmingham (lecturer and senior lecturer), and since 1996 he has been the Hamilton Harty Professor of Music and Head of School at Queen's University, Belfast. He has written extensively on many aspects of Czech music, in particular the life and works of Dvořák and the music of the Prague Provisional Theatre. His most recent publications include a book on Dvořák's Cello Concerto and articles on the National String Quartet and Mozart in the Twentieth Century. He is also well-known as a critic and broadcaster who has worked for *The Independent*, *The Times*, *Opera Magazine* and the *BBC Music Magazine*, as well as BBC Radios 3 and 4.

Briony Williams is from New Zealand where she did her first degree. She immigrated to the UK in 1994. She is currently completing a PhD at the Royal Academy of Music, on Lieder by women composers of the Berlin Sing-Akademie. Besides research, she also teaches around London and works as a freelance accompanist, mainly with singers, with a particular interest in non-mainstream repertoire, particularly by women across the centuries.

Susan Youens is a Professor of Musicology at the University of Notre Dame. She is the author of six books on the Lieder of Franz Schubert and Hugo Wolf: *Retracing a Winter's Journey. Schubert's Winterreise* (Ithaca and London: Cornell University Press, 1991), and five books published by Cambridge University Press – *Schubert: Die schöne Müllerin* (1992), *Schubert's Poets and the Making of Lieder* (1996), *Schubert, Müller and 'Die schöne Müllerin'* (1997), *Hugo Wolf and his Mörike Songs* (2000) and *Schubert's Late Lieder: Beyond the Song-Cycles* (2002).

Editorial Note and Acknowledgements

The question as to whether or not Goethe was a musical poet has perplexed generations of his critics. Though recent criticism has brought this topic into focus, in many minds the question still remains unresolved. The difficulty of making a conclusive appraisal of an artist is frequently the measure of his greatness. Such an appraisal of Goethe is however, problematical, for in a sense he becomes enigmatic, vacillating in his musical convictions and shifting emphasis in his underlying musical philosophy. This kind of equivocation, which Goethe makes throughout his life, is rooted in far deeper intellectual and aesthetic grounds than in a rigid appraisal of strophic song, as is traditionally claimed. At the base of his musical thinking there is a deep-rooted and sophisticated dualism. This duality is seen in Goethe's response to Beethoven whom he considered more energetic and yet more inward than any other artist he had ever met. This type of double perspective characterizes Goethe's musical theory and his whole attitude to musical creativity. On the one hand he envisages music as an embodiment of a genuine aesthetic and spiritual experience; on the other hand, he is obsessed with the idea that a musical work can never free itself from abstract ideas. In other words, Goethe was concerned with the perennial question about the nature of art that has plagued Western artists and theorists for centuries: is music cognitive or affective? Placed in this context, Goethe's musical response becomes clear and his aesthetic claims become more intelligible. His views on music, which emanate from observations in novels, letters and other writings, command interest beyond the insight they offer into his cognitive and affective response to music and make a vaulable contribution to the social and cultural history of music and its reception.

Goethe's literary works which were set to music, chiefly as Singspiele and Lieder, from the 1770s onwards, serve to demonstrate most clearly his complex and many-faceted relationship to music. Like Schubert, Goethe strove to realize his early operatic ambitions, yet his contribution to opera was historically less decisive and less productive than his contribution to the German Lied. In his *Tages-und Jahreshefte* of 1805 Goethe spoke of music as 'the true element from which all poetry springs and to which it returns'. He saw lyric poetry as in some sense incomplete without music. His famous ballad, 'Der Erlkönig', written in 1782, reveals the characteristics of a musical score: the characters speak in carefully differentiated rhythms which form a colourful fabric of contrasting voices. These rhythms, augmented by the staccatos of the galloping horse's hooves, were what enticed so many composers to set the poem. Goethe's private rapport with music comes to the fore in the musicality of his language – a quality which magnetically attracted composers to his works. Such works as Berlioz's *La damnation de Faust*, based on Gérard de Nerval's translation, Mendelssohn's *Die erste Walpurgisnacht*, Liszt's *Faust-Symphonie* and Schumann's *Requiem für Mignon*, testify to the great importance for musicians of two of Goethe's literary works in particular: the verse drama *Faust* and the novel *Wilhelm Meisters Lehrjahre*. The latter contains the characters of Mignon and the Harper, whose songs, embedded within the narrative, have had an enduring fascination for composers throughout the 19th century and well into the 20th reaching as far as Charles Ives, Othmar Schoeck, Hanns Eisler, Ernst Krenek and Winfried Zillig and beyond, and has resulted in a long line of compositions of extraordinary stylistic diversity. Goethe's verse has acted as a catalyst to the Lied just as the poetry of Petrarch did to the 16th-century madrigal: the world of feeling and imagination unlocked by his poetry has been explored and musically developed in many different directions.

Ten of the lectures given here were delivered at the conference, Goethe: Musical Poet, Musical Catalyst, during my tenure as Post-Doctoral Fellow at the National University of Ireland, Maynooth. It was an honour to be granted this position and to be welcomed so wholeheartedly within the department. My chief gratitude must go to my colleagues in Maynooth and to the students who attended these lectures: it was a delight to see their supportive faces among the audience. In the months before the conference I was guided and assisted in Maynooth's ways by Marie Breen. During the conference I could not have received more willing and able assistance from Adele Commins, Catherine Ferris, Daniel Apalaghie and Kellyann McGrory: to say I am grateful is to understate the case. Heartfelt thanks to Barra Boydell, Gerard Gillen, Moray McGowan, Jan Smaczny and Harry White, who chaired sessions with characteristic grace and charm, and to Gerard Gillen, whose broad perspective and magnanimous attitude made my time as Post-Doctoral Fellow such a happy experience.

Several institutions and people have supported me throughout the work on the conference. The Peace II Programme, administered by ADM/CPA, granted me the opportunity to forge links north and south of the border. The first collaboration took place in Trinity College Dublin between the Department of Germanic Studies, Trinity College Dublin and the Department of Music, University of Ulster, Jordanstown; the second brought together two Music Departments, those of NUI Maynooth, and the Queen's University of Belfast. The aim of these North-South partnerships is to organize an educational project that will support cross-border social and cultural regeneration through education and the arts. This conference provided a channel for this work and united the fields of academic research and musical performance. This volume reflects the European dimension of research in the humanities, which produces scholarship that ranges across disciplines and national boundaries. I owe a depth of gratitude to Paddy Logue, whose continual encouragement, good will and foresight made the collaboration between two north and south universities possible: this volume would not have been feasible without him. Thanks are due to Margaret Flood and Mary Kelly for their financial advice, and I should especially like to express my appreciation of Pauline Perry's immense kindness. Special thanks are due to the Austrian Ambassador, Dr Harald Miltner, the German Ambassador, Dr Gottfried Haas, and Dr Matthias Müller-Wieferig of the Goethe Institute.

I owe a great debt of gratitude to many people who have supported me throughout the work on this book. If I had not had the good luck to meet Dan Farrelly, I doubt if this book would have existed. His undergraduate lectures on Goethe's *Faust* at University College Dublin awakened my interest in a poet who will be my companion throughout life. Whatever may be felicitous in my writing and translation owes much to his generous guidance.

Naturally, my very warm thanks are due to all contributors, whose presence at the conference was a joy and inspiration, as is their continued friendship. Special thanks are due to my keynote speaker Nicholas Boyle; Goethe was lucky in his lovers and his friends; we can now add to that glory such a biographer. It was a happy privilege for me to translate Adolf Nowak's essay on Mignon's exequies and have the volume graced by Susan Youens' erudite preface. I am especially grateful to Jeremy Adler for giving me the opportunity to try out a portion of my article in a lecture to the English Goethe Society at King's College London in November 2003, and to Martin Swales for the valuable suggestions he made to me on that occasion. I am indebted to the Neue Pinakothek, Munich, for the portrait of Goethe by Joseph Karl Stieler; the Goethe Institute in Düsseldorf for Carel's ink drawings of Mignon and the Harper; to the Sächsische Staatsoper and Zentrum für Theaterdokumentation, Dresden, for permission to reproduce the *Faust* and *Fidelio* photographs; to Edition Argus for allowing me to translate an essay from *Musik in Goethes Werk: Goethes Werk in der Musik* (Schliengen: 2003); to Bloodaxe Books for their permission to publish Micheal O'Siadhail's 'Hopscotch' and to Universal Edition for their permission to publish Webern's, 'Gleich und Gleich', op.12, no.4 and 'Weiß wie Lilien', op.19, no.1. Special thanks are due to Michael Casey, who performed the feat of transmitting the contents of innumerable music manuscript pages into the serviceable memory of Sibelius; I am grateful for his unfailing good humour and valiant persistence at the computer keyboard.

I am especially grateful to the musicians who illustrated our lectures so admirably: Mairead Buicke, Anna Devin, and Colette Boushell; special thanks are due to Kathleen Tynan, Sam McElroy and Dearbhla Collins for their first performance of *Mignon und der Harfner*; to Dearbhla Collins for her unfailing professionalism and engaging performances; to Francis Collins for the musical sensitivity of her Beethoven Lieder and to Alison Hood for her inspiring performance of the Beethoven Bagatelles. My thanks are due to Tony Carver and the Queen's Consort, Alan Costello and the Maynooth Chamber Choir, for their North/South performance of Schumann's *Requiem für Mignon*. I am especially grateful to Colman Pearce, whose good humour and musical gifts combined to elicit the best from those who worked with him; to John Feeley, William Dowdall, William Butt and John Lynch for the magical recital of the Schubert/Matiegka Quartet for Flute, Viola, Violoncello & Guitar (D94). Their performance is a memory to cherish. I am deeply grateful to Gerard Gillen, who brought the breadth of his musical vision to his fine organ interpretations of Mendelssohn. I wish to acknowledge Peter Jankowsky, whose dramatic reading provided a wonderful platform for the performance of Schumann's *Requiem für Mignon*. Special thanks are due to Micheal O'Siadhail, whose energy of mind and characteristic way of reaching out to everyone in his company, coupled with the artistic power of his poetry, resulted in a reading unparalleled among those I have attended.

I am indebted as ever to friends and family: to my mother for her constant love and gentle affirmation: no words can express my gratitude. To my father, for his enthusiastic attendance at both conferences, and to my daughter, Bláthnaid: how miraculous and perfect she is. Finally, my work on this book and on the conference, along with my previous endeavours, has benefited from the unfailing encouragement of Seóirse Bodley. From his profound understanding of human nature and from his immense musical gifts I have received so much.

List of Abbreviations

I Periodicals

GJb	Goethe-Jahrbuch
JAMS	Journal of the American Musicological Society
JGG	Jahrbuch der Goethe Gesellschaft
MT	The Musical Times
MQ	The Music Quarterly
NCM	Nineteenth Century Music
NZfM	Neue Zeitschrift für Musik

II Editions

AG	*Artemis-Gedenkausgabe der Werke, Briefe und Gespräche*, ed. Ernst Beutler, 24 vols, rev. ed (Zurich: Artemis-Verlag, 1960-71).
BA	*Berliner Ausgabe Poetische Werke. Kunsttheoretische Schriften und Übersetzungen*, ed. Siegfried Seidl, 22 vols (Berlin/Weimar: Aufbau, 1960-78).
HA	*Hamburger Ausgabe. Goethes Werke*, 14 vols, ed. Trunz (Munich: Beck, 1988).
HABr	*Goethes Briefe, Hamburger Ausgabe*, ed. Karl Robert Mandelkow (Hamburg: Wegener, 1962).
MA	*Sämtliche Werke nach Epochen seines Schaffens. Münchner Ausgabe*, ed. Karl Richter, 20 vols (Munich: C. Hanser, 1985ff).
NG	*The New Grove Dictionary of Music and Musicians*, 20 vols, eds Stanley Sadie/ John Tyrell, 2nd edn (London: Macmillan, 2001).
WA	*Weimar Ausgabe. Goethes Werke*, 143 vols, eds Gustav von Loeper, Erich Schmidt, Hermann Grimm et al. (Weimar: Hermann Böhlau, 1887-1912).

List of Figures

Figure 2.1	Karl Friedrich Zelter, Lithograph by Ludwig Hein from the Oil Painting by Karl Begas.
Figure 2.2	Zelter's Setting of Goethe's 'Das Gastlmahl' enclosed in the correspondence (in Goethe's and Zelter's own hand).
Figure 2.3	The Wooden House on the Gickelhahn at Ilmenau. (Photograph, author's own.)
Figure 2.4	Opposite the Wooden House on the Gickelhahn at Ilmenau. (Photograph, author's own.)
Figure 2.5	Portraits of Goethe and Beethoven by Joseph Karl Stieler (1781-1858).
Figure 3.1	Two Beethoven masks. Life mask by Franz Klein, 1812. Death mask (the so-called Hippocratic face) by Joseph Danhauser, 1827.
Figure 5.1	*Fidelio*, Sächsische Staatsoper Dresden: 7/8 October 1989: The Main Set.
Figure 5.2	*Fidelio*, Sächsische Staatsoper Dresden: 7/8 October 1989: Rocco's office and postroom.
Figure 5.3	*Fidelio*, Sächsische Staatsoper Dresden: 7/8 October 1989: The guardroom.
Figure 5.4	*Faust*, Staatsschauspiel Dresden, 28/29/30 August 1990: Martha's house as a doll's house-GDR apartment.
Figure 5.5	*Faust*, Staatsschauspiel Dresden, 28/29/30 August 1990: Goethe applies the wig and make-up which signals Faust's blindness.
Figure 5.6	*Faust*, Staatsschauspiel Dresden, 28/29/30 August 1990: Mephisto with characteristic Gustav Gründgens skullcap and make-up.
Figure 5.7	*Faust*, Staatsschauspiel Dresden, 28/29/30 August 1990: The 'Lemuren' lay the railway track (the production's version of Faust's land reclamation project).
Figure 5.8	*Faust*, Staatsschauspiel Dresden, 28/29/30 August 1990: Goethe as Prompter has Faust rehearse three versions of the famous 'freies Land' verse.
Figure 5.9	*Faust*, Staatsschauspiel Dresden, 28/29/30 August 1990: The final scene: Faust unwigged: Faust and Mephisto deliver Goethe's 'Envoi' as they walk down the railway tracks towards the audience.
Figure 12.1	Franz Ludwig Catel, 'Mignon dressed as an Angel', Ink Drawing (1799).
Figure 12.2	Franz Ludwig Catel, 'The Harper in his Cell', Ink Drawing (1799).

List of Illustrations

Cover Design   Portrait of Johann Wolfgang von Goethe
(1828)
Joseph Karl Stieler (1781-1858).
Oil on canvas. 78,0 x 63,8 cm.
Reproduced by kind permission by Neue Pinakothek, Munich.

Joseph Stieler painted his portrait of Goethe on commission from Ludwig I of Bavaria. In 1828, carrying a letter of recommendation from the King, the artist travelled to Weimar to begin the preliminary portrait work. Goethe's diaries relate the details of Stieler's stay in Weimar, as well as details of the sittings. Three preliminary studies still exist. Stieler depicted the poet and scholar Goethe as a half-figure sitting at his desk. His upper body is turned frontally to the viewer, while his head is turned to the right, glancing sideward out of the picture confines. The static collectedness of the entire composition and the precise depiction of the facial features are thereby eased and given a more life-like quality.

The poet is holding in his right hand a piece of paper upon which the last lines of a poem written by Ludwig I can be read. The King was the author of a goodly number of passionate poems, which were mostly written in antique metre. He used twenty-eight of his couplets as inscriptions to Carl Rottmann's Italian cycle in Munich's Hofgarten. Goethe's clutching of Ludwig's poem in his hands marked a certain reverence for the King and his poetic creations – no small honour, as Goethe's artistic judgment carried great weight. Other colleagues were not quite as restrained when it came to criticism and mockery of Ludwig's rather awkward verses.

List of Musical Quotations

Example 1.1	Eberl, 'Meeresstille' und 'Glückliche Fahrt'.
Example 1.2	Dietrichstein, 'An die Entfernte'.
Example 1.3	Kruft, 'Lied aus Wilhelm Meisters Lehrjahre'.
Example 1.4	Czerny, 'Der Erlkönig'.
Example 2.1	Zelter, 'Wandrers Nachtlied'.
Example 2.2	Zelter, 'Rastlose Liebe'.
Example 3.1	Beethoven, 'Marmotte' op.52, no.7.
Example 3.2	Beethoven, 'Mailied', op.52, no.4.
Example 3.3	Beethoven, *An die ferne Geliebte*, op.98, no.2, bars 1-31.
Example 3.4	Beethoven's Klavierlied 'Mignon', op.75, no. 1, bars 14-17.
Example 3.5	Beethoven, *Egmont*: Incidental Music to 'Komm süßer Schlaf'.
Example 4.1	Reichardt, 'Kennst du das Land'.
Example 4.2	Zelter, 'Kennst du das Land'.
Example 4.3	Beethoven, 'Kennst du das Land', bars 1-34.
Example 4.4	Zelter, 'Ich denke dein'.
Example 4.5	Zelter, 'Nähe des Geliebten'.
Example 4.6	Reichardt, 'Ich denke Dein'.
Example 4.7	Beethoven, 'Andenken', bars 33-49.
Example 4.8	Beethoven, 'Ich denke Dein'.
Example 4.9	Beethoven, Sechs Variationen: Lied mit Veränderungen, WoO 74, Variation 2, *primo* and *secondo*.
Example 4.10	Beethoven, *Sechs Variationen*, Variation 3 *primo* and *secondo*.
Example 6.1	Tomášek, 'Heidenröslein'.
Example 6.2	Tomášek, 'Mignons Sehnsucht'.
Example 6.3	Tomášek, 'Erlkönig'.
Example 7.1	Bettina von Arnim, 'An Luna'.
Example 7.2	Bettina von Arnim, 'Ach neige, du Schmerzenreiche'.
Example 8.1	Anton Webern, 'Blumengruß'.
Example 8.2	Anton Webern, 'Gleich und Gleich', op.12, no.4.
Example 8.3	Anton Webern, Tone Row, op.19.
Example 8.4	Anton Webern, 'Weiß wie Lilien', op.19, no.1, bars 1-15.
Example 10.1	Schumann *Requiem für Mignon* op.98(b), Monotonal Reading
Example 10.2	Schumann *Requiem für Mignon* op.98(b), Directional Reading
Example 10.3	Schumann *Requiem für Mignon* op.98(b), Directional Reading with Text Overlaid
Example 10.4	Schumann *Requiem für Mignon* op.98(b), Thematic Relationships.

List of Tables

Table 3.1	Juxtaposition of Goethe's *Werther*, Letter 10 May 1771, and 'Mailied' 1771.
Table 3.2	Juxtaposition of Goethe's 'Mailied' and Beethoven's Dramaturgy for his Setting of 'Mailied'.
Table 3.3	Beethoven, *Egmont*, Entreacte III. Allegro, *Marcia vivace*.
Table 3.4	Beethoven's Letter from Heiligstadt, 10 October 1802
Table 3.5	Egmont's monologue, 'Komm süßer Schlaf' and Goethe's Stage Directions.
Table 3.6	Goethe, 'To Ferdinand Hiller', 10 February 1827.
Table 4.1	Goethe, 'Nähe des Geliebten' (1795).
Table 4.2	Friederike Brun, 'Ich denke Dein'.
Table 4.3	Matthisson, 'Ich denke Dein'.
Table 6.1	Productions of Goethe's plays *Faust* and *Egmont* in the Provisional Theatre.
Table 6.2	Goethe, 'Der Fischer'.
Table 7.1	Bettina von Arnim, 'Wer sich der Einsamkeit ergibt'.
Table 7.2	Bettina von Arnim, 'An Luna'.
Table 8.1	Goethe, 'Blumengruß'.
Table 8.2	Goethe, 'Gleich und Gleich'.
Table 8.3	Two Songs from Goethe's Chinesisch-Deutsche Jahres- und Tagezeiten, op.19.
Table 10.1	Schumann, *Requiem für Mignon*, op.98(b), Distribution of Text.
Table 10.2	Schumann, *Requiem für Mignon*, op.98(b), Text and Outline of Key Scheme.

Message from the Ambassador of the Federal Republic of Germany
Dr Gottfried Haas

I would like to congratulate the Department of Music of NUI Maynooth on hosting this conference entitled 'Goethe: Musical Poet, Musical Catalyst'. Particular recognition must go here to Dr Lorraine Byrne, who initiated the conference and saw this whole project through to the end so splendidly.

After a very successful conference last year at Trinity College Dublin on Goethe and Schubert, it was an excellent idea to use the momentum and venture even further into this field, as there obviously remains much to be discovered.

This conference was an international event, gathering prominent speakers and musicians from several European countries, including Germany. It bridged the gap between academic theory and artistic practice by integrating performance and academic reflection. Finally, it was also a truly interdisciplinary event, as it combined – once again – musicology and Germanistik (German studies).

To both subjects, music and German language, I attribute a particular importance. Language is the key to understanding a country and a culture. And I am pleased with the fact that all seven universities in Ireland offer German studies. Equally, music is certainly a form of art that is particularly suited to crossing borders and being understood by the people of all countries and cultures. German language and music have through the centuries often existed in some kind of symbiosis. At times, music may actually have served as a medium to transport German literature.

Robert Schumann once defined this unique relationship as follows:

> 'Musik ist die höhere Potenz der Poesie.'
> (Music is the higher power of poetry)

Whether this statement holds up in the light of two days of a high-level academic exchange is up to the reader of these conference proceedings to decide.

Hopscotch

Our chalked figure of boxes squared
off and interlocked. Overlappings
of sides, t-shapes, half-shared
divides. A groundwork for high jinks.

'Your go!' And everyone hunkers to watch
if I toe the line. Footfall vigil.
Is this why the Germans call hopscotch
'playing a game of heaven and hell'?

Such passion for limits and thresholds.
Johnston's shop in Pettigo, its entrances
In both counties. A foot in two worlds.
Abutment and frontier. Old ambivalences.

Or the way sometimes exact same sounds
seem to slide and play with words;
a child is riddling out how 'bounds'
means 'confines' and 'bounces forwards'.

Then, the pivot homewards. Our swift
About-face. Thrill and crisis of turning;
One ankle clasped, one hand aloft,
Frail balance of gravity and yearning.

A skittish jump. Again our spreadeagle
Heavy-footed landings astride a border.
Stop-go momentum of hop and straddle.
That need of lines. That leap's desire.

Micheal O'Siadhail

Caprice

1
Vibes that want to jar or risk the duo,
Passing notes too harsh, out of sync,

Mismatched phrasings, uneven tempo,
Clashes as melody hovers on the brink.

O the ease of steady lines! One to one.
Unnerved at every interrupted cadence

It took me years to trust to resolution.
Richness of each mended dissonance.

Caprice and ruses of wild love-making,
Flirted anticipations, playful tension,

Rising sounds retarded enough to hone
An urge, keep accelerating and braking

Pleasure. A quaver held in suspension.
Offbeat discords prime a sweeter tone.

2
Delicious liberty of notes to rove
Extempore
Con amore
As in between the lines we wove
Inaudible noise
Of a middle voice
Underwrites our undersong,
Cantus firmus
Holding us
In melodic progression, headstrong
Silent tenor,
Our rapport.

3
A trace in us, an echo of some tonality,
Whatever loves us before we ever loved,

What loneness ours even as we roved
Out, still signs its key in you and me.

Three decades everything shared and joint.
Flesh of my flesh, bone alongside bone;

More and more together and still alone,
Lines ripening in unison and counterpoint

We hold a pitch and measure as best we can.
The more our rock and rhythm correspond

The longer we long, the further on beyond,
Desire homing towards where desire began

As though from its beginning a tune returns;
Glory of our music how our music yearns.

Micheal O'Siadhail

Preface
Susan Youens

From the late eighteenth-century to the present day, Goethe looms large on the landscape of Western music. Opera, secular oratorio, song: composers of the major genres of vocal music owe him massive debts. Certainly song scholars encounter him at every turn. Goethe, steeped in musical culture from his youth to the end of his days, attracted Lieder composers from the time his first poems were published, and not only in the German-speaking world. Benjamin Britten's setting of 'Um Mitternacht' in the century just past is a work of the first magnitude, less well-known than it should be, and there are Goethe songs in a plethora of languages, from A to Z. In 1885, when Ernst Challier brought out his *Grosser Lieder-Katalog. Ein alphabetisch geordnetes Verzeichniss sämmtlicher Einstimmiger Lieder mit Begleitung des Pianoforte*, the tabulation of Goethe songs was already imposing. From this 1,382-page tome, we discover 'best-sellers' such as 'Nähe des Geliebten' (sixty-two settings, pp.620-21), 'Nur wer die Sehnsucht' (forty-seven settings, pp.643-44), and 'Erlkönig' (twenty-six settings, p.227) as evidence of a burgeoning repertoire, with more to follow. Challier's list was, of course, quite incomplete, as we have long known, although Goethe still awaits his Günter Metzner, whose twelve-volume catalogue, *Heine in der Musik*, is an invaluable resource for scholars. I will never forget my first visit to the 'Dichter-Komponist' catalogue at the Stadtbibliothek zu Berlin music collection, where I discovered file drawer after file drawer filled with index cards which record thousands of settings, ample evidence of Goethe's impress on the world of music. How many singing Mignons are there on Planet Earth? – enough for mass choruses of wandering waifs with tragic origins and preternatural knowledge. Every 'hunter-gatherer' expedition I make to add to my storehouse of songs results in more Goethe settings whose existence I had not known before, and I expect that this tale will be repeated throughout my life, happily so. From

Kleinmeister to the accredited 'greats', few composers passed by Goethe without appropriating him for music.

My own bird's-eye view of Goethe features Schubert most prominently, given the seventy-four Schubert-Goethe songs and the great writer's role in the 'miracle year' extending from late 1814 through 1815, when the young composer was as if drunk on Goethe's words. By the time Schubert came onto the scene, Goethe was a demi-god; the young war-poet Theodore Körner was not the only one to own busts of Goethe and Schiller and to venerate the still-living writer with great fervor. It is fascinating to watch (and hear) Schubert 'take on' Goethe from the moment he came into full-fledged compositional maturity at the extraordinary age of seventeen in songs from the tiny, poignant 'Die Spinnerin' (eleven bars, repeated through seven verses) to works as challenging as 'An Schwager Kronos' and 'Erlkönig'. In the multiple versions of single poems, for example, 'Nur wer die Sehnsucht', Schubert both approaches Goethe with utmost seriousness and appropriates him for the composer's own agendas. What, we hear him asking himself, is the suitable musical garb for the enigmatic Mignon? A harmonically tortured permutation of the folk-like Lied, or a flowing, Italianate song of the sort to which the Harper sings his torment, or (one of the most beautiful things Schubert ever wrote) the B minor duet which begins op.62? Who could fail to be fascinated by these multiple Mignons and Harpers? – certainly not the composer Seóirse Bodley, who adds his eloquent voice to those who have contemplated this evergreen subject and this extraordinary duet.

One of my favourite examples of Schubert returning to a poem by Goethe and engaging it in a different way is the two versions of 'An den Mond', the first composed in August 1815 as a strophic song, the transformation of *Volkstümlichkeit* into something radiant. (It is irresistible to speculate which verse or verses gave rise to the musical strophe in a strophic setting such as this one. It is my guess that the eighteen-year-old composer, already wise beyond his years, was most struck by the remembrance of 'happy and dark times' and by the evocation of a persona walking in solitude between joy and sorrow. The way in which the word 'Schmerz' leaps upward, startled, ambushing the singer's line and transforming the tonic pitch into something else harmonically, is all-too-accurate a register of surprise attacks by pain in real life.) When he returned to the poem that same year, it was clearly with the intent of expanding, 'unpacking', if you will, the poem's riches. This time, he makes of the 'Labyrinth der Brust' at the end something unforgettable, the singer's music first drawn inside the labyrinth of the piano's heart and then calmly walking the night in beauty from on high. Every time I return to one of the Schubert-Goethe songs, I am struck by jewelled details and musical-architectural wonders I had not seen before; for example, when I recently revisited this composer's setting of 'Ganymed', op.19, no.3 ('Dem Dichter gewidmet'), I realized that the first vocal gesture – the placement of the first word 'Wie' on the downbeat and its prolongation throughout three beats – constitutes a dazzled expression of wonderment. 'How' indeed does such transcendence happen?

But I digress (always tempting when Goethe and Schubert beckon). If these are troubled times for the world at large, they are halcyon times for those who love to contemplate the works of one of the world's greatest literary figures and the music born from his words. In Nicholas Boyle's massive, marvellous biography, we learn not only of Goethe himself, but the intellectual-artistic-political-social contexts in which he moved, and here, we share in Boyle's reflections on the novel which made such a deep impression on the nineteenth century: *Wilhelm Meisters Lehrjahre*. In Boyle's stimulating account, this novel marks a major station in the evolution of Goethe's thinking about religion, from early sympathy for the figure of Christ (while, however, refusing to identify himself as Christian) to deeper critique; along the way, his alternative faith in 'the gods' also fails to survive the passage of time. And yet, Boyle locates in this crucial work precursors to Goethe's later return to theistic language. In Nowak's essay, we are told of diverse influences on Mignon's requiem: the Protestant tradition of the *Trauerfeier*, the Egyptian tradition of embalming the bodies of the dead, and the historical requiem-in-music, with reference to Anton Rubinstein's *Requiem* and Max Bruch's *Trauerfeier für Mignon*, op 93, among others. Lorraine Byrne has carefully dissected (and exploded) many of the hoary old legends distorting what we know of Goethe's involvement with music and musicians; she is continuing that exemplary project in her latest work on Goethe's long relationship with the composer Carl Friedrich Zelter. Amanda Glauert is similarly rectifying prior accounts of Beethoven's view of song. 'Ich schreibe ungern Lieder', he once famously grumbled, but the lyrical impulse was integral to his music, as Glauert demonstrates in full in a forthcoming book, and the way in which Beethoven garbs Goethe's 'Ich denke dein' in music is a case in point of a complex Poet-Composer relationship. In another revisionary endeavour, Briony Williams casts the relationship of Bettine von Arnim and Goethe in a new and welcome light, that of a muse transformed from stereotypical passivity to reciprocal creativity. Goethe and Beethoven were often invoked in the same breath as like Prometheus-figures, and the familiar pairing of these two giants is at issue in Moray McGowan's piece on *Fidelio* and *Faust* against the recent backdrop of political upheaval in East Germany in 1989/1990. The simultaneous phenomena of distance and affinity are explored in Claus Canisius's essay. It is very moving to read Canisius's careful tracing of the encounters, both personal and artistic, of these two men, from Beethoven's first Goethe songs in the style of the second Berlin song-school to the triumph of Beethoven's *Egmont* music. Goethe's presence in other places, later times, other people's creative endeavours, is the subject of Jan Smaczny's, Gareth Cox's and Otto Biba's essays. In Smaczny's article on the little-known and fascinating theme of Goethe and the Czechs due consideration is finally being paid to Vaclav Jan Tomášek's Goethe songs, and I was fascinated to discover that Fibich and Smetana were Goethe composers. From Cox's discussion of Anton Webern's indebtedness to Goethe, a frequent presence in Webern's correspondence, thought, and music we learn that Webern saw links between Goethe's *Farbenlehre* and his own twelve-tone compositional techniques. Otto Biba enlightens us all about Goethe's knowledge of music in the Habsburg realm, his personal relations with the Austrian emperor and the music-loving nobility circa 1800, and Goethe songs in late eighteenth-century Austria. In sum, what this volume demonstrates so richly are Goethe's multitudinous transactions with the world of music, both past and present. The *Nachklänge* of such greatness are long-lived.

A: Goethe's Musical Aesthetics

1 | Goethe in the Vienna Music Scene of his Era
Otto Biba

When works of Goethe first became known in Vienna, and when Goethe reception first began there, has not yet been thoroughly investigated. In 1776 a production of *Erwin and Elmire* marked the first performance of a play by Goethe on the stage of the Burg Theatre.[1] This is to be seen as a sign of visible acknowledgement of the poet At that time Vienna was experiencing, and had experienced, the Werther fashion.[2] The Werther fever[3], was, of course, weaker than in some parts of Germany: enthusiasm for the cult of feeling was also characteristic of Vienna of the 1770s. But the immediate production of parodies and travesties[4] accompanied successful literary works of this kind in Vienna, and inhibited any drastic results of the Werther enthusiasm. In her memoires,[5] the writer Caroline Pichler (1769-1843) relates:

> Mich ließ der Werther, als Roman, kalt, so lebhaft mich die psychologische Wahrheit der Charaktere, die tiefe Kenntnis des menschlichen Herzens, die Naturschilderungen usw. anzogen.

Her mother had – as long as she considered her too impressionable and too immature – withheld from her two books that were widely read at the time: Goethe's *Werther* and

---

[1] Helmut Barak, 'Goethe im Hofburgtheater', in: *Goethe und Österreich* (Vienna, 1999), p.98.
[2] Gustav Gugitz, 'Die Wiener Stubenmädchenliteratur von 1781', in: Emil Karl Blümml – Gustav Gugitz: *Altwienerisches* I (Vienna, 1921), pp.28-64 (p.38).
[3] Gustav Gugitz, *Das Wertherfieber in Österreich* (Vienna, 1903).
[4] Barak has collected examples, partly with relevance to music, pp.87-196.
[5] Caroline Pichler, *Denkwürdigkeiten aus meinem Leben*, ed. Emil Karl Blümml, 1 (Munich, 1914), p.139. '*Werther*, as a novel, left me cold though I found the psychological truth of the characters, the profound understanding of the human heart and the descriptions of nature etc. extremely attractive.'

Wieland's *Agathon*. At about the age of twenty or twenty-one she recounts how she read them:

> [...] und sowohl meine Mutter als ich selbst mussten uns wundern, daß der Eindruck, welchen diese Werke auf mich machten, ganz dem erwarteten oder gefürchteten entgegengesetzt war. [...] Meine Phantasie, deren Aufregung man hauptsächlich gefürchtet hatte, blieb ruhig.[6]

Goethe's world of feeling was familiar, but people were not carried away by it. For a relatively short time it was a fashion to follow, but one soon returned more or less to the *terra firma* of sober reality. Nothing illustrates this more clearly than Caroline Pichler's judgement. Around 1790 her mother, almost certainly on the basis of her own experience, was afraid that Goethe's *Werther* would cause her daughter an emotional upset. But this was not the case.

This is the background against which the first Goethe settings by Viennese composers are to be seen. They chose texts characterized by feeling and emotion, which, sufficiently supported by music, brought Goethe into the music repertoire as a poet belonging to the *Empfindsamkeit* era. It is not surprising, therefore, that in a song collection published in 1778 with works of the Court Pianist Joseph Anton Steffan (1726-1797)[7] – the piano and music teacher of the children of the Imperial family – the first Goethe song contained[8] in it is 'Lotte auf Werthers Grab'. Thus the Werther fashion can also be traced in music and brought Goethe to the attention of composers. It is worth noting that the volume contains a setting of 'Das Veilchen auf der Wiese by Gleim', but in fact the poem, wrongly attributed to Johann Wilhelm Ludwig Gleim (1719-1803), is by Goethe. The Viennese were familiar with the text since 1776, as a song of Goethe's heroine in *Erwin und Elmire*. In Part Three of this collection, which appeared in 1780, we again find a setting of the poem 'Das Veilchen auf der Wiese' by Karl Frieberth[9], who had a career an opera singer, most notably under Joseph Haydn at the court of Prince Esterházy. He was conductor of choirs in important Viennese churches and was also known as a composer. As with all the other songs in this volume, the name of the poet is omitted.

---

[6] ibid. '[...] and both my mother and I were surprised that the impression these works made on me was just the opposite of what was expected or feared. [...] My imagination, the agitation of which one had most feared, remained calm.'

[7] *Sammlung Deutscher Lieder für das Klavier.*[...] I (Vienna: Joseph Edler von Kurzböck, 1778), N.5. Copy consulted in the Archiv der Gesellschaft der Musikfreunde in Vienna, Cat. N. VI 4203 (Q 10633).

[8] ibid., N.16

[9] *Sammlung Deutscher Lieder für das Klavier.* [...] III (Vienna: Joseph Edler von Kurzböck, 1780), N.14. Copy consulted in the Archiv der Gesellschaft der Musikfreunde in Vienna, Cat. N. VI 3974 (Q 5579).

In Goethe's poem the violet wished to be plucked by a beloved young shepherdess and pressed to her bosom. But it is trodden on and so dies through her: 'And if I die, at least I die through her, at her feet', as we read at the end of the poem or song. That love finds fulfilment in death must have been a fascinating theme that was often taken up by composers of this time. It is not surprising therefore that in 1785 Wolfgang Amadeus Mozart went back to this Goethe text (KV 476): 'Das Veilchen. Vom Göthe' appears in his manuscript.[10] The term 'vom [von dem] Göthe' shows that he was very familiar with the name Goethe, that he knew it intimately. Ulrich Konrad supposed that the basis for the composition was not a text edition of *Erwin und Elmire*, nor any other literary publication, but rather Frieberth's setting which appeared in 1780.[11] Fulfilment of love in death was a theme with which Mozart was often preoccupied, including the G minor aria of Pamina in *Die Zauberflöte*. His setting of Goethe's 'Veilchen' can therefore be seen, on the one hand, as part of a chain of a musical tradition beginning in Vienna in 1778,[12] and, on the other hand, as a central theme in his work.[13]

---

[10] Facsimile edition with an epilogue by Alfred Einstein (Vienna-Leipzig, Zürich, 1936.) An identical facsimile edition done by collotype and with the same commentary was published without the publisher's name and undated. On a label glued to the inside cover it was claimed that this manuscript was 'the first collotype reproduction of the original'. There were 100 numbered copies. The text of this label mentions that supposed 'chance' mentioned in footnote 13 below. It says: 'Only in one single case has that ideal combination of the purist musician and the greatest poet come about by chance: in 'Veilchen'. (Nur in einem einzigen Fall ist jene ideale Verbindung des reinsten Musikers mit dem größten Dichter durch Zufall zustande gekommen: im 'Veilchen'.) Copies consulted in the library of the Gesellschaft der Musikfreunde in Vienna, Cat. Nos 23619/161 and 23620/161.

[11] Ulrich Konrad – Martin Staehelin, 'allzeit ein buch', in: *Die Bibliothek Wolfgang Amadeus Mozarts* (Wolfenbüttel, 1991), p.110.

[12] Max Friedländer has some examples of still earlier settings outside the Viennese area: *Gedichte von Goethe in Compositionen seiner Zeitgenossen*, ed. Max Friedländer (Weimar, 1896), pp.12-17.

[13] Against this Ilija Dürhammer maintains: 'It is likely that Mozart had not had Goethe in mind, and that Mozarts 'Veilchen' setting was more due to chance' ('auch mehr einem "Zufall" zu verdanken'). (Ilija Dürhammer: ' "Göthe's musikalisches Dichter-Genie". Goethes Bedeutung für die österreichische Musikgeschichte von Mozart bis Mahler', in: *Goethe und Österreich*, p.66 and p.78). This opinion is not to be suppressed here even if, because of the broader considerations he has outlined, the author cannot agree with it.

Example 1.1 Eberl, 'Meeresstille, Glückliche Fahrt'

The sensibility of the Rococo period reflected in the theme of the lover's yearning that leads to death (symbolized by an experience of nature), but also love and yearning for their own sake is evident in the four Goethe poems which Anton Eberl (1765-1807) chose for the six 'Songs with piano accompaniment'[14], op.23, published in 1804: 'Nähe des Geliebten', 'Der Fischer', 'An die Entfernte', 'Meeresstille – Glückliche Fahrt' (see example 1.1). Eberl was a piano teacher and composer in Vienna and several of his works were falsely circulated under Mozart's name, which is understandable because to a large extent he followed Mozart's musical idiom. It is worthy of special attention that in his Opus 23 he combined, for the first time, both Goethe poems – 'Meeresstille' und 'Glückliche Fahrt' – in one composition. Beethoven did the same in 1814/15 in his Opus 112, which, without Eberl as a precursor, would be unthinkable. With this combination Eberl was the first to see Goethe's lyrical poetry under the aspect of musical drama. It was not until Franz Schubert that also Goethe's dramatic ballads or his dramatic poems became interesting for Austrian composers. Indeed, Eberl's Opus 23 was also a precursor for Franz Schubert: he, too, had set 'Der Fischer' und 'Nähe des Geliebten'. At the same time, Eberl should not be seen as a direct model for Schubert – even if it is possible that Schubert knew Eberl's settings – but rather as a precursor: Schubert belongs to an already different age, for he approaches the setting of these texts with completely new presuppositions and with different intentions. On 9 April 1804 Eberl sent Goethe a copy of his six songs op.23.[15] Characteristically, Goethe didn't reply. But when on 30 January 1806 Josef Friedrich Freiherr von Retzer, with whom Goethe often corresponded on theatre business, sent Goethe a letter[16] recommending that Eberl be warmly received in Weimar, Goethe responded. He was welcomed 'at the Weimar Court both because of this recommendation and because of his talent, and I hope, when he left us, that he was not unhappy with the reception', Goethe wrote to Freiherrr von Retzer[17]. This was a more or less official reception given to a travelling composer as was customary at courts interested in the arts. But that doesn't mean that the visit gave rise to a profound discussion of song style and song composition, since it was not a private visit to Goethe.

---

[14] *Gesaenge mit Begleitung des Pianoforte von Anton Eberl. Works* 23 (Vienna: Kunst- und Industrie-Comptoir, No. 298, 1304). Copy consulted in the Archiv der Gesellschaft der Musikfreunde in Wien, Cat. N. VI 11987 (Q 5425).
[15] Eberl's letter is published in: *Goethe und Österreich. Briefe mit Erläuterungen* II., ed. August Sauer (Weimar, 1904), p.76.
[16] ibid., p.20.
[17] ibid., p.21.

Example 1.2 Dietrichstein, 'An die Entfernte'

In 1811 Graf Moriz von Dietrichstein (1775-1864) published sixteen settings of Goethe poems (two of them duets) in Vienna and dedicated them to the poet[18]. Quite apart from its musical quality, this edition is worthy of attention, firstly, because Dietrichstein called the poems he has chosen 'Lieder' and, secondly, because it is dedicated to Goethe. On 23 January 1811 the composer sent a copy of this edition to Goethe. He described himself as 'enthused by your immortal Lieder' – so, again, not poems, but Lieder – and 'far removed from the illusion that I possess those excellent qualities which distinguish Herr Reichardt from all others'. It was clever to mention Reichardt, whom Goethe, as also later Carl Friedrich Zelter (1758-1832), so admired. For Reichardt (like Zelter) represented the Berlin Lieder school whose approach to song composition was fundamentally different from that in Vienna. Goethe was familiar with the Berlin School, whereas the song aesthetic of the Viennese was to a large extent foreign to him. Still, on 23 June 1811 Dietrichstein received an effusive thank-you letter from Goethe who was in Karlsbad. He assured Dietrichstein that the songs had given him much pleasure:

> Ohne dass ich im Stande bin ein Kunsturtheil über jene Compositionen zu fällen, darf ich doch soviel sagen, dass mir sowohl ihre Anmut als eine gewisse Eigenheit des Charakters sehr viel Vergnügen gemacht hat. Es gibt zu interessanten Betrachtungen Anlaß, wenn man sieht, wie der Componist, indem er sich ein Lied zueignet [gemeint: aneignet] und es auf seine Weise belebt, der Poesie eine gewisse Vielseitigkeit ertheilt, die sie an und für sich gar nicht haben kann; woraus denn erhellt, dass etwas Einfaches und beschränkt scheinendes, wenn es nur wirksam ist, zu den manigfaltesten Productionen Anlaß geben kann.[19]

---

[18] *XVI Lieder von Göthe in Musik gesetzt und dem Dichter gewidmet vom Grafen Moriz von Dietrichstein* (Vienna: Artaria, No. 2120, 1811). Copy consulted in the Archiv der Gesellschaft der Musikfreunde in Vienna, Cat. No. VI 11975 (Q 7549).

[19] *Goethe und Österreich. Briefe mit Erläuterungen*, pp.77-79. 'Without my being in a position to judge the compositions aesthetically, may I say that their charm and a certain original character made them very pleasing. It gives rise to interesting reflections when one sees how the composer, when he makes the song his own and brings it to life in his own way, gives the poetry a certain many-

Goethe's very noteworthy and fundamental aesthetic comments reveal the extent to which he was inspired by Dietrichstein's songs. He continues:

> Sehr angenehm würde es mir seyn, diese Lieder von dem Componisten selbst oder in seiner Gegenwart vorgetragen zu hören, weil sie dadurch gewiß nur gewinnen können. Indessen haben unsere Sänger und Musiker sie mit viel Liebe und Aufmerksamkeit behandelt und mir dadurch manche vergnügte Stunde gemacht.[20]

In this letter Goethe mentions twice that he would like to get to know Dietrichstein personally.

Was it Dietrichstein's social standing at the centre of a literary and musical circle in Vienna that drew such a detailed response from Goethe, or were there artistic reasons for the response? If one asks this question it is in the understanding that Dietrichstein was a very able composer and was acknowledged as such. He is not to be seen as a nobleman who, out of ambition or a misplaced enthusiasm, wanted to try his hand at composition. He had a perfect technical grasp of music and was in fact artistically gifted. He was also aesthetically educated and in these Lied settings, one can detect the subtle influence of Reichardt to please Goethe, to whom he wished to give a token of his devotion[21]. Goethe knew how to savour this. To explain it more simply: Dietrichstein's Lieder are situated between Mozart and Schubert. They are far removed from Rococo sentiment, but the music is still the handmaid and not an equal partner of the text.

This aesthetic – which requires more of music than empathy with the sensibility of the text and is less interested in an additional or new interpretation of the text – is more advanced than Beethoven's early Goethe Lieder: the 'Mailied', op.52/4, published in 1805 but of a much earlier date; 'Aus Goethes Faust', op.75/2; and the three songs from 1810, op.83. This is further corroborated by the fact that there seems to be no answer from Goethe when Beethoven sent him his cantata 'Meeresstille und Glückliche Fahrt', op.112. Here in Opus 112, which dates from the years 1814/15, Beethoven is striking out independently. The music rises with the aid of the text only to leave it behind, having achieved independence. It was the same (of course, to a much more modest degree) with Eberl's setting of both of these poems, but also in the tone painting ('der Wandrer bebt' or 'mit dumpfem Rauschen die Welle steigt') of his 'Nähe des Geliebten'. On the other hand, Eberl's 'An die Entfernte' – a strophic song, in contrast to the two

---

sidedness which it can in no way have of itself. This makes it clear that something that seems simple and limited can, if it is effective, give rise to the most manifold productions.'

[20] ibid. 'It would be very pleasant for me to hear these songs performed by the composer, or at least in his presence, because they could thereby only be enhanced. In the meantime our singers and musicians have treated them with much love and attention and so have given me many an hour of pleasure.'

[21] *Goethe und Österreich. Briefe und Erläuterungen*, p.77.

mentioned – is again in the tradition of *Emfindsamkeit* songs such as Beethoven's 'Mailied' and equivalent settings of other early poems of Goethe.

Can we say that Eberl and Beethoven had to share the fate of hearing no response from Goethe to settings of this kind? For Beethoven it was the case that 'I, too, have to remind you of myself', as he wrote to Goethe on 8 February 1823, after he had received no reaction to his 'Meeresstille und Glückliche Fahrt'. Beethoven wrote:

> beide schienen mir ihres Kontrastes wegen sehr geeignet auch diesen durch Musick mittheilen zu können, wie lieb würde es mir seyn zu wissen, ob ich passend meine Harmonie mit der Ihrigen verbunden, auch Belehrung welche gleichsam als wahrheit zu betrachten, würde mir aüßerst willkommen seyn. [22]

Even his assurance – 'wie hoch würde ich eine allgemeine Anmerkung überhaupt über das komponiren oder in Musick sezen Ihrer Gedichte achten!'– did not help.[23] What Beethoven had sent him did not belong to Goethe's musical world. He avoided a long written discussion about it – as he had already done with Eberl – but he also wanted to avoid making a short negative reply. Whereas the Lieder compositions were made to be performed privately or in a semi-public musical salon, this particular work, with its cantata character, belonged to the few Viennese settings of Goethe texts to be performed in the concert hall. The first performance took place on 25 December 1815 in the Großer Redoutensaal. In February 1822 this work was published in Vienna by Sigmund Anton Steiner. It is well worth noting that the Leipzig composer Friedrich Rochlitz (1769-1842), who corresponded with Goethe and was appointed Court Councillor by the Grand Duke of Weimar, wrote a review[24] in which he gave this work high praise. He was very attracted by this music which, with its tone painting, assumed an independent role – which, for Goethe, was too much of a good thing.

In contrast to Beethoven's cantata and to Eberl's settings, Dietrichstein's Lieder corresponded to Goethe's musical world. For us this is all the more remarkable because we are still captive to hero-worship. We busy ourselves with Goethe, Beethoven and Schubert but fail to see that we are better able to see the relationship between these three if we also take Eberl and Dietrichstein into account.

The same applies to the Goethe settings by Nikolaus Freiherrn von Krufft (1779-1818), a composer who today is completely forgotten, but whose Lieder and chamber music are as fine as any composed in Vienna at the beginning of the nineteenth century.

---

[22] *Ludwig van Beethovens Briefwechsel. Gesamtausgabe*, ed. Sieghard Brandenburg, 5 (Munich: 1996), p.36. 'both seemed to me to be communicable through music. How nice it would be for me to know whether I have succeeded in combining my harmony with yours; even instruction, which I would accept as truth, would be extremely welcome.'

[23] ibid. 'how highly I would value any sort of general comment at all about the composing or setting of your songs!'

[24] *Allgemeine Musikalische Zeitung*, 24 (Leipzig, 1822), columns 674-76.

In 1812 he published 25 Lieder with piano accompaniment and a significant foreword dated February 1812:

> Was die musikalische Behandlung dieser Texte betrifft, so hatte ich dabey einen dreyfachen Zweck vor Augen: Richtige Declamation in dem Geiste der Gedichte und mit Beziehung auf alle Strophen; möglichste Klarheit und Abründung der Melodie; unabhängige Clavier-Begleitung, so viel sich dieß mit der erforderlichen Unterstützung der Stimme vereinigen ließ.[25]

These are strophic songs in which the music is neither subordinate nor dominant but plays a role equal with that of the text. They are, as the composer writes in the foreword:

> in den klassischen Dichtern Deutschlands geschöpft; bey einigen derselben, z.B. der Würde der Frauen, dem Troste in Thränen, dem Liede aus der Ferne, dem Liede aus Meisters Lehrjahren – traf ich in der Wahl mit sehr ausgezeichneten Tonsetzern zusammen; viele derselben wurden, so viel mir bekannt, noch nie componirt.[26]

Goethe is represented with three poems: Stylistically these Lieder are closer to Schubert's than to Dietrichstein's strophic Lieder. For anyone who wants to place Schubert's Goethe settings in the proper context of the period, knowledge of these Lieder by Krufft is indispensable.

---

[25] *Sammlung deutscher Lieder mit Begleitung des Claviers. Der verdienstvollen Sängerin Therese Fischer zugeeignet vom Freiherrn Niklas von Krufft* (Vienna: Anton Strauß, 1812). Copy consulted in the Archiv der Gesellschaft der Musikfreunde in Vienna, Cat. No. VI 3752 (Q 6406). 'With regard to the musical treatment of these texts I had a three-fold aim in mind: correct declamation in the spirit of the poems and in relation to all the strophes; the greatest possible clarity and roundedness of the melody; independent piano accompaniment, insofar as this was compatible with the support required by the voice.'

[26] ibid. 'drawn from the classical writers of Germany; some of the poems – like "Würde der Frauen", "Trost in Thränen", "Das Lied aus der Ferne", the Lied from *Wilhelm Meisters Lehrjahre* – coincided with the choice made by other, excellent composers; many of the poems, so far as I know had never yet been set to music at all.'

Example 1.3 Krufft, 'Lied aus *Wilhelm Meisters Lehrjahre*'

Amongst the many Viennese composers who set Goethe texts to music, Johann Christoph Kienlen (1783-1829), originally from Bavaria, must also be highlighted, although he belonged to the Viennese musical world only in 1808, when he worked as theatre conductor in Pressburg (today Bratislava), and again from 1811 to 1816 when he was opera director and theatre conductor in Pressburg and Baden-Wien. Already in 1810, while working briefly in Munich, he published twelve Goethe Lieder in Leipzig.[27] Kienlan's setting of 'Heidenröslein', is, according to Max Friedländer[28], 'of all [settings of this text] the nearest to that of Schubert'. Around 1813/14 twenty of Kielen's songs were published in Vienna[29], seven of which have texts by Goethe: 'Der Rattenfänger', 'Lied des Mephistopheles aus Faust', 'Ritter Curts Brautfahrt', 'Wechsel-Lied zum Tanze', 'Trost in Thränen', 'Wer kauft Liebesgötter', 'An Mignon'. His simple and unpretentious settings correspond exactly to the ideal of the Berlin Lieder School and thus to that of Goethe and his musical models, Reichardt and Zelter. It is no wonder that Goethe was interested in Kienlen, supported him and in 1815 recommended him for work in Frankfurt.[30] The Goethe settings of Ignaz von Mosel (1772-1844) have a similar character, although we don't know whether Goethe knew them. Like Kienlen, Mosel had, on the one hand, set texts with which we are familiar from Schubert, and, on the other hand, composed poems which we would never have expected to be set. For us the Goethe settings in the Lieder dedicated to Michael Vogl and published in 1820 are of particular interest.[31] Michael Vogl is known to us above all as a dedicatee and interpreter of Schubert songs. These settings of the poems 'Sehnsucht. Aus dem Roman: Wilhelm Meisters Lehrjahre', 'Jägers Abendlied', 'Rastlose Liebe' were also set by Schubert, though in a very different way.

Out of this rich supply of material one final reference should be made to the Goethe settings of the Beethoven pupil, Carl Czerny (1791-1857), best known as a composer for piano. These settings were composed in the years 1810/11 and were not published,

---

[27] *Zwölf Lieder von Göthe mit Begleitung des Piano-Forte in Musik gesetzt und Ihro Majestät der Königin von Baiern Friederike Wilhelmine Caroline in aller tiefster Ehrfurcht gewidmet* (Leipzig: Ambros Kühnel, Plattennummer 818, 1810). Copy consulted in the Archiv der Gesellschaft der Musikfreunde in Vienna, Cat. No. VI 12502 (Q 6286). There was a copy of this edition also in Goethe's library.

[28] Max Friedländer, p.133.

[29] *Zwanzig Lieder mit Begleitung des Piano-Forte in Musik gesetzt und Seiner Kaiserlichen Hoheit dem Allerdurchlauchtigsten Erzherzog Rudolph von Oesterreich in allertiefster Ehrfurcht gewidmet* (Vienna: Pietro Mechetti, 228, 1813/14). I consulted Kienlen's copy dedicated to the Archduke Rudolph in the Archiv der Gesellschaft der Musikfreunde in Vienna, Cat. No. VI 12503 (Q 10544).

[30] *Goethe und Österreich. Briefe und Erläuterungen*, p.XXXVI.

[31] *Sechs Gedichte für eine Singstimme mit Begleitung des Piano in Musik gesetzt und Herrn Michael Vogel* [recte: Vogl] *k.k. Hof-Opern-Sänger gewidmet* (Vienna: S. A. Steiner & Comp., 3014 1820). Copy consulted in the Archiv der Gesellschaft der Musikfreunde in Vienna, Cat. No. VI 12651 (Q 7321).

though this does not at all mean that they were not performed[32]: 'Des Mädchens Klage', 'Das Geheimnis' und 'Der Erlkönig' (see example 1.4). What the young composer produced leads us into a new era: his understanding of the Lied is that of Schubert. While he does not match Schubert's achievement either in invention nor in artistic quality, he shares with him the ability to exhibit completely new possibilities for setting Goethe's texts. They are, to begin with, through the tone painting in a completely independent piano part, not in line with Goethe's aesthetic but are pointing to the future. If we were tracing lines of development, they would lead from Eberl via Czerny – and partly via Krufft – to Schubert.

Reference to these selected works of all the composers before, and contemporary with, Schubert is not only important for highlighting the strength of Goethe's presence in the Viennese music scene of his time. These songs also show us that Schubert's Goethe settings are to be seen in an historical perspective which reveal two aesthetic trends which needed to be described here. That Schubert trod a path that did not correspond to Goethe's own aesthetic ideas about music and genre has often been discussed. But it is important to know that Schubert was not alone in this respect and was still less a pioneer. What was new in Schubert was that he set so many ballads and dramatic texts of Goethe which account for a higher percentage of his Goethe settings than with any other composer mentioned here. It is also important to remember that Goethe must have looked on the Schubert settings of his texts at least with good will, despite the fundamental aesthetic distance, for, according to the censorship laws which were tightened up as a result of the Congress of Vienna, the name of the dedicatee could only be put on the title page of a publication with his written permission. If Schubert dedicated his three Lieder op.19 'respectfully to the poet'[33] there must have been a written permission from Goethe. It is a pity that it has been lost, but that it existed cannot be denied. It was not an acknowledgement by Goethe of Schubert's Lieder style, but it was a proof of his respect for the composer.

Did the Viennese public make the aesthetic distinctions that Goethe did or could have done? Not likely, because it loved variety, newness – it sought new ideas, new conceptions and happily waited for something different, whatever it might be.

---

[32] Czerny's manuscript is in the Archiv der Gesellschaft der Musikfreunde in Vienna, Cat. Musikautographe Carl Czerny 27a

[33] 'dem Dichter verehrungsvoll' is the formulation used on the title page of the first edition which appeared with Anton Diabelli & Co. in Vienna.

Example 1.4 Czerny, 'Der Erlkönig'

Goethe's presence on the Viennese music scene naturally affected the stage as well. In 1796, the director of the orchestra of the Vienna Court Theatre, Paul Wranitzky (1736-1808), asked Goethe whether he would entrust to him the setting of Part Two of the *Zauberflöte* that Goethe was working on. The poet thought very highly of Wranitzky's *Oberon, König der Elfen*, and consented in principle. There were other reasons why the libretto remained a fragment and could not contribute to Goethe's presence on the Viennese music scene.[34] When the enthusiastic friend and patron of music, Joseph Franz Maximilian Fürst von Lobkowitz (1772-1816), advertised a richly endowed competition for opera libretti and asked Goethe to preside over the jury, Goethe declined, but he consented to look through the most deserving of the manuscripts that were to be sent to him. We don't know what became of this, and there was no recommendation by Goethe of an opera libretto for Vienna. 'May it please you to find time to come to Austria', wrote Lobkowitz in this context. 'I am convinced that you will find Vienna interesting in various ways, and Vienna won't fail to appreciate its guest.'[35] It is worth adding that Lobkowitz had earlier already been in contact with Goethe over musical issues concerning the Weimar Court Theatre.

In relation to musical drama, Goethe was present in Vienna for the first time in 1780. We can name here the following examples of operas with texts either by Goethe or in imitation of him. Usually it is stated, without any distinction, that the text is by Goethe. In the year 1780 the three-act opera *Claudine von Villa Bella* by Ignaz Beecke (1733-1803) had premiered in the Hofburgtheater; the opera remained on the programme and was also performed in the Kärntnertortheater. Franz Schubert's Singspiel *Claudine von Villa Bella*, D 239, composed in 1815 and unfortunately partly lost, was not staged in a public theatre. There is some evidence that there was a private performance (at least of some numbers) in a *Haustheater*.[36] Similarly it is a matter of regret that nothing came of the project of a setting of *Claudine von Villa Bella* by the Haydn pupil, Anton Polzelli (1763-1855), because Goethe gave advice for its composition.[37] On the other hand, in 1830 *Claudine von Villa Bella* by Joseph Drechsler was performed. *Scherz, List und Rache*, a

---

[34] Goethe was assuming that the second part of the *Zauberflöte* would be played in conjunction with the first part, but since the latter was, at the time, only being presented in Schikaneder's Vorstadttheater, Goethe would have had to apply to the Baron Braun, the Theatre Director. It was unlikely that Braun would suddenly stage Part One for that reason alone. A further impediment would have been the competition with a rival theatre. The question of censorship would have played a part: Goethe would have had to submit his sequel to the Viennese authorities for their approval. It is certain that they would have required some changes. For further correspondence on this project see *Goethe und Österreich. Briefe und Erläuterungen*, pp.3-8.

[35] ibid., pp.44-48.

[36] For further discussion of this theme see Otto Biba, 'Schubert's Position in Viennese Life', *NCM* (1979), *NCM* 3/2 (1979), pp.106-13.

[37] ibid., p.XXXVI

German opera with Goethe's text and music by Peter von Winter, had its premiere in Vienna in 1784. In 1794 Goethe's Singspiel *Erwin und Elmire*, published in 1788 (the previous year there was a revision of the drama which had been performed at the Wiener Burgtheater as early as 1776) with music by Josef Martin Ruprecht (1756-1800), was given its first performance in the Kärntnertortheater.

In the Freihaustheater directed by Emanuel Schikaneder, the German version of an Italian opera with words by Goethe and music by Domenico Cimarosa (1749-1801) was produced with the title *Die vereitelten Ränke*. The Singspiel *Jery und Bätely* with words by Goethe and music by Conradin Kreutzer (1780-1849) had its premiere in 1810 in the Hofburgtheater. Around 1812, during the time he was opera director and conductor in Pressburg and Baden-Vienna, Johann Christoph Kienlen's Singspiel with Goethe's text, *Scherz, List und Rache*, was written[38] and must have had its premiere in one of the two theatres – and thus in the outskirts of Vienna. After nothing came of a *Faust* project of Beethoven's, Josef Bernard wrote a *Faust* libretto – a version of Goethe – for Louis Spohr (1784-1859); his big two-act *Faust* opera, written in Vienna in 1813, had its premiere in Prague in 1816 and its first Viennese performance in 1818 in the Theater an der Wien. In 1827 it was also in rehearsal in the Kärntnertortheater. In the Theater an der Wien in 1816 the five-act melodrama of Ignaz Seyfried (1776-1841) had its premiere (with August Ernst Klingemann's version of Goethe's text). It remained a success right into the second half of the nineteenth century.[39]

Of the music for Goethe's plays we need only refer to Beethoven's *Egmont* music, op.84, with an overture and nine vocal and instrumental numbers for which he was commissioned by the Hofburgtheater in 1809. Since the composer was not finished on time, the play received its first performance there in 1810 without Beethoven's music, which finally came to be heard for the first time in the fourth performance. It is, right up to the present day – but now only in the concert hall – the best known music to a dramatic text of Goethe.

---

[38] See Othmar Wessely in: *Die Musik in Geschichte und Gegenwart. Allgemeine Enzyklopädie der Musik* 7 (Kassel-Basel-London-New York, 1958), column 885.
[39] This overview is taken largely from Anton Bauer: *Opern und Operetten in Wien* (Graz-Köln, 1955).

2 | Goethe and Zelter: An Exchange of Musical Letters
Lorraine Byrne

Goethe's Musicality Revealed

Goethe's correspondence with Zelter, which began in 1799 and lasted until 1832, the year in which both friends died, is an important source for the poet's understanding of music, and testifies to his musical intelligence. In order to survive life, Goethe was convinced that a person needed the soothing power of music, above all song, and in his letters to Zelter the poet's genuine need for music in his life is apparent. He regularly attended concerts and soirées, and when approaching sixty he organized a *Singschule* in his house to make music under his direction. Goethe's interest in vocal music led him to compose a rhythmic setting of 'In te, Domine, speravi' for four-part choir. A year later, in the winter of 1813/14, he asked Zelter to compose a setting of 'In te, Domine speravi' for the same medium in exchange for some quodlibets for his *Liedertafel*.[1] The composer acquiesced and, in comparing the two renditions, Goethe recognized the influence of the Baroque composer, Jommelli, on his own compositional style.[2]

Goethe's *Hauskapelle* was the fulfilment of a dream he wrote about in *Wilhelm Meister*. In this novel he saw himself as Serlo, who:

> ohne selbst Genie zur Musik zu haben oder irgendein Instrument zu spielen, wußte ihren hohen Wert zu schätzen [...] Er hatte wöchentlich einmal Konzert, und nun hatte sich ihm durch Mignon, den Harfenspieler und Laertes, der auf der Violine nicht ungeschickt war, eine wunderliche kleine Hauskapelle gebildet.[3]

---

[1] Goethe to Zelter, 26 December 1813, *MA* 20.1, p.326.
[2] Goethe to Zelter, 23 February 1814, *MA* 20.1, p.333.
[3] *Wilhelm Meisters Lehrjahre*, *HA* 7, Book 5, Chapter 1, p.283. Serlo 'knew how to appreciate the high value of music without having a genius for it or playing any kind of instrument; [...] he had one

Figure 2.1 Carl Friedrich Zelter, Lithograph by Ludwig Hein from the Oil Painting by Karl Begas

concert a week and now through Mignon, the Harper, and Laertes, who was good at playing the violin, he had formed a wonderful little *Hauskapelle*.'

Through Goethe's letters to Zelter we know what music was performed and how his house-music was arranged. The first part of the programme was always dedicated to sacred music; the secular works were usually followed by songs dealing with 'nature and the world' and finally – as was the preference of the poet – the evening ended with the performance of humorous songs.[4]

In addition to his *Hauskapelle* Goethe attended concerts regularly, yet constant musical activity alone was not enough for the poet. After performances he consulted Zelter about the music he had heard and so we witness his spiritual response to music and his sincere concern to understand the art. The history of music interested Goethe as part of the chronicle of human culture, and his correspondence with Zelter reveals his desire to obtain a picture of musical development in general. In a letter to Zelter dated 14 January 1819, Goethe records a series of instructional recitals in Berka, where Schütz played to him every day for three to four hours at his request:

> in historischer Reihe: von Sebastian Bach bis zu Beethoven durch Philipp Emanuel, Handel, Mozart, Haydn, durch, auch Dusseck und dergleichen mehr.[5]

In a similar fashion, he urged the twenty-two-year old Mendelssohn to play him pieces in chronological order and then to explain what each composer had done in order to further the art. While Goethe's relationship with both musicians reveals a certain reliance on an interpreter to bring music alive to him, the poet's modest technical skill in music should not be taken as definite proof that the poet was 'unmusical'. Goethe's lack of skill in score reading and performance did not result from a lack of musicality, but arose from his late start in learning an instrument. While Goethe grew up with music, he was fourteen before he learned to play the piano; flute and cello were studied in later years. Goethe refers to his incomplete musical education in his correspondence with Zelter, yet, conscious of this handicap, he was industrious in acquiring a greater knowledge of the art.

Goethe's love for the melismatic melodies of Bach and Handel reveals the independence of his musical judgement and suggests how his opinion on setting words to music is not as conservative as is traditionally held. His own perception of Bach stands in complete contrast to the social aspect of music-making and performance. Lying down with his eyes shut in the Juno room of his Frauenplan house, in a state of heightened experience, Goethe listened attentively to Schütz's interpretations of Bach's

---

[4] See, for example, Goethe's letters to Zelter on 15 September 1807, *MA* 20.1, p.163 and 16 December 1807, *MA* 20.1, p.168.

[5] Goethe to Zelter, 4 January 1819, *MA* 20.1, p.550. 'in historical sequence selections from Sebastian Bach to Beethoven, including Philipp Emanuel, Handel, Mozart, Haydn, Dusseck too, and other similar composers'.

preludes and fugues. This took place in November 1818.[6] Even before this significant encounter he acclaimed Fräulein Hügel's performance of Bach in 1815, many years before Mendelssohn's Berlin performance of the *St Matthew Passion* in 1829 heralded the revival which brought Bach's music to the attention of the public at large. The signficance of Goethe's encounter with the music of Bach is apparent in a letter to Zelter in 1827, where he again records the private recitals in Berka and describes how his entire attention was directed at the transacoustic background of the music:

> Wohl erinnerte ich mich bei dieser Gelegenheit an den guten Organisten von Berka; denn dort war mir zuerst, bei vollkommener Gemütsruhe und ohne äussere Zerstreuung, ein Begriff von eurem Grossmeister geworden. Ich sprach mir's aus: als wenn die ewige Harmonie sich mit sich selbst unterhielte, wie sich's etwa in Gottes Busen, kurz vor der Weltschöpfung, möchte zugetragen haben, so bewegte sich's auch in meinem Innern, und es war mir, als wenn ich weder Ohren, am wenigsten Augen und weiter keine übrigen Sinne besässe noch brauche[7]

Listening to Schütz's performance, Goethe experienced the very essence of Bach's music, its inner coherence and timelessness. When Goethe speaks of eternal harmony, he is, of course, alluding to the classical idea of a numerically structured cosmic harmony, which he believed to have witnessed upon hearing Bach's music. He describes Bach's instrumental music as resounding metaphysics, as the revelation of *musica mundana*, which gave him a sense of inwardly participating in the cosmic order. Within the framework of Goethe's *Theory of Sound*, enclosed in a letter to Zelter in 1826, the music of Bach would be classified in terms of numerical laws. In this way it contrasts with the anthropocentric, organic dimension of music, whose medium is the human voice, and with which Goethe ultimately had greater affinity.

As with his scientific studies, Goethe's portrayal as an *Augenmensch* is complementary to his musicality, for he often translated the effect music had upon him into pictorial terms. Various images contained in the correspondence show how Goethe sought to capture the gestures of music pictorially, in a way which altogether matched the basic nature of music. During his visit in 1830, Mendelssohn reports that upon hearing the beginning of Bach's Overture in D Major, Goethe visualized a Baroque feast in tableau form. While scholars have interpreted this form of criticism as a lack of technical ability,

---

[6] See Goethe's letter to Zelter, 4 January 1819, *MA* 20.1, p.549.
[7] See Goethe to Zelter, 17 July 1827, Enclosure, *MA* 20.1, p.1021. 'On this occasion I of course, recalled the good organist of Berka; for it was there, in perfect repose and without extraneous disturbance, that I first formed an idea of your great maestro. I said to myself, it is as if the eternal harmony were conversing with itself, as it may well have done in God's breast just before the creation of the world; that is the way it moved deep within me, and it was as if I neither possessed nor needed ears, nor any other sense – least of all, the eyes. See also Zelter's letter to Goethe, 9 June 1827, *MA* 20.1, p.1003.

Goethe's method of approach is embedded in the universality of interdisciplinary thinking. His form of musical appreciation revealed relationships which a more academic approach might possibly not have reached. An example of this is his manner of thinking in analogies, which he drew between music, architecture and colour, and which transcended the limits of the individual arts. Goethe considered Leonardo's *Last Supper* to be the first fugue in the visual arts and it is reasonable to assume Goethe was open to synaesthesia. In his letters to Zelter Goethe openly acknowledged this visual orientation and he took cognizance of this when listening to music. Unlike Carl Philipp Emanuel Bach who saw the gestures of music-making as a positive contribution to the communication process, Goethe held them to be a disturbing secondary phenomenon, which could divert attention from the unreserved reception of music if they were not in harmony with the music performed. With chamber music the communication between players enhanced the performance, but in opera the orchestral players should be hidden, for their gestures interfered with the musical drama.

Goethe regarded not the eye but rather the ear as the sense organ, which permits the most direct access to the individual's innermost being. When Goethe found himself incapable of making more than a partial pictorial transformation of a quartet by Mendelssohn, whom he greatly esteemed, he described how it remained 'in den Ohren hängen'. It remained on his ear until he had time to assimilate it. Conversely, when Mendelssohn played through the first movement of Beethoven's Fifth Symphony during his 1830 visit, Goethe immediately remarked, 'Das bewegt aber gar nichts, das macht nur staunen'.[8] Goethe's verbal inadequacy in the face of Beethoven's Fifth is not an example of the poet's musical conservatism, as is usually claimed. Like Zelter, Goethe recognized Beethoven's brilliance as a composer and admired him with awe.[9] Beethoven's music had a diffuse emotional effect upon Goethe: some of it remained beyond rational grasp and was therefore incomprehensible. Interestingly, for Zelter, such incomprehensibility was part of its appeal and in a letter to Goethe in 1831, he considered, 'Das ist der Vorteil den man beim Genie voraus und davon hat: es beleidigt und versöhnt, es verwundet und heilt; man muß mit.'[10] Yet musical enjoyment, which Goethe described to Zelter as a balanced relationship between sensuality and intellect, was, for him, tantamount to intelligibility. By not being accessible to the intellect, Beethoven's instrumental music embodied the daemonic for Goethe, something he had

---

[8] Andreas Eichhorn, 'Goethe als Musikhörer', in: *Goethe Chorlieder* (Frankfurt am Main, 1998), p.27. 'That does not move one at all, it only causes astonishment.'
[9] Zelter to Goethe, 14 September 1812, *MA* 20.1, p.286.
[10] Zelter to Goethe, 6 April 1831, *MA* 20.2, p.1462. 'This is the advantage we derive from genius: it offends and reconciles, it wounds and heals; one must go along with it'.

always inwardly rejected and once defined for Eckermann as that 'was durch Verstand und Vernunft nicht aufzulösen ist'.[11]

One of the most interesting documents in Goethe's communication with Zelter is his interest in music as an acoustic phenomenon and his discussion of major and minor tonalities. That Goethe was the leader in this discussion, and not reliant on Zelter's opinion, is evident in his letters to Schlosser where the debate is continued. In contrast to Schlosser, Goethe questions the association of the minor mode with melancholy, and he relates major and minor tonalities to the duality in human nature. For Goethe, the major mode was an expression of all that is objective and connects the soul to the outer world, and the minor tonality is the mode of introspection and concentration. The poet's preoccupation with musical polarity is revealed through his correspondence with Zelter, and it is clear that he does not always accept the composer's opinion. While Zelter's conciliatory response brought the debate to a halt, Goethe reopened the discussion a year before his death, and it is Zelter who agrees with Goethe's musical opinion.[12] Goethe's first formal papers on music commenced in 1805, with his translation of Diderot's *Neveu de Rameau*.[13] What is most significant about Goethe's writing about music is that he is not merely recycling his reading and the views of others, but is giving his own experienced, passionately felt, existentially authentic insights. In the notes to this work he recognized the depth of his own musical response, and his research on the French composer awakened his interest in other theorists. In a letter to Zelter on 4 January 1819, he mentions his discovery of the theoretician, Johann Mattheson, a contemporary of Bach, whose monumental folio *Der Vollkommene Capellmeister* he was reading.[14] The fact that Goethe was interested in the theoretical background and sought appropriate expert advice strikes us as extremely modern. Inspired by the acoustician, Ernst Chladni and the scientist Ernst Meyer,[15] he sketched a treatise on acoustics. Goethe's *Tonlehre* is contained in his correspondence to Zelter on 9 September 1826, where he encloses it for the composer's consideration.[16] Although fragmentary in form, Goethe's *Tonlehre* is interesting, for it reveals how he approaches music in a scientific way in order to gain a deeper insight into the art.

---

[11] Eckermann, 2 March 1831, (Stuttgart, 1998), p.486. 'that which cannot be accounted for by understanding and reason'.
[12] See, for example, Goethe's letters to Zelter on 22 June 1808, *MA* 20.1, pp.184-85; 31 March 1831, *MA* 20.2, p.1460 and Zelter to Goethe, 14 April 1831, *MA* 20.2, p.1463.
[13] Goethe to Zelter, 19 June 1805, *MA* 20.1, p.102.
[14] Goethe to Zelter, 4 January 1819, *MA* 20.1, p.550. See also Zelter's letter to Goethe, 2 June 1819, *MA* 20.1, p.561.
[15] Goethe to Zelter, 31 January 1803, *MA* 20.1, p.33.
[16] Goethe to Zelter, 9 September 1826, *MA* 20.1, p.952.

Figure 2.2 Zelter's Setting of Goethe's 'Das Gastmahl' enclosed in the correspondence (in Goethe's and Zelter's own hand)

Goethe's independent and ingenious reflections upon music, as exemplified by the tonality controversy with Zelter or by his draft of a system of acoustics, derive not least from his opinion that the sensual effect which music exercised upon his imaginative faculty was more important than preconceived aesthetic dogma. For Goethe, theory was the critical penetration of sensual perception, of what is audible as music. In countering Zelter, who held the minor to be a deficient mode on empirical, scientific grounds, it is interesting that Goethe should have used the musician's ear as an argument: 'Was ist denn eine Saite und alle mechanische Teilung derselben gegen das Ohr des Musikers?'[17] The primary encounter was of paramount importance to Goethe, followed by knowledge through reflection. Thus Goethe gave priority to listening to music. To Friederike Helene Unger Goethe named three qualities which characterized his listening to music: his conviction regarding the unique affective power of music, the frame of mind in which he listened to music, and listening as far as possible, 'unreservedly' and 'repeatedly'. Goethe placed great emphasis on repeated listening, not only because of the importance of increased familiarization, but rather that in the phase of actually coming to grips with the music, described by Goethe as 'Nachdenken' (a reflective process), repeated hearing provided him with several chances to check his first impressions and deepen them. Goethe's personal experience of this phenomenon is described in his letters to Zelter; on one occasion he attended three performances of Mozart's *Il Seraglio* in order to gain access to the music. In 1824 he opens up a discussion of Handel's *Messiah* inspired by his reading of J. F. Rochlitz's theoretical study of the work.[18] He arranges a performance of Handel's *Messiah* in his home and attends rehearsals to test out what he has read. He discusses the work with Zelter and relates how his understanding becomes clearer in performance.

Scholars far too seldom realize what extraordinary wide-ranging knowledge of the repertoire Goethe possessed. It included the music of Palestrina, which he had encountered for the first time during his journey to Italy; Byzantine vocal music; and composers right up to his own time, such as Hummel, Beethoven, Schubert, and Mendelssohn. Numerous operas, which had been performed under Goethe's theatre direction in Weimar, were likewise at his hand. Goethe's correspondence with Zelter bears testimony to his catholic taste in music and contradicts the perception that the poet blindly accepted Zelter's musical opinions. While Goethe admired Zelter's musicological writing and compositions he also recognized the limits of his abilities. In May 1815 he suggests Zelter write a History of Music in the same vein as Winkelmann's

---

[17] Goethe to Zelter, 22 June 1808, *MA* 20.1, p.186. 'For what is a string and all its mechanically produced division in comparison with the ear of a musician?'

[18] Rochlitz, *Die Entwickelung des Messias*, in *Für Freunde der Tonkunst*, Goethe to Zelter, 8 March 1824, *MA* 20.1, p.788. See also Zelter to Goethe, 20-23 March 1824, *MA* 20.1, p.796; Goethe to Zelter, 27 March 1824, *MA* 20.1, p.798 and 28 April 1824, *MA* 20.1, p.803.

classical histories[19] but, like their plans to write a cantata for the Reformation Jubilee,[20] Goethe eventually drops the idea, recognizing Zelter's talent was realized in smaller forms. Even here Goethe did not acclaim Zelter blindly: in a letter to the composer on 14 October 1821, Goethe asks permission to reinstate the poet as he alters the musical rhythm of Zelter's setting of 'Derb und Tüchtig'.[21] While the beginning of Goethe's correspondence with Zelter is marked by his dependence on the composer, frequently Goethe opened up their musical discussion and, as his knowledge grew, gradually this reliance diminished. When Zelter tells Goethe that Milton's tragedy first induced Handel to write his *Samson*, Goethe is intrigued but finds Handel's treatment closer to the Bible than Milton's text which, in his opinion, approached very closely the purport and style of ancient Greek Tragedy.[22] Following a performance of a Greek choir at the Easter services in 1808, Goethe remarks on the close relation between the Russian hymns and Sistine chants, and asks Zelter about the origins of Byzantine music.[23] Zelter's reply reveals that Goethe's musical knowledge had surpassed him in this area and he corresponds with the philologist F. A. Wolf on the music in Constantinople. At the end of their correspondence Zelter himself recognized the reversal in their roles, and in a letter to the poet he admits: 'you are the only person I know, whose musical judgement offers unique insight and value'.[24]

Zelter's relationship with Goethe

Zelter's relationship with Goethe has been looked at askance, the blunt Zelter being falsely blamed for Goethe persisting in eighteenthcentury concepts of musical aesthetics and 'ignoring' composers like Schubert and Berlioz. Ossified into an object of philology, the pedantic tutor of Mendelssohn, Loewe, Nicoli and Meyerbeer, and a solid monument to a philanthropic sense of responsibility to education, today Zelter's name is only raised in association with Goethe or with composers such as Schubert or Mendelssohn. In comparing a composer of ability with a composer of genius, it is not surprising that Zelter comes out of it badly. If we compare the canon of Zelter's compositions with Schubert's compositional oeuvre, the difference between the two composers is clear, without our even listening or reading through it. Yet, looked at in their own light, Zelter's songs are as good as any Lieder to be found by a contemporary composer other than Schubert, but in performance and musicology we continually

---

[19] Goethe to Zelter, 17 May 1815, *MA* 20.1, p.383.
[20] Goethe to Zelter, 14 November 1816, *MA* 20.1, p.476.
[21] Goethe to Zelter, 14 October 1821, *MA* 20.1, p.670.
[22] Goethe to Zelter, New Year's Eve 1829, *MA* 20.1, p.1299.
[23] Goethe to Zelter, 20 April 1808, *MA* 20.1, p.173. Zelter to Goethe, 2 May 1808, p.179.
[24] For further development of this theme, see Lorraine Byrne, *Schubert's Goethe Settings* (Aldershot: Ashgate, 2003), pp.10-14, and 426-28.

underrate his music through such comparisons. In making this observation I am not espousing a Zelter renaissance but am interested in responding to the history of the German Lied against the wider background of German cultural history. Like Reichardt, Zelter's was a philosophical and a sociological approach to the definition of musical goals. His desire to find a language capable of communicating emotional experience in its simplest and purest form bore something of the same cultural message, as did the nascent ideas of German classicism. Goethe and Zelter recognized song as the innermost unity of poetry and sound. Goethe's first letter to Zelter on 26 August 1799 praises the unity of words and music in Zelter's Goethe settings and the composer's true inclination for making much of their spirit his own.[25] Zelter describes his compositional process to the poet; the correspondence is laden with attachments – suggestions of poems to be set – some of which were taken up: 'Um Mitternacht' and 'Gleich und Gleich' received their setting this way. The correspondence records settings of some particularly demanding poems of Goethe such as the varied interpretations of 'Harpers Klage' composed in 1795 and in 1816, as well as programmatic scenes and musical tableaux such as 'Johanna Sebus'.[26]

In the correspondence there are many references to popular settings such as 'Wandrers Nachtlied' ('Über allen Gipfeln', see example 2.1): in 1814 Goethe praises a performance by the tenor, Carl Moltke at his *Hauskapelle*[27] and in 1820 he cites it along with 'Johanna Sebus', 'Um Mitternacht' as 'die reinste und höchste Malerei in der Musik'.[28]

Figure 2.3 The Wooden House on the Gickelhahn at Ilmenau

---

[25] Goethe to Zelter, 26 August 1799, *MA* 20.1, p.7.
[26] See, for example, Goethe to Zelter, 6 March 1810, *MA* 20.1, p.228.
[27] Goethe to Zelter, 22 April 1814, *MA* 20.1, p.344.
[28] Goethe to Zelter, 2 May 1820, *MA* 20.1, p.599. 'the purest and highest style of word-painting in music'.

Figure 2.4 Opposite the Wooden House on the Gickelhahn at Ilmenau

Example 2.1 Zelter, 'Wandrers Nachtlied'

The correspondence also records Goethe's response to settings of deeply thoughtful poems like 'An die Entfernte', which Zelter composed plainly and strophically, as well as his enthusiasm for)'s 'Rastlose Liebe', which is remarkably progressive, starting with precipitate declamation and building up to furious, emphatic octave rises (see example 2.2):

Example 2.2 Zelter, 'Rastlose Liebe'

Zelter's musical ability is continually called into question by scholars, yet his letters to Goethe reveal a reflective musician. When he asks Goethe to translate from Latin Jungius' *Harmonie* he rewards the poet by discussing the fundamental principles of harmony discussed in relation to the music of Hans Leo Hassler and Palestrina. Later when Goethe sends him a manuscript of 247 chorales by Pachelbel, Zelter considers Pachelbel's achievement in relation to other composers of chorales from Luther up to Sebastian Bach.[29] Zelter's correspondence with Goethe chronicles the composer's artistic growth and the impact he had on the musical life of Berlin. In December 1808 he founded the Berlin *Liedertafel*, a choral society of twenty-five men – which inspired the formation of other such societies. In addition he established various institutes for teaching church and school music in Königsberg (1814), Breslau (1815) and Berlin (1822) and a student 'collegium musicum vocale' in 1830. When he was founder of the Royal Academy of Religious Music in Berlin (1822) and director of the Sing-Akademie (1823), numerous works were staged under his direction. The correspondence chronicles performances of such works as Bach's motets and cantatas, Handel's oratorios, Graun's *Der Tod Jesu*, Haydn's *Creation* and *Seasons*; Beethoven's Oratorio, *Christus am Ölberge*, and Mozart's *Requiem*. Under his guidance, the Sing-Akademie became a model for the performance of early sacred choral works with instrumental accompaniment, provided by the *Ripienschule,* which he founded in 1809. Zelter drew his profound understanding of musical works and sources from the extensive collection of music in the Sing-Akademie Archives and thereby gained a reputation as an authority on early sacred music. In recognition of this he received an honorary doctorate from the University of Berlin in 1829 and was appointed Professor of Music of the Akademie der Künste in Berlin the following year.

Two years before his death, Zelter admitted to the poet, '[Ich kann] nicht ohne Töne leben',[30] and Zelter's discussion of concerts attended provides a valuable chronicle of concert life in Berlin at the beginning of the nineteenth century. His letters provide an important musical record of the music performed in public concerts in Berlin, which included performances of Rossini's *Tancredi, Wilhelm Tell, Othello, The Siege of Corinth* and *La Donna del Lago*; Spontini's *Olympia, Cortes* and *La Vestale*; and Spohr's *Macbeth*.[31] Zelter shared Goethe's love of the human voice and his letters carry detailed descriptions of performances such as those of Anna Milder-Hauptmann in Gluck's *Iphigénie en Tauride*; as Emelina in *Die Schweizerfamilie* and Pamina in the *Zauberflöte*; Henriette Sontag's performances of Susanna in Mozart's *Figaro* and Desdemona in

---

[29] Zelter to Goethe, 4 April 1824, *MA* 20.1, p.800.
[30] Zelter to Goethe, 4 March 1830, *MA* 20.2, p.1330. 'I cannot live without music'.
[31] See, for example, Zelter's letters to Goethe: 27 August 1818 *MA* 20.1, p.543; 7 June 1820, *MA* 20.1, p.617; 21 July 1820 *MA* 20.1, p.625; 27 January 1830, *MA* 20.21, p.1310; 26 October 1830, *MA* 20.2, p.1383; 1 November 1830 *MA* 20.2, p.1387; 27 October 1831, *MA* 20.2, p.1560.

Rossini's *Othello*, and he acclaims Wilhelmine Schröder-Devrient as the leading lady in Ferdinand Reis's opera, *Die Räuberbraut*.[32] Like Goethe, Zelter criticized the virtuoso cult of individualism, which degrades the musical work to a mere vehicle for the demonstration of technical and artistic dexterity and so works against the listener's purely musically-oriented interest. At first Zelter complained about the extravagant reception of Paganini's concerts of his violin concerti, yet when he heard him perform he acclaimed not only his technical virtuosity as a performer, but also his individuality, his grace and intellectual force.[33] Other performances of note include concerts given by Moscheles and Hummel, whom Zelter describes as 'ein Summarium jetziger Klavierkunst indem er Echtes und Neues mit Sinn und Geschick verbindet'.[34] Goethe envies musical activities such as Moser's Quartet evenings in Berlin, and Zelter continually makes an effort to include him. He continually introduced composers and performers to Goethe and a year before both artists died, he wrote to the poet, 'Dein redlicher Anteil an meinen Produktionen ist mir immer gegenwärtig, so wie ich Dich unter unsern Zuhörern denke'.[35] Zelter's role as inspector of public music education made him attentive to the needs of musicians. And he objected to the high fees Rossini and Spontini received in comparison to the orchestral players.[36] He was acutely aware of this on a trip to Vienna in the summer of 1819, during which time he really embraced the musical life of the city. He tells Goethe how Beethoven is praised to high heavens and Haydn is forgotten, though his spirit lives among the Viennese. He relates how Rossini is in vogue and he attends many performances including *La Gazza Ladra*. He meets Beethoven and Grillparzer,[37] befriends Weigl and Salieri, and, astonishingly, he says none of Salieri's pupils surpass their master.[38] The letters contain many topical issues, some directly related to his own work such as the quarrels over the new Berlin

---

[32] See, for example, Zelter's letters to Goethe on 13 September 1812, *MA* 20.1, p.284; 28 October 1827, *MA* 20.1, p.1074 and 12 April 1830, *MA* 20.2, p.1342; 10 May 1830, *MA* 20.2, p.1356 and 12 February 1831, *MA* 20.2, p.1445.

[33] See, for example, Zelter to Goethe, 17 April 1829, *MA* 20.1, p.1218; 14 May 1829, *MA* 20.2, p.1227. Goethe to Zelter: 17 May 1829, *MA* 20.2, p.1230 and 9 November 1829, *MA* 20.2, p.1275.

[34] Zelter to Goethe, 23 May 1826, *MA* 20.1, p.922; 'an epitome of contemporary pianoforte playing, for he combines what is genuine and new with feeling and skill.' See also Zelter to Goethe, 30 April 1821; *MA* 20.1, p.657; 27 November 1824, *MA* 20.1, p.823; Goethe to Zelter, 14 October 1821, *MA* 20.1, p.671.

[35] Zelter to Goethe, 14 April 1831, *MA* 20.2, p.1464. 'Your honest, sympathetic interest in my music is ever present with me, just as I think of you as one of our audience'

[36] Zelter to Goethe, 19 June 1825, *MA* 20.1, p.854 and 19 May 1831, *MA* 20.2, p.1475.

[37] Zelter to Goethe, 14 & 15 September 1819, *MA* 20.1, pp.584-85.

[38] Zelter to Goethe, 22 & 29 July, 1819, *MA* 20.1, p.568 and p.573.

Hymn Book. Others more striking include Beethoven's use of the metronome and the question of authorship in Mozart's *Requiem*.[39]

Zelter's correspondence with Goethe throws light on the background to the Bach revival. A chart of Baroque composers which he draws up for Goethe reveals his extensive knowledge of the period and includes such musicians as Schütz, Schien and Scheidt, Rosenmüller, A. Scarlatti, Pachelbel and Telemann.[40] In their correspondence of 1827, Goethe is fascinated by Zelter's observation of Couperin's and Vivaldi's influence on Bach's compositional style, and during his trip to Vienna, the composer considers how 'Mozart steht viel näher an Sebastian Bach als Emanuel Bach und Haydn'.[41] He informs Goethe of Mozart's enthusiastic reception of Bach in Leipzig at a time when Hiller considered Bach's music dated and raises the question of Baroque influence on Mozart's style.[42] Zelter sends Goethe some autographs of Sebastian Bach, discusses the musical irony in Bach's biblical settings and comments on the inward nature of Bach's music. There is extensive documentation of the rehearsals for the first performance of the *St Matthew Passion*. Zelter relates to Goethe how, 'Felix hat die Musik unter mir eingeübt und wird sie dirigieren wozu ich ihm meinen Stuhl überlasse'[43] and from the orchestral pit he watched Mendelssohn with pride.[44] Although in one letter he calls out to Bach, 'Ich habe dich wieder ans Licht gebracht',[45] he only steps in to conduct a second performance because Felix was giving a series of organ recitals in London and he does not hide from Goethe how the reviews are different, but not intolerably so.[46]

Zelter's letters to Goethe provide a fascinating account of Mendelssohn's development as a composer. He introduces Felix to Goethe in the winter of 1821/22 and after the visit his letters chronicle Mendelssohn's development. He describes 'sein erstaunliches Klavierspiel'[47] and recounts Mendelssohn's compositional progress with delight. Between 1822 and 1826 he records the composition of Mendelssohn's dramatic works: *Die wandernden Komödianten*; *Der Onkel aus Boston oder Die beiden Neffen*; *Die Hochzeit des Camacho*; a Gloria in E flat Major and a Magnificat in D Major for solo voices, choir

---

[39] Zelter to Goethe, 10 May 1831, *MA* 20.2, p.1475 and enclosure to Zelter's letter to Goethe, 10 August 1827, *MA* 20.1, p.1021.

[40] Zelter to Goethe, 4 April 1824, *MA* 20.1, p.800.

[41] Zelter to Goethe, 28 July 1826, *MA* 20.1, p.937. 'Mozart stands much nearer to Sebastian Bach than to Emanuel Bach and Haydn.'

[42] Zelter to Goethe, 28 July 1826, *MA* 20.1, p.936.

[43] Zelter to Goethe, 9 March 1829, *MA* 20.2, p.1207. 'Felix has studied it under me, and is going to conduct it, for which I am giving up my desk to him'.

[44] Zelter to Goethe, 12 March 1829, *MA* 20.2, p.1209.

[45] Zelter to Goethe, 9 June 1827, *MA* 20.1, p.1005. 'I've brought you to light again'.

[46] See, for example, Zelter to Goethe, 9 March 1829, *MA* 20.2, p.1207.

[47] Zelter to Goethe, 11 March 1823, *MA* 20.1, p.729. 'his marvellous piano playing'

and orchestra; the Piano Quartet in C Minor, op.1; his Concerto in A Minor for piano and string orchestra; his Double Piano Concerto in A flat Major; his Octet in E flat Major, op.20, and the first movement of his String Quintet, no.1 in A Major, op.18. Characteristically, Zelter recounts Mendelssohn's 'schöner Fleiß'[48] without any trace of jealousy, admitting, 'Weiß ich selber nichts Rechts zu machen, halte ich doch meine Jünger an';[49] he relates how Mendelssohn's development positively delights him and after a private performance of his fourth opera in 1824 he admits, 'Von meiner – schwachen Seite kann ich meiner Bewunderung kaum Herr werden, wie der Knabe der so eben 15 Jahre geworden ist mit so großen Schritten fortgeht'.[50] Goethe responds with delight, recalling Felix's performance of his Piano Quartet in D Major, op.3, which he dedicated to the poet during his visit to Weimar in 1825,[51] and a year later he sends thanks to Felix for the splendid copy of his aesthetic studies.[52] Mendelssohn's travels to Paris in 1825 and 1832, to Scotland in 1829, and his Italian Journey in 1830 are all documented and discussed in Goethe and Zelter's letters.

Zelter's humility is evident in his letters to Goethe and it is clear that he recognized the limits of his musical abilities. He recalls how he practised the violin unwearyingly in his youth, performing Tartini's, Benda's, Celli's, and Corelli's concerti in public; at the same time he recognizes the limits of his technical ability.[53] The experience of these years informed his writing of instrumental music including the Viola Concerto in E flat Major.[54]

In 1808 Zelter described his music as 'kleinen Herrlichkeiten'[55] to the poet Goethe, admitting, 'Könnte ich nur an etwas Großes kommen. Meine Jahre gehn dahin und es wird – nichts'.[56] At the same time he was well able to celebrate those around him. In a letter to Goethe on Christmas Eve 1825, Zelter acclaims a performance of Weber's *Euryanthe*. He compares the unfavourable reception of this work in Vienna and Dresden to the warm reception and encouragement the composer received in Berlin. He praises

---

[48] Zelter to Goethe, 10 December 1824, *MA* 20.1, p.828. The quote continues: 'Sein schöner Fleiß ist die Frucht einer gesunden Wurzel'. 'His admirable industry is the fruit of a healthy root'.

[49] Zelter to Goethe, 17 March 1822, *MA* 20.1, pp.694-95. 'Even if I myself fail to produce anything much myself, I keep my students focussed'.

[50] Zelter to Goethe, 8 February 1824, *MA* 20.1, p.785. 'From where I stand, I can hardly master my surprise, at a youth just fifteen years old, progressing so quickly.'

[51] Goethe to Zelter, 21 May 1825, *MA* 20.1, p.844.

[52] Goethe to Zelter, 11 October 1826, *MA* 20.1, p.954.

[53] Zelter to Goethe, continuation of letter dated 7 May 1831, p.1468.

[54] Carl Friedrich Zelter (1752-1832) Concerto for Viola and Orchestra in E flat Major (Munich Chamber Orchestra with Harold Schlichtig as soloist and conductor), CD 7 61959 11 070878.

[55] Zelter to Goethe, 3 February 1803, *MA* 20.1, p.33. 'small glories'

[56] ibid. 'Could I but achieve something great! My life is passing and nothing comes of it'.

Weber's intense industry[57] and is delighted by the celebrations after the performance, remarking:

> Daß ich altes Stück dabei nun auch immer sein muß braucht Dich nicht zu wundern, weil ich nicht der Narr sein will mit den Schmälern zu Winkel gehn und mich am Wohlergehn Eines Menschen in der Welt zu ärgern.[58]

A remarkable example of his humility is found in Zelter's letter to Goethe on 11 June 1826, where he compares his own setting of a poem by Voss to a setting by his student, Fanny Hensel, and admits, 'sie [hat] es in der Tat besser getroffen als ich'.[59]

Conclusion

Goethe and Zelter spent a staggering thirty-three years corresponding or, in the case of each artist, over two thirds of their lives. Zelter's position as Director of the Sing-Akademie in Berlin and Goethe's location in Weimar resulted in a considerable correspondence. The 891 letters that passed between these artists contain an important historical record of the music performed in public concerts in Berlin and in the private and semi-public soirées and matinees of the Weimar court at the beginning of the nineteenth century.

Goethe's letters offer a chronicle of his musical development, from his Classical Weimar years to the final months of his life. While the beginning of Goethe's friendship with Zelter is marked by his dependence on the composer, Goethe's awareness of the gap in his musical knowledge inspired him to develop, and gradually his reliance on Zelter diminished. Although they remained life-long friends, Goethe moved away from the composer on many points and at an early stage in their correspondence he recognized the composer's limitations. He perceived Zelter as an unsuitable composer for *Der Zauberflöte Zweiter Teil* and for *Faust*, and though they originally planned to write an oratorio together which could stand beside Handel's *Messiah*, he was aware that the composer could not realize this aim. Zelter's name is usually linked with Goethe, as a composer of his settings, yet what Zelter offered Goethe and bequeathed to history was much more than this. As Kayser and Reichardt correctly realized, Goethe found in Zelter the musical correspondent he had been seeking. In Zelter he found an intelligent and reflective musician whose natural outspokenness, sharp wit and ironic sense of humour engaged the poet. Zelter's unceasing energy, his passionate devotion to music,

---

[57] Zelter to Goethe, 24 December 1825, *MA* 20.1, p.889.

[58] ibid. 'You need not wonder that an old artist like myself must always be at hand on these occasions, for I am not such a fool as to go into a corner with begrudgers or to be put out by the prosperity of anyone in this world'.

[59] Zelter to Goethe, 11 June 1826, *MA* 20.1, p.933. 'She has really caught the spirit of it better than I have.'

and the profound shocks that he suffered, drew Goethe to him. Their correspondence grew increasingly intimate, and the strength of their friendship is shown in Goethe's letter to Zelter about the suicide of his stepson Karl Flöricke. Here he used the familiar pronoun 'du'. Zelter was one of the few people after 1800 with whom Goethe shared this form of address. Goethe's trust is reflected in the openness with which he discusses his various artistic ventures with Zelter. His letters to Zelter offer important insights into the creation and reception of his work, and the richness of themes raised in them establishes this group of letters as being amongst the finest in all of Goethe's correspondence.

A year before he died Goethe wrote to Humboldt that for him in his later years everything became 'mehr und mehr historisch'.[60] In Zelter's final letter to Goethe, he shares this consciousness, writing: 'es wäre recht artig, wenn man von Jahrhundert zu Jahrhundert auf die Oberwelt zurückkehren könnte, welches Korn aufgegangen und fortgegangen ist?'[61] Like Goethe, Zelter felt compelled to express his artistic ideas in writing – in reviews and music criticism in such journals as *Deutschland, Lyceum der schönen Künste* and the *Allgemeine musikalische Zeitung* – but, above all, he was aware of his bequest to music history through these letters. The original German texts, first published in three sizable volumes between 1834 and 1836 by Friedrich Wilhelm Riemer in *Briefwechsel zwischen Goethe und Zelter in den Jahren 1796-1832*, were prepared with Goethe's collaboration. Both artists consciously handed down their letters. To borrow Goethe's words, the letters 'sind so viel wert, weil sie das Unmittelbare des Daseins aufbewahren'.[62] They open the door to Goethe's and Zelter's musical lives. As Goethe once wrote:

> Briefe gehören unter die wichstigen Denkmäler, die der einzelne Mensch hinterlassen kann. Lebhafte Personen stellen sich schon bei ihren Selbstgesprächen manchmal einen abwesenden Freund als gegenwärtig vor, dem sie ihre innersten Gesinnungen mitteilen und so ist auch der Brief eine Art von Selbstgespräch. Denn oft wird ein Freund, an den man schreibt, mehr der Anlaß als der Gegenstand des Briefes.[63]

---

[60] *HABr*, 4, p.463. 'more and more historical.'
[61] Zelter to Goethe, 22 March 1832, *MA* 20.2, pp.1633-34. 'It would be nice from century to century if we could come back to earth [and see] which seed sprouted and blossomed.'
[62] *Dichtung und Wahrheit, Anhang, Aricsia der Mutter*. 'are worth so much because they preserve the immediacy of existence'
[63] *Schriften zur Kunst, Winkelmann und sein Jahrhundert, Vorrede*. 'Letters belong to the most important monuments which the individual can leave behind him. Living people conjure up for themselves the image of an absent friend to whom they communicate their innermost thoughts. Thus the letter is a kind of conversation with oneself. Often the friend to whom one writes is more the reason for the letter than the object of it.'

Portraits of Beethoven and Goethe by Joseph Karl Stieler (1781-1858)

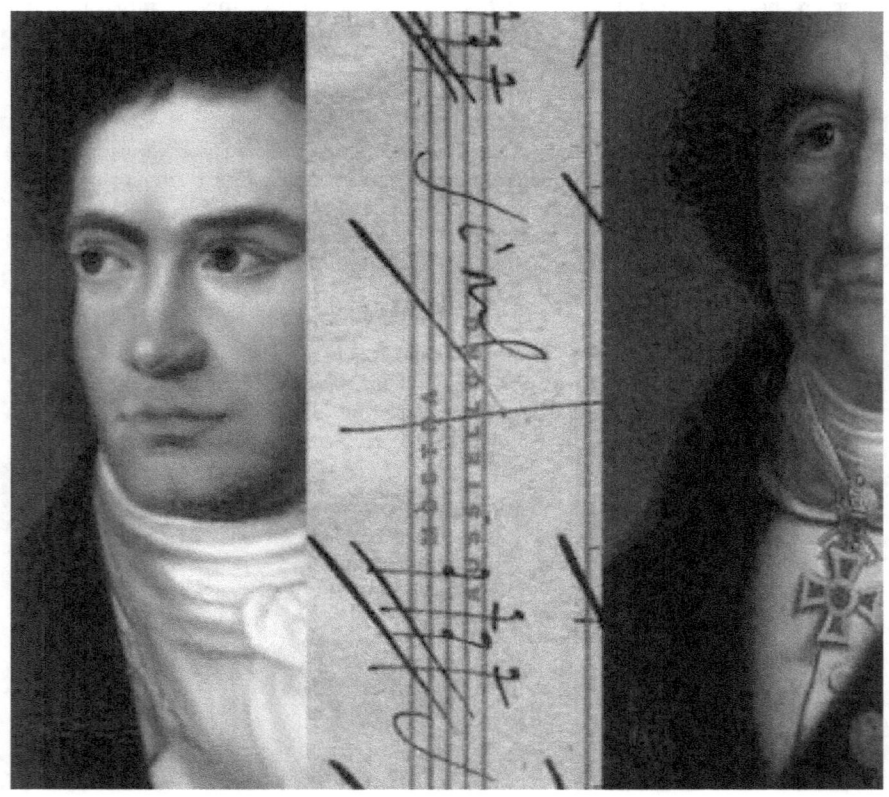

B: Goethe and Beethoven

3 | Göthe and Beethowen: Men of Genius between Distance and Affinity
Claus Canisius

When Goethe and Beethoven met in the Bohemian health resort Teplitz in July 1812, a great deal of mutual curiosity was involved. Due to the great difference in their ages – the poet was twenty-one years older than the composer – this personal interest in the beginning had naturally been somewhat unsymmetrical. Beethoven knew quite a few of Goethe's works even when he was still a child. 'Seit meiner Kindheit kenne ich Sie', he wrote in a letter to Goethe in April 1811.[1] The young Beethoven was musically educated and intellectually guided by Christian Gottlob Neefe, a former student of Johann Adam Hiller. Beethoven got to know Goethe's early poems and probably also the novel, *Die Leiden des jungen Werthers*. But at that time Goethe could hardly have been acquainted with Beethoven's early compositions written at about the age of eleven and published in 1783. Goethe was then working as an appointed Saxonian councillor of legation in Weimar and privately preoccupied with studies of anatomy.

One of Beethoven's earliest Goethe settings is the song 'Marmotte', op.52, no.7, from the Shrovetide play, *Das Jahrmarktsfest zu Plundersweilen*. This 'Klavierlied' of a frolicsome street Arab dates from about 1790. Goethe wrote four strophes each of which consisted of merely two lines plus a refrain in colloquial French 'avecque la marmotte' and its melodious variation, 'avecque si, avecque la marmotte':

---

[1] Ludwig van Beethoven, *Briefwechsel. Gesamtausgabe* (Munich: G. Henle Verlag, 1996), II, Letter no. 493, p.185. Hereafter referred to as *Briefwechsel*.

Example 3.1 Beethoven, 'Marmotte', op.52, no.7

2. Ich hab' geseh'n gar manchen Herrn,
   avec que la marmotte.
   Der hat die Jungfrau gar zu gern,
   avec que la marmotte. (Refrain)

3. Hab' auch geseh'n die Jungfer schön,
   avec que la marmotte.
   Die täte nach mir Kleinem seh'n!
   avec que la marmotte. (Refrain)

4. Nur laßt mich nicht so geh'n, ihr Herrn,
   avec que la marmotte,
   Die Burschen essen und trinken gern,
   avec que la marmotte. (Refrain)

Beethoven seemed to be inspired especially by the refrain and followed Goethe's poetic pattern in applying the simple strophic structure of the so-called Berliner Liederschule. He embroidered the monostrophic setting by adding a short postludium. Beethoven captures the histrionic charm of this dramatic farce by setting a hurdy-gurdy pattern in the piano accompaniment.

Since it is written in strophic form, Beethoven's composition enables the singer to capture the substance of the lyric by varying the expression in each verse. On the face of things the poetic substance of Goethe's 'Marmotte' song, the begging for food of a travelling street Arab, seems to be rather plain. There is, however, some vitality in this episode. Let us cast a glance at Goethe's stage directions. Marmotte was successful in appealing for money. His audience gave him some coins. But Marmotte's rival, the boy that plays the zither, also claims some of the pennies thrown by the listeners: 'Er hat mir meinen Kreuzer (a sort of threepence) genommen.' But Marmotte replies: 'Ist nicht wahr, ist mein.' The two boys now begin a fight at the end of which the defiant Marmotte is the winner and the weeping zither-player the looser. Beethoven has captured this episodical detail by composing abrupt *sforzati* in the refrain. As a sort of syncopation on the second half of the bar, they disturb the melancholic mood that Beethoven establishes at the beginning of this *Klavierlied*.

The other Goethe setting in Beethoven's *Liederheft*, op.52, the 'May-Lied' was originally entitled 'Mayfest'. (Later on the inauthentic title 'Mai-Gesang' emerged, probably for the sake of distinguishing this lyric from Goethe's second 'Mailied' (Zwischen Weizen und Korn', 'Amid Oats and Corn'). The Maylied in question was written in 1771 in Strasbourg and dedicated to Goethe's sweetheart Friederike Brion. It reminds one of a certain passage in *Die Leiden des jungen Werthers* written in 1774. Goethe, however, dates Book One of his novel back to 1771, exactly the same year in which the lyric in question was created. We recall how Werther's frame of mind depends on the four seasons: he feels depressed in autumn, for example, but happy in springtime (see table 3.1).

Goethe's 'Maylied' comprises nine strophes of four lines each. In a letter to Breitkopf & Härtel Beethoven reveals his approach to this poem. He did not set to music every detail of Goethe's synaesthetic apotheosis of love and nature. Instead he concentrated on capturing the general mood of the poem. 'Aus ihr hat er sich ein Ganzes gedacht', he wrote to his publishers, curiously referring to himself in the third person – something he occasionally used to do when he wanted to bolster his self-confidence.[2]

---

[2] Joseph Müller-Blattau, *Goethe und die Meister der Musik* (Stuttgart, 1969), p.47. 'He beheld the structure of the song in its entirety'.

Table 3.1 Juxtaposition: Goethe's *Werther*, Letter, 10 May 1771 and 'Mailied' 1771

Werther

Am 10. Mai
Eine wunderbare Heiterkeit hat meine ganze Seele eingenommen,
gleich den süßen Frühlingsmorgen, die ich mit ganzem Herzen
genieße. Ich bin allein und freue mich meines Lebens in dieser
Gegend, die für solche Seelen geschaffen ist wie die meine.
Ich bin so glücklich, mein Bester, so ganz in dem Gefühle von
ruhigem Dasein versunken, daß meine Kunst darunter leidet.
Ich könnte jetzt nicht zeichnen, nicht einen Strich, und bin nie
ein größerer Maler gewesen als in diesen Augenblicken.
Wenn das liebe Tal um mich dampft und die hohe Sonne
Oberfläche der undurchdringlichen Finsternis an der meines
Waldes ruht und nur einzelne Strahlen sich in das innere
Heiligtum stehlen, ich dann im hohen Grase am fallenden Bache
liege und näher an der Erde tausend mannigfaltige Gräschen
mir merkwürdig werden; wenn ich das Wimmeln der kleinen Welt
zwischen Halmen, die unzähligen unergründlichen Gestalten
der Würmchen, der Mückchen näher an meinem Herzen fühle
und fühle die Gegenwart des Allmächtigen

10 May
A wonderful serenity has taken possession of my entire soul,
as these sweet spring mornings have, which I am enjoying with my
whole heart. I am alone and rejoicing in my life in these parts,
which were created for just such souls as mine. I am so happy, dear
friend, so absorbed in this feeling of peaceful existence, that
my art is suffering. I could not draw now, not a single line,
and yet I have never been a greater painter than in these moments.

When the vapours rise about me in this lovely valley, and the sun
shines high on the surface of the impenetrable darkness of my forest,
and only single rays steal into the inner sanctum, and I lie in the long
grass by the tumbling brook, and lower down, close to the earth,
I am alerted to the thousand various little grasses; when I sense
the teeming of the little world among the stalks,
the countless indescribable forms of the grubs and flies,
closer to my heart, and feel the presence of the Almighty.

'Mailied'

1. Wie herrlich leuchtet
Mir die Natur!
Wie glänzt die Sonne!
Wie lacht die Flur!
2. Es dringen Blüten
Aus jedem Zweig
Und tausend Stimmen
Aus dem Gesträuch.
3. Und Freud und Wonne
Aus jeder Brust.
O Erd', o Sonne!
O Glück, o Lust!
4. O Lieb', o Liebe!
So golden schön,
Wie Morgenwolken
Auf jenen Höhn,
5. Du segnest herrlich
Das frische Feld,
Im Blütendampfe
Die volle Welt.
6. O Mädchen, Mädchen,
Wie lieb ich dich!
Wie blickt dein Auge!
Wie liebst du mich!
7. So liebt die Lerche
Gesang und Luft,
Und Morgenblumen
Den Himmelsduft,
8. Wie ich dich liebe
Mit warmem Blut,
Die du mir Jugend
Und Freud' und Mut
9. Zu neuen Liedern
Und Tänzen gibst.
Sei ewig glücklich,
Wie du mich liebst!

Table 3.2: Juxtaposition of Goethe's 'Mailied' and Beethoven's Dramaturgy for his Setting of 'Mailied'

Beethoven's Dramaturgy	Goethe
(Verses 1-3) Wie herrlich leuchtet mir die Natur, wie glänzt die Sonne, wie lacht die Flur! Es dringen Blüthen aus je-dem Zweig und tausend Stimmen aus dem Gesträuch, und Freud' und Wonne aus jeder Brust: o Erd', o Sonne, o Glück, o Lust!	1. Wie herrlich leuchtet Mir die Natur! Wie glänzt die Sonne! Wie lacht die Flur! 2. Es dringen Blüten Aus jedem Zweig Und tausend Stimmen Aus dem Gesträuch 3. Und Freud und Wonne Aus jeder Brust: O Erd', o Sonne! O Glück, o Lust!
(Verses 4-6) O Lie-be, o Lie-be! so gol-den schön, wie Morgen-wolken auf je-nen Höh'n! du segnest herrlich das frische Feld im Blüthen-dampfe die volle Welt, (*forte*) o Mäd-chen, Mäd-chen, wie lieb' ich dich! Wie blickt dein Au-ge, wie liebst du mich!	4. O Lieb', o Liebe! So golden schön, Wie Morgenwolken Auf jenen Höhn! 5. Du segnest herrlich Das frische Feld, Im Blütendampfe Die volle Welt. 6. O Mädchen, Mädchen, Wie lieb' ich dich! Wie blickt dein Auge! Wie liebst du mich!
(Verses 7-9) So liebt die Ler-che Ge-sang und Luft, und Morgen-blumen den Himmels-duft, wie ich dich lie-be, mit warmen Blut, die du mir Ju-gend und Freud' und Muth zu neuen Liedern und Tän-zen giebst, sei e-wig glücklich, wie du mich liebst, sei (*sforzato*) e-wig glücklich, wie du mich liebst, sei e-wig glücklich, (*piano*) wie du mich liebst!	7. So liebt die Lerche Gesang und Luft, Und Morgenblumen Den Himmelsduft, 8. Wie ich dich liebe Mit warmem Blut, Die du mir Jugend Und Freud' und Mut. 9. Zu neuen Liedern Und Tänzen gibst. Sei ewig glücklich, Wie du mich liebst!

Beethoven rearranged Goethe's original material into three strophes of twelve lines each. In some lines he changes Goethe's rhythm and punctuation, omits exclamation marks and stops, and puts in commas. The last two lines 'Sei ewig glücklich, Wie Du mich liebst!' he repeats twice for the sake of musical enhancement at the climax of his setting (see table 3.2).

After having changed the original order of Goethe's poem, Beethoven could no longer strictly apply the stereotypical strophic structure of the Berlin Liederschule. In accordance with his dramaturgy he modified this arrangement by composing an introduction and an interlude. The latter he inserts twice between the strophes. The introduction is a dolce bicinium setting, embroidered with chromatic intervals, which foreshadows the vocal line and brings a certain tinge of happiness to the setting. In the interlude Beethoven evokes the mood of springtime by using a motif that imitates the singing of birds. Apart from the piano introduction and the interlude, Beethoven wrote a simple piano accompaniment consisting exclusively of a chorale-like setting (a sort of 'Kantionalsatz' with the chorale melody in the part of the soprano. See example 3.2).

In relation to the Kantionalsatz Beethoven follows the conventions of the Berliner Liederschule, although he modifies the piano accompaniment towards the end of the setting. In the final strophe Beethoven obviously follows Goethe's inspiring line 'die du mir Muth zu neuen Tänzen gibst', in writing a dance rhythm. Beethoven concludes the dramaturgical climax, the triple repetition of Goethe's line, 'sei ewig glücklich, wie du mich liebst', by adding a coda with *sforzato* accents and abruptly changing dynamics. These *subito*-effects are typical for Beethoven's personal style throughout his different periods of production. But they also seem to correspond with Goethe's character, as it were. In *Dichtung und Wahrheit* Goethe says about himself that he had been driven by his mental nature from one extreme to another.[3]

After Beethoven had settled down in Vienna and studied with Joseph Haydn, he wrote in 1796, two arias which were to be integrated into the *Komisches Singspiel, Die schöne Schusterin*, by Ignaz Umlauf. In the aria, 'O welch ein Leben', for tenor and orchestra, Beethoven applied the principle of the *Kontrafaktur* – a technique of musical self quotation – by using the same vocal line he had composed in his Goethe setting of the 'Maylied'.

---

[3] *Dichtung und Wahrheit*, WA II, 7, p.110

Example 3.2 Beethoven, 'Mailied', op.52, no.4

Beethoven's *Liederheft* op.52 originally included a setting of Schiller's first version of the Lied 'An die Freude' (1785). This setting is mentioned in 1793 by Bartholomäus Fischenich, Professor of Jurisprudence in Bonn, in a letter to the poet's wife, Charlotte. The composition, however, got lost. Beethoven had planned to use the entire text, which is structured like a Greek ode in eight strophes for the protagonist and four verses for the choir. It is very likely that Beethoven has failed here to complete a Klavierlied encompassing Schiller's entire text. He probably withdrew the composition, which had in fact already been offered by Beethoven's pupil Ferdinand Ries to the publisher Simrock in 1803. Carl Czerny has handed down Beethoven's reservations about the suitability of Schiller's poetry for settings: 'Seine Dichtungen sind für den Musiker äußerst schwierig [...] Da ist Goethe viel leichter'.[4]

In fact, Beethoven has only written two Schiller settings: 'Gesang der Mönche' from the play *Wilhelm Tell*, a three-part setting of only twelve bars, and the famous choral finale of the Ninth Symphony. In the latter, Beethoven has widely changed Schiller's Lied, 'An die Freude'. He wrote out two incomplete versions of the Lied 'An die Freude', dated 1785 and 1803, and in following the model of the Dorian poet, Pindar, he transformed these excerpts into a Greek ode.

In contrast to these two Schiller settings, Beethoven has composed about thirty settings of Goethe's texts. My brief consideration of two Schiller settings reveals the tremendous difference that Beethoven must have felt in the texts of these Weimarian classicists, the works of both of whom he read over and over again. It also demonstrates Beethoven's talent for dramaturgy in the poetry he had chosen for his settings.

But for what reason did Beethoven prefer setting Goethe's texts to music rather than those of Schiller? Bettina von Arnim – *une émissaire romantique* between the poet and the composer – has handed down to posterity Beethoven's opinion of Goethe's lyrics:

> Goethes Gedichte behaupten nicht allein durch ihren Inhalt, sondern auch durch ihren Rhythmus eine große Gewalt über mich; ich werde gestimmt und aufgeregt zum Komponieren durch diese Sprache.[5]

However, in view of the two Goethe settings we have analysed, the rhythm seems to play a less important role than the general mood conveyed by the poem in question. Beethoven apparently refers to this element by saying, 'ich werde gestimmt'.

---

[4] *Czernys Erinnerungen an Beethoven*, ed. by G. Schünemann, in *Neues Beethoven-Jahrbuch*, IX, 1939. It is extremely difficult for a musician to set his poetry to music [...] this is much easier in the case of Goethe'.

[5] Joseph Müller-Blattau, *Goethe und die Meister der Musik* (Stuttgart, 1960) p.47. 'Goethe's poems have great power over me - not only through their contents but also through their rhythm. His language puts me in the right mood and stimulates me to compose'.

In February 1810 Beethoven offered his publishers Breitkopf & Härtel *12 Gesänge Mit Begleitung des Klawier's, beynahe alle durchkomponirt*. Four months later, 6 June 1810, he repeats his offer and points out that some of his compositions were Goethe settings. He especially recommends 'Kennst du das Land' because it should make a great impression on people who listen to it.[6] A month before Beethoven wrote this letter, he had been visited by Bettina von Arnim in Vienna. He had just completed the two Goethe settings 'Kennst du das Land' and 'Trocknet nicht, Tränen der ewigen Liebe', and sang both to Bettina, also playing the piano part for her. Presumably, Bettina was impressed by this authentic presentation and was apparently one of those people mentioned by Beethoven in his letter to Breitkopf & Härtel. When Bettina left him to go to Weimar, Beethoven asked her, 'Sprechen Sie dem Goethe von mir'.[7]

In the two quoted letters to his publishers, it is remarkable that Beethoven uses the term 'durchkomponieren'. He also proudly communicates that he had already received favourable feedback from some listeners even before the setting had been published. Obviously Beethoven had intended to make a special artistic impact in his Klavierlied op.75, no.1. An analysis of the setting shows he took great pains to capture the essence of the poem as well as to follow Goethe's own analysis of the technical and emotional background of 'Kennst du das Land'. In the complete edition of Goethe's works, the poem is specified as a ballad entitled 'Mignon'. Goethe himself has defined the essence of this poetic genre:

> Das geheimnißvolle der Ballade entspringt aus der Vortragsweise. Der Sänger [...]bedient sich daher aller drei Grundarten der Poesie [lyrisch, episch, dramatisch] [D]ie Elemente [sind] noch nicht getrennt, sondern wie in einem lebendigen Ur=Ei zusammen [...], das nur bebrütet werden darf, um als herrlichstes Phänomen auf Goldflügeln in die Lüfte zu steigen.[8]

In the passage that directly follows the opening strophes of the third book of *Wilhelm Meisters Lehrjahre* Goethe meticulously describes a performance he heard by the young singer 'Mignon', who accompanied herself on the zither. As we gather from *Dichtung und Wahrheit* II, Book VII, as well as from a conversation handed down by Eckermann on 18 September 1823, all his poems are based on personal experience. Eventually Goethe maintains in *Dichtung und Wahrheit* that even his entire publications are 'fragments of a great confession' – an adaptation of a dictum by Martin Luther. In view of these

---

[6] *Briefwechsel*, II, no.423, p.105 and no. 445, p.126.
[7] Franz Götting, *Chronik von Goethes Leben. Bibliography* (Frankfurt am Main, 1963), p.67. 'Tell the man Goethe about me'.
[8] 'Ballade', 'Betrachtung und Auslesung', *WA* I, 41, p.223. 'The mystery of the ballad has its roots in performance. The singer applies the three basic categories of poetry, the lyrical, the epic and the dramatic. [...] The elements are not separated. They are, so to speak, united in an egg which has to be brooded over before being able to rise into the air as a golden-winged phenomenon'.

statements, Goethe's description of the background of his 'Mignon' poem should be understood from an autobiographical point of view. But what does Goethe actually describe? He discusses the discrepancy between the two elementary versions of music: a spontaneously improvised performance of non-notated music and music that is fixed in notation, the frame of which of course is petrified, as it were. Goethe was aware of this problem. He experienced it himself, when he collected folksongs in the Rhine area, which he had listened to and had later on written down in Strasbourg. The key passage of Goethe's poetic discussion reads as follows:

> Er ließ sich die Strophen wiederholen und erklären, schrieb sie auf und übersetzte sie in's Deutsche. Aber die Originalität der Wendungen konnte er nur von Ferne nachahmen. Auch konnte der Reiz der Melodien mit nichts verglichen werden[9]

the key sentence being, 'Aber die Originalität der Wendungen konnte er nur von Ferne nachahmen'.[10]

The general problem with non-notated music as against music which has been written down has been extensively pursued by Ferrucio Busoni in his 'Entwurf einer neuen Ästhetik der Tonkunst' (1906). His essay is based on Goethe's aesthetics as well as on those of Ernst Theodor Amadeus Hoffmann (and was, incidentally, later commented upon by Arnold Schoenberg). Busoni points out that the composer's inspiration is automatically impaired by the notation of his musical ideas:

> Jede Notation ist schon Transskription eines abstrakten Einfalls. Mit dem Augenblick, da die Feder sich seiner bemächtigt, verliert der Gedanke seine Originalgestalt.[11]

Busoni concludes that it is up to the interpreter to reinstate the composer's originality. In the course of the description of the background of 'Kennst du das Land' the protagonist, 'Wilhelm', asks 'Mignon' to repeat her performance. Thus 'Wilhelm' could notice precisely the changing of her timbre in darkening her voice and that she created an air of mystery and enchanting desire on reciting certain lines. Goethe's juxtaposition of his fixed version of 'Kennst du das Land' and his description of 'Mignon's' live performance is a stroke of genius. It renders virtually two versions of the poem. The first one is the description of Mignon's singing – a challenge to our imagination – and is a sort of 'work in progress'. It varies according to the changing

---

[9] *Wilhelm Meisters Lehrjahre*, Book III, Chapter 1, *WA* I, 21, p.234. 'He asked her to repeat it, explain it; then he wrote it down and translated it into German. But, for the originality of the phrases he could only manage a pale imitation. Nothing could compare with the charm of the melodies.'
[10] 'But, for the originality of the phrases he could only manage a pale imitation of the turns of phrase.'
[11] Ferrucio Busoni, *Entwurf einer neuen Ästhetik der Tonkunst* (Frankfurt am Main, 1974), p.29. 'Every notation is a transcription of an abstract idea. From the moment the quill is seized, the idea loses its original form.'

emotional situations, especially in the case of the line 'Lass uns ziehn!' In the second version, however, placed before the 'work in progress' is the lyric established by the poet.

Busoni assumes that the destination of the musical art is to be 'free and to be freed from classical restrictions such as symmetry or harmonic rules'. In this matter Beethoven is one of his declared representatives of the avant-garde. Busoni believes that Beethoven achieved the aim of structural freedom especially in introductions to his greater works, (such as the fugue in the 'Hammerklaviersonate').

Beethoven followed the poetic drive of the *Sturm und Drang* period when he wrote his Goethe setting of 'Kennst du das Land'. He changed the key from A major to A minor and thus darkened the timbre in keeping with Goethe's description of Mignon's interpretation. Beethoven literally followed Goethe's description in several other details. No other composer has set to music the triple repetition of the poem's last line, 'Lass uns ziehen', in three different settings.[12] However, in the case of line five, the emphatic question, 'kennst *du* es wohl?', Beethoven followed his own ideas. In writing a sort of counterpoint setting, as it were, he applied an historical principle of vocal polyphony. At the early age of ten Beethoven became acquainted with this technique by studying Bach's *Das Wohltemperierte Clavier*. We encounter the technique of a double counterpoint setting later on in the Klavierlied of the Jeitteles setting, 'Wo die Berge so blau', in *An die ferne Geliebte* (op.98, no.2). The role of the singer and that of the pianist are completely exchanged. Beethoven, as it were, turns the vocal part and the instrumental part upside down: contrary to all convention, the singer supports the bass line as a vocal pedal point, whereas the pianist takes over the vocal line. Example 3.3 might demonstrate how Beethoven transcends the conventions of his time:

---

[12] Akio Mayeda, 'Kennst du das Land', *Zur Musik der Dichtung und zur Poesie der Musik*, in: *Musik in Goethes Werk. Goethes Werk in der Musik* (Schliengen, 2003), p.234.

Example 3.3 Beethoven, 'An die ferne Geliebte', op.98, no.2, bars 1-31

Returning to the Mignon 'Klavierlied', we see how Beethoven once again applied a sort of counterpoint setting by changing the conventional roles of the piano accompaniment and the vocal part. The emphatic question in the line 'Kennst du es wohl' is anticipated in the two-bar setting for piano solo:

Example 3.4 Beethoven's Klavierlied 'Mignon' from Sechs Gesänge von Göthe, op.75, no.1, bars 14-17

The setting of these four bars could also be defined as a medieval technique that follows a principle of rhetorical ornament: the *repetitio diversae vocis*, an element of the *colores* described by Johannes de Garlandia (13th century).

In the first bar of this interlude Beethoven prescribes a *crescendo* followed instantly by a *diminuendo* (bar 14). In the following two bars (16 and 17) he prescribes the same dynamics in the vocal line but he intensifies this prescription in regard to the vocal idiosyncrasy. A singer, unlike a pianist, is able to perform a *messa di voce* on a single note in the tradition of the Italian belcanto. This *messa di voce*, the 'placing of the voice', is exactly what Beethoven applied in the case of the personal pronoun 'du' within his setting of the emphatic question, 'Kennst du es wohl?'

This detail shows – *pars pro toto* – Beethoven's precision in his approach to Goethe's lyric. His interlude for piano solo, anticipating Mignon's suggestive question, is technically rooted in old music. Yet it might be considered as a stroke of revolution in the history of the 'Klavierlied'. But it can also be understood as a historical step of emancipation of instrumental music from vocal music in the sense of a *musica humana* that expresses meaning without words.

In any case, Beethoven did not really pay too much attention to Goethe's poetical discussion of the problem of non-notated music and *res facta* music. He just took Goethe's description literally and created an inspired work. Goethe is said to have disapproved of Beethoven's unconventional approach to his poem *'Mignon'*. In referring to the title of my paper 'Göthe and Beethowen: Men of Genius between Distance and Affinity',[13] I think that in the case of Beethoven's 'Mignon' setting we have come exactly to the issue of 'distance' between these two classical figures. Distance in the historical sense of Marcus Tullius Cicero's *'de amicitia': distantia tanta est unter eos morum studiorumque*[14] means as much as dissimilarity rooted in different habits and scientific activities. There was indeed a great deal of dissimilarity between Göthe and Beethowen. The poet was oversensitive with regard to the integrity of his *Sprachmelodik* in musical settings of his lyrics. On the other hand, the musician postulates, 'Der Tonsetzer muss sich über den Dichter zu erheben wissen', as Carl Czerny has handed down in his 'Mitteilungen über Beethoven'.[15]

In the environs of their artistic neighbourhood – Beethoven played for Goethe; and Goethe, as director of the Weimarian theatre, performed Beethoven's *Fidelio* as well as his music to *Egmont* – Goethe's and Beethoven's *distantia* gradually converted to an *affinitas* in the sense of an intellectual affinity.

In a letter to Marianne v. Willemer on 12 October 1821, Goethe comments on his esteem for Beethoven. This reflection was made in response to a letter from Marianne which she had written the month before, and where she says about Beethoven:

> Er hat Sie ganz verstanden, ja man darf sagen: derselbe Geist, der Ihre Worte beseelt, belebt seine Töne.[16]

---

[13] The title reflects the original spelling used by Goethe and Beethoven. It is used here by the author to suggest how they perceived everything as work in progress.
[14] Laelius, see *de amicitia*, § 74. 'On friendship': such is the distance between them of morals and education.
[15] *Czernys Erinnerungen an Beethoven*, ed. by G. Schünemann, in *Neues Beethoven-Jahrbuch*, IX, 1939. 'The composer should rise in rank above the poet when setting one of his texts to music'.
[16] Liselotte Blumenthal in: *Johann Wolfgang Goethe*, Munich 1979, p.234. 'He has understood you completely. You could even say: The same spirit that inspires your words gives life to his music.'

This passage corresponds with Ernst Theodor Amadeus Hoffmann's written remarks on Beethoven's music to *Egmont*, published in the *Allgemeine Musikalische Zeitung*, 1813:

> Jeder Ton, den der Dichter anschlug, klang in seinem Gemüte, wie auf gleichgestimmter, mitvibrierender Saite, wider.[17]

In his letter to Marianne Goethe also complains that, in the contemporary *Lied* settings, the poet's spirit has only rarely been captured. Upon listening to the works in question one merely might learn something about their composer's style and their actual frame of mind. But Goethe concedes that he also found delightful settings which mirrored his ideas and intensified them in the sense of 'expansion and contraction'. Goethe here uses the wording of his maxim of the metamorphosis, 'ausdehnen und zusammenziehen', the principle of polarization in the sense of diastole and systole that has its roots in the ideas of Immanuel Kant. And on top of this statement Goethe confesses:

> Beethoven hat darin Wunder gethan, und es war ein glücklicher Einfall, die Musik zu Egmont durch kurze Zwischenspiele dergestalt zu exponieren, dass sie als Oratorium aufgeführt werden kann.[18]

The main issue in this passage is twofold: Goethe's dictum, 'Beethoven hat Wunder gethan', is probably the highest praise that he ever bestowed on any contemporary artist. He admires Beethoven's congenial adaptability in regard to a symbiosis of poetry and music. On the other hand, Goethe perceives an aspect of transcendentalism in Beethoven's incidental music op.84 and imagines that Beethoven's *Egmont* settings might be performed separately from the drama as a sort of oratorio.

I return now to the artistic cooperation between Goethe and Beethoven in the case of *Egmont*. What are the technical and emotional preconditions, which led to this symbiosis of poetry and music? Let us glance at the dramatic structure and, following the principles of the school of hermeneutics – the art of interpretation, established by Martin Heidegger and Hans-Georg Gadamer – we must analyse the very end of the drama. Unlike Goethe's other protagonists – Werther, Tasso, Faust, for instance – Egmont dies as a hero. Surrounded by Spanish soldiers with halberds, Egmont exclaims:

> Es blinken Schwerter; Freunde, höhern Mut! Im Rücken habt ihr Eltern, Weiber, Kinder! [...] Schützt eure Güter! Und euer Liebstes zu erretten, fallt freudig, wie ich euch ein Beispiel gebe.[19]

---

[17] *Allgemeine Musikalische Zeitung*, 21 July 1813, XV/29, pp.473-81. 'Every note, which the poet touched, resounded in his soul, like strings tuned to the same pitch and vibrating together.'

[18] *Goethe Briefe*, Weimar, 12 July 1821, *WA* I, 8, p.305. 'In this respect Beethoven was miraculous, and it was an enginious idea to use entreactes in music to *Egmont* in such a way it can be performed as an oratorio.'

Goethe's drama was criticized by Schiller, who remarked about the closing scene that it was:

> aus der wahrsten und rührendsten Situation [...] durch einen Salto mortale in eine Opernwelt versetzt.[20]

Goethe, himself, must have sensed a bit of structural weakness in his historical drama, for it does not really deal with historical problems but with Egmont's daimonic character and private intricacies. And apparently for this reason Goethe rather often resorts to music in his stage directions. The final one following Egmont's monologue, 'Sweet sleep', is remarkably extensive and is reminiscent of a libretto. It is a variation of Lessing's metaphor of sleep being one of the brethren of death Beethoven has composed this lyric on sleep, happiness and madness as a melodrama – a technique which had already been used by his teacher, Neefe.

In 1809 Beethoven occupied himself for nine months with the musical setting of *Egmont*, and the work was commissioned by the Vienna Court Theatre. Apart from the two Clara songs, Goethe requires music in three of his stage directions. In addition to this Beethoven composed the overture and four entracte settings. This masterly composed instrumental music naturally links the five acts of the drama. But to enhance this function Beethoven wrote detailed stage directions into the bargain. He had obviously analysed Goethe's texts to which his settings refer.

Beethoven announced in a letter to Goethe on 12 March 1811, the transmission of the score of the *Egmont* settings:

> Sie werden nächstens die Musik zu Egmont [...] erhalten, diesen herrlichen Egmont, den ich, indem ich ihn ebenso warm als ich ihn gelesen, wieder durch sie gedacht, gefühlt und in Musik gesetzt habe.[21]

---

[19] *Egmont*, Act Five, Scene, Four, *WA* I, 8, p.305. 'Swords are flashing; courage, friends! Behind are your parents, your wives, your children! [...] Protect your homes! And to save those who are most dear to you, be ready to follow my example, and to fall with joy.'

[20] Lieselotte Blumenthal, *Johann Wolfgang Goethe, Artemis Gedenkausgabe*, 10 (Munich, 1969), p.231 'One feels hurled by a *salto mortale* out of a pure and moving situation into the world of the opera'.

[21] *Briefwechsel*, II, no.493, p.185. 'You will soon receive my music for Egmont, this wonderful Egmont which I read and felt and set to music thinking warmly of you.'

Table 3.3 Beethoven, *Egmont*, Entreacte III, Allegro. Marcia vivace

Allegro
Beethoven's score, stage direction:

'Das Orchester fällt gleich nach den letzten Worten von Clärchen ein: So laß mich sterben! Die Welt hat keine Freuden auf diese!' noch ehe der Vorhang herunter gefallen ist, welcher langsam herunter gelassen wird, so daß er erst gegen Ende des zweiten Taktes gänzlich herunter fällt. [22]

The orchestra enters just after Clärchen's final words: 'So let me die! The world has no joy after this' before the curtain has fallen, which is slowly lowered, so that it comes down completely just at the end of the second bar.

Marcia vivace. Allegro
Beethoven's score, stage direction:

'Die Schauspieler treten schon während der Musik hier von zwei Seiten heraus, schleichen sich immer langsam näher der Vorderbühne, bis die Musik geendigt, als dann fangen sie an zu sprechen, jedoch anfangs sehr langsam und furchtsam'.[23]

While the music plays, the actors step forward from both sides, slowly they creep closer to the front of the stage until the music is over, at which point they begin to speak, however very slowly and timidly at the beginning

Goethe:
Beginning of Act IV

Jetter: He! Pst! He, Nachbar, ein Wort!
Zimmermeister: Geh deines Pfads und sei ruhig.
Jetter: Nur ein Wort. Nichts Neues?
Zimmermeister: Nichts, als daß uns von Neuem zu reden verboten ist.
Jetter: Wie?
Zimmermeister: Tretet hier ans Haus an. Hütet Euch! Der Herzog von Alba hat gleich bei seiner Ankunft einen Befehl ausgehen lassen, dadurch zwei oder drei, die auf der Straße zusammen sprechen, des Hochverrats ohne Untersuchung schuldig erklärt sind.
Jetter: O weh![24]

Jetter: Hist neighbour, - a word!
Carpenter: Go your way and be quiet.
Jetter: Only one word. Is there nothing new?
Carpenter: Nothing except that we are anew forbidden to speak.
Jetter: How?
Carpenter: Step here, close this house. Take heed! Immediately on his arrival, the Duke of Alva published a decree, by which two or three, found conversing together in the streets, are without trial, declared guilty of high trason.
Jetter: Alas!

---

[22] *Gesänge und Zwischen-Akte zu Goethe's 'Egmont' für das Piano-forte von L. v. Beethoven*, op.84 (Breitkopf & Härtel in Leipzig.) Quoted in E.T.A. Hoffmann, *Schriften zur Musik* (Munich, 1977), p.461.
[23] ibid.
[24] *Egmont, WA* I, 8, Act IV, p.244.

Goethe received Beethoven's handwritten score containing all the stage directions on 23 January 1812. Some of Beethoven's remarks concern the musical performance: an immediate entry of the full orchestra at the end of the scene, for instance. Other instructions refer to technical details such as exact timing for the fall of the curtain or the extinction of a lamp. Other remarks explain musical details, such as the entry of a trumpet as a symbol of freedom. But there are also genuine stage directions concerning the actors – how they are supposed to walk or to speak. In the case of the Entreacte III Marcia vivace Beethoven notes: 'Die Schauspieler treten schon während der Musik hier von zwei Seiten heraus, schleichen sich immer langsam näher der Vorderbühne, bis die Musik geendigt, als dann fangen sie an zu sprechen, jedoch anfangs sehr langsam und furchtsam'.[25] This instruction is amazing. One might ask why does Beethoven, after having composed the incidental music for *Egmont*, then wish to play the part of a stage-manager. And was this accepted by Goethe? (Incidentally, Beethoven was experienced in stage music. In 1789 he played the viola in the orchestra of the court in Bonn and thus got to know a great deal about the contemporary opera repertoire.)

Reflecting on the composer's relationship to literature, it seems that Beethoven was disposed to plunge into the works of his predilection. In the case of Goethe's writings – his library contained 24 volumes by Goethe – he even seemed to identify himself with the protagonists. Beethoven is said to have known Goethe's novel *Die Leiden des jungen Werthers* by heart. He was obviously fascinated by the beautiful language that Goethe employed to depict nature mirrored in Werther's soul. In any case Beethoven takes Goethe's preface to *Werther* literally and 'draws consolation from his sorrows and lets the little book be his friend'. When Beethoven wrote a postscriptum of a letter from Heiligenstadt he adapted several passages from *Werther* (see table 3.5). This example might demonstrate that Beethoven really knew his 'Goethe' and that 'he read and felt and thought warmly of him', as he says in his letter to Goethe. We are now able to understand Beethoven's music for *Egmont* with all the amazing remarks, instructions and explanations as a sort of *Gesamtkunstwerk* that foreshadows somewhat Richard Wagner's approach to stage music. We also might understand more clearly Goethe's special 'organic' aspect in respect to Beethoven's music op.84 in the sense of 'zusammengezogen und erweitert'. Beethoven's music set to *Egmont* and the composer's detailed stage directions improve the dramaturgy of Goethe's play. This was fully accepted by Goethe.

---

[25] *Gesänge und Zwischen-Akte zu Goethe's 'Egmont'*, p.461. 'The actors enter from both sides, the music is still playing. They creep slowly down stage till the music stops, then they begin to speak, but initially they speak slowly and timidly.'

Table 3.4 Beethoven's Letter from Heiligenstadt

(He draws consolation from Werther's sorrows)

> Heiligenstadt am 10ten Ocktober 1802 so nehme ich den Abschied von dir – und zwar traurig – ja die geliebte Hoffnung - die ich hierher nahm, wenigstens bis zu einem gewissen Punckte geheilet zu seyn – sie muß mich nun gänzlich verlassen, wie die Blätter des Herbstes herabfallen, gewelckt sind, so ist – auch sie für mich dürr geworden, fast wie ich hierher kam gehe ich fort – selbst der Hohe Muth – der mich oft in den schönen Sommertägen beseelte – er ist verschwunden'.[26]

Beethoven adapted in this postscriptum three different passages from Goethe's Werther:

> Und ich –und ich gehe ohne Hoffnung, ohne Zweck heraus und kehre wieder heim, wie ich gekommen bin.[27]

> Ja, es ist so. Wie die Natur sich zum Herbste neigt, wird es Herbst in mir und um mich her. Meine Blätter werden gelb, und schon sind die Blätter der benachbarten Bäume abgefallen[28].

> Eine Wunderbare Heiterkeit hat meine ganze Seele eingenommen, gleich den süßen Frühlingsmorgen, die ich mit ganzem Herzen genieße.[29]

Let us now look at Goethe's stage directions in regard to Egmont's monologue 'Sweet sleep'.[30] I have put Goethe's stage direction, 'Der Schall wird stärker' (The music grows louder and louder), and the following three sentences in brackets because Beethoven did not take these directions into consideration when composing the melodrama:

---

[26] 'Heiligenstadt, 10 October 1802. 'I take leave of you, and sadly. The hope I cherished to be healed at least to certain extent must now forsake me entirely. The autumn leaves fall and yellow, so too everything has withered for me, I leave here almost as I came – the enthusiasm – which often animated me on blissful summer days – has disappeared.'

[27] Book II, 30 November 1772. 'And I – I go out with no hope or purpose at all, and return home as I departed.'

[28] Book II, 4 September 1772. 'Yes, that is how it is. As nature's year declines into autumn, it is becoming autumn within me, and all about me. My leaves are yellowing, and already the leaves of the nearby trees have fallen.'

[29] Book I, 10 May 1771. 'A wonderful serenity has taken possession of my entire soul, as these sweet spring mornings have, which I am enjoying with my soul.'

[30] *Egmont*, Act V, Prison, *WA* I, 8, p.303.

Table 3.5 Egmont's monologue 'Komm süßer Schlaf' and Goethe's Stage Directions

Egmont (allein)	Egmont (alone)
(Er setzt sich aufs Ruhebett. Musik)	(He sits down on his couch. Music)
Süßer Schlaf! Du kommst wie ein reines Glück ungebeten, unerfleht am willigsten. Du lösest die Knoten der strengen Gedanken, vermischest alle Bilder der Freude und des Schmerzes; ungehindert fließt der Kreis innerer Harmonien, und eingehüllt in gefälligen Wahnsinn, versinken wir und hören auf zu sein.	Sweet sleep! Like purest happiness most willingly you come unbidden, unimplored! You loosen every knot of rigid thought, you mingle all images of joy and pain; unobstructed flows the circle of inner harmonies and wrapped in fond delusion, we sink and we cease to be.
(Er erschläft; die Musik begleitet seinen Schlummer. Hinter seinem Lager scheint sich die Mauer zu eröffnen, eine glänzende Erscheinung zeigt sich Die Freiheit in himmlischem Gewande, von einer Klarheit umflossen, ruht auf einer Wolke. Sie hat die Züge von Klärchen und neigt sich gegen den schlafenden Helden. Sie drückt eine bedauerende Empfindung aus, sie scheint ihn zu beklagen. Bald faßt sie sich, und mit aufmunternder Gebärde zeigt sie ihm das Bündel Pfeile, dann den Stab mit dem Hute. Sie heißt ihn froh sein, und indem sie ihm andeutet, daß sein Tod den Provinzen die Freiheit verschaffen werde, erkennt sie ihn als Sieger und reicht ihm einen Lorbeerkranz. Wie sie sich mit dem Kranze dem Haupte nahet, macht Egmont eine Bewegung, wie einer, der sich im Schlafe regt, dergestalt, daß er mit dem Gesicht aufwärts gegen sie liegt. Sie hält den Kranz über seinem Haupte schwebend: man hört ganz von weitem eine kriegerische Musik von Trommeln und Pfeifen: bei dem leisesten Laut derselben verschwindet die Erscheinung. [Der Schall wird starker. Egmont erwacht; das Gefängnis wird vom Morgen mäßig erhellt. – Seine erste Bewegung ist, nach dem Haupte zu greifen; er steht auf und sieht sich um, indem er die Hand auf dem Haupte behält.)]	He falls asleep; the music accompanies his slumber. Behind his bed the wall seems to open, a brilliant apparition enters. Liberty in celestial garments, bathed in brilliant light, rests upon a cloud. She has Clare's features and inclines towards the sleeping hero. Her demeanour expresses compassion, she seems to lament his fate. She soon composes herself and, with an encouraging gesture, shows him the sign of authority: the bundle of arrows, the staff and hat. She tells him to be of good cheer and, while she points out to him that his death will bring about freedom for the Provinces, acknowledges him conqueror and hands him a laurel wreath. As the wreath comes near his head, Egmont makes a movement like one stirring in his sleep so that he is now lying facing her. The wreath hovers in his hands above his head. Away in the distance warlike music of drums and pipes is heard. At the slightest sound of this the apparition vanishes. [The sound becomes louder, Egmont wakes up, the prison is lit up with a moderate morning light. His first movement is to put his hand to his head: he rises and looks about keeping his hand on his head.]

Example 3.5 Beethoven's Incidental Music to 'Komm süßer Schlaf'[31]

---

[31] For translation see Table 3.5.

In the closing scene Goethe's stage direction is rather short: 'Drums. As he advances between the guards towards the door in the background, the curtain falls. The music joins in, and the scene closes with a symphony of victory.' Beethoven did supply this symphony. He chose instrumentation similar to that of the finale of his fifth symphony, completed in the year 1808, just before he commenced the music to *Egmont*. The instrumentation requires a full orchestra: piccolo, 2 flutes, 2 oboes, 2 clarinets, 2 bassoons, 2 trumpets, 4 horns, timpani and strings. In a letter to his publishers Beethoven sarcastically describes the quality of sound in the fifth symphony: 'The finale of the symphony is written for 3 trombones and a piccolo, not for 3 drums, but it will make more noise, and noise of a better quality than if there were six.' In the symphony of victory Beethoven does not require trombones but four horns instead.

Some Biographical Notes

Goethe visited Beethoven for the first time on 19 July 1812 while both were taking a cure at Teplitz. The year before, Goethe had become acquainted with Beethoven's setting of the two songs from *Egmont* in a version for voice and piano accompaniment. In Teplitz Goethe was now bent upon meeting Beethoven in the flesh as the legendary improvising pianist. After they had made a trip to the nearby health resort, Bilin, Beethoven played for Goethe on 21 and 23 July. Goethe noted in his diary 21 July 1812: 'Abends bei Beethoven. Er spielte köstlich'. (With Beethoven in the evenings. He played superbly.) This sentence is laconic. But it expresses high praise through its use of the adverb 'köstlich' which essentially means delightful but implies that Beethoven's performance was 'one of great value'. Goethe had already been deeply impressed by Beethoven's personality at their first meeting in the public wine restaurant 'Im goldenen Straus' at Teplitz. The same day, 19 July 1812, he wrote to his wife Christiane):

> Zusammengefaßter, energischer, inniger habe ich noch keinen Künstler gesehen. Ich begreife gut wie er gegen die Welt wunderlich stehen muß. [32]

In this dictum Goethe obviously judges Beethoven by his outward appearance. In comparing him with other artists, he employs the adjective 'zusammengefaßt' (in the comparative form 'zusammengefaßter'). Goethe uses the same word in his description of Raphael's skull which he saw in Rome in April 1781: 'Eine so schön als nur denkbar zusammengefasste abgerundete Schale'.[33] In this passage from the *Italienische Reise*

---

[32] To Christiane) from Goethe, Teplitz, 19 July 1812, *WA* IV, 23, p.45. 'I have never seen an artist with more composure energy and inwardness. I can well understand how he felt estranged from the world.'

[33] *Italienische Reise* Bericht, April. 'Das Römische Karneval', *WA* I, 32, p.327. 'A skull like a beautifully polished shell.'

Goethe also mentions Franz Joseph Gall, who wrote a theory of phrenology. In following this school Goethe developed phrenological ideas of his own. Few months after he had seen Raphael's skull in Rome he wrote to the physiognomist Lavater, that he considered the bones of the human skeleton as a 'text' in which all life of human being could be expressed: 'Zugleich behandle ich die Knochen als einen Text, woran sich alles Leben und alles Menschliche anhängen läßt'.[34]

Beethoven's forehead has been described by contemporaries as a 'Kugel', a noun which is difficult to translate into English (globe, sphere). (See figure 3.1.)

After Goethe left Teplitz for Karlsbad, he wrote to Zelter on 2 September 1812 and reported on his encounter with Beethoven. He speaks of the musician's stupendous talent and mentions his progressing deafness with great sympathy. Goethe observed that Beethoven's loss of hearing did not mean the loss of his musical ear. But he noticed that Beethoven's deafness impaired his social life and made him even more laconic than he had already been. But there is also a very critical note in Goethe's letter:

> allein er ist leider eine ganz ungebändigte Persönlichkeit, die zwar nicht ganz Unrecht hat, wenn sie die Welt detestabel findet, aber sie freylich dadurch weder für sich noch für andere genußreicher macht. [35]

In other words, Goethe was utterly shocked by Beethoven's unrefined manners. Goethe's note points out the social 'distance' between the two men of genius in the very sense of Cicero's *distantia tanta est inter eos morum* (dissimilarity rooting in different habits). Goethe's critical note also mirrors the contemporary notion of education. Wilhelm von Humboldt, for example, defines 'Bildung' (education) as magnanimity that is rooted in the striving after morals and that also might influence men's character.[36] Friedrich Hegel goes a step further by saying that a person who indulges in particularism lacks the capacity for abstraction, a deficiency ultimately caused by lack of education.

---

[34] Goethe to Lavater, Weimar, 14. November 1781, *WA* IV, 5, p.217
[35] Goethe to Zelter, 2 September 1812, *WA* IV, 23, p.89. 'but he is unfortunately a quite untamed personality. He is not entirely unjustified in finding the world detestable, but at the same time he doesn't thereby make it more pleasant for himself or others.'
[36] *Gesammelte Schriften*, VII, 1.

Figure 3.1 Two Beethoven masks. Life mask by Franz Klein, 1812. Death mask (the so-called Hippocratic face) by Joseph Danhauser, 1827

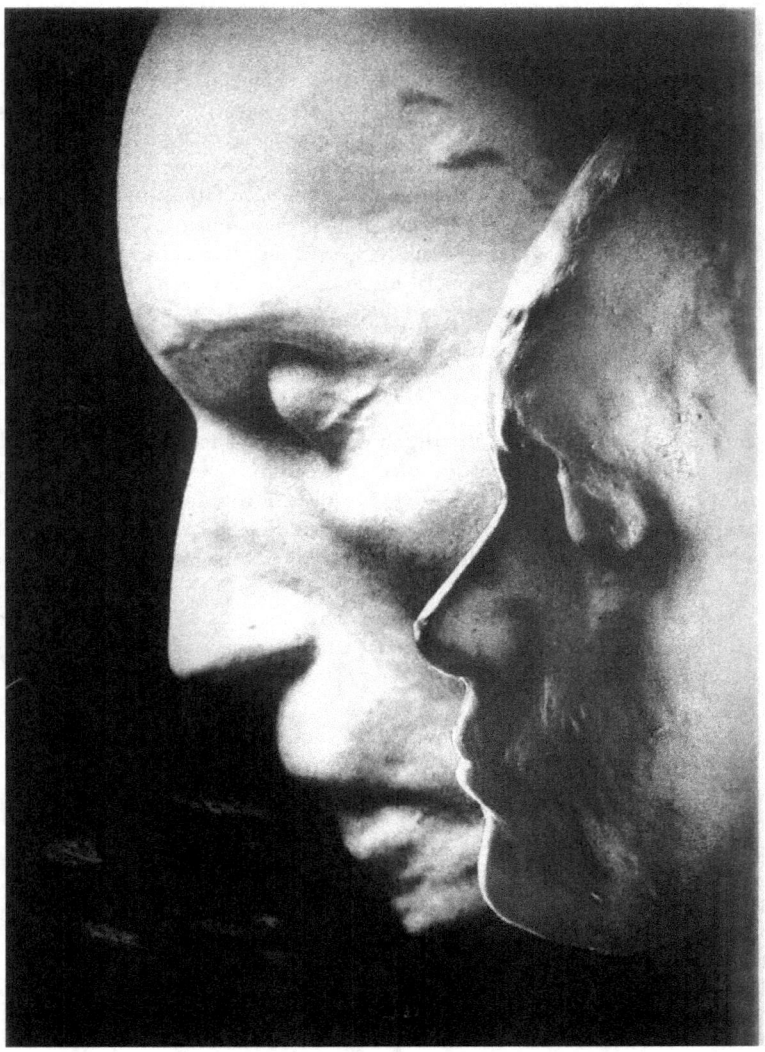

Goethe was obviously irritated by the discrepancy between Beethoven's imposing talent and his blind scorn of society. In his *Tagebücher* he merely notes on 8 September 1812: 'Beethovens Ankunft. Mittag für uns. Beethoven.'[37]

'Ira furor brevis est' (anger is a short rage) says Horace in one of his 'epistles'. In his archive Goethe stored some manuscripts of Beethoven's letters and also of his Lied settings. He inscribed the composer's name on them in red ink. When the young Ferdinand Hiller, a pupil of Hummel, in spring 1827 was sent from Weimar to visit Beethoven in Vienna, Goethe wrote a lyric on the young musician and his teacher. The first strophe is an apotheosis of musical talent and music as the medium of communication:

Table 3.6 Goethe, 'To Ferdinand Hiller', 10 February 1827

Ein Talent das jedem frommt	You have taken possession of
Hast du in Besitz genommen,	A talent that serves everyone
Wer mit holden Tönen kommt,	Whoever comes with sweet song
Überall ist der willkommen.	Is welcome everywhere. [38]

Ferdinand Hiller has handed down the composer's last utterances to posterity. Beethoven asked the young musician about Goethe's state of health and in answering this question with good news, Ferdinand Hiller also mentioned the poem that Goethe had written as an accompaniment on his journey to Vienna. Beethoven then bestowed upon Hiller his intellectual testament: 'Man muß die Kunst immer fortpflanzen'.[39]

After Beethoven had died, on the 26 of March 1827, Goethe commented upon a church ceremony in Prague in commemoration of Beethoven's death. Goethe's sentence is laconic and yet renders a final tribute to the composer: Hier ist [...] der für Beethoven veranstalteten Todtenfeier ehrend Erwähnung zu tun.[40]

---

[37] Goethe, *Tag- und Jahreshefen*, 8 September 1812. *WA* III, 4, p.320.
[38] Goethe, 'To Ferdinand Hiller', Weimar, 10 February 1827, *WA*, I, 4, p.276.
[39] Russell Martin, *Beethovens Locke* (Beethoven's Hair) (Munich, 2000), p.26. 'One always has to propagate the matter of art'
[40] Lesarten, *WA* I, 42, 1, p.50. 'Here I must honour Beethoven by mentioning the ceremonies which were held in celebration of his death.'

4 | 'Ich denke dein': Beethoven's Retelling of Goethe's Poetry
Amanda Glauert

When Beethoven died the poet Grillparzer mourned him as 'der letzte Meister des tönenden Liedes'; he invited the German people to join him as 'wir stehen weinend an den zerrissenen Saiten des verklungenen Spiels'. The one note of consolation he offered in his funeral oration, as he looked at the 'dahingeschwundenen Glanz heimischer Kunst', was the reminder that Goethe still lived, the poet who represented the other half of the nation's heart.[1] Hovering beneath the surface of Grillparzer's eloquent tribute seems to lie regret for a cultural fulfilment that never quite happened. With the image of the 'tattered strings' he evokes a piano broken by Beethoven's efforts to express more than wood and gut might bear, while he seems to consign Goethe to a half-life now that these efforts are silenced. Grillparzer referred to Beethoven's solitary existence – 'Er blieb einsam, weil er kein Zweites fand'.[2] Our thoughts immediately turn to the composer's unrequited loves. But the lack of a 'second I' also suggests a lyricist's lament over the absence of a listening ear, over the absence of a sympathetic response to give the artist back to himself, and make him and his listeners one.

Beethoven despised those who merely wept at his music and he seems to have been disappointed at Goethe's response when he played to him on the occasion of their meeting at Teplitz in 1812. According to Bettina von Arnim, Beethoven upbraided the poet directly for weeping rather than applauding:

> Aber von Euch, Goethe, lasse ich mir dies nicht gefallen; wenn mir Eure Dichtungen durch's Gehirn gingen, so hat es Musik abgesetzt, und ich war nicht stolz genug mich auf

---

[1] Franz Grillparzer, *Sämtliche Werke*, III (München, 1964), p.882. When Beethoven died Grillparzer mourned him as 'the last master of resounding song'; he invited the German people to join him in 'weeping beside the tattered strings of the silent instrument' […] as he looked at the 'vanished splendour of native art'. Michael Hamburger (ed.), *Beethoven: Letters, Journals and Conversations* (London, 1951), p.269.

[2] ibid., p.883. 'he could find no second I'. ibid., p.270.

gleiche Höhe schwingen zu wollen wie Ihr, aber ich habe es meiner Lebtag nicht gewußt [...]. Ihr müßt doch selber wissen, wie wohl es thut, von tüchtigen Händen beklatscht zu sein; wenn Ihr mich nicht anerkennen, und als Euresgleichen abschätzen wollt, wer soll es dann tun?[3]

Even in this small anecdote we see signs of the conflicts that mark out a lyricist's realm. On the pages of his *Missa Solemnis* Beethoven wrote, 'Vom Herzen – Möge es wieder – zu Herzen gehn!'[4] These words invoke the lyricist's ideal of music passing as sympathetic resonance along a chain of fellow feeling, telling or sounding out what has already been felt or heard – so that it can be felt or heard again. Yet in the scene from 1812 Beethoven is seen representing music to Goethe as a product of reflection, which passes through and is held by the brain before being offered up for recognition and applause. Therefore, when Beethoven sent Goethe settings of his poetry it is clear he wanted him to respond to new works of creation, to a retelling of his lyrics, not just to the continuing resonances of the poet's own emotion.

Knowing that Goethe was suspicious of song-setting being viewed as an act of 'componieren' (composing) rather than 'betonen' (sounding),[5] it is almost certain that the poet would have taken Beethoven's words, 'wenn mir Eure Dichtungen durch's Gehirn gingen'[6] as a challenge. The sense of confrontation in the Teplitz scene is confirmed by what we experience with Beethoven's 1809 setting of Goethe's 'Kennst du das Land'. The poet complained that here Beethoven made Mignon sing an operatic aria rather than a song.[7] If true, then Beethoven could be denying Mignon her role as a natural lyricist, as one who sings within a continuum of echoes, passing on what she has heard or what resonates within her – whether as hymn or folksong. Goethe called these two, hymn and folksong, the centres of true music-making. As he said in his *Maximen und Reflexionen*:

Die Heiligkeit der Kirchenmusiken, das Heitere und Neckische der Volksmelodien sind die beiden Angeln, um die sich die wahre Musik herumdreht. Auf diesen beiden Punkten

---

[3] Hermann von Pückler-Muskau, 'Briefwechsel zwischen Pückler und Bettina von Arnim', *Aus dem Nachlaß des Fürsten Pückler-Muskau: Briefwechsel und Tagebücher*, ed. Ludmilla Assing, 1 (Bern: Lang, 1873) pp.92-93. 'From you, Goethe, I won't stand for this. When your poems passed through my brain, they produced music and I was proud enough to desire that I might rise to the same height as yourself. But never in my life did I know whether I had done so [...] You yourself must know how pleasant it is to be applauded by hands which one respects: if you don't recognize me and consider me as your equal, who will?' ibid., p.117.

[4] This appeared over the head of the Kyrie, as quoted in *The Beethoven Compendium*, ed. Barry Cooper (Thames and Hudson, London, 1996), p.256. 'From the heart may it go to the heart'.

[5] See Heinrich W. Schwab, *Sangbarkeit, Popularität und Kunstlied* (Regensburg, 1965) p.44 and Hans Joachim Moser, *Goethe und die Musik* (Leipzig, 1949), p.92.

[6] Pückler-Muskau, p.92. 'when your poems passed through my brain'.

[7] See Schwab, p.52, quoting from letter of Goethe to Tomášek of 1822.

beweist sie jederzeit eine unausbleibliche Wirkung: Andacht oder Tanz. Die Vermischung macht irre, die Verschwächung wird fade [...] so wird sie kalt.[8]

Whether we consider Beethoven's 'Kennst du das Land' to be a song or aria, the composer seems to place Mignon on a cusp between hymn and folksong, as though she cannot settle on the true direction of her music. Reading Goethe's description of Mignon's performance of 'Kennst du das Land' in his novel *Wilhelm Meister*, it does suggest that her mood oscillates, as she changes from conveying a 'solemn grandeur' and 'weightiness and mystery' 'to pressing forward with promise or entreaty'.[9] One notes the weightiness of Goethe's opening line 'Kennst du das Land, wo die Zitronen blühn', compared to the skip of James Thomson's 'Bear me, Pomona! To thy citron groves', the poem which provides one of Mignon's background echoes.[10] Goethe's comma after the words 'Kennst du das Land' creates a more obvious pause within the first line, separating off the first two metrical feet; though as the comma's effect is carried forward into the shorter fifth and sixth lines, the separation of the two iambs begins to imply an acceleration rather than a slowing of rhythmic energy:

> Kennst du das Land, wo die Zitronen blühn,
> Im dunklen Laub die Gold-Orangen glühn,
> Ein sanfter Wind vom blauen Himmel weht,
> Die Myrte still und hoch der Lorbeer steht,
>
> Kennst du es wohl?
> Dahin! Dahin
> Möcht' ich mit dir, o mein Geliebter, ziehn.

Beethoven might be right to suggest that Mignon dances inside as she sings these rhythms. Yet for Goethe it was still crucial that the composer should chose a clear song-tendency as a basis for his realization of her performance of the poem – whether hymn or dance – not sway between the two as suggested by the contrasts in Beethoven's song.

---

[8] Goethe, *Maximen und Reflexion* 489. 'The numinous nature of church music, the cheerfulness and playfulness of folk-melodies are the two pivots of true music. At these two focal points music always and inevitably leads either towards reverence or else to dance. Any mixture of the two is confusing, dilution is boring and [...] the result is coldness.' Translation from Johann Wolfgang von Goethe, *Maxims and Reflections* (Harmondsworth, 1998), p.64.

[9] Johann Wolfgang von Goethe, *Wilhelm Meister's Apprenticeship*, ed. and trans. Eric A. Blackall (Princeton, New Jersey, 1995), p.84.

[10] Taken from James Thomson's poem 'Summer' published in 1746, as identified by Frederick Sternfeld, *Goethe and Music: A List of Parodies* (New York, 1954), p.34. 'Bear me, Pomona! To thy citron groves; /To where the lemon and the piercing lime, /With the deep orange, glowing through the green, / Their lighter glories blend. Lay me, reclin'd,/ Beneath the spreading tamarind, that shakes, Fann'd by the breeze, its fever-cooling fruit.'

The opening of Beethoven's song[11] (see example 4.3) bears some resemblance to the stately style of Reichardt's 'Kennst du das Land',[12] the setting which appeared in the original publication of Goethe's novel (see example 4.1). Yet Reichardt keeps the ebb and flow of emotional movement much more within the bounds of a single song-statement. In his song that statement simultaneously unfolds across two notions of time. The quaver rest after 'Land' outlines a pause on the dominant and hints at a rhetorical imperfect cadence, in a way that draws attention to the melody as a series of small-scale articulated moments – a kind of declamatory utterance that emerges most clearly in bars 18 and 19. Yet the composer also projects the implied cadence on the dominant in bar 2 as part of a larger-scale harmonic movement to the cadences in bars 8 and 16, which begin to emphasize the dominant more and more strongly. Thus the small-scale pause for breath in bar 2 is carried forward, via the elision of phrase-ending in bar 4, to the biggest pause for breath in bar 16, to be followed by a release of tension as the bass Ab of bar 17 directs the line from the dominant back towards the tonic. Reichardt thus encloses his song within one large shape, like an inhalation and exhalation of breath, even while outlining intermediary pauses that shift our focus from the large to the small-scale rhythmic and melodic phrasing.

Zelter's 'Kennst du das Land'[13] (example 4.2) can be analysed in similar terms, though his pause on 'Land' in bar 2 actually takes us into a different key, from G to the dominant of E minor, a key that returns in an extended passage from bars 18 to 24. His song thus operates on two harmonic levels as well as two rhythmic planes. Zelter's rhetoric of pausing on the dominant in bars 4, 6 and 14 is more obvious and exaggerated than Reichardt's, and the notion of one extended breath has to be aided by the rippling keyboard figuration from bars 6 to 12. The composer's struggle to hold the song to one hymn-like statement is much nearer the surface, and one notes how Zelter inflects his song with performance instructions to bring out the sense of shape. Yet the symmetry of one intake of breath to bar 14, and then the letting out of breath with a return towards the tonic over the next 13 bars, remains.

Looking at these two songs from Goethe's close friends helps to prepare us for the significance of Beethoven's challenge to the poet (example 4.3). For Beethoven begins to turn upside down Reichardt's and Zelter's concept of 'sounding out' or 'uttering through the breath' almost from the first bar of his song. In example 4.3 the melodic statements constantly turn back upon themselves, rather than unfolding in steady hymn-like succession. In the first two bars of his song, Beethoven reverses Reichardt's and

---

[11] Beethoven, *Sämtliche Lieder*, ed. Helga Lühning, *Neue Beethoven-Gesamtausgabe* (München, 1990), pp.96-97.
[12] Johann Friedrich Reichardt, *Goethes Lieder, Oden, Balladen und Romanzen mit Musik*, ed. Walter Salmen, *Das Erbe deutscher Musik*, LVIII (München-Duisberg, 1964), p.105.
[13] Carl Friedrich Zelter, *Fünfzig Lieder*, ed. Ludwig Landshoff (Mainz, 1932), p.47.

Zelter's melodic rise to the dominant by a melodic dominant ascending to tonic. He introduces a harmonic move to the dominant with the imperfect cadence in bar 4, but with the condensed repetition of the whole phrase from bars 5 to 7 this move seems suspended in time – an impression that is reinforced by the shifting harmonic textures from bar 8. The phrasing from bars 8 to 13 continues the rhythmic pattern of the three-bar phrase from bars 5 to 7, yet harmonically these phrases do not connect as part of one overarching progression. When the piano articulates its rhetorical imperfect cadence in bars 14 and 15, we might say it is not just asking 'where is the land?' but perhaps more crucially 'where is Mignon's song?' The piano's rhythmic motif, echoed by the voice, takes us back to the beginning – but the beginning of what? The answer Beethoven provides from bar 18 is not conclusive. Harmonically, the breath is exhaled from bar 18 with a series of perfect cadences onto the tonic, but rhythmically Beethoven takes us into a different song. From bar 18 we seem whirled into an instantly invoked 'dance around the maypole'. Such a leap from one song to another requires that we interpret the pause in bar 17 as infinitely extendable. The first song has been frozen into silence and the silence must be filled from bar 18 by whatever lies at hand – by melodic and rhythmic formulae that indicate closure without diminishing the memory of that earlier silence.

Example 4.1 Reichardt, 'Kennst du das Land'

Example 4.2 Zelter, 'Kennst du das Land'

In his novel *Wilhelm Meister* Goethe showed both Mignon and the Harper making lyrics out of what they could not express; Beethoven's 'Kennst du das Land' could claim to be doing the same with musical means. A three-fold repetition of the composer's strange hymn/dance combination directs us remorselessly to the same point of silence between the two. As all performers know, communication often depends upon the effective treatment of pauses, and here Beethoven makes sure that his performers and listeners adapt themselves to his unusual managing of silence:

Example 4.3 Beethoven, 'Kennst du das Land', bars 1-34

So was Goethe right to cast doubts on the validity of this song and on Beethoven as singer? Goethe himself believed that the flight of the lyric had to be evoked through remixing the elements of epic, dramatic and lyrical expression, as a performer responded to the 'Ur-Ei' offered by the poet.[14] His own responses to other people's lyrics brought profound transformations that marked both his separation from and identification with the sources of his inspiration. His poem 'Ich denke dein' of 1795 resulted from just such an act of creative reinterpretation – or from a series of reinterpretations, for more than one artist was involved in the chain of lyric responses leading up to Goethe's poem.[15]

Table 4.1 Goethe, 'Nähe des Geliebten' (1795)

Ich denke dein, wenn mir der Sonne Schimmmer Vom Meere strahlt; Ich denke dein, wenn sich des Mondes Flimmer In Quellen malt.	I think of you, when the shimmer of the sun Shines on me from the sea; I think of you, when the glimmer of the moon reflects in streams.
Ich sehe dich, wenn auf dem fernen Wege Der Staub sich hebt; In tiefer Nacht, wenn auf dem schmalen Stege, Der Wandrer bebt.	I see you, when the dust rises On distant paths; In deep night, when the wanderer stumbles On the narrow path.
Ich höre dich, wenn dort mit dumpfem Rauschen Die Welle steigt. Im stillen Haine geh ich oft zu lauschen, Wenn alles schweigt.	I hear you, when waves rise up With a dull roar. I often go to listen in the still grove, When all is silent.
Ich bin bei dir, du seist auch noch so ferne, Du bist mir nah! Die Sonne sinkt, bald leuchten mir die Sterne. O wärst du da!	I am with you, however far away you might be, You are near me! The sun sinks, soon the stars will come to light me. O that you were here![16]

Certain features in Goethe's poem offer to bring the chain to completion, but others invite further questions. Having taken his listener from 'thinking' of the beloved, to 'seeing' and 'hearing' her, in an emotional progression that Goethe felt made good the looseness of previous poetic versions,[17] the silence of the grove in the third verse of his poem awakens doubts about the success of his poetic conjuration. By the end we do not

---

[14] See Schwab, p.32, quoting from Goethe's discussion of the 'ballad', in: *Über Kunst und Altertum*, III (1821).
[15] See Max Friedländer, 'Goethes Gedichte in der Musik', *GJb*, 17 (1896), pp.176-94 (p.193).
[16] Translations of Goethe's, Brun's and Matthisson's 'Ich denke dein' poems, author's own.
[17] See Sternfeld, *Goethe and Music*, p.107.

know if the beloved is with the poet or not; in the final verse he asserts, 'I am with you', but then pleads, 'O that you were here'.

Such issues of 'presence' versus 'absence' were close to Beethoven's heart – as man and artist – as we know from his settings of Matthisson's *Adelaide* and of Jeitteles's song-cycle *An die ferne Geliebte* ('To the distant beloved'). In responding to Goethe's 'Ich denke dein' Beethoven could be said to be drawing the poet onto his own musical territory. The dialogue between poet and composer becomes more subtle still if we bear in mind that Goethe was inspired to write his poem by a melody, by Zelter's setting of Friederike Brun's version of 'Ich denke dein':

Table 4.2 Friederike Brun, 'Ich denke dein'

Ich denke dein, wenn sich im Blütenregen Der Frühling malt Und wenn des Sommers mild gereifter Segen In Ähren strahlt.	I think of you, when Spring paints itself In blossoms of rain And when summer's mildly ripened blessing Shines forth in ears of corn.
Ich denke dein, wenn sich das Weltmeer tönend Gen Himmel hebt Und vor der Wogen Wut das Ufer stöhnend Zurükke bebt.	I think of you, when the roaring ocean lifts itself towards the heavens and before the rage of the waves the groaning shore Moves backwards.
Ich denke dein, wenn sich der Abgrund rötend Im Hain verliert Und Philomelens Klage leise flötend Die Seele rührt.	I think of you, when the abysses of the grove Disappear into reddening light and Philomela's piping lament gently Moves the heart.
Beim trüben Lampenschein, in bitterm Leiden Gedacht ich dein, Die bange Seele flehte, nah am Scheiden: Gedenke mein!	By the dim lamplight, in bitter grief I remembered you, The fearful soul pleaded, near to parting: Remember me!
Ich denke dein, bis wehende Cypressen Mein Grab umziehn; Und auch in Tempe's Hain soll unvergessen Dein Name blühn!	I think of you, until the waving cypresses Encircle my grave; And also your name shall flower unforgotten In Tempe's grove.

Goethe responded enthusiastically to the musicality of the rhythms in Brun's poem, even though he said he felt compelled to refine the nature of her descriptive content. Brun's poetic rhythms ebb and flow around the basic shape of the 'ich denke dein' phrase itself; this was her response to the mesmeric rhythms one finds in her friend Matthisson's 'Ich denke dein' poem:

Table 4.3 Matthisson, 'Ich denke dein'

Ich denke dein	I think of you
Wenn durch den Hain	When through the grove
Der Nachtigallen	The nightingale
Akkorde Schallen.	Pours out roulades.
Wann denkst du mein?	When do you think of me?
Ich denke dein	I think of you
Im Dämmerschein	In the twilight
Der Abendhelle	Of an evening glimmer
Am Schattenquelle.	At the shadowed spring.
Wo denkst du mein?	Where do you think of me?
Ich denke dein	I think of you
Mit süsser Pein	With sweet pain
Mit bangem Sehnen	With fearful yearning
Und heissen Tränen.	And with hot tears.
Wie denkst du mein?	How do you think of me?
O denke mein	O think of me
Bis zum Verein	Until we are united
Auf besserm Sterne!	On a better star!
In jeder Ferne	In that far place
Denk' ich nur dein.	I will think only of you.

If Matthisson's rhythms here could be called dangerously 'sing-song', Brun's give time for reflection in the way they expand and then fall back to the 'ich denke dein' rhythm itself for the second and fourth line of each stanza. This sense of an 'opening out' before 'falling back' is reflected in the progress of Brun's descriptive imagery, which expands from blossoms and corn, to oceans and waves, before retreating into twilight, lamplight, and then death.

Example 4.4 Zelter, 'Ich denke dein'

As one can see from example 4.4,[18] Zelter captures an essential simplicity in the ebb and flow of Brun's poem, as he makes his melody circle around a single pitch – the dominant B. The four repeated B's that begin the second half of the stanza in bars 3 and 4 underline this purposeful reduction of the melodic compass, as does the melodic pointing of B within the postlude. The melody is almost reduced to standing on one spot. In his poetic response to Zelter, Goethe traces a progressive stilling and quieting of the senses, until from the expectant silence at the end of the third verse he claims his union with the beloved. Knowing that Goethe conceived this poem to Zelter's melody, one can connect the poet's silence of communion quite explicitly with the internal stillness of Zelter's melodic arch. However, it is interesting that when, in 1808, Zelter came to respond to Goethe's poem in his turn, he felt something more extraordinary was needed.

Goethe's 'wanderer stumbling on the narrow path' does suggest a dangerous route to the silent grove. Yet the tortuousness of Zelter's new 'Ich denke dein' melody[19] (see example 4.5) comes as rather a shock after the simplicity of example 4.4. The almost Bachian twists and turns of the vocal line suggest that Zelter felt some act of compositional virtuosity was needed to top the chain of lyrical improvisations on the 'Ich denke dein' theme. Reichardt was actually much more successful in his melodic response to Goethe's poem in 1795.

Looking at example 4.6 one can see how the rather exaggerated melodic gesture of the first two bars of Reichardt's song[20] – with the anguished diminished fifth interval and sighing appoggiatura – is progressively smoothed out and reduced in the simpler phrases from bar 7 to the end. Within each verse and across the four verses, the performers have the opportunity to press forward or linger, to make their own fluid movement between anxiety and calm. Reichardt was not offering a final completion of Goethe's poem – in fact he published another version in 1809. Instead he seemed to be pushing for the chain of improvisation to be extended further through challenging his performers' responses.

And what of Beethoven's place in the 'Ich denke dein' chain? Some will know his emphatic response to the mesmeric rhythms of Matthisson's original Ich denke dein poem.[21] After three verses where the energy of the instrumental-style sequences seems more and more ready to burst the confines of vocal melody, in the final verse of his song Beethoven makes the piano begin a series of free extensions on the 'Ich denke dein' or 'o denke mein' rhythm, as one can see in example 4.7.

---

[18] Zelter, *Fünfzig Lieder*, p.75.
[19] ibid., p.32.
[20] Reichardt, *Goethes Lieder, Oden, Balladen und Romanzen mit Musik*, p.22.
[21] Beethoven, *Sämtliche Lieder*, p.84.

Example 4.5 Zelter, 'Nähe des Geliebten'

Example 4.6 Reichardt, 'Ich denke dein'

Example 4.7 Beethoven, 'Andenken', bars 33-49

For Beethoven this was one kind of answer to Goethe's evocation of silence – a return to Matthisson's mesmeric rhythms, and thus – as in 'Kennst du das Land' – a filling of silence with rhythm rather than song-like melody.

Example 4.8 Beethoven, 'Ich denke dein'

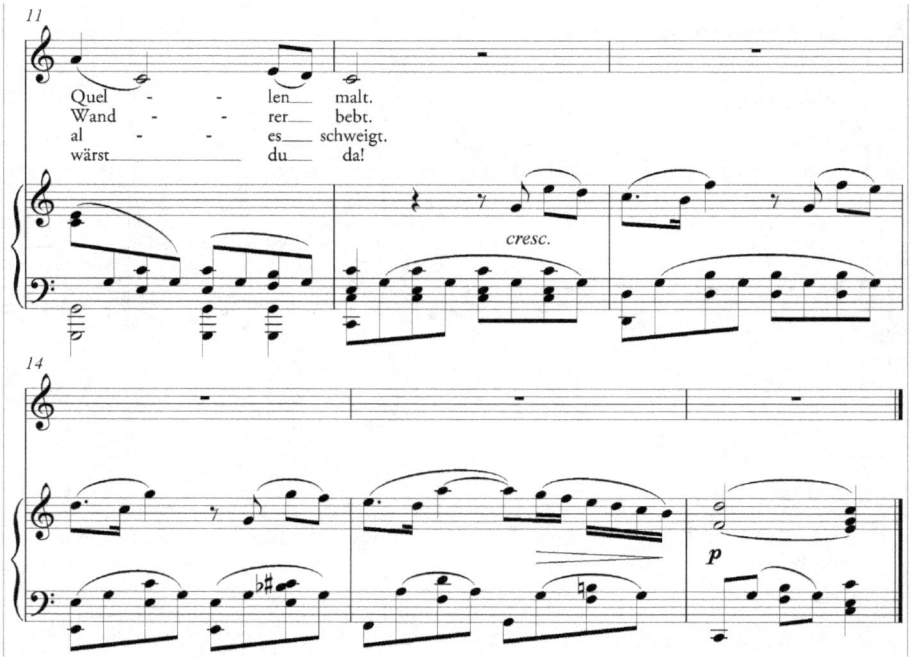

In fact Beethoven never addressed Goethe's Ich denke dein directly through song. If one looks in Erk-Böhme's *Deutscher Liederhort* of 1893[22] there is a song-version attributed to Beethoven (see example 4.8), but what is offered is in fact an editorial reconstruction of the melody Beethoven used as the basis for his variations for piano duet WoO74, first published in 1805. I do not know whether this song-melody was ever publicly performed as a song-rendering of Goethe's poem. One can imagine a certain amount of vocal improvising taking place between Beethoven and the two sisters, Josephine Deym and Therese Brunsvik, who were the dedicatees of the variations. Performed as a song the melody is surprisingly effective, in this case living up well to the melodic expectations established by Reichardt and Zelter. Indeed the similarities of example 4.8 to the melodic and harmonic construction of Reichardt's setting (example 4.6) are striking, except that in Beethoven's melody the particular shape associated with the words 'Ich denke dein', which comes in bars 2, 6, 8 and 12 of Reichardt's song, is also referred to in bars 4 and 10. Thus Beethoven's song-melody is marked every two bars

---

[22] Erk-Böhme, *Deutscher Liederhort* (Leipzig, 1893-94), II, p.82.

by the sighing appoggiaturas of his 'Ich denke dein' motif. It is just as well that Beethoven breaks up his two-bar shapes into one-bar figures in the postlude; this provides a vital contrast, a balancing effect after so much repetition. The postlude's return to melodic poise ensures that the song continues to behave like a song, even if one also senses that Beethoven is reflecting on what makes a song through his insistent use of appoggiaturas.

Beethoven's formal answer to the question of how to write a song that is simultaneously a commentary on song-writing, was to compose a set of variations. In his piano duet WoO 74 one can see how instrumental variation techniques allow the composer to expand and refine the analysis of melodic gesture that is inherent in example 4.8. In Variation 2 the overriding symmetry and sweep of the song's six-bar song-phrases is highlighted by decorative semiquavers in the *secondo* part, while two-note figures in the *primo* part bring an atomization of the original appoggiatura shape. In example 4.9 melodic outlines are dissolved and intensified simultaneously in a play of presence and absence that connects directly to Goethe's poem.[23] In the first version of these variations, from 1799, Beethoven followed Variations 1 and 2 with what became Variations 5 and 6,[24] so that the crucial third verse of Goethe's poem corresponded to Beethoven's turn to the minor in Variation 5, and his evocative reassembling of the vocal line at that point over an almost Schubertian bed of harmony. After 1803, when Beethoven added Variations 3 and 4 to the set, Variation 3 added another landmark before Variation 5's return to song-like utterance. In Variation 3 each player offers up a two-bar fragment, as though remembering a part of the 'Ich denke dein' melody, and then both have to call on the embodiment of their listening self, the other player, to join in and make the parts into a whole (see example 4.10).[25] Such a cooperation of 'halves' is shown to open the way for the fuller communion of Variation 5, and then for the comic but entirely harmless dismemberment of phrases in Variation 6.

---

[23] Beethoven, *Werke für Klavier zu vier Händen*, ed. Hans Schmidt, *Neue Beethoven-Gesamtausgabe* (Munich-Duisberg, 1956), pp.40–41.
[24] ibid., preface.
[25] ibid., pp.42-43.

Example 4.9 Beethoven, *Sechs Variationen: Lied mit Veränderungen,* **WoO 74, Variation 2,** *primo* **and** *secondo*

Beethoven's Retelling of Goethe's Poetry 123

Example 4.10 Beethoven, *Sechs Variationen*, Variation 3, *primo* and *secondo*

The further melodic triumphs of the coda, as Beethoven's instrumental lines expand and contract around the persistently returning two-bar song-shape, might seem a final tribute to the sisterly cooperation of Josephine Deym and Therese Brunsvick. But I would also like to think that in calling upon the bridging of a gulf between partners, Beethoven was offering his own distinctive contribution to the 'Ich denke dein' chain. His representation of the gulf between a poet and his 'second I' in the third variation is as vivid and poignant as Goethe's description of gondoliers singing to each other across the waters in Venice:

> Je ferner also die von einander sind desto reizender ist das Lied, wenn der Hörer zwischen ihnen beiden ist, steht er am rechten Flecke [...] ich ging zwischen ihnen auf und ab, so daß ich immer den verliess der zu singen anfangen sollte und [mich] dem wieder näherte der aufhörte [...] Wie lebendig wird mir nun diese Melodie, über deren Toten Buchstaben wir uns sooft den Kopf zerbrochen haben. Gesang eines Einsamen in die Ferne und Weite, dass ihn ein andrer gleichgestimmter höre, und ihm antworte.[26]

In these variations Beethoven found his own ways of showing the poignancy of singer and listener meeting across silences, in a union that is best achieved by pulling away from each other. By doing so we can say he was able to unite and pull away from Goethe, his equal, in the manner he so desired.

---

[26] Johann Wolfgang von Goethe, 'Tagebuch der italienischen Reise für Frau von Stein 1786', in: *Sämtliche Werke*, ed. Norbert Miller and Hartmut Reinhardt (Munich, 1990), III.1, pp.9-158 (pp.116-117). Translated as Goethe's letter to Charlotte von Stein of 7 October 1786, in: *Letters from Goethe* ed. and trans. M. von Herzfeld and C. Melvil Sym (Edinburgh, 1957), p.178: 'The farther they are from each other, the more delightful the song, and between the two is the best spot for the listener [...] I walked up and down between them, always away from the one whose turn it was to sing and towards the one who was stopping [...] This tune over whose dead notes we have often puzzled in vain, now seems so alive to me, this song that one solitary man sends out into the distance for another who feels as he does, to hear and answer him.'

5 | *Fidelio* and *Faust* in the German 'Wende' of 1989/90
Moray McGowan

Both Beethoven's *Fidelio* and Goethe's *Faust* had, in the course of the nineteenth century, become central constitutive elements of German national culture, and they remained so in the twentieth. The Cold War turned them into contested trophies. Thus throughout the German Democratic Republic's forty-year history from 1949 to 1989, high on the East German state's cultural agenda was to claim itself, and not the supposedly neo-fascist successor regime in the West, to be the true heir and custodian of the 'Erbe', this cultural heritage. Subsequently, and consequently, during the German 'Wende' of 1989/90 (a problematic term, but used here to denote the implosion and disappearance of the GDR), both works had productions with remarkable, ambivalent relationships to their historical moment.

The productions of *Fidelio* and *Faust* that concern us here both took place in one East German city, Dresden. It was here that the 'Wende' can be said to have begun, even though subsequent events in Leipzig and Berlin have become and remained more famous. It was on the streets of Dresden that violent dispersal of demonstrations was replaced, in early October 1989, by the first acts of dialogue between the forces of order and the still unrecognized organizations of popular protest, and it was at the Dresden Staatsschauspiel that representatives of the theatre workers of the GDR, who had a significant if ambivalent role in the protest movement, took what became the emblematic collective public stance of the GDR's protesting artists, with the famous text 'Wir treten aus unseren Rollen heraus', read from the stage after every performance in the Staatsschauspiel from 6 October 1989, the night before the state's fortieth birthday, until late November of that year.[1]

---

[1] *'Wir treten aus unseren Rollen heraus'. Dokumente des Aufbruchs Herbst '89*, collected by Angela Kuberski (Berlin 1990), p.39. 'We are stepping out of our roles.' The version read out from 6 October onwards was a revision of one originally read on 4 October.

Fidelio in Dresden, 7 and 8 October 1989

The weekend of 7 and 8 October 1989 in Dresden saw the remarkable concatenation of three already interconnected sets of events: firstly, the celebrations to mark the GDR's fortieth birthday; secondly, a series of protest demonstrations and reactions to them by police and party; thirdly the premiere, in the Sächsische Staatsoper, the city's opera house (usually called the Semperoper after its architect Gottfried Semper), of Christine Mielitz's production of Beethoven's opera of oppression and liberation, *Fidelio*. What was represented on stage both echoed and challenged what was happening on the streets and in the city's corridors of power. Briefly, thrillingly, opera, production, reception and extra-theatrical reality resonated together.[2] But this conjuncture of art and life at a historic moment also offers a case study in the uneasy and temporally contingent relationship of appositeness, art, monument and kitsch.

Beethoven's opera charts a movement from imprisonment to freedom, despotism to justice. Mielitz's production related the opera unmistakeably to GDR realities, though with a heart-stopping closeness she could hardly have anticipated when planning or even rehearsing it. For meanwhile, in early October 1989, in the police cells and temporary holding stations of Dresden, scenes of violence against its citizens by representatives of a regime in its death throes were being played out. At the same time on the streets of Dresden, a genuinely popular movement turned from inchoate and sometimes violent protest to peaceful, purposeful, democratic action. Also at the same time, leading figures within the local hierarchy of the Sozialistische Einheitspartei Deutschlands (SED), the ruling party in the GDR, decided against the use of military force against their own people, and in favour of dialogue. This decision sent a crucial signal to protesters in other cities, especially Leipzig (where the security forces were still issued with live ammunition on 9 October[3]): peaceful demonstration was possible, representations might be listened to. The following day, Monday 9 October, saw the weekly Leipzig demonstration grow from 10,000 the previous week to 70,000[4]; the GDR revolution as a mass, popular, peaceful movement was truly underway. In this sense, 7-8 October 1989 in Dresden is the crucial catalytic moment of the East German 'Wende'.

---

[2] See: Wolfgang Lange, 'Als fulminantes Zeitstück. Zu *Fidelio* von Beethoven in Dresden', *Theater der Zeit*, 45 (1990), 2, pp.48-50 (p.48); Friedrich Dieckmann, *Glockenläuten und offene Fragen. Berichte und Diagnosen aus dem anderen Deutschland* (Frankfurt/Main, 1991), p.65.

[3] See Herbert Wagner, *20 gegen die SED. Der Dresdner Weg in die Freiheit* (Stuttgart & Leipzig, 2000), p.17.

[4] Figures from Uwe Schwabe, 'Chronik', in: *Wir bleiben hier. Erinnerungen an den Leipziger Herbst '89*, ed. Thomas Ahbe, Michael Hofmann, Volker Stiehler (Leipzig, 1999), pp.129-228. Figures vary from source to source, but the dramatic rise in participation is unquestionable.

Let me, therefore, briefly trace the events of early October in Dresden[5], in order then to bring out their multi-layered relationship to Mielitz's production, its first performances and their reception. By summer 1989, mass dissatisfaction in the GDR had reached an intense pitch. Thousands of citizens trying to leave the GDR occupied West German embassies in other Eastern Block countries, including that in Prague in September. When these squatters were permitted to emigrate to the West, reports that the special trains would pass through Dresden led, in early October, to several nights of angry protest around the railway station, escalating violence and escalating police response.

Hans Modrow, *Bezirkssekretär* (district chief) of the SED, was under strong pressure to maintain tight control in the run-up to the 7 October celebrations of the GDR's 40th birthday. Party leader Erich Honecker had explicitly urged wholesale suppression of dissent, and the *Ministerium für Staatssicherheit*, the *MfS* or *Stasi*, had begun preventative arrests.[6] A tank division was put on alert. The army, called in by Modrow, came on the streets on 5 October. The railway station remained a gathering and sparking point for protests, which, though, now involved not just embittered would-be emigrants, but others peacefully demanding reforms in the GDR itself, a stance which, not for the first time, was interpreted in *MfS* reports as a more serious threat to the GDR's integrity. The party, the *MfS* and the police now concentrated on maintaining order and a semblance of state loyalty on 7 October. But they failed to stop the demonstrations that evening. One, singing the *Internationale* and chanting 'Wir bleiben hier', 'We're staying here', marched right past the City Hall, where Mayor Berghofer was hosting the fortieth anniversary celebration.

A further demonstration was planned for the *Theaterplatz*, directly in front of the Semperoper, for 3 pm on 8 October. A telegram from Honecker urged: 'Alles ist im Keim zu ersticken.'[7] The demonstration was violently dispersed, and 150 demonstrators arrested, including members of the Semperoper ensemble itself.[8] At this stage, Modrow too was still endorsing violent action and arrests.

---

[5] Karin Urich, *Die Bürgerbewegung in Dresden 1989/90* (Cologne, Weimar, Vienna, 2001) offers the definitive account of the events of early October in Dresden, drawn on extensively here. See also: Wagner, *20 gegen die SED*, pp.10-19; Thomas Rosenlöcher, *Die verkauften Pflastersteine. Dresdner Tagebuch* (Frankfurt/Main, 1990), pp.19-27.

[6] On the *MfS* and police preparations for 'Jubiläum 40', see Armin Mitter & Stefan Wolle (eds.), *'Ich liebe euch doch alle…'. Befehle und Lageberichte des MfS. Januar-November 1989* (Berlin 1993), pp.187-89.

[7] Quoted in Urich, p.177. 'everything must be nipped in the bud.'

[8] For example, a three-page statement by Köhler, a Semperoper stage technician, on his arrest and treatment after this *Theaterplatz* demonstration, is among the papers of Schönfelder, Intendant of the opera, in the Sächsisches Hauptstaatsarchiv (Sächs. HstA, Staatsoper Dresden, 2. Abgabe, Nr. 16).

Shortly after 6pm on 8 October, the local *MfS* General Horst Böhm rang the *SED-Bezirksleitung* for approval to use force to disperse a further demonstration of some 5,000 marching from the railway station into the town. Modrow, though, was at the opera. Around 8pm about 1500 demonstrators were surrounded by police on *Prager Strasse*. This windswept pedestrian zone between high-rise blocks of prefabricated public housing, with a large black statue of Lenin at its focus, symbolized the socialist dream. Confrontation here between the 'Volk' and the 'Volkspolizei' sharply exposed the bankruptcy of the SED's claim to be a people's party. Police began to isolate groups of demonstrators; the crowd, singing 'Dona nobis pacem', 'We shall overcome' and the *Internationale*, refused to disperse. This time, though, the cycle of violence was interrupted. A group was chosen, later called the 'Gruppe der 20', who succeeded in negotiating a peaceful end to the demonstration that evening and also in getting an audience with mayor Berghofer in the city hall the following morning.

While this development still depended, crucially, on the actions of two senior regional SED members, Modrow and Berghofer, who were, of course, trying to retain power by strengthening their reputation as reformers, nonetheless the pattern of violent suppression of popular protest had been broken: a crucial signal that was immediately understood in Leipzig the following day. In less than a week, from 3 to 9 October 1989, the potential if not yet actual face of GDR politics and society had been transformed.

At the climax of this week of tense political drama, Christine Mielitz's Dresden production of Beethoven's *Fidelio* had its premiere. This production had been justified to the cultural authorities as a work of the humanist canon to mark a dual anniversary: the two hundredth of the French revolution and the fortieth of the founding of the GDR. From the founding of the GDR, opera had an explicit role to play in the construction of the new socialist nation[9], and Beethoven, we have already noted, was central to the 'Erbe' that the GDR contested bitterly with the West German Federal Republic. In 1952 the SED used the 125th anniversary of Beethoven's death to attack 'die amerikanischen Kulturbarbaren und ihre Lakaien': in Bonn (Beethoven's birthplace, and since 1949 the West German capital): 'werden Beethovens erhabene Forderungen nach Frieden und Völkerfreundschaft mit Füßen getreten.'[10] In 1970, GDR Minister of Culture Klaus Gysi wrote: 'Beethoven belongs to us', because 'he too struggled

---

[9] See the numerous examples cited in Joy Haslam Calico, ' "Für eine neue deutsche Nationaloper": Opera in the Discourses of Unification and Legitimation in the German Democratic Republic', in: *Music and German National Identity*, ed. by Celia Applegate & Pamela Potter (Chicago & London, 2002), p.190-204.

[10] Quoted in Dietrich Staritz, *Geschichte der DDR 1949-1985* (Frankfurt/Main, 1985), pp.58-59. 'the American cultural barbarians and their lackeys' are using Bonn 'to trample underfoot Beethoven's sublime calls for peace and friendship between the peoples'.

inexhaustibly against the injustices and arbitrariness of the ruling classes.'[11] *Fidelio*, or extracts from it, were standard fare at official events such as the opening of the Palast der Republik in East Berlin on 23 April 1976.[12]

Precisely this complacent appropriation of artists such as Beethoven made it hard for works of what the GDR saw as its 'Erbe' to be refused performance, even if their potential for explosive critique was actually apparent. Mielitz had to attend several meetings at up to *Bezirksleitung* level, including with Modrow himself, to gain approval for her production: 'Die ahnten natürlich, daß da etwas auf sie zukommt. Aber nicht einer hat wirklich gewagt, das zu verbieten.'[13]

Beethoven began *Fidelio* in the revolutionary excitement of the mid 1790s, and its theme of wrongful incarceration and the powerful music of the prisoners' chorus have 'compelled associations with principles of political liberty', as David Dennis says in his study of *Beethoven in German Politics*.[14] In Ernst Bloch's words: 'Jeder künftige Bastillensturm ist in *Fidelio* intendiert.'[15] But, Dennis continues, 'the famous trumpet call announcing salvation at the hands of an aristocratic redeemer complicates reception of this "rescue opera" as a piece of revolutionary propaganda.' It espouses humane values, enlightenment and liberty, but these are realized through a representative of the existing order, the Minister, Don Fernando, who rights the wrongs committed by the despotic prison governor Pizarro.

Moreover, *Fidelio* is a work whose invocation of high-minded but abstract ideals makes it susceptible to being harnessed to mutually contradictory causes. At the Congress of Vienna in 1815 it served to celebrate Metternich's restoration of the old order in Europe. By the 1830s its reception as the opera of the German nation, as a key performance of German nationalist aspirations, was well underway.[16] The National Socialists enthusiastically appropriated this tradition; Richard Eichenauer, in the journal

---

[11] 'Zum Beethoven-Jahr 1970', *Musik und Gesellschaft* 20 (1970), 2; quoted in David B. Dennis, *Beethoven in German Politics 1870-1989* (New Haven & London, 1996), p.181. Despite its title, Dennis's otherwise thorough account does not mention Mielitz's production.

[12] See Christoph Dieckmann, 'Der sterbende Schwan. Berlins Palast der Republik, Symbol des deutschen Umgangs mit Geschichte, wird 25 Jahre alt', *Die Zeit*, 19 April 2001, p.72.

[13] ' "Freiheit, Gleichheit, Brüderlichkeit – wo gibt es das denn?" Ein Gespräch mit Christine Mielitz', Semperoper 9 (1995), pp.14-15. 'They sensed, of course, that something awkward was coming their way. But not one dared actually to ban it.' See also: ' "Wie schlecht die Welt auch ist, es gibt Träume": Im Gespräch mit Regisseurin Christine Mielitz', *Dresdner Neueste Nachrichten*, 7.10.1999; quoted in Urich, p.168.

[14] Dennis, p.27.

[15] Ernst Bloch, *Das Prinzip Hoffnung* (Frankfurt/Main, 1959), III, p.1296. 'Every future storming of the Bastille is inherent in *Fidelio*.'

[16] See Elisabeth Eleonore Bauer, *Wie Beethoven auf den Sockel kam* (Stuttgart, 1992), pp.173-201.

Music and Race, calls *Fidelio* 'the first truly Nordic opera'.[17] These are reminders that concepts such as 'freedom' are intrinsically empty and can be filled many ways, and secondly that in the performing arts, the contexts of production, performance and reception are crucial variants of a work's constantly reconstituted 'meaning'. Against the political background of Dresden in early October 1989 sketched above, what then were the characteristics of Mielitz's production of *Fidelio*?

The minutes of a 'Discussion of the concept and model for *Fidelio*' on 25 January 1989 report Mielitz's declared rationale for the production: The French Revolution had led Beethoven to the conclusion that:

> im Grunde [tötet] jede Revolution sich selber. Was aber eigentlich nicht sein sollte. [...] Man kann sich mit dem 'Fidelio' heute nicht hinter einem Mantel- und Degenstück verstecken [...] Pizarro ist ein Beamter des Geheimdienstes, ein an eine bestimmte Richtung gebundener Mensch, der von seiner Sendung überzeugt ist. Er ist nicht 'böse' schlechthin, sondern er hat sich eingerichtet in einem schauerlichen Ort. Der Minister kommt nicht aus einem fremden Staat, sondern dem Bestandteil eines Staates.
>
> Das Stück ist aktuell und kommt uns allen zu [...] Wir dürfen nicht feige sein und sagen, was wir zu sagen haben. Es darf nichts unter den Teppich gekehrt werden.'[18]

This is a courageous conception, even as late as January 1989, given that of the twenty-four people present at this meeting some, almost certainly, will have been *MfS* informers. Mielitz's direct engagement with GDR conditions is also apparent in her suggestions for the set made at the same meeting: 'hohe Wände, einmal in Schwarz, einmal in Betonstruktur, grau [...] Auf der Drehscheibe Wachturm [...] 3 Gitterwände (Betonpfeiler mit Drahtzaunfeldern)'.[19] The set for the actual production in October adhered to this closely.

---

[17] Quoted in Dennis, p.138.

[18] Document in the Archives of the Semperoper, dated April 1989 (no explanation for the three-month delay in recording these minutes is given): 'Every revolution essentially destroys itself. But that does not need to be the case. [...] Doing 'Fidelio' today, one cannot hide behind a cloak-and-dagger style production. [...] Pizarro is a secret police officer, someone tied to a particular orientation, who is convinced of his mission. He is not 'evil' in an absolute sense, but has rather made himself at home in a terrible place. The Minister does not come from a foreign state, but is part of the state itself. / The piece [the opera] is contemporary and concerns us all [...] We cannot be cowardly; we must say what we must say. Nothing must be swept under the carpet.'

[19] 'High walls, some in black, some in a concrete texture, grey [...] On the revolving stage a watch tower [...] Three high walls of wire (concrete pillars with wire fencing stretched between them)'.

Figure 5.1 *Fidelio*, Sächsische Staatsoper Dresden, 7/8 October 1989: The Main Set

Beethoven's themes of loss of liberty, dignity and justice, and the struggle to regain them, were thus played on a set of walls, wire and watchtowers under neon light (see figure 5.1).[20] Marcelline, the daughter of prison warder Rocco, dutifully, even with a sense of enjoyment, controls the prisoners' mail, removing photographs and books (see figure 5.2). In the prison governor's office stand rows of the very truncheons with which, in early October, close to and sometimes within sight of the opera house, the Dresden police severely beat up demonstrators (see figure 5.3).

---

[20] The set and costumes were designed by Peter Heilein. My remarks on the production's visual signals are based on photographs from the archives of the Sächsische Staatsoper and a video of the production in the Zentrum für Theaterdokumentation of the Akademie der Künste, Berlin.

Figure 5.2 *Fidelio*, Sächsische Staatsoper Dresden, 7/8 October 1989: Rocco's office and postroom

Figure 5.3 *Fidelio*, Sächsische Staatsoper Dresden, 7/8 October 1989: The guardroom

From the start, Mielitz had planned and rehearsed a production that would unmistakeably refer to GDR conditions and experience. But given the events on the streets outside, the beatings, the transportations to Bautzen prison, the general climate of suspicion, surveillance and shock, the extent of the production's immediacy was both extraordinarily prescient and extraordinarily intense.[21]

Nonetheless, Mielitz does not, as the opera reaches its climax, submerge her critique in a wash of undifferentiated humanist pathos. For example, when the Minister Don Fernando to whom Rocco now transfers his loyalties issues a general pardon, the gratitude expressed by Mielitz's chorus of prisoners and relatives is muted and dutiful rather than effusive or spontaneous. A gracious pardon from a relatively enlightened representative of power is no substitute for democratic rights. As the liberated prisoners step forward to fraternize with the audience, they find themselves still stopped by a fence. Perhaps most disturbingly of all, the freed Florestan carries the same briefcase and wears the same lapel emblems as the Minister himself.

It is of course difficult to know how many of the production's cautionary emphases were picked up by the audience. The premiere was interrupted repeatedly by tumultuous applause, for example at the question: 'O Freiheit! Kehrest du zurück?' ('O Freedom! Will you return?') Almost certainly, long term restrictions on their freedom, compounded by the immediate shock of the demonstrations and the state's harsh response on those very same early October days, meant that for the audience in the Semperoper that weekend emotional identification overcame critical reflection. The closing applause, lasting twelve minutes, may well have been for the production's emotive signals as much as its musical quality or its critical differentiation, its moments of aesthetically productive refusal simply to mirror either events on the streets or their popular interpretation. Thus the production was in part a victim of the historical processes it seemed so resoundingly to articulate and which were giving it such thrilling immediacy. In 1995, Mielitz recalls her concern 'daß der Theaterabend an dieser unmittelbaren Konfrontation mit der Realität zerbrechen würde', for if art echoes life too closely, 'kann Kunst auch einfach aufhören.'[22]

What, meanwhile, was the local SED leadership doing? The answer to that suggests that Mielitz's production was not the only staging of *Fidelio* in Dresden that weekend. Possibly presciently, the SED leadership had scheduled their fortieth anniversary

---

[21] This is confirmed by all the contemporary reviews; as well as those cited elsewhere in this paper, see e.g. Kerstin Leiße, 'Vieles ist auf Erden zu tun, tue es bald!' *Union*, 12.10.1989; Friedbert Streller, 'Das Prinzip Hoffnung als Triebkraft des Lebens', *Sächsische Zeitung*, 10.10.1989.

[22] '"Freiheit, Gleichheit, Brüderlichkeit – wo gibt es das denn?"', p.15. 'that the theatre evening might have come to grief in this direct confrontation with reality', for if art echoes life too closely, 'art can simply cease to be.'

reception in the town hall on 7 October to coincide with the premiere at the Semperoper. Modrow noted later:

> Damit hatten wir eine Begründung geschaffen, die Festlichkeit zum DDR-Geburtstag vom Kunstereignis zu trennen. Das gab es bis dahin nicht. Semperopern-Premieren galten bisher geradezu als heilig.[23]

Thus, by skulking in the town hall, Modrow and his fellow SED dignitaries avoided being confronted with a staging of *Fidelio* that would have uncomfortably resembled the reality on which their grip was rapidly slipping. But through a conjunction of ironies, precisely in the town hall they could not avoid being confronted with a surge of mass popular energy that, just as uncomfortably for them, resembled a staging of *Fidelio*. Moreover, it took place on a stage of the SED's own making. For in the 1950s a huge open space was cleared in front of the town hall for those performances of mass solidarity that were fundamental to the state's identity and self-legitimation.[24] Now, though, on 7 October, around 8pm, whilst the performance of *Fidelio* in the Semperoper which had begun at 7 was reaching its first climax, the prisoners' chorus towards the end of Act One, Hans Modrow recalls pushing aside a heavy curtain in the town hall:

> Über den Rathausplatz auf die Leningrader Straße ging in relativ schnellem Schritt eine grössere Menschenmenge, geordnet, völlig lautlos, man sah in Bildausschnitt weder rechts noch links das Ende. Nun kamen auch andere Festgäste ans Fenster. Peinlichkeit. Wachsende Unruhe. Der Empfang war quasi zu Ende. Jetzt plözlich drangen Rufe hinein: 'Wir sind das Volk!' 'Schämt euch!'[25]

In this defiant march past on a space designed for marches past, the demonstrators take at its word, and throw back in its face, the SED state's claim to be the heir of the humanist 'Erbe'. Whilst Modrow and the other functionaries peer out through the curtain, the demonstrators stage their version of the emancipatory energies of *Fidelio*. At least retrospectively, Modrow's version of this moment is also narrated in terms of a

---

[23] Hans Modrow, *Ich wollte ein neues Deutschland* (Munich, 1999), p.272. 'That gave us a reason to separate the festivities for the GDR's birthday from the artistic event. That was unprecedented. Premieres in the Semperoper had hitherto been considered as practically sacred.'

[24] See Corey Ross, 'Staging the East German "working class": representation and class identity in the "workers' state" ', in: *Representing the German nation. History and Identity in twentieth-century Germany*, ed. Mary Fulbrook & Martin Swales (Manchester, 2000), pp.155-71; Friedrich Dieckmann, *Dresdner Ansichten: Spaziergänge und Erkundungen* (Frankfurt/Main, 1995), p.23.

[25] Modrow, *Ich wollte ein neues Deutschland*, p.273. 'Across the Rathausplatz towards the Leningrader Straße a large mass of people were marching with relatively rapid steps, orderly, completely silently, from our framed viewpoint we could see the end of the column neither on the right nor the left. Now other guests at the celebrations came over to the window. Embarrassment. Growing unrest. The reception was effectively over. Now suddenly cries could be heard: 'We are the people!' 'You should be ashamed!'

theatrical or filmic event, viewed from an elevated position like a theatre box, through a curtain, the protesters a framed and choreographed body of marchers. 'Die französische Revolution verstand sich als ein wiedergekehrtes Rom', argues Walter Benjamin[26]: that is, actors in processes of profound historical change depend on existing models and narratives to shape and direct their actions. Could one not observe, in some of the actions on 7 and 8 October and certainly in the subsequent narratives of those events, political actors who understood themselves and their circumstances in terms of Beethoven's *Fidelio*? Modrow and Berghofer were determined to be the Minister Don Fernando rather than Pizarro (the latter role would seem best filled by the hawkish *MfS* General Horst Böhm). On the GDR national stage, Honecker's brief successor Egon Krenz, who tried to cling to power by applying 'Wende', the term of the moment, to his desperate rearguard actions in October and early November 1989, might be seen as manoeuvring himself into Don Fernando's role.[27] Don Fernando, after all, offers an amnesty and the rectification of abuses (including the punishment of a corrupt subordinate, Pizarro) whilst leaving the existing order unchanged.

Modrow did not attend the opera on 7 October, and on the afternoon of 8 October he still endorsed a tough line against the demonstrations. But at 6pm on 8 October he went to the opera, sat through a production of *Fidelio* whose references to the GDR in general and to the events in Dresden in particular are unmistakable. In Berghofer's words, ten years later:

> Modrow weilte in der Semper-Oper, in der zweiten Aufführung von *Fidelio*, wo auf der Bühne dasselbe stattfand wie auf den Straßen.[28]

At the prisoners' words: 'Sprecht leise, haltet euch zurück/Denn wir sind belauscht mit Ohr und Blick',[29] the audience, instead of applauding, stood in silent tribute. Some eyewitnesses, at least, recall that at this moment Modrow and his party stood in silent tribute too.[30] Here too, Mielitz's production, whether by artistic intuition or chance, was

---

[26] 'Über den Begriff der Geschichte', in: *Gesammelte Schriften*, I/2: Abhandlungen (Frankfurt/Main, 1980), p.701. 'The French Revolution understood itself as the return of Rome.'

[27] On 18 October 1989, the day after he replaced Honecker, and again on 5 November: see Christina Schäffner, 'Sprache des Umbruchs und ihre Übersetzung', in: *Sprache im Umbruch. Politischer Sprachwandel im Zeichen von 'Wende' und 'Vereinigung'*, eds Armin Burkhardt and K.P.Fritsche (Berlin and New York, 1992), pp.135-53 (pp.138-44).

[28] ' "So konnte es nicht weitergehen." Redaktionsgespräch mit Wolfgang Berghofer', *Dresdner Hefte. Beiträge zur Kulturgeschichte* 59 (1999), pp.52-59 (p.57). 'Modrow was in the Semperoper, in the second performance of *Fidelio*, where the same was happening on stage as on the streets.'

[29] 'Speak softly, be restrained/For we are under surveillance by ears and eyes.'

[30] So, at least, Hella Bartnig, 'Dramaturgin' at the Semperoper, recalled the moment in an interview with the author on 22 January 2002; see also the version of events offered by Heinz Magirius, *Die Semperoper in Dresden* (Berlin, 2000), p.303. Martin Walser recalls events slightly differently:

remarkably prescient: she altered the conclusion slightly to make clear that Don Fernando's decision to free the prisoners is motivated by the appearance and temper of the masses calling for change. As they threaten to swamp him, he joins in their final chorus.[31]

The exact relationship of this artistic experience to Modrow's processes of political decision-making is of course impossible to determine, but the coincidence is remarkable. That evening, 8 October, he agreed to a process of dialogue that broke the circle of violence and opened the way to reform. Moreover, the parallels between work, stage realization and contemporary reality which were achieved with this historic production of *Fidelio* were no less remarkable for not, of course, being complete.

But can the thrill of a moment of theatre in a specific moment of history be preserved by repeating it unchanged? What meanings does this production generate when, having returned to the repertoire in the mid-1990s, it continues to be performed, with unchanged staging, though a varying cast of singers (for example on 4, 6 and 11 October 2004, on the fifteenth anniversary of the momentous events that surrounded its premiere), when the real contours of the GDR revolution are a fading memory?

In GDR times, arguably, though the Semperoper was not free of commercial pressures, it came as close as such an institution was ever likely to to a democratization of opera-going, with tickets at 18 marks and 80,000 subscriptions for local people, plus dedicated performances for youth, union and other groups. Moreover, the characteristic GDR public perception of the theatre as one of the rare spaces for the articulation of collective dissent, created a strong sense of solidarity between audience and performers. This reached its peak in 1989 in many theatres, but this moment of solidarity, harmony, even mourning for the failed socialist experiment, was wedded to the historic moment of the GDR's collapse. A decade or more later, the opera no longer expresses so unambiguously the interests of the people who experienced the emotions it articulates. The moment of revolutionary euphoria is now not theirs, but a traded commodity. The voice that, on that extraordinary weekend, spoke for them and with them, now speaks of them; that it does so, unchanged, in their masks, only intensifies the irony. Since 1989,

---

'Dem ersten Auftritt des Chors folgte ein fast den Abend unterbrechenden Beifall. Schräg unter uns, in der Staatsloge, wurde auch geklatscht. Ich glaube, Hans Modrow war dabei.' Walser: 'Kurz in Dresden. Einige Szenen aus dem deutschen Frühling im Herbst', *Die Zeit*, 20.10.1989, p.74; quoted from the reprinted version in *Union*, 25.11.1989, p.5. 'The first chorus was followed by applause which almost stopped the show. Diagonally below us, in the official box, they were clapping too. I think Hans Modrow was amongst them.' The parallels between Modrow's and Don Fernando's response to the pressure of mass opinion, however, remain valid, whichever version is true.

[31] A point noted in many reviews, e.g. Frank Geißler: 'Keine Spur von Sentimentalität', *Sächsische Neueste Nachrichten* 11.10.1989.

the Semperoper has necessarily adapted to the Federal Republic's practices and prices. To see the 'Private performance' of *Fidelio* on 26 October 2001, for example, you would have had to contact Drescher Incoming & Tourismus GmbH or Dr. Augustin Studienreisen GmbH. In October 2002 a tourism website offering tickets for the forthcoming performance on 18 December 2002 explained the price of €116 per ticket in *Preisklasse 3* thus: 'Die Kartenpreise enthalten Gebühren von Zwischenhändlern und weichen daher stark vom aufgedruckten Originalpreis ab.'[32] The thrilling political immediacy of Mielitz's *Fidelio* has itself become captive to the supply and demand mechanisms of a speculative market.

When *Fidelio* is performed today, visiting audiences can vicariously relive a 'Wende' they were never part of, an experience heightened by the proximity of those Dresdeners in the contemporary audience who are still moved to tears by the reenactment of a doubly historic moment. Without a single onstage sign being changed, the extraordinary conjunction of art and life on 7 and 8 October 1989 becomes kitsch, precisely because of art's Janus-faced potential not only to convert experience into the narrative through which and as which the experience can be recalled, but also to offer a spurious pseudo-participation in the historical experience of others. In 1995, Mielitz denied that reviving the production was an anachronism, arguing that oppression and longings for freedom remain universal human experiences.[33] But precisely the apparent specificity of reference that made and makes Mielitz's production historic hinders (or will do so for as long as the events of 1989 remain part of what its audiences think they remember) the wider application she claims for it.

It is not just commercial pressures, though, which have changed the meanings of this production of *Fidelio*. Friedrich Dieckmann, comparing 1989 with 1849, notes that 'in Dresden, wieder einmal, fand die Revolution als Oper, fand die Oper als Revolution statt.'[34] Once the process whereby art converts experience into narrative is underway, the signifier uncouples itself from the initially signified, and gains a wider descriptive force that, while apparently explanatory, actually aids the accession to dominance of a particular narrative of history. *Fidelio* becomes the GDR revolution as a whole, the GDR revolution as a whole a version of *Fidelio*. So for example, in October 2000, an article by Klaus von Dohnanyi on ten years of German unification refers thus to the night, a month after the *Fidelio* production in Dresden, on which the Berlin Wall was opened:

---

[32] www.dresden.citysam.de. 'The ticket prices include middlemen's charges and therefore differ markedly from the original price printed on the tickets.'
[33] 'Freiheit, Gleichheit, Brüderlichkeit – wo gibt es das denn?', p.15.
[34] Dieckmann, *Glockenläuten*, p.66. 'in Dresden, again, the revolution took place as opera, and the opera as revolution.'

the night of 9 November, 1989, was to become the most unusual night of freedom. Like in the last act of *Fidelio* the people came out, blinded by the television floodlights, still unable to believe that they had cast off their chains; they drove, they tumbled across to the West, through the gates in the wall that, just a few minutes earlier, had been an insuperable barrier.'[35]

As Dohnanyi stresses, the euphoria of 9 November was still relatively inchoate, was not yet directed at unification or the Deutsche Mark. Champions of a reformed socialist GDR fought on: every night from 29 October 1989 onwards members of the Semperoper delivered a statement after each performance associating themselves and their production of *Fidelio* with the popular protests: 'Der Wille des Volkes sei geachtet! [...] Es ist angetreten, ein demokratisches Land zu errichten, das ein sozialistisches sein kann und wird'.[36]

But *Fidelio*'s paeans to freedom are sufficiently unspecific for the thrilling theatrical moment of 7 and 8 October 1989 to be progressively re-read until it becomes but a first step in the teleologically rescripted history of the 'Wende' as a triumphal progression towards unification and the victory of Western values. Federal Chancellor Helmut Kohl's first key public appearance in the GDR after 9 November 1989 was on 19 December 1989 in Dresden. His 10-point plan for German unification had already secured him the initiative, and now his promise of 'blühende Landschaften' ('blossoming landscapes') meant that there was little doubt who was now meant to go down in history as the GDR's Don Fernando. On 22 December at the Brandenburg Gate, he restaged the opening of the Wall in front of the world media, reasserting the monopoly of official politics after the unscripted popular moments of 9 November at the Berlin Wall, of the Leipzig Monday demonstrations, and of the weekend of 7/8 October in Dresden. On 7/8 October 1989, *Fidelio*, as the artistic reflection of a political reality, could at least discomfort the authorities of the city in which it was performed. Today, the narrative of the GDR revolution as a version of *Fidelio* causes no such discomforts.

---

[35] 'Unity: 10 formative years. Tranformed nation adjusts to reality after euphoria of 1990', *Perspectives* [Newspaper of the German Embassy, Ottowa], 7 (2000), p.3 at: http://www.germanembassy-ottowa.org/news/Perspectives/fall2000/unity.html.

[36] Quoted from the version in the *Sächsische Neueste Nachrichten*, 11.11.1989. 'Let the will of the people be respected! [...] They have set out to establish a democratic country, which can and will be a socialist one.'

Faust in Dresden, 28, 29 and 30 August 1990

Wolfgang Engel's production of both parts of *Faust* over three consecutive evenings is an engagement with the Faust myth as it resonates in his own age, an age for which the transcendent themes and scenes seem less central than those of social vision and historical dialectic. (This does not mean the production reduces the play to social, let alone socialist realism.) The production engages with the ideological encrustations of his state's particular perception of the Faust theme, the work and how it should be performed, and is thus also a continuation of a dialogue with other interpretations and performances of the work. Conceived as a bitter parody of the yawning gulf between the staging of the state and its actual condition, in the circumstances in which it finally reached the stage it became also a wry valediction to the socialist dream.[37]

Engel began rehearsal for *Faust* in early 1988, eventually premiering the production in August 1990. Throughout most of its rehearsal period, therefore, his production accompanied the unravelling of the East German state and the values it represented; Engel had initially taken up *Faust* as a tiresome duty no leading German director could escape; it became, in his hands and in his production's historical moment, an engagement with a central myth of the GDR's self-image. By the time the production could actually be performed, it became, literally, an 'Abkündigung', an envoi or leave-taking for GDR socialism.

In the GDR, the contested 'Erbe' generated contradictions with regard to *Faust*. On the one hand, it led to productions which sought to strip the play of its Wilhelmine and National Socialist accretions, and also of any trace of Gustav Gründgens's influential reading of Mephistopheles (the actor, director and theatre manager Gründgens, briefly discredited as a Nazi fellow traveller, had settled in the West and continued his portrayal of Mephistopheles as the Pied Piper in an influential production in Hamburg in the late 1950s).[38] There were moves in the GDR to play *Faust* as Volkstheater, popular theatre, with as little pomp and pathos as possible (ironically, something which Wagner had called for in *Faust* but which had been swept aside as the play was recruited to serve imperial Germany's self-aggrandizement). But there were also strongly conservative pressures, precisely since the GDR wished to be seen as sustaining the national canon. Hence, from the beginning, both political support and generous funding were available for the preservation of the heritage Weimar and its poets represented as the 'Symbol für

---

[37] This section is indebted to Ulrich Kühn's analysis of this production, but focuses more on the relationship to the GDR's Faustian self-myth: 'Eine Brust voller Seelen. Faust als DDR-Intellektueller auf Identitätssuche', in: *Im Auftrieb. Grenzüberschreitungen mit Goethes 'Faust' in Inszenierungen der neunziger Jahre*, ed. Hans-Peter Bayerdörfer (Tübingen, 2002), pp.31-62.

[38] See Daniel J. Farrelly, *Goethe in East Germany 1949-1989. Towards a History of Goethe Reception in the GDR* (Columbia, SC, 1998), p.89.

ein edleres und humaneres Deutschland' (SED chairman Otto Grotewohl in 1949[39]). But it was accompanied by close scrutiny of productions of *Faust* by the highest political circles. A concept of 'Werktreue', faithfulness to the work, emerged that related to conservative staging practice as much as actual adherence to a text which, played in full, would subvert comfortable expectations as surely as the most experimental approach.

Ironically, too, the appropriation of *Faust* for the humanist tradition that East German socialism saw itself as continuing, was often couched in language, and often lay claim to aspects of the text, which recalled the National Socialist reception. The socialist conception of Faust as representative of the energies of the masses, unleashed in the workers' and peasants' state GDR, echoed the National Socialist view of Faust as the man of action, and of 'das Faustische' as ruthless pursuit of a national purpose: now, under socialism, of course, not of the 'völkisch' or racist nation, but of the class-based socialist nation. Faust's land reclamation project in *Faust II* and his vision of 'Auf freiem Grund mit freiem Volke stehn',[40] once 'perhaps the most quoted Faust line of Fascist *Germanistik*',[41] were now harnessed to a new, socialist project.

SED leader Walter Ulbricht's much-quoted cry, 'Faust III sind wir!' ('Faust III, that's us!') may be apocryphal. But in a speech in 1962 he anchored his, and the SED's, vision of the whole of Germany as a peaceful and prosperous land in a series of direct references to *Faust II*. He quotes:

> Ein Sumpf zieht am Gebirge hin,
> Verpestet alles schon Errungene;
> Den faulen Pfuhl auch abzuziehn,
> Das letzte wär das Höchsterrungene. (11559-62)[42]

He relates this directly to the antinational and reactionary forces in the Federal Republic who had turned their part of Germany into a foul capitalist morass of exploitation and warmongering. This swamp must be drained, to which end Ulbricht offers the hand of

---

[39] Quoted in Deborah Viëtor-Engländer, *Faust in der DDR* (Frankfurt/Main, New York, Bern, Paris, 1987), p.20. 'Symbol for a more noble and humane Germany'. The following section is indebted to Viëtor-Engländer's authoritative study of GDR *Faust* reception (on and off stage) up to, but not including, Engel's production. See also Bernd Mahl, *Goethes 'Faust' auf der Bühne (1806-1998)* (Stuttgart, 1998), pp.192-236.

[40] *Faust. Der Tragödie zweiter Teil* (Stuttgart 1970), p.208: verse 11580. 'Standing on freedom's soil, a people free'. Quotations from *Faust* will be from this edition and identified by verse numbers in the text; English translations from the version by Philip Wayne (Harmondsworth, 1959).

[41] Kirsten Belgum, Karoline Kirst-Gundersen & Paul Levesque, ' "Faust im Braunhemd": *Germanistik* and Fascism', in: *Our 'Faust'. Roots and Ramifications of a Modern German Myth*, eds Reinhold Grimm & Jost Hermand (Madison, 1987), pp.153-68 (p.159).

[42] 'A marshland flanks the mountainside, /Infecting all that we have gained / Our gain would reach its greatest pride / If all this noisome bog were drained.'

friendship to the working people of the West. Faust, he argues, comes to recognize that only the collective labour of a free people leads to the highest happiness. He quotes *Faust II* again:

> Solch ein Gewimmel möcht' ich sehn,
> Auf freiem Grund mit freiem Volke stehn!
> Zum Augenblick dürft' ich sagen:
> Verweile doch, du bist so schön!
> [...]
> Im Vorgefühl von solchem hohen Glück,
> Genieß' ich jetzt den höchsten Augenblick.' (11579-11586)[43]

Ulbricht notes at this point that Goethe leaves the results of this collective labour unclear. Goethe had no choice, he suggests, because in the emergent capitalist world in which Goethe was writing, 'konnte der dritte Teil des *Faust* auch noch nicht geschrieben werden.' Only now, one hundred and more years later, have the working people of the GDR begun to write this third part, and the unification of the whole German people in a peace loving and socialist state 'wird diesen dritten Teil des *Faust* abschliessen'.[44]

This posturing, comic in retrospect, nonetheless epitomizes the insecurely possessive view of *Faust* held by the party faithful. Some productions met official approval by presenting *Faust* as a drama of the people, set in a late bourgeois age in transition to a post-bourgeois and implicitly socialist one, others by reiterating the conception of man (sic) as creator of his own historical destiny, Faust not as unworldly intellectual, but as practical man, challenger and conqueror of the world: the Columbus of his age.

Such conceptions of *Faust*, a re-import, essentially, of 'das Faustische' in proletarian guise, remained firmly part of the GDR's image of itself, and productions which deviated from it long continued to provoke sanctions. Bertolt Brecht and Egon Monk's staging of *Urfaust*, the fragmentary early version of the play, in Potsdam in 1952, which viewed Faust as an unheroic, untrustworthy charlatan, drew attacks from Ulbricht himself[45], and was withdrawn after only a few performances. Similarly, Adolf Dresen and Wolfgang Heinz's *Faust I* in 1968 fell foul of party nervousness towards cultural unorthodoxy in the aftermath of the Soviet invasion of Czechoslovakia. Dresen's Faust was a neurotic, nervous, inhibited, sometimes hysterical intellectual, far from the Renaissance man striding to new deeds and instigating human progress demanded by

---

[43] 'Such busy, teeming throngs I long to see, / Standing upon freedom's soil, a people free. / Then to the moment could I say: / Linger you now, you are so fair! [...] Foreknowledge comes, and fills me with such bliss, I take my joy, my highest moment this.'

[44] Quoted in Viëtor-Engländer, pp.59-61: 'the third part of *Faust* could not yet be written [...]' The whole German people 'will complete this third part of *Faust*'.

[45] See e.g. his speech 'Die Aufgaben der Intelligenz beim Aufbau des Sozialismus in der DDR' of 27 May 1953, quoted in Viëtor-Engländer, p.154.

Alexander Abusch, deputy chairman of the Council of Ministers, in October 1968, during a discussion of the production at the highest level.[46]

Only gradually did official reactions to unorthodox productions of *Faust* become more tolerant, though this was, arguably, more a function of the state's disintegration than of an actively endorsed pluralism. By the latter 1980s, the state's abandonment of its own ideals was now so far progressed that it could no longer afford to engage seriously with artistic questioning of these ideals or their realization. By then it would have been highly improbable for the Staatsrat to convene a special meeting to discuss a *Faust* production.

In these contexts – firstly, of a relatively more open but still fundamentally conservative official concept of what constituted legitimate stagings of the national drama, and, secondly, of a state and the ideals which underpinned it, in deep and probably terminal crisis – Wolfgang Engel began rehearsing his production of both parts of *Faust* in Dresden in 1988. This production was eventually premiered over three evenings on 28, 29, and 30 August 1990 (28 August being Goethe's birthday), in the brief lacuna, the liminal moment, when the GDR's fate was sealed but not yet executed: after the elections of 18 March 1990 had produced a clear majority for unification on the basis of the capitalist market economy, and the currency union of 3 June 1990 had hastened the collapse of the GDR economy and made its complete helplessness inevitable, but before the final demise and disappearance of the GDR on 3 October 1990, when it was swallowed up into the new, enlarged, but constitutionally essentially unaltered Federal Republic.

The production had four guiding conceptions with major implications for its structure: firstly, that *Faust I* and *Faust II* are a single whole: many of the cuts and re-orderings of the dialogue and scenes, and the division between the three evenings, sought to draw the themes, figures and action of the two plays together.

Secondly, there is the conception that the whole universe of the play emanates from Faust's consciousness, expressed visually in the way that his study remained alluded to in the staging throughout (e.g. by the presence of his writing desk). What we see on stage is the drama of a mind at a moment of turmoil and transition in European culture. This is one of several ways in which the performative aspect of the *Faust* drama is explicitly foregrounded

Thirdly, Faust's declaration that he has 'zwei Seelen, ach, in meiner Brust'[47] is stripped of its encrustations with cliché (a similar problem to that posed for any production of *Hamlet* by the 'To be or not to be' soliloquy) and taken literally: there are two Fausts, almost always on stage together, played by Christoph Hohmann and by

---

[46] Quoted in Viëtor-Engländer, p.162.
[47] 'Two souls, alas, are housed within my breast': *Faust / Part One*, translated by Philip Wayne (Harmondsworth 1949), p.67.

Wolfgang Engel himself. They speak Faust's lines sometimes in unison, sometimes just out of synchronization, sometimes separately, as a form of externalized inner dialogue, or to differentiate a moment of public utterance from an inner train of thought. Moreover, there is, in this production, no Mephistopheles figure (at least, not until nearly the end of the third evening). His lines are distributed between the two Fausts. Thus the often-voiced idea that Faust and Mephistopheles are dialectically or symbiotically inseparable is staged explicitly. In Engel's production, they coalesce into one Faust, but this one Faust, having two souls in his breast, is externalized into two physically distinct yet psychologically conjoined Faust figures. Simultaneously unifying and doubling the drama's central figures unsettles over-familiarity, breaks up over-long monologues and refocuses audience attention. It too foregrounds the inherent theatricality of the Faust figure as both agent and onlooker. Finally, it reinforces the duality, one might say the concentricity, rather than binary polarity, of good and evil.[48]

These radical interventions might well upset purists, though in fact ever since 1829, when Ludwig Tieck bowdlerized the text, cut the anti-clerical sideswipes and added his own prologue, it is rare for productions of *Faust* not to make substantial changes. Goethe himself, when directing, freely cut and transposed his own and others' texts.[49] He understood very well the necessary difference between any dramatic text and its possible realizations even in its own time, let alone 200 years later. Repeatedly, he stressed his *Faust*'s incommensurability, its resistance to exhaustive interpretation, even its unperformability, and essentially set it free for directors and theatres to do what they could, and would, with it. And after all, and above all, his *Faust*, accreted over some sixty years, was itself a text in dynamic process, reordering, modernizing, artistically intervening and re-engaging with a disparate, shifting corpus of material in a situation of continuous change. In its own epoch, the sixty years of extraordinary flux that lay either side of the year 1800, Goethe's *Faust* shapes its material into the protean form necessary to engage with the onset of modernity in European culture and the first great crisis of Enlightenment rationalism. Recognizing the implications of this through a critical engagement with the material is arguably more relevant to the work's living achievement than a dogmatic 'Werktreue' that regards the text as a sacrosanct work of genius. Engel, via a close though certainly adventurous, in a Barthean sense writerly reading of Goethe's text and of the history of its subsequent reception, engages with another epochal historical transition, namely the endpoint of an experimental attempt to create a

---

[48] Henriette Harnisch, 'Variations in the political appropriation of classics in GDR theatre at the time of the collapse of the GDR and the unification of Germany' (PhD, Sheffield, 2000), pp.206-10, suggests that this aspect of Engel's production was influenced by Gründgens's *Faust* film of 1960.

[49] According to Eudo C. Mason, Goethe himself sometimes transferred lines between Faust and Mephistopheles; see, for example, *Goethe's Faust: its Genesis and Purport* (Berkeley, 1967), p.181.

utopian society which, as we saw from Ulbricht's speech, claimed to be that glimpsed in Faust's vision.

Engel's production sought to explore the mental and spiritual condition of GDR society, especially its intellectuals and artists, in its state of final crisis. His production, and the staging by Frank Hänig and costumes by Jutta Harnisch, mixed the timeless with the specifically contemporary.[50] There were many allusions to GDR reality – Valentin appears in the uniform of the 'Nationale Volksarmee'; the scene between Mephistopheles, Gretchen and Martha is set in a doll's house version of a GDR 'Plattenbau' high-rise block (see figure 5.4); part of the 'klassische Walpurgisnacht' resembles a carnevalesque satire of the sterile, self-congratulatory rituals of the socialist state's celebration of the heroic worker; Faust and Mephistopheles's introduction of paper money to the bankrupt imperial court becomes an introduction to credit- and debit-card culture, complete with ATMs.

Figure 5.4 *Faust*, Staatsschauspiel Dresden, 28/29/30 August 1990: Martha's house as a doll's-house GDR apartment

[50] Principal source for analysis of the production's textual and visual aspects: *Wolfgang Engel inszeniert Goethes "Faust" am Staatsschauspiel Dresden 1990*, dokumentiert von Dieter Görne, 2 volumes (Berlin, 1991), which permits precise study of the cuts and transpositions undertaken by Engel and his dramaturge Görne.

But Engel also changed elements of his planned staging which seemed, with the flux of history, to be now too facile: A huge thousand DM note which had hung at the back of the stage for the paper money scene was removed after the currency reform of 3 June 1990 and does not feature in the premiered version in August. Moreover, though *Faust*, like Schiller's *Wilhelm Tell*, turns out to be full of references to walls, borders and imprisonment which immediately resonated with GDR audiences, some of the original text's references, such as 'Diese Mauern, diese Wände / Neigen, senken sich zum Ende' (6695-6) are cut as too crudely referential.[51]

But the fourth guiding conception of Engel's production is the crucial one. Engel's approach to *Faust* and to the task of directing *Faust* at this moment in his state's history can be most clearly brought out by focusing on a key scene on the third evening, that is, in the second half of *Faust II*: the scene, more accurately, pair of scenes, where Faust's vision of a utopian future is followed by his death.

Early in *Faust I*, Faust wagers with Mephistopheles that should he ever be satisfied with what the latter offers, should he ever ask that the moment remain, then he becomes Mephistopheles's to do with him as he will. Late in *Faust II*, Faust experiences a vision that leads him to cry out:

> Zum Augenblicke dürft' ich sagen:
> Verweile doch, du bist so schön! [...]
> Im Vorgefühl von solchem hohen Glück
> Genieß' ich jetzt den höchsten Augenblick (11581-6)[52]

Let us remind ourselves of Faust's vision:

> Eröffn' ich Räume vielen Millionen,
> Nicht sicher zwar, doch tätig-frei zu wohnen [...]
> Solch ein Gewimmel möcht' ich sehn,
> Auf freiem Grund mit freiem Volke stehn! (11563-4, 11579-80)[53]

The last line, like most celebrations of freedom, is eminently quotable, eminently removable from context, endlessly malleable. It was central to National Socialist as well as Communist appropriations of *Faust*. A life which is 'nicht sicher zwar, doch tätig-frei' could, in the early nineteenth century, refer to venture capitalism or the North American frontier; or, in the early twenty-first, to the Blairite enterprise society beyond the nanny state.

---

[51] 'In the end our walls, our ceiling, / Will be ruined, crumbled, reeling'.
[52] 'Then to the moment could I say: / Linger you now, you are so fair! [...] Foreknowledge comes, and fills me with such bliss, / I take my joy, my highest moment this.'
[53] 'I work that millions may possess this space, / If not secure, a free and active race. [...] Such teeming throngs I long to see, / Standing on freedom's soil, a people free.'

But already in Goethe's play this vision is, in fact, deeply ambivalent. Firstly Faust's vision is of a future whose prospects of realization are qualified by the conditional 'dürfte' (might/would be able to), hence Mephistopheles's belief that Faust has lost the wager is premature. Secondly, the freedom the vision promises is not to be had without costs ('nicht sicher zwar') – this is, after all, reclaimed land behind a presumably breachable floodwall. Thirdly, it has not involved a revolution of property rights or any other kind of rights on existing land, but is, rather, an act that in a real historical context would represent an old order alleviating its problems of overpopulation by exporting them. Fourthly, the project requires 'tausend Hände' but 'ein Geist', a labouring mass and an executive elite; the earth is being transformed by slaves in a system of antagonistic social relations,[54] and 'tätig-freies Wohnen' is only a visionary promise, somewhere far ahead. At the same time, fifthly, in Faust's vision 'freedom' is neither an abstract ideal nor a gift granted to passive recipients, as it is for example in *Fidelio* by a minister arriving *ex machina*. Instead, it is the result of the communal effort of the masses. Sixthly, though, the aging Faust who speaks these words is already blind, and it is partly but not only the blindness of the prophetic seer: during his final speech, he hears what he takes to be workers tilling the new-won land, but they are in fact digging his grave. Thus his vision is surrounded by and perhaps rests on, illusion. Moreover, this is not the end of the play; it is followed by his death, his soul apparently in the clutches of the devil, but then also by his apotheosis and salvation.[55] Thus the celebration of freedom articulated in these much quoted lines is already substantially qualified, hedged in by, shot through with ironies, in Goethe's play, and Engel's production emphasizes this.

In Goethe's text, Faust is saved by a quasi-religious apotheosis under the aegis of 'das Ewig-Weibliche' (the Eternal Feminine), during the salvation scene that closes the whole work. However, we do not need here to add to the huge volume of would-be elucidation of this ambiguous term, since Wolfgang Engel has not only cut the wager from the Prologue (necessarily, since he has merged the Mephistopheles figure with that of his two Fausts). His approach to the conclusion of the play is equally radical. He also cuts the whole of the two final scenes, Faust's burial and ascension.[56] This was not uncommon in GDR productions, which, however, usually ended not with Mephistopheles's final invocation of 'das Ewig-Leere' ('Eternal Emptiness'), but with

---

[54] See Thomas Metscher, 'Faust's End: On the Present Significance of Goethe's Text', in: Grimm & Hermand, *Our 'Faust'* pp.22-46.

[55] This section is indebted to Klaus Berghahn, 'Georg Johann Heinrich Faust: the Myth and its History', in: Grimm & Hermand, pp.3-21, especially p.19.

[56] According to Harnisch, p 222, Engel had originally planned to retain Goethe's final scene, but as a tragic promenade past crucified heroes of human history from Christ through Rosa Luxemburg to the Unknown Soldier, before rejecting this as too heavily symbolic.

Faust's final monologue preceding it, that is, with the utopian vision. Engel's new final scene in contrast undergoes a number of further crucial modifications. Firstly, Engel introduces Goethe as a figure in the drama, merging the figures of the Wanderer (Goethe's nickname in the 1770s) and Sorge (Care) into one, who proceeds quite literally to apply the make-up to Engel, as Faust, which signifies his blindness (see figure 5.5):

Figure 5.5 *Faust*, Staatsschauspiel Dresden, 28/29/30 August 1990: Goethe applies the wig and make-up which signals Faust's blindness

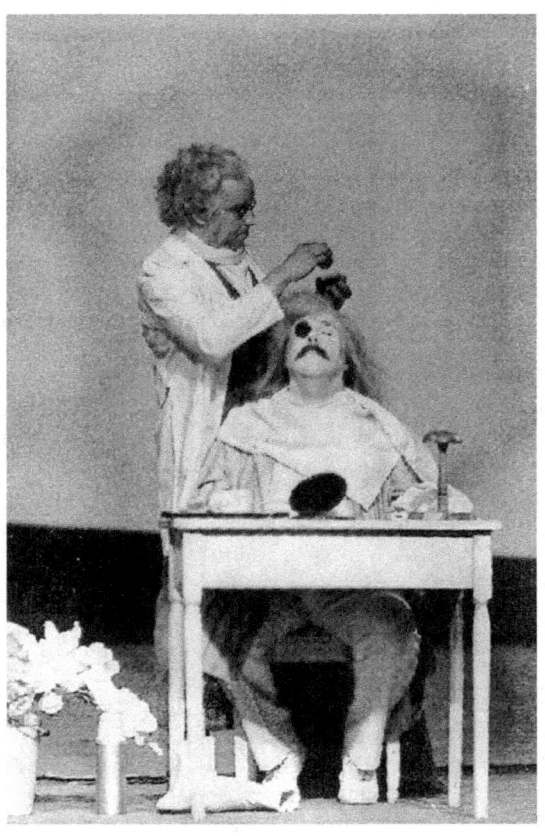

Secondly, this signals a re-separation of the Faust (Wolfgang Engel) and Mephistopheles (Christoph Hohmann) figures, the latter now donning the skullcap and facial make-up that directly, and in the GDR, provocatively, associate him with the most famous German Mephistopheles, Gustav Gründgens (see figure 5.6):

Figure 5.6 *Faust*, Staatsschauspiel Dresden, 28/29/30 August 1990: Mephisto with characteristic Gustav Gründgens skullcap and make-up

At the moment when Faust attempts his rapacious intervention into history, ruthlessly disposing of Philemon and Baucis, he becomes both blind and separate from Mephistopheles (visually distinguishable, speaking separate lines), while at the same time Mephistopheles acquires power over him.

Faust's fatal delusion, taking the noise of the 'Lemuren' digging his grave to be the spades of the workmen labouring on his land reclamation project, is represented on stage by the laying of a railway track, section by section, from upstage down towards the footlights and the auditorium (see figure 5.7):

Figure 5.7 *Faust*, Staatsschauspiel Dresden, 28/29/30 August 1990: The 'Lemuren' lay the railway track (the production's version of Faust's land reclamation project)

Engel then replaces the 'freies Land' verse with a dialogue in which Goethe, peeping like a prompter from behind a half-open door (see figure 5.8), has Faust try out three other versions, before settling on the one we find in the published text (they are in fact all versions to be found in Goethe's own variants):

Faust:	Solch ein Gewimmel möcht ich sehn,
	Auf eignem Grund und Boden stehn!
Goethe:	Auf wahrhaft eignem Grund und Boden stehn.
Faust:	Solch ein Gewimmel möcht ich sehn,
	Auf wahrhaft eignem Grund und Boden stehn!
Goethe:	Auf wahrhaft freiem Grund und Boden stehn.
Faust:	Solch ein Gewimmel möcht ich sehn,
	Auf wahrhaft freiem Grund und Boden stehn!
Goethe:	Auf freiem Grund mit freiem Volke stehn.
Faust:	Solch ein Gewimmel möcht ich sehn,
	Auf freiem Grund mit freiem Volke stehn.[57]

---

[57] Quoted from *Wolfgang Engel inszeniert Goethes 'Faust' am Staatsschauspiel Dresden 1990*, unpaginated. The four variants translate: 'Standing on my own soil and property […] Standing on what would

Figure *Faust*, 5.8 Staatsschauspiel Dresden, 28/29/30 August 1990: Goethe as Prompter has Faust rehearse three versions of the famous 'freies Land' verse

Thus Engel's treatment, in this closing scene, of this – especially in the GDR, recalling Ulbricht's *Faust II* speech – most ideologically charged line of the play, both ensures it maximum attention and renders it relative, one of a number of possible goals, possible outcomes of historical processes. Its ideological accretions are thus sharply silhouetted. Moreover, the blindness of a man who believes to the end that those who are digging his grave are labouring for his ideals evokes the blindness, real or willed, of Honecker and the SED leadership in its final phase.

Now we see another reason there is no salvation scene in Engel's *Faust*. Rejecting apotheosis, Engel is rejecting ideologically invoked closure, Ulbricht's and his successors' false utopias. Faust's vision is as much autocratic as democratic, but now Faust is dead; there will be no grand socialist project, no *Faust III*. Engel's *Faust*, whose genesis as a production closely coincided with the death throes of the East German socialist state, is its epitaph.[58] Additionally, in *Faust I*, Faust drinks a magic potion to

---

truly be my own soil and property […] Standing on what would truly be freedom's soil and property […] Standing on freedom's soil, a people free.'

[58] One of several, of course, including Heiner Müller's montage of *Hamlet* and his own *Hamletmaschine* at the Deutsches Theater Berlin, also in 1990.

escape *tedium vitae*; magic is what, just before this final scene, he abjures. Engel's production is a melancholy acknowledgement that the GDR version of socialism was not science, but astrology, quack medicine. As Faust dies, Mephistopheles fills a balloon with Faust's breath and bursts it. Mephistopheles's life principle, 'das Ewig-Leere', worthless, meaningless delusion, has seemingly triumphed.

This, though, is not quite the end of Engel's version of *Faust*. Instead it is a signal for Engel, as Faust, to remove the wig Goethe had applied to him and tiptoe cautiously, hand in hand with Mephistopheles, down the railway tracks from stage back to stage front, towards the audience. This is a richly ambivalent closing image: The railway tracks recall the onset of the industrial age, Germany's first railways coming into being around the time of Goethe's death: a material image of the intellectual and cultural transition Goethe's life and work spanned, encapsulated and expressed (see figure 5.9):

Figure 5.9 *Faust*, Staatsschauspiel Dresden, 28/29/30 August 1990: The final scene: Faust unwigged: Faust and Mephisto deliver Goethe's 'Envoi' as they walk down the railway tracks towards the audience

Railway tracks both divide and unite: progress and destruction as dialectical twins. The tracks also suggest both a closed linear model of historical development – a criticism of the simplistic version of the Marxist view of history adopted in the GDR's official pronouncements about itself and its future – and its opposite, an openness: the tracks point directly into the audience, but do not otherwise specify their destination. Not without a rueful echo of *The Wizard of Oz*, Faust and Mephistopheles walking down them towards the audience are taking the path of history into an uncertain future, that of the audience, sitting in a GDR theatre in August 1990, after the fall of the wall and the collapse of the SED, after the elections of March 1990 which represented a decision for unification, after the currency union of 3 July 1990 which sealed the fate of the GDR economy, and only weeks before the final dissolution of the GDR on 3 October 1990.

There is a further self-referential ambiguity: not only does Goethe the author appear as a figure in the drama, and participate, sometimes, as a director or at least a prompter, but the empirical director of the production, Wolfgang Engel, now appears too. Anticipating, both literally and metaphorically, his curtain call before the curtain has fallen, Engel removes his Faust wig, and steps out of his role. 'Wir treten aus unseren Rollen heraus', the ensemble of the Staatsschauspiel Dresden declared from the stage in the crucial weeks of October and November 1989, and now their director is walking down the tracks towards the audience, abandoning the separate, ambiguous role of the theatre worker between protest and privilege, to become part of the audience who are now at the sharp end of history, facing the future towards which, open or not, they are being driven with the inevitability of a runaway train.

Thus though Engel cuts the salvation scene, his ending does not exhaust itself in reapplying to the GDR Goethe's jaundiced view of the utopian social engineering inspired by the French Revolution.[59] Instead, his ending recalls Brecht's epilogue to *Der gute Mensch von Sezuan*, which declares that the ending is 'kein rechter Schluß' ('not a proper ending') and calls on the audience to work one out for themselves. Engel closes not with Mephistopheles's scornful 'Ewig-Leere', but with the 'Abkündigung' ('Envoi') Goethe wrote for *Faust* around 1800, but subsequently cut:

> Vielleicht, daß sich was Beßres freilich fände –
> Des Menschen Leben ist ein ähnliches Gedicht:
> Es hat wohl Anfang, hat ein Ende, Allein ein Ganzes ist es nicht.
> Ihr Herren, seid so gut und klatscht nun in die Hände![60]

---

[59] For this reading of *Faust* as a conservative critique of modernity, see, most recently, Michael Jaeger, *"Fausts Kolonie". Goethes kritische Phänomenologie der Moderne* (Würzburg, 2004).

[60] Quoted from *Wolfgang Engel inszeniert Goethes "Faust" am Staatsschauspiel Dresden 1990*. 'It may well be that one could come up with something better. It's like human life: It has a beginning and an end,

The altered gendering of the ending, the direct replacement, as the vast work's final idea, of 'das Ewig-Weibliche' with 'Ihr Herren' cannot be accidental or insignificant. Certainly, this is an Envoi to the GDR, and to the GDR theatre in its ambivalently symbiotic relationship with the state.[61] But additionally, I would argue that just as 'das Ewig-Weibliche' may not relate to specific biological or even cultural gender, so too the homoeroticism signalled from the beginning of the production in the smacking kiss with which the two Fausts greet each other[62], may be primarily allegorical too.[63] Honecker's Germany was a 'Herrenstaat', Kohl's hardly less so. Goethe's text, whose prologue is dominated by the 'Herr', the Lord, closes with a scene where the female principle reigns in multiple forms; but it is a female principle constructed by, and for the salvation of, a male world. Arguably, with the deletion of this final scene, Engel declares that the option of self-absolution on the part of the at least allegorically and perhaps empirically patriarchal perpetrators of history via transcendent intervention by an idealized matriarchal principle, must be abandoned. In the context of the widely observed gendering of unification, the ending is a sarcastic act of congratulation to Western triumphalism, an ending which deletes the allegorical feminine, the self-interested celebration of a nurturing utopia, only to reinstate it as an absent presence for the audience, the railway tracks of history pointing directly at their heads and hearts, to find new ways to fill out.

Conclusion

The immediately evident differences between Christine Mielitz's production of *Fidelio* and Wolfgang Engel's of *Faust* can, of course, be partly explained by the utterly different scale, scope, degrees of textual richness and ambiguity of the two works; partly, too, they reflect the different individual styles of their directors. But the two productions also offer case studies in strongly contrasting alternatives of what theatre was and could be during the rapidly changing historical and political circumstances of the 'Wende' period. Mielitz's *Fidelio* focuses, in a moment of intense political emotions, on the immediate fate of the protesters, and was thus, as we have seen, linked with extraordinary

---

but it doesn't add up to a whole. Gentlemen, be so good as to clap your hands now!' (my translation: MMcG)

[61] As pointed out by Heinz Klunker, ' "Faust international": Das Staatsschauspiel Dresden nimmt mit Goethes Klassiker Abschied vom DDR-Theater', *Deutsches Allgemeines Sonntagsblatt*, 7.9.1990, quoted in *Wolfgang Engel inszeniert Goethes 'Faust' am Staatsschauspiel Dresden 1990*, 2, pp.136-38.

[62] The fact that cutting the final scene also removes Mephistopheles's ogling of the angels' buttocks would tend to strengthen the argument that Engel is not seeking facile camp effects.

[63] Peter Konwitschny's production of Handel's *Tamerlan* in Halle in April 1990 explored still more directly the gendering of the unification process by underlining the links between masculinity, power and aggression.

specificity to the days of its premiere on 7 and 8 October 1989. But this premiere took place early enough in the 'Wende' period for the remarkable speed and scale of the paradigm shifts of the 'Wende' not to influence its form, though they certainly influenced its reception. Engel's *Faust* production, which addresses the relationship between the whole socialist project the GDR represented and the humanist aspirations from which it drew its legitimacy, was exposed, throughout most of its rehearsal period, to precisely these paradigm shifts. A theatre production's survival in the repertoire can rarely be attributed to a single cause and is often at least partly a matter of economics. But productions of a given society's canonical repertoire are part of that society's process of engaging with its narratives of collective understanding; and history is, we know, written by the victors. In that light it is paradoxical, perhaps, but all too understandable that while Engel's critical engagement with a whole historical epoch and the conception of progress that underlay it, is the richer production of the two, semiotically, aesthetically, intellectually, it is the emotional immediacy of Mielitz's production which has survived in the repertoire, but survived to a large degree as a museal re-enactment (and thus the very opposite) of this immediacy.

C: Goethe as Musical Catalyst

6 | Goethe and the Czechs
Jan Smaczny

Goethe among the musical Czechs is a multi-layered and at times frustratingly patchy tale. For example, while Goethe is a potent presence in Czech culture in the first part of the nineteenth century, as the numerous song settings of his poetry by Tomášek attest, he retreats into a somewhat hazy middle distance in what has come to be termed as the national revival in the latter half of the century, a situation that requires explanation. While there had been more than stirrings of a broad cultural awareness of Goethe among the Czechs from the late eighteenth century onward, the heyday of the national revival dates, more or less, from the founding of the Prague Provisional Theatre[1] in 1862. This precursor of the Czech National Theatre, which now stands as the principal architectural ornament of nineteenth-century Prague on the banks of the Vltava, opened its doors on 18 November 1862 and had a mission to perform plays and opera exclusively in Czech. Inevitably its repertoire tended to favour native writers in Czech rather than the classics of German drama, although many of the latter were given in translation.

There were, however, a number of anomalies in play at this juncture. Several major figures of the national revival, both literary and musical, the latter including the composers Bedřich Smetana and Zdeněk Fibich, spoke German as their first language. In the case of these two composers, the situation was determined by their relatively comfortable middle-class backgrounds. Dvořák, on the other hand, from a decidedly poor, rural, working-class background, spoke Czech as his first language; indeed, he was unusual in coming both from a more or less impoverished background *and* being a first-language Czech speaker. While the main thrust of this contribution is orientated to

---

[1] The title in Czech was the 'Královské zemské prozatímní divadlo' which translates as the 'royal provincial provisional theatre'.

musical connections between Goethe and the Czechs,[2] it is, for the sake of a more complete picture, desirable and necessary to reflect on Goethe's legacy among the Czechs as both a philosophic and literary phenomenon, the latter present, not just in influence, but also in terms of the reception and contemporary significance, within the national revival, of such works as *Faust* and *Egmont*.

Zdeněk Fibich (1850-1900) was perhaps the most intellectually engaged of all the composers of the Czech national revival; a pronounced modernist when it came to musical theatre, he wrote the first thorough-going Czech Wagnerian Music Drama, based on Schiller's *The Bride of Messina*, and revived Benda's epoch-making melodramas *Ariadne* and *Medea* in 1875. This pioneering revivalism was not limited to performance and eventually led to his own trilogy of scenic melodramas, *Hippodamie*, lasting a near *Ring*-like three nights in an attempt to realize, as he and his later librettist, Anežka Šulcová, saw it, the full potential of Wagner's theories of music drama.[3] Rather earlier in his career – Fibich was a child prodigy who conducted his first symphony at the age of thirteen – he had set numerous German texts, in fact, a large majority of his songs. Leipzig trained, Fibich was drawn to the poetry of Chamisso, Eichendorff, Heine, Lenau, Rückert and, indeed, Goethe. His nineteen settings of Goethe were made between 1866 and 1871, and he also set for mixed chorus Goethe's 'Über allen Gipfeln ist Ruh'. His settings were not composed as parts of cycles, although three, including Mignon's 'Kennst du das Land', were included in a collection entitled *Jarní paprsky* (Spring sunbeams, 1884). His interest in Goethe was not just confined to settings of poetry: while in Leipzig (1865-67) he provided entr'acte music for *Clavigo* and a parody duet for tenor and bass based on *Faust*; there is also a 'Gypsy song' for solo and chorus composed for a production of *Götz von Berlichingen* (1869). These Goethe settings all belong to the 1860s when Fibich's career might easily have taken him to employment in Germany; as his fortunes prospered in Prague, however, we find, a familiar pattern among Czech composers, Fibich turning more and more to native texts with national resonance.

Bedřich Smetana (1824-1884) showed little interest in text setting until after the opening of the Provisional Theatre when he began forging the line of operas that were the chief propellant of the national revival. There are, however, a few German song settings from 1853, including texts by Wieland and Rückert, though none by Goethe. Unfortunately, Smetana's overture to *Doktor Faust*, one of his few genuinely witty pieces,

---

[2] The most substantial survey of Goethe and Bohemia, Johannes Urzidil's *Goethe in Böhmen* (Esptein Verlag: Vienna and Leipzig: 1932) [hereafter Urzidil], mentions music rarely and Tomášek hardly more than peripherally.

[3] For further information about Fibich's activities in opera and melodrama in English, see Jan Smaczny, 'The operas and melodramas of Zdeněk Fibich (1850-1900)', *Proceedings of the Royal Musical Association*, CIX 1982-3, pp.119-33.

does not have a direct Goethe connection since it was composed for a production in 1862 of a puppet play of the same name by Kopecký. Goethe's *Faust*, however, was certainly in the air in the early 1860s in Prague. In 1862 Gounod's *Faust* had proved enormously popular with audiences in Prague's German theatre and extended its hegemony over Czech audiences in the Prague Provisional Theatre. From its premiere in Czech, on 6 July 1857, until the final closure of the Theatre in 1883,[4] Gounod's *Faust* was given complete 115 times, along with six performances of separate acts, outstripping in popularity any non-Czech operas and being trumped only by Smetana's *The Bartered Bride*, which was given 116 times.[5] Additionally, in 1861 the Czech Dramatic Theatre had put on successful performances of Goethe's *Faust*, Part One. A year later, on 6 December 1862, Prague's St Cecilia Music Society, one of the Czech capital's most imaginative concert-giving bodies, gave a performance of Schumann's *Scenes from Faust*.[6]

In fact, Goethe's first appearance on the stage in Czech in Prague had been with the first part of *Faust* in 1855 in a translation by Josef Jiří Kolar (Kolar was the translator of choice in both plays and opera in mid-century; he also translated, among a number of plays by Schiller, his *Wallenstein* trilogy – a cycle with understandably poignant significance for the Czechs); he was also a fine actor and took the role of Mephistopheles in this production. This landmark production was followed by *Goetz von Berlichingen* in 1856 and *Egmont* in 1858.

The nature of Czech-language theatre in mid-century Prague needs some supplementary explanation. In this period the Czech capital was changing from a primarily German-speaking city into one in which Czech became the majority language. There had been a continuous tradition of German theatre and opera since the late eighteenth century in the Estates Theatre originally built by Count Nostitz in 1783. Described as a 'National Theatre', it was sold by Nostitz's son to the Bohemian Estates in 1789. Productions in German took place here until 1888 when the company transferred to a new theatre near Prague's main station (it was renamed the 'Smetana Theatre' after the Second World War and yet again renamed after the Velvet Revolution when it became the home of the state opera company). Nostitz's theatre still exists today and was completely rebuilt (it closed for renovation for eight years and reopened in 1990); it is now mainly associated with Prague's newest musical industry, namely giving frequent performances of Mozart's better-known operas, in a way appropriate since the theatre management in Nostitz's day commissioned and gave the premiere of *Don Giovanni*.

---

[4] The National Theatre was opened for the first time in the summer of 1881 but burned down by accident days later; the rebuilding of the structure took place in hardly more than two years.

[5] For details of performance statistics in the Provisional Theatre see J. Smaczny, *The daily repertoire of the Prague Provisional Theatre* (Prague: Miscellania Musicologica, 1994) [hereafter Smaczny].

[6] I am grateful to Karl Stapleton for supplying this information.

There was no permanent home in Prague for plays and opera in Czech until the so-called Provisional Theatre was opened on 18 November 1862.[7] Productions in Czech were sporadic throughout the earlier part of the century, some, on relatively regular occasions in the 1850s held in the German Theatre. These, largely matinee events, were given on a hand-me-down basis where sets and costumes were concerned and often fell victim to the management dropping the curtain if a production overran.

The Provisional Theatre, a handsome if decidedly small structure, designed by Ignac Ullmann, an ingenious architect responsible for many of the architectural endeavours of the national revival, is now only visible as the back part of the National Theatre which succeeded it. While it is tempting to give the impression that the Provisional Theatre was the kind of temple to culture that its instigators had hoped it would be and the rather more high-minded historical accounts of the national revival have tended to favour,[8] the reality is somewhat different. The management which ran the theatre were extremely practical when it came to the profits they were charged with maintaining, since they were engaged on short-term renewable contracts.[9] Aspects of populist entertainment, such as tight-rope walking, and gymnastic displays were mounted alongside plays and opera. As an indication of the nature of taste among Provisional Theatre audiences, Smetana's populist, rabble-rousing first opera, *The Brandenburgers in Bohemia*, was a great deal more popular than the rather more lofty, if ravishingly lyrical, *Dalibor*. Reflecting the public predilection for the spectacular, it is little surprise to find Smetana and his librettist, Karel Sabina, incorporating a circus scene into their first comedy, *The Bartered Bride*. The nature of foreign repertoire also reflected a demotic tone: while Verdi and Gounod were certainly popular, the audiences for the operettas of Offenbach, Johann Strauss and others, particularly in the summer seasons, were among the largest to be found in the theatre.[10] This is, to a large extent, explained by the nature of the audience. The intentions of the founders of the Provisional Theatre had been inclusive of the new working classes drawn in to Prague from the provinces by the industrial revolution; thus high art was tempered by popular repertoire.

This might, to an extent, explain Goethe's somewhat disappointing track record in the Provisional Theatre:

---

[7] The title of the Provisional Theatre arose from its status as a stand-in structure for the planned, and much larger, National Theatre.
[8] See Josef Bartoš. *Prozatímní divadlo a jeho opera* [The Provisional Theatre and its opera] (Prague: 1938).
[9] For further information concerning the theatres of Prague in English see John Tyrrell, *Czech Opera* – in particular 'Theatres' (Cambridge: CUP, 1988), pp.13-59 [hereafter Tyrrell].
[10] For figures relating to performance see Smaczny, pp.135-37.

Table 6.1 Productions of Goethe's plays *Faust* and *Egmont* in the Provisional Theatre

	Faust	*Egmont*
1863	0	1
1864	0	0
1865	3	2
1866	1	2
1867	1	0
1868	2	1
1869	2	0
1870	1	1
1871	0	0
1872	2	1
1873	2	0
1874	2	2
1875	0	0
1876	1	1
1877	0	1
1878	1	1
1879	1	1
1880	0	1
1881	3	3
1882	2	0
Totals	24	18

The statistics are simple enough: the first performance of a play by Goethe was of Egmont, though apparently without Beethoven's music on 29 December 1863.[11] Faust was given for the first time on 15 March 1864; the performance was accompanied by Lindpaintner's overture and music, and the splendour of the occasion was advanced by its being the translator-actor J.J. Kolar's last stage performance as Mephistopheles.

---

[11] Figures for the list of performances of Goethe plays in the Provisional Theatre are derived from a ms. list compiled by J. Smaczny from material in the Theatre Centre of the Czech National Museum.

In the succeeding twenty years of the theatre's existence *Egmont* and *Faust* performed an elegant two-step with 1865 something of a bumper year: *Egmont* was given twice with Beethoven's overture and incidental music (13 March; 22 July), and *Faust* three times (30 October; 5 and 23 November), each time with Lindpaintner's incidental music. In 1874 the number of performances was reversed with three performances of *Egmont* (27 February; 30 April; 4 May) and two of *Faust* (17 May; 27 November). But generally, performances were rarities in the repertoire, one or two a year, until 1881 when both were given three times (*Egmont*: 8 March; 23 May; 24 September; *Faust*: 13 February; 12 March; 13 May). Bearing in mind the theatre management's ready tendency to reflect public response, it is possible that the overwhelming popularity of Gounod's operatic treatment of *Faust* froze the play off the stage; there is also the question that in a repertory company of actors adopting roles that settled fairly quickly, performances of *Faust* perhaps fell victim to the retirement of actors. It is possible to discount theories of anti-Germanism relating to the repertoire since Schiller, to take but the most prominent example, was frequently performed in the theatre. Apart from opera, *Faust* had other incarnations on the Czech stage, namely a series of parodies. These included one entitled *Doctor Faust and his little home-made hat* by Hopp and another by members of theatre's company.[12] Ironically, these might have guaranteed the sporadic performances of *Faust* the play as a way of touching base, a means of reminding the ready audiences for parodies of the fountainhead for their enjoyment.

Goethe on stage in the Czech lands was not just a metropolitan phenomenon: performances of *Faust* and *Egmont* were given in provincial theatres in Hradec Kralové and Brno in the nineteenth century. Once Kolar's translation was felt to be somewhat dated, a new one of very real literary distinction was provided by Jaroslav Vrchlický – a kind of Czech Tennyson who was arguably the greatest native Czech poet, and certainly the most prolific, of the nineteenth century. Vrchlický was an avid translator of literary epics from the Renaissance to his present day.

The fact that there are no Czech Goethe operas is not surprising, even apart from the comprehensive popularity of Gounod's *Faust*. Subject matter for both comic and serious opera was overwhelmingly related to national material. Where composers did tend toward non-national material, the leanings favoured mid-nineteenth-century modernism, in other words subjects suitable for Wagnerian music drama – Schiller's *The Bride of Messina* provided Fibich and his librettist, Otakar Hostinský, with the basis for the most thorough-going Czech music drama of the national revival; for his epic retelling of the Hippodamie legend in melodrama over three nights Fibich used suitably classically-orientated libretti by Vrchlický; the same author also provided Dvořák with the text for his last opera, *Armida*, based on episodes from Tasso's *Gerusalemme liberata*.

---

[12] *Doktora Fausta domácí čepička* first given on 13 October 1864.

There was, however, one occasion when Czech musical nationalism's founding father and Goethe came together. In Smetana's musical treatment of 'Der Fischer' (in Czech, Rybář) we encounter one of the real curiosities of the Czech national revival. A very popular entertainment in Prague in the 1860s and 70s was the so-called živý obraz – better known to English-speaking audiences by its French title, the *tableau vivant*. Capitalizing on the popular appeal of these entertainments, Smetana contributed to a concert designed to raise funds for the completion of St Vitus Cathedral.[13] For a concert on 12 April 1869, Smetana provided the music for three *tableaux vivants*; the first was an arrangement of music from *The Bartered Bride* – which included the first chorus – a suitably uplifting presentation entitled the *Judgement of Libuše* (Libušin soud), based on an episode from Czech historical mythology, and a treatment of Goethe's 'Der Fischer'. This last is best described as a melodrama in which the poem, against a musical background with an eye-catching backdrop enhanced by atmospheric lighting, is recited. This single 'setting' of a text of Goethe by Smetana poses a conundrum since it is, to all intents and purposes, a reduction of the opening of Wagner's *Das Rheingold*. Although this preludial portion of *Der Ring* was not premiered until 22 September 1869, some months after the debut of *Rybář*, its vocal score had been published eight years earlier (1861). Smetana's homage to Wagner's evocation of the depths of the Rhine was almost certainly prompted by the nature of the poem itself, presented here in a somewhat histrionic translation mirroring the Czech version Smetana used:[14]

Table 6.2 Goethe 'Der Fischer'

Der Fischer	Rybář	The Angler
Das Wasser rauscht', das Wasser schwoll,	Znívody šum a dme se proud,	The water roars, the water swells,
Ein Fischer saß daran,	Tam rybář na břeh sed,	A fisher sits nearby.
Sah nach dem Angel ruhevoll,	Zřel za udicí klidně v hloub	Calmly he looks at his rod,
Kühl bis ans Herz hinan.	A jeho srdce – led.	Calm, too, is his heart.
Und wie er sitzt, und wie er lauscht,	A jak tu tiše naslouchá,	And as he sits and as he looks
Teilt sich die Flut empor:	Vod rozčeří se klín	The waves rise and part.
Aus dem bewegten Wasser rauscht	A ve vln šumu pozvedá	Out of the roiling waters,
Ein feuchtes Weib hervor.	Se vlhké ženy stín.	A woman rises from the depths.

---

[13] Although begun in the late middle ages, the structure that bears the name of St Vitus standing on the castle height in Prague by the nineteenth century was still without a substantial proportion of its nave and west end. The cathedral was eventually completed in 1929.

[14] Czech translation by Otakar Zich.

The metaphysical seduction that ensues is too well known to require further elucidation, but the poignant point for Prague audiences is the image of the woman from the waters who draws the fisherman into her welcoming depths. Watery things are afoot, and the concert at which this version of 'Der Fischer' was premiered was given in a hall on the Sophie (Žofín) Concert Hall on an island in the river Vltava, the Rhine equivalent for Czech audiences. Perhaps, more importantly, the water imagery that Smetana evokes so successfully via Wagner is the start of an inheritance prompted by Goethe which bore rich fruit. Smetana's symphonic poem *Vltava*, from the cycle *My Country* (Má vlast) makes use of this kind of water imagery and, the greatest of all Czech evocations of watery depths, Dvořák's opera *Rusalka*, is soaked in the atmosphere that rises mist-like from this curious piece.

What is clear, where the Czech tradition is concerned, is that Goethe's influence is apparent, if somewhat sporadic, and also subtly inherent. In fact, Goethe's influence among the Czechs at its most significant might best be described as endogenous, an influence that grew within the development of the national revival. For evidence of this influence, it is necessary to look back toward the late eighteenth century and Goethe's relationship with Johann Gottfried Herder whose writings, both philosophical and otherwise, not only underpinned the politics of the Czech national revival, but provided part of the seed corn of that revival.[15] A seminal episode in advance of influence was the period in 1771 when Goethe went into the countryside of Alsace in search of German folksong. Of the twelve songs that Goethe sent to Herder three found their way into the philosopher's influential collection 'Folksongs from many lands' (*Volkslieder* 2 vols, 1778-79 which is better known under the title, *Stimmen der Völker in Liedern* (1807)). In his landmark biography, Boyle was exaggerating only a little when he described Goethe as '[…] one of the very first field-workers in German folklore'.[16] Goethe's model and the fruits of his labours proved to have significance well beyond the borders of Germany.

Although it is far too easy to over-rate, particularly in the cases of Smetana and Dvořák, the role of Czech folksong in the national revival, a vital source for the Czech self-image was founded on folksong collecting. Jan Harrach's initial instructions to potential composers of Czech opera for the Provisional Theatre was the distinctly Herderian command that comedies should make use of the songs of the Slavic peoples of Bohemia, Moravia and Silesia.[17] Among the Slavs, the Czechs came to formal folksong collecting relatively late; the Russians had been hard at it in the early nineteenth century followed in short order by the Poles, the Ukranians and the Slovenians. The

---

[15] See ed. René Welleck, trans. Peter Kussi, *The Meaning of Czech History by Tomás G. Masaryk* (Chapel Hill: The University of North Carolina Press, 1974), pp.28-36.
[16] See Nicholas Boyle, *Goethe: the Poet and the Age*, I (Oxford: OUP, 1991), pp.98-99.
[17] See Tyrrell, pp.209-10.

first significant stirrings in the Czech lands were prompted by an official Austrian body, the Gesellschaft der Musikfreunde of Vienna. This institution charged provincial governments within the Austrian empire with fostering the collecting of folksong. An early result was a volume of *Böhmische Volkslieder* published in 1825 and edited by Jan Ritter z Rittersberku and Friedrich Dionys Weber, which comprised 300 Czech songs, 50 German songs and 50 instrumental dances.[18] Of greater local significance for the Czechs were the activities of the poet František Ladislav Čelakovský who, heavily influenced by the philosophy of Herder and Goethe,[19] sought to bring about a renaissance of the Czech language through the revival of folk poetry. While Herder was certainly crucial in providing inspiration for Čelakovský, the most important influence was the poetry of Goethe: without doubt, *Faust*, about which Čelakovský wrote at length, but in the case of his approach to folk poetry and his own work, the poetry and Volkslied style promulgated by Goethe. Čelakovský's three volumes of *Slavonic Folksong* (Slovanské národní písně), published between 1822 and 1827, and comprising mainly verse with only a few melodies, were, in a sense, the first pebbles dislodged in what rapidly turned into an avalanche. Key ventures were the folksong collecting activities of František Sušil and Karel Jaromír Erben: Sušil eventually published some 2500 Moravian folksongs (published in seven instalments it was complete by 1860: *Moravian folksongs with tunes included with the text*; Moravské národní písně s nápěvy do textu vřaděnými); Erben did much the same in volume for Bohemian folksong (tunes 1862, texts 1864: *Czech folksongs and nursery rhymes*; Prostonárodní české písně a říkadla). As well as providing the Czechs with the authentic article, Erben produced, in 1853, a sensationally successful volume of ballads based on folk sources entitled *A Garland of National Tales* (Kytice z pověstí národních, 1853). Erben was a huge admirer of Goethe and had translated 'Erlkönig' into Czech. In many ways the atmosphere of this, one of the most popular and famous of Goethe's works, hovers over the poems of Erben's Garland, notably the 'Water Goblin' (Vodník). One of the most atmospheric and successful of Dvořák's four late symphonic poems based on poems from Erben's *Garland*[20] was a version of the *Erlkönig*-shaded 'Water Goblin'.

While Goethe's influence, whether endogenous or by proxy as in the case of Erben on Dvořák, was crucial in the Czech national revival, there is a much more material link between his poetry and the Czechs in the shape of the forty-three Goethe settings by Václav Jan Křtitel Tomášek (1774-1850).[21] Tomášek's long life spanned the late classical

---

[18] ibid.
[19] See Artur Závodský, *František Ladislav Čelakovský* (Prague: Melantrich, 1983), pp.144-61.
[20] Dvořák set lines of Erben's text to music, without text, would be used as the main thematic material of these symphonic poems.
[21] These forty-three settings comprise thirty-four solo songs, three duets and four duos; in addition, there are two there are two dramatic scenes based on texts from *Faust*. The only extensive

period, early romanticism and the somewhat faltering early days of the national revival. Tomášek's musical education was a classic of the Bohemian type: from a far from wealthy mercantile family, he was taught music, as so many were, in the rural locality, graduating at nine to elementary school in Chrudim – a small town – where he studied singing and the violin. In his early teens he gained a scholarship to the Minorite monastery in Jihlava – had he been born a generation earlier he might well have studied, as did so many others, in a Jesuit seminary, but the order had been dispersed in 1775. From here, Tomášek went to Prague to Gymnasium in the Lesser Town (Malá strana) and went on to study, among other subjects, philosophy and law at the Charles University. A formative musical experience in Prague in 1790 was a performance of Mozart's *Don Giovanni*.

With no conservatory in Prague at this stage, music for Tomášek was largely a self-taught art. In 1806 he was appointed as music tutor to the aristocratic Buquoy family; Count Buquoy was a man of broad humanist sympathies and an acquaintance of Goethe.[22] This loose-limbed appointment enabled Tomášek to travel extensively in Austria and Germany where he had the opportunity to meet many of Europe's musical luminaries. Many of those he did not meet on his travels beat a path to his door in Prague once he had become established as the city's undisputed musical doyen. His pupil, the critic Hanslick, referred to him as Prague's 'Dalai Lama' or 'musical Pope';[23] among these visitors were Berlioz, Wagner, Paganini and Clara Schumann. We know about the former visits abroad, and much else, since Tomášek tells us in his autobiography, an extensive and fascinating document, published in six issues of the Prague periodical *Libussa* between 1845 and 1850.[24] The period covered by these reminiscences runs from Tomášek's childhood to 1824. It is little exaggeration to say that Tomášek name-dropped for Bohemia while exhibiting a healthy flair for gossip: there were visits to the failing Haydn in 1808, the near completely-deaf Beethoven in 1814, and in 1822 a significant appointment with Goethe.

Before considering this high point in Tomášek's life, a brief word on the nature of his muse and influences. He was an ardent, not to say devout, Mozartean and an

---

consideration of these settings in English is to be found in Kenneth DeLong, 'Jan Václav Tomášek's Goethe Lieder', *Kosmas* 7 (1988), pp.71-90.

[22] See Urzidil, pp.169-70.

[23] See Eduard Hanslick, *Aus Meinem Leben* (Berlin: Allgemeiner Verein für Deutsche Literatur, 1911), p.25.

[24] V. Tomášek, 'Selbstbiographie', *Libussa* (Prague: 1845-50). There is no complete English translation of this source available although excerpts are printed in A. Loft, 'Excerpts from the Memoirs of J.W. Tomáščhek', *MQ* xxxii (1946), pp.244-64. An annotated Czech translation, which was used as the basis of the sections relating to Tomášek's memoirs in this article, exists: see Zdeněk Němec, *Vlastní Životopis V.J. Tomáška* [complete autobiography] (Topičova edice v Praze: Prague, 1941) [hereafter Němec].

admirer, via his studies with Forkel, of J.S. Bach. The musical life of Prague during his lifetime was not as fecund as might be supposed from snapshots of the city in Mozart's later years or, indeed in the national revival. There were few of the institutions that were to guarantee the musical health of Prague later in the century. Indeed, so limited were the opportunities for promising musicians, that the haemorrhage of talent so evident through the eighteenth century continued into the early years of the nineteenth. Tomášek, himself, was unusual in being one of the few who stayed at home; many of his pupils, including Voříšek, Dreyschock and Hanslick, all left to seek their fortunes elsewhere. The most significant institution arrived with the founding of the Prague Organ School in 1830 largely designed to fill the gap left when the Jesuit seminaries were abolished in the late eighteenth century; the consequent decay in the standards of church music was not lost on the founders of this institution which eventually educated the likes of Dvořák and Janáček. Apart from these ventures, musical endeavour in Prague might be described as having fallen into a kind of post-Mozartean gloom in the early decades of the nineteenth century.

Tomášek himself was always ready to espouse the virtues of his beloved Mozart and German music while frequently excoriating Italian composers and their taste, yet his music, once he had reached compositional maturity, from about 1807, has a distinctly early romantic cut. His numerous piano works often bear a generalized resemblance to Schubert, a feature shared by his greatest composing pupil, Jan Hugo Voříšek, and one which was more a case of parallel development than specific influence.

Tomášek's relationship with Goethe's poetry was long lasting. It is interesting, if sadly salutary, to reflect that, despite the large number and excellence of his Goethe settings, the songs on which the Czechs focused in the national revival of the 1860s tended to be from Tomášek's fairly extensive groups of Czech settings, made in order to remind the composer of his native language spoken before he learned German.[25] A more fruitful influence on the later Czechs was his various sets of piano pieces: Eclogues, Dithyrambs and Capriccios; revived by Karel Slavkovský in the 1870s, they had a conspicuous impact on Dvořák.

Concerning Tomášek's relationship with Goethe, the modern reader can lean to a considerable extent on the composer's own words since there is ample reference to the poet in Tomášek's autobiography. Tomášek informs us of the extent of his interest in Goethe as follows: 'I wrote several sets of songs which I sold by subscription', adding with relish, 'I wrote them with taste and love'. 'In the seventh set, which I dedicated to Goethe, there are three ballads.'[26] Tomášek was thanked handsomely by Goethe for the songs and the dedication, the poet telling him that 'Your songs are the best I have come

---

[25] Němec, p.190.
[26] Němec pp.238ff.

across in years';[27] since this was written in 1820, Goethe's comment would have included Beethoven and Schubert in this appraisal.

In 1822 Tomášek had the opportunity to meet Goethe who was staying in the west Bohemian town of Cheb (Eger). Tomášek attended on the poet and was greeted cordially; after much conversation, he performed a number of his settings, the first of which was 'Heidenröslein'. Tomášek's setting may lack the epigrammatic qualities of Schubert's, but it has unquestionable charm and freshness including a delightful yodelling effect at the end of the first line. There is one point of close contact with Schubert's setting, in that the treatment of the word 'Röslein' is identical in rhythm and melodic shape. A point of difference from Schubert's approach is that he does not treat the poem exclusively strophically: for the climax in the third verse, Tomášek goes for minor key drama (see example 6.1).

The last song Tomášek performed for Goethe in this impromptu recital was 'Mignons Sehnsucht' (see example 6.2). A graceful, dignified setting, it is, unlike Schubert's, entirely strophic, a point that clearly appealed to Goethe and evoked the following approbation:

> You understand the poem – Goethe said this to me after listening to the last-named song; he also said clearly that he was entirely satisfied with my setting of the song [...] It seems strange to me that both Beethoven and Spohr so completely misunderstood the song when they composed it. The distinctive mark in the same place in each verse, I would think, was enough to tell composers that what I expect from them is simply a song [Lied]. Evidently, Mignon by her very nature could not sing an aria, but only a song.[28]

The variety in Tomášek's Goethe settings is considerable and, as a whole, the collection of songs represents the finest body of Czech Lied settings in the first part of the nineteenth century. While Goethe clearly approved of Tomášek's uncomplicated approach to his Lied-inspired verse, we do not know the poet's view of the Czech composer's treatment of 'Erlkönig' (see example 6.3). Schubert's superbly dramatic setting will always take pride of place, and those of Loewe and Franz are likely to claim precedence in terms of performance history, but Tomášek's certainly stands high in this company. Effectively through-composed, it develops wonderful impetus and climaxes, with a clear metronome-mark increase, in an Allegro assai dash to the double bar. Eschewing Schubert's expressionist clinching of the drama, Tomášek repeats the final words, placing 'todt' at the top of a bold diminished chord followed by a Neapolitan cadence which unleashes savage descending chromatics in the piano part.

---

[27] Němec p.239.

Example 6.1 Tomášek 'Heidenröslein'

Example 6.2 Tomášek 'Mignons Sehnsucht'

Example 6.3 Tomášek 'Erlkönig'

7 | Maker, Mother, Muse: Bettina von Arnim, Goethe and the Boundaries of Creativity
Briony Williams

Bettina von Arnim has long been seen as a 'muse' to male creators such as Goethe, Beethoven and the Grimm brothers. She herself could be seen to have assisted in immortalizing this role through her semi-fictitious epistolary accounts of her relationships with these men. Her rewriting of much of the correspondence has earned her a great deal of controversy in historical terms, due to the resulting questionable veracity of her account. Bettina herself courted this controversy when she wrote in her introduction to *Goethes Briefwechsel mit einem Kinde*:

> [...] treten Sie abermals hier zwischen mich und das Vorurteil derer, sie schon jetzt, noch eh' sie es kennen, dies Buch als unecht verdammen und sich selbst um die Wahrheit betrügen.[1]

This has been assumed to mean that Bettina intended the letters to be taken as reality; but Bettina also gives a hint of her intentions in the book when she wrote to the Weimar Chancellor, Friedrich von Müller, 'ich spreche nicht von [Goethe], ich spreche zu ihm'.[2] These two statements immediately problematize the defining concepts of our use of the term 'muse' in relation to the complex figure of Bettina. What exactly was she intending, creatively speaking, in her works? How are we to see her relationship with Goethe? Some answers can be found through exploring the three ways in which Bettina responds to Goethe artistically – through the correspondence, through her poems and

---

[1] Bettina von Arnim, *Goethes Briefwechsel mit einem Kinde*, in *Sämtliche Werke*, ed. Waldemar Oehlke (Berlin, 1920-22), III, unpaginated. 'you should ignore the prejudice of those, who before they are acquainted with the book, condemn it as not genuine and thus deceive themselves of the truth.'

[2] Quoted in Ann Willison Lemke, *Bettine's Song: The Musical Voice of Bettine von Arnim, neé Brentano* (diss., Indiana University, 1998), p.154. 'I do not speak of [Goethe], I speak to him.'

through her musical compositions. These last two 'primary' creative activities reveal a great deal about Bettina's own relationship to, and view of, the role of muse.

One difficulty in defining Bettina as a muse in the common conception of the term is that the connection between Bettina and Goethe neither resulted directly in a poem by Goethe, nor is described, at least at face value, in realistic terms in the published correspondence. How, then, did this relationship work in reality?

The word 'muse' has often come to define a passive role, particularly of a woman who inspires a male creator in his artistic endeavours, often with herself as the object of his artistic scrutiny. Kimberley Marshall sums up popular contemporary definitions when she writes:

> Late-medieval descriptions of the Muses show them making music, inspiring through example as mentors in the specialized disciplines they came to represent. Unfortunately, during the intervening centuries these powerful archetypes have been reduced to an insipid allegory for artistic inspiration.[3]

Those far more active connotations of the original Greek Muses that were still present in medieval thought are recorded by Ferdinand Comte:

> The Muses created what they sang about. By praising the gods, they completed their glory; by boasting of valiant warriors, they wrote their names in history. In this way they collaborated in the ordering of the world [...] The disciples of Pythagoras celebrated the Muses as the keepers of the knowledge of harmony and the principles of the universe which allowed access to the everlasting gods.[4]

Here the word 'access' is, I believe, of prime importance in redefining Bettina's response, in particular to Goethe, in more active terms.

Goethe's acquaintance with Bettina's family had already extended over two generations. Bettina's grandmother was the acclaimed novelist Sophie von La Roche, whose first published book, *Die Geschichte des Fräuleins von Sternheim*, was an overnight success, and is considered to be the model for Goethe's *Die Leiden des jungen Werthers*. Goethe himself wrote of Sophie, 'Sie war die wunderbarste Frau, und ich wußte ihr keine andre zu vergleichen.'[5] Through Sophie's salons, Goethe also met her daughter Maximiliane, Bettina's mother. Goethe was considerably attracted to the young woman. Bettina discovered this fact when she read Goethe's correspondence with Sophie, and it seems to have inspired her to take something of the same role. She began writing to Catherina von Goethe, the poet's mother, in 1806, and after meeting Goethe himself in

---

[3] Kimberley Marshall, ed., *Rediscovering the Muses: Women's Musical Traditions* (Boston, 1993), p.xix.

[4] Ferdinand Comte, *The Wordsworth Dictionary of Mythology* (Ware, 1994), p.135.

[5] Johann Wolfgang von Goethe, *Dichtung und Wahrheit* (Stuttgart, 1884), p.445. 'She was the most wonderful woman, and I know of no other who can compare with her.'

1807, began a correspondence with him as well. Both letter exchanges are 'documented' in Bettina's book, *Goethes Briefwechsel mit einem Kinde*.

The letters are saturated with Bettina's views on creativity. Interestingly, she seems to see the act of creation as always being reciprocal – whether it is between two artists, or between an artist and his or her inspiration. In the correspondence with her brother, published as *Clemens Brentanos Frühlingskranz*, Bettina talked of the 'four pillars' of her soul – Goethe, Arnim, music and nature.[6] All four are, in Bettina's view, capable of interplay. Even nature not only inspires but is inspired. Bettina's image of the shepherd playing his shawm is an example of this view, as he is so in tune with nature that he not only copies the echo he hears, but teaches it new melodies. And music is inspired by words, but the reverse is equally true. The model of creative reciprocity in place in the exchange between Bettina and Achim von Arnim prior to their marriage – where Achim would send her poems, which she would then set to music, which would, in turn, inspire him to add more verses – was not only an exchange between the two creators, but between their creations as well. Not only did Achim inspire Bettina to compose, but his poetry inspired her music in a much more direct way.

This whole notion of inspiration arising from within the work itself is apparent in Bettina's own poetry. It would seem very clear that Bettina is intending a direct response to specific Goethe poems – the most obvious is 'Wer sich der Einsamkeit ergibt', in which the first verse is a direct quote from the Harper's song in *Wilhelm Meisters Lehrjahre*. Other poems are less obvious, but still seem to draw their own parallels, for example, the untitled poem in which the narrator stands atop his hill, viewing the scene below, and yearning for the sight of the lost beloved's rooftop:

> Auf diesem Hügel überseh ich meine Welt!
> Und könnt ich Paradiese überschauen,
> Ich sehne mich zurück nach jenen Auen,
> Wo Deines Daches Zinne meinem Blick sich stellt,
> Denn der allein umgrenzet meine Welt.[7]

One cannot help but be reminded of 'Schäfer's Klagelied'. Other examples include Bettina's 'Lied des Hemdchens', a story of what can only be attempted rape, with its overtones of 'Heidenröslein', or 'Das Königslied', which, like 'Der König in Thule', is the story of a king coming to terms with an event in his life before his death.

'Wer sich der Einsamkeit ergibt' is a particularly interesting example, not only because it opens with a direct quotation from the Harper's song, but also because of its overt statements regarding Bettina's views on the relationship between an artist and a muse. In this parody she has distanced herself from ordinary mortals, from the 'masses',

---

[6] Lemke, op.cit., p.1.
[7] Arnim, op.cit., IV, p.149.

and has endowed upon herself the role of priestess in the quasi-religious experience which she believes music to be and as she continually describes it to Goethe in the *Briefwechsel*.[8] Like the original Greek muses, the persona of Bettina within the poem is the medium for communication between the artist and heaven – she gives a gift of 'the flame of life'. And it does not end there – she lays wreaths at the altar, that is to say she offers her own creations as part of the dynamic of the relationship, and in so doing, achieves immortality for both herself and the artist. Although this could be seen simply as an indication of Bettina's search for historical permanence, the most interesting aspect of this view of the muse is its possibility for neverending reciprocity – a conceptualization of creativity that is a model of a type of creativity which, in Riane Eisler's words, moves the process 'from a linear, cumulative view to a more cyclic, or spiralic one, where repetition and recombination play an important role.'[9]

---

[8] Bettina von Arnim, *Goethes Briefwechsel mit einem Kinde*, op.cit. See for example the letters dated Winkel 7. August, pp259-263, and 24. July, pp.232-34.

[9] Riane Eisler and Alfonso Montuori, 'Creativity, Society and the Hidden Subtext of Gender: Toward a New Contextualized Approach', forthcoming in *Social Creativity* eds A. Montuori and R. Purser (Hampton Press:Creskill, NJ), III.

Table 7.1 Bettina von Arnim, 'Wer sich der Einsamkeit ergibt'

Wer sich der Einsamkeit ergibt,	He who devotes himself to solitude
Ach der ist bald allein;	Alas, is soon alone.
Ein jeder lebt, ein jeder liebt	Everybody lives, everybody loves,
Und läßt ihn seiner Pein.	And leaves him to his sorrow
Wer sich dem Weltgewühl ergibt,	He who devotes himself to the milling crowd
Der ist zwar nie allein.	Is, admittedly, never alone
Doch was er lebt und was er liebt,	What he experiences and what he loves
Es wird wohl nimmer sein.	Is mere allusion
Nur wer der Muse hin sich gibt,	He who devotes himself to the Muse
Der weilet gern allein,	Is willingly alone
Er ahnt, daß sie ihn wieder liebt,	He senses that she returns his love
Von ihm geliebt will sein.	And that she wants to be loved by him
Vergöttlicht Lust und Pein.	Deifies pleasure and pain,
Sie kränzt den Becher und Altar,	She crowns the chalice and altar
Was sie ihm gibt, es ist so wahr,	What she gives him is so true
Gewährt ein ewig Sein.	It gives eternal being.
Es blüht hell in seiner Brust	The brilliance of life's flame
Der Lebensflamme Schein.	Blossoms bright in his breast
Im Himmlischen ist ihm bewußt	In the heavenly he becomes conscious of
Das reine irdsche Sein.[10]	The purity of earthly being.

At times, in Bettina's life, the term 'muse' seems to be almost interchangeable with the term 'role model'. Bettina herself had a number of role models who could be seen as fulfilling both functions. She grew up in an environment conducive to creative achievement in women. The most important of these was, of course, her grandmother Sophie von La Roche. Not only was Sophie an internationally well-known literary figure even before Bettina was born, she was also financially independent as a result of her writing. Her husband, Georg Michael von La Roche had published a book anonymously, *Briefe über das Mönchswesen*. It was a politically critical book, and despite the anonymity, his authorship was well-known, and his views lost him his job and career. Overnight, Sophie became the breadwinner of the family with her continuing publications. From 1785 she published almost one volume per year until her death in 1807. Her work

---

[10] Bettina von Arnim, *Werke und Briefe* (Frechen, 1963), IV, p.125.

encompasses novels, travel memoirs, epistolary novels and, in the two years before her death, two volumes of an autobiography.

There are a number of interesting parallels between Sophie and Bettina, not only through their choices for creative expression – for example, the epistolary novels – but also through their life choices. Both of them married comparatively late and chose partners whom they thought would encourage them in their quest for self-expression. Both women also published most of their output later in life, due to early pressures in their roles as wife and mother. The fact that these other gendered roles encroached on their creative lives means that Bettina's views on marriage and motherhood need to be taken into account when considering her perception of the gendered role of muse.

Regarding gender issues, two different interpretations of Bettina emerge. One is that she was not interested in her own role as a woman, being far more concerned with her role as an artist. Gert Mattenklott is an advocate of this viewpoint. She names individual women such as Rahel Varnhagen von Ense, Caroline von Schlegel and Bettina von Arnim as being exceptions to the general gendered silence in Germany at that time, but argues that these women were more interested in the rights of the individual to artistic expression than their right as a woman to be heard.[11] Yet all of these women fulfilled the role of muse as well as original creator, and were aware of this duality. Surely it is possible that the two perspectives are not mutually exclusive. Despite the emphasis on individual expression, it seems to be the case that these women were aware of the difficulties facing them culturally through their choice to be outspoken. They were also acutely aware of the differences in their means and outcomes of expression from those of men. At one point Bettina wrote to Achim von Arnim, 'nun sagen meine Lehrer zwar, daß ich nicht dumm sei, sondern besser verstehe wie mancher Mann, aber daß noch viel, viel Zeit dazu gehört, bis ich etwas kann.'[12]

Another view of Bettina is as an outspoken advocate of women's issues, as she was on many other social matters. The difficulty with this view is that women's issues per se do not feature in her writing, although it could be said that there are a number of indirect references. There is, for example, the account of how she and her sister dressed as men to travel to Weimar:

> Jetzt rat' Sie einmal, was der Schneider für mich macht. Ein Andrieng? – Nein! – Eine Kontusche? – Nein! Einen Joppel? – Nein! Eine Mantille? – Nein! Ein paar Boschen? – Nein! Einen Reifrock? – Nein! Einen Schlepprock? – Nein! Ein Paar Hosen? – Ja! – Vivat –

---

[11] Gert Mattenklott, 'Romantische Frauenkultur: Bettina von Arnim zum Beispiel', in: *Frauenliteraturgeschichte: Schreibende Frauen vom Mittelalter bis zur Gegenwart*, eds Hiltrud Gnüg and Renate Möhrmann (Stuttgart, 1985), p.123.

[12] Quoted in Lemke, p.31. 'My teachers say that I'm not stupid, and that although I understand many things better than a man, it will be a long long time before I can do anything as well as a man can.'

jetzt kommen andre Zeiten angerückt – und auch eine Weste und ein Überrock dazu. Morgen wird alles anprobiert, es wird schon sitzen, denn ich hab' mir alles bequem und weit bestellt, und dann werf' ich mich in eine Chaise und reise Tag und Nacht Kurier durch die ganzen Armeen zwischen Feind und Freund durch; alle Festungen tun sich vor mir auf, und so geht's fort bis Berlin, wo einige Geschäfte abgemacht werden, die mich nichts angehn. [13]

In highlighting the issue of male costume as camouflage, Bettina is, I believe, making a very strong statement about how aware she is of gender constructs and limitations in what she achieves. Thus it would seem that Bettina was fully aware of the necessity of action in encouraging freedom of expression for women, but consciously chose to address these issues through her artistic works. Certainly she appears to have thought very carefully of her options before marriage to the poet, Achim von Arnim. Bettina was afraid that the move would stifle her creative endeavours but the apparent environment of mutual inspiration between poet and musician assured Bettina that her creativity would be nurtured. Unfortunately, this was not to be the case – Bettina became confined in a world of domesticity, financial struggle and – worst of all – her husband's neglect of her creativity. That she understood this in terms of her gendered role in the society of the time is evident from her advice to Philip Hössli that marriage is 'für das Weib das Einzige, für den Mann blos eine Epoche.'[14]

Despite Bettina's frequent depression and feelings of creative inadequacy during her marriage, she was a highly successful mother – all seven of her children survived into adulthood, a rare occurrence at the time. In such a case, it seems difficult to accept Sally Winkle's view of the adoption of 'subordinate' roles for women leading to the loss of their 'active capability to resolve, lead, create or transform.'[15] Bettina seems to have brought her creative self to almost all of these roles in a consciously active and successful way that turned them into primary roles. Although Bettina herself does not seem to have attached the notion of creativity to these other roles, she does make one interestingly explicit comparison between the creativity of a mother and an artist in the passage in the *Briefwechsel* where she describes music as 'Mutterwärme'. She writes that

---

[13] Bettina von Arnim, *Sämtliche Werke*, III, p.6. 'Now guess what the tailor is making for me. An Adrian? No! – A Paduasoy? No! – A Boddire? No! – A Mantilla? No! – A training-gown? No! – A Pair of trousers? Yes! – Hurrah! (Other times are now coming) – and a waistcoat and coat too. Tomorrow everything will be tried on; it must set well, for I have ordered everything to be made full and easy; and then I throw myself into a chaise, and courier-like travel day and night through the entire armies, between friend and foe [...]' Translation from Bettina von Arnim, *Goethe's Correspondence with a Child* (London, 1837-39).

[14] Quoted in Lemke, p.48 'the be-all and end-all for the wife, but for the husband it is simply an epoch.'

[15] Sally A. Winkle, *Woman as Bourgeois Ideal: A Study of Sophie von la Roche's 'Geschichte des Fräuleins von Sternheim' and Goethe's 'Werther'* (New York, 1988) p.95

music is a mother of twins: 'eins hatte sie an der Brust, und das andre wiegte ihr Fuß im Takt, während sie ihr Lied sang.'[16]

Although Bettina was most well-known as an author, her own desire was to be a composer. Music, she felt, expressed what words could not, and she wrote to the poet Caroline von Günderode that she felt more at home within the rhythms of music than those of words.[17] It was through composition that she felt most able to converse with other artists – mostly, of course, Arnim and Goethe, and to a lesser degree, with other poets. Formal composition, however, was difficult for Bettina throughout her life, and she constantly struggled to commit her ideas to paper and permanence. She was known as a great improvisational singer – Ludwig Tieck was one of those who admired her talent – and this seems very clear in the structure of her songs. Improvisation could be defined as instantaneous composition in response to a larger context and certainly her melodies seem to unfold in direct and immediate response to a particular text. Bettina's description of her composition methods outline this process:

> Jetzt macht mir's Freude zu komponieren. – Hymnen der Diane, Päane an Dionysos, von Stolberg übersetzt. – Ja, das macht mir Freude, ich klettere am Abend aufs Dach von der Waschküche, dort erfind' ich die wunderlichsten Wendungen. Der Himmel rötet sich davon vor tiefem Mitgefühl, und die Sterne drängen sich herbei und lauschen, und Hoffmann lauscht auch, er ist unser nächster Nachbar. Meine Stimme ist durchdringend, wär mein Geist es auch! – Hoffmann kommt am Morgen in die Stunde, kann meine Melodie halb auswendig, was ich mit Bleistift notiert habe, kann er meist besser als ich – über Metrum streiten wir zwar nicht; denn er will durchaus, es soll sein, wie ich's ursprünglich singe, Takt und Auftakt kommen in Subordination und dürfen nicht ihre herkömmliche Observanz mehr geltend machen, er sagt, wenn ich mich hineinstudiere, so wird's der Musik eine neue Bahn brechen. Närrischer Kerl! Will mir schmeicheln, mir Mut machen zum Lernen; weiß ich doch, daß er's mir weismacht, so trägt's doch meine Begeistrung unendlich hoch![18]

---

[16] Arnim, *Sämtliche Werke*, III, p.235. 'she had one at her breast, the other she rocked rhythmically with her foot while she sang her song.'

[17] Quoted in Bettina Brand, *Komponistinnen in Berlin* (Berlin, 1987), p.32. 'Ich hab oft darüber gedacht, daß Musik so leicht und gleichsam von selbst sich melodisch ins Metrum füge, die doch vom Verstand weit weniger erfaßt und regiert wird wie der Sprache, die nie ohne Anstrengung das Metrum des Gedankens ergründet und entwickelt.' I have often thought how music, which fits so naturally and melodically into the metre, is less easily grasped and governed by the intellect; just as language can never, without effort, be fathomed and developed by thought.

[18] Bettina von Arnim, *Ein Lesebuch*, ed. by Christa Bürger and Birgit Diffenbach (Stuttgart, 1987), p.45. 'Now it gives me a great deal of joy to compose – hymns to Diana, paens of praise of Dionysos, translated by Stolberg. Oh yes, it gives me so much joy. In the evening I climb up onto the roof from the laundry, there I invent the most wonderful idioms. The sky blushes with deep empathy, and the stars gather round and listen, and Hoffmann listens too – he is our closest neighbour. My voice carries, if only my spirit did as well! Hoffmann comes to the lesson the next morning; he already knows my melody half from memory – the part I had written down in pencil

Because of the improvisatory nature of much of Bettina's music-making, her songs have often been dismissed, from Liszt, who wrote to Marie D'Agoult, 'Ces *Lieder* qu'elle vient de publier et de dédier à Spontini ne valent pas grand chose,'[19] to Max Friedländer, who rather condescendingly acknowledges her 'für eine Dilettantin erfreuliche Begabung'.[20] Of the approximately eighty songs in existence, most are fragments. Nine songs were published in her life-time – two in works by Achim von Arnim, and one collection of seven songs, dedicated to Spontini, director of the Royal Opera.[21] All display the same hallmarks of unconventionality.

The two Goethe settings chosen for discussion are prime examples of this refusal to adhere to mainstream compositional rules. They were written approximately twelve years apart – 'Ach Neige' in 1810, 'An Luna' in about 1822. 'An Luna' was written for the singer and actress Amalie Neumann, upon the request of Philipp Hössli, a law student who was a close friend of Bettina's. The copy in his notebook is dated 28 June 1822. On the surface, the poem of 'An Luna' (see table 7.2) could be seen to be an evocation of feminine archetypes, from Luna – the moon, a very common symbol of feminine purity – to the maiden asleep beneath the male gaze. But even here there are echoes of the active muse. In the first verse, Luna has awoken the poet – that is, she has given him both consciousness and the ability to create his verses. She raises him to her side and shows him the object of his inspiration, his beloved asleep in her bed. Her own history is also invoked through the Endymion myth. Luna has inspired the persona of the poet, who in turn inspires Goethe, Bettina, the performer, and ultimately the listener. But according to Bettina, the circle can also work in reverse, so that the listener can redirect the response of the performer, which in turn literally changes the meaning and content of both music and poetry, all the way back to the Endymion myth. In the myth, Luna saw the shepherd Endymion asleep among his sheep as she went on her nightly rounds, and fell for his beauty. She thereupon went to Zeus and asked if Endymion could be granted eternal youth and eternal life. Zeus granted her wish, and Endymion slept on for eternity, dreaming that he held the moon in his arms, while Luna seduced him nightly. Certainly the kind of eroticizing of the muse role inherent in the

---

he knew better than I. We scarcely argued about the timing, because he wanted the whole thing to be as I had originally sung it; the beats and upbeats are of lesser importance and make the established rules irrelevant. He says, if I apply myself to my studies, then music may break new ground. Foolish fellow He compliments me so that I'm motivated to learn; I know that he says these things to keep my enthusiasm at the very highest pitch!'

[19] M. Daniell Ollivier, ed. *Correspondance de Liszt et de la Comtesse D'Agoult 1840-1864*, (Paris, 1934), p.321. 'Those songs that she has just published and dedicated to Spontini are of no great value.'

[20] Max Friedländer, in Arnim, *Sämtliche Werke*, IV, p.299. 'A pleasant talent for an amateur.'

[21] At the time, Spontini had been accused of offending the king and booed out of the opera house. Bettina's dedication was at once a political statement and a gesture of support.

myth is completely in character for Bettina; and given Bettina's penchant for reading her own life in terms of myths, it becomes possible to begin to understand how past and present, conscious and unconscious, intertwine in creative interchange.

Table 7.2 Bettina von Arnim, 'An Luna'

Schwester von dem ersten Licht	Sister of the sun
Bild der Zärtlichkeit im Trauer!	Picture of tenderness in mourning!
Nebel schwimmt mit Silberschauer	Mist swims in silver shimmers
Um dein reizendes Gesicht.	Around your lovely face.
Deines leisen Fußes Lauf	The tread of your soft foot
Weckt aus tagverschloßnen Höhlen	Awakens from caves that shut out the day
Traurig abgeschiedne Seelen,	Sad isolated souls,
Mich, und Nachtgevögel auf.	Me, and nocturnal birds.
Forschend übersieht dein Blick	Your glance, searchingly surveys
Eine unermeßne Weite:	A boundless expanse
Hebe mich an deine Seite,	Raise me to your side
Gönn' der Schwärmerei dies' Glück.	Grant my zeal this happiness.
Und in wollustvoller Ruh	And in peaceful ecstasy
Säh der weitverschlagne Ritter	The knight, driven far, would, through
Durch das gläserne Gegitter	The glass barrier, keep watch over
Seines Mädchens Nächten zu.	His lady as she slept.
Des Beschauens holdes Glück	The sweet happiness of contemplation
Mildert solcher Ferne Qualen;	Assuages the torments of such distance
Und ich sammle deine Strahlen	And I gather your rays
Und ich schärfe meinen Blick;	And I focus my gaze
Hell und heller wird es schon	It becomes bright and brighter already
Um die unverhüllten Glieder	Around the unveiled limbs
Und sie zieht mich zu sich nieder	And she draws me down to her
Wie dich einst Endymion.[22]	As once Endymion did to you.

---

[22] Ann Willison Lemke, ed., *Von Goethe inspiriert*, (Kassel, 1999), p.12.

Example 7.1 Bettina von Arnim, 'An Luna'

The cyclic nature of the story is picked up by Bettina in her setting of 'An Luna', where the opening accompaniment is harmonically static. The almost constant use of the dominant seventh chord removes any feeling of climax and repose. Even the ending is open, hovering about the dominant. Despite the harmonic stasis, however, 'An Luna' is tonally ambiguous. Because there is no introduction and no postlude, the ambiguity of the final chord of each verse blurs the strophic boundaries until the very end, when the questioning half-close becomes at last apparent. This continuous feel makes the music almost glide, and the rests in both voice and piano seem a particularly poignant cessation of movement. Bettina also, through irregular rhythmic movement, blurs where text lines begin and end. The accompaniment is deliberately neutral, a framing device that is representational of the 'larger context' that is the performance space for the emotional improvisation of the singer. The text dictates the structure: therefore we cannot define structure in the usual musically analytical terms. It is as if all the accepted defining components have been removed – harmonic direction, formal symmetry – so that we are left with what is, in a sense, a return to the original lyric. In her music, Bettina has created a bridge between listener and text, thereby enabling our access to artistic experience in a way that has been seen historically as inherent to the role of muse. If we accept this as a definition of muse, Bettina has been successful in her aims.

The other song, 'Ach Neige' [23](example 7.2) raises a different set of questions, but again, Bettina's musical language could be seen to arise from her belief in cyclic creativity. Bettina did not want to set all of *Faust*, but she did write an Overture – one of the only two textless compositions she is known to have written. Unfortunately this is, at present, lost, along with settings of 'Was ist die Himmelsfreud' in ihren Armen', 'Der König von Thule', and two songs known only as 'Zwei glückliche Melodien zum *Faust*'. One of these 'good melodies' may be the setting of Faust's declaration of love to Gretchen in the garden, 'Ich schaud're nicht', which appears in the Spontini collection. It is interesting that Bettina chose to set direct speech from *Faust*, as well as some of the more obvious songs.

---

[23] Ed. Renate Moering, *Von Goethe inspiriert* (Kassel, 1999).

Example 7.2 Bettina von Arnim, 'Ach neige, du Schmerzenreiche'

While writing 'Ach Neige', Arnim wrote to Goethe, 'ich meine es müßte gut sein denn es hat mich innig gerührt.'[24] She also told her husband, 'Mein Lied [...] hat mich viel Mühe gekostet.'[25] Formally, the song is a mixture of linear development and sectional compartmentalization. It has the effect of introducing what Ruth Solie has called 'narrative gaps'. Not only is each section an immediate response to a changing emotional context, the listener also has the impression that we are within a larger story, that other history and experience are implicit in the breaks. The space that is thus constructed is not so much a performance space, as in the case of 'An Luna', but rather

---

[24] Quoted in Lemke, *Von Goethe inspiriert*, p.56. 'I think it must be good, because it has moved me deeply.'

[25] ibid., p.56. 'My Lied [...] has cost me great effort.'

a narrative space. This narrativity, however, is more flexible than it may at first appear. We are accustomed to an Ariadne's thread of chronology, in which structural events conform to a linear, conscious time, occuring in logical response to textual and musical material. But 'Ach Neige' seems to follow a circular, subjective time, in which, as in the subconscious, all events are concurrent and present. This can result in musical language that is 'incorrect' under the rules of mainstream response. The odd intrusion of major tonality at the end of bar 2 is one example. C minor has barely been established before two fleeting beats of the relative major interrupt, only for C minor to close over again instantly. (See example 7.2, bars 1 to 3.) This moment of warmth could be seen as an almost physical presence of the person whom Gretchen addresses, and would thus be an overlapping chronology, a reminder that this is not simply Gretchen's tale. The same effect seems to be in place at the end of the section, when Bettina chooses to highlight rhythmically the word 'deine', in sein' and deine Not' (bars 9 to 11). We are taken back into an earlier time frame and forced to remember that Gretchen speaks to Mary, who in some ways mirrors her. In the same way, there are moments that project the listeners forward – the sudden unison accompaniment at 'deines Sohnes Tod' seems autobiographical in its maternal empathy (bars 4 to 7). The very ending, too, with its major tonality (bars 38 to 42), involves us in an implicit assumption of our fore-knowledge of Gretchen's redemption. Gretchen is not aware of this, but we know of her rebirth as the *Ewig-Weibliche*, creative source.

Despite Bettina's unconventionality as composer, or perhaps because of it, she can reveal a richer font of creativity than may be at first apparent. Her goals seem to have been not so much to produce repertoire, but to open up new routes and new directions through her discourse with other creators. Suzi Gablik sums up this partnership in art when she writes:

> when art is rooted in the responsive heart, rather than the disembodied eye, it may even come to be seen, not as the solitary process it has been since the Renaissance, but as something we do with others.[26]

---

[26] Gablik, Suzi, 'Making Art as if the World Mattered', *Utne Reader*, 34 (1989), p.76.

8 | *Blumengruß* and *Blumenglöckchen*: Goethe's Influence on Anton Webern

Gareth Cox

Anton Webern and Goethe. The influence which Goethe's poetry and other writings had on Webern is a topic which could hardly be ignored by Webern scholarship. Hans and Rosaleen Moldenhauer's path-breaking biography of 1978[1] is sprinkled liberally with references to Goethe as are other earlier biographies to a lesser extent, such as those by Friedrich Wildgans and Walter Kolneder.[2] Certain writers have gone further and considered Webern's reception of Goethe's philosophical and scientific theories on nature in detail, in particular Angelika Abel[3], Karlheinz Essl[4] and Barbara Zuber[5]. As Moldenhauer notes, 'the German thinker who exerted the strongest influence upon Webern was Goethe'[6]. It is hardly surprising that a composer with Webern's privileged background would have been well versed in the works of Goethe. He would obviously have read Goethe's classics at school, and during his time at university in Vienna from

---

[1] Hans and Rosaleen Moldenhauer, *Anton von Webern: A Chronicle of his Life and Work* (London: Victor Gollancz, 1978).

[2] Friedrich Wildgans, *Anton Webern* (London: Calder & Boyars, 1966); Walter Kolneder, *Anton Webern: Genesis und Metamorphose eines Stils* (Vienna: Österreichischer Bundesverlag, 1974). See also Juri and Valentina Cholopov, *Anton Webern: Leben und Werk* (Berlin: Henschelverlag, 1989), pp.164-69.

[3] Angelika Abel, Weberns und Goethes Methodik der Farbenlehre: Zur Kompositionstheorie und Ästhetik der Neuen Wiener Schule (Wiesbaden: Steiner, 1982). See also Abel, 'Musik als Sprache: Über Webern und Goethe', *Neue Zeitschrift für Musik*, 144/12 (1983), pp.10-13.

[4] Karlheinz Essl, Das Synthese-Denken bei Anton Webern: Studien zur Musikauffassung des späten Webern unter besonderer Berücksichtigung seiner eigenen Analysen zu op.28 und 30 (Tutzing: Hans Schneider, 1991).

[5] Barbara Zuber, 'Reihe, Gesetz, Urpflanze, Nomos: Anton Weberns musikalisch-philosophisch-botanische Streifzüge', *Musik-Konzepte Sonderband: Anton Webern II*, ed. Heinz-Klaus Metzger & Rainer Riehn (Munich: edition text + kritik, 1984), pp.304-36.

[6] Moldenhauer, p.276.

1902 to 1906, while studying music history under Guido Adler, he took subsidiary courses in German literature which included many lectures on Goethe. In this paper I will discuss some of these influences and consider his published Goethe settings from 1903, 1917 and 1926 as the songs of op.12 and op.19 occupy significant positions in his oeuvre.

Webern spent much of his life as a professional conductor, and in Vienna in March 1932, to mark the centenary of Goethe's death, with his *Singverein* in the Konzerthaus he conducted settings of Goethe-inspired works: Brahms's *Beherzigung* and *Gesang der Parzen*; Beethoven's *Meeresstille und Glückliche Fahrt*; Mendelssohn's *Erste Walpurgisnacht* and Krenek's *Der Triumph der Empfindsamkeit*. A week later he conducted Wagner's *Faust* Overture with the Wiener Sinfonieorchester as part of the Goethe-Feier des Deutschen Volkstheaters.[7] On a minor note we know that he spent many evenings with Siegfried Altmann, a Goethe scholar who was also the director of the Israelitic Institute for the Blind in Vienna where Webern taught in the 1920s.[8] In his diaries and letters Webern often quotes from such works of Goethe as: *Metamorphose der Pflanzen*, *Die Farbenlehre*, *Gespräche mit Eckermann*, and *Wilhelm Meisters Lehrjahre*. He liked to cite passages from Goethe's correspondence with Schiller with which he could identify, for instance, that Goethe spent weeks revising his little poems[9] (consider Stravinsky's aphorism about how Webern 'inexorably kept on cutting out his diamonds').[10] In a letter to Jone in 1936 discussing his Piano Variations op.27 he reminded her that Goethe had once stated to Eckermann that he had been thinking about a poem for 40 years.[11] Webern was intrigued by *Faust* and in 1911 in a letter to Schoenberg he described a production in Berlin saying that there is probably nothing in the art of poetry approaching its marvels and that, at the end, he continually heard Mahler's music (this uncanny premonition just days before Mahler's death in Vienna).[12] After 1918 he always carried a copy of *Faust* with him[13] having in 1903 marked Hugo Wolf's death in his diary with the closing words 'Es kann die Spur von meinen Erdetagen/Nicht in Äonen untergehen'[14] and in 1929, on arriving at a highpoint in his career with recognition and publishing success, Webern quotes in his diary from Goethe's *Italienische Reise*, that art is becoming for him like

---

[7] Listed in Regina Busch, 'Verzeichnis der von Webern dirigierten und einstudierten Werke', in Metzger, p.412.
[8] Moldenhauer, p.287.
[9] ibid., p.129. Or Goethe's admonition to Schiller that only inner withdrawal could provide the fertile soil for creative productivity. ibid., p.295.
[10] Igor Stravinsky, *Die Reihe*, 2, ed. Herbert Eimert (Vienna: Universal Edition, 1955), p.7.
[11] *Anton Webern: Briefe an Hildegard Jone und Josef Humplik*, ed. Josef Polnauer (Vienna: Universal Edition, 1959), p.34.
[12] Moldenhauer, p.144.
[13] Wildgans, p.92.
[14] Moldenhauer, p.57. 'the trace of [my] days on earth cannot perish in aeons'.

second nature.[15] However, his literary hero is not spared when making a point about the difficulty people have grasping a musical idea during one of his lectures in 1933: 'Goethe – was hat ihm gefallen? Zelter! Schubert schickt ihm den "Erlkörig" – er schaut ihn gar nicht an'.[16]

Most importantly however, is the enormous influence on Webern of Goethe's philosophical and technical theories on nature and botany, in particular the significance of *Zur Farbenlehre* and *Metamorphose der Pflanzen*. Webern was a man obsessed with nature. He was never happy to be away from his home and family in Austria and loved with a passion his native homeland of Kärnten. He spent long summer holidays mountain climbing, and there are numerous photos of Webern hiking in the Austrian Alps. He was happiest in the garden with his plants and flowers[17] and was delighted that his house in the Mödling suburb had access to the Wienerwald at the end of the street. His annotations in his sketchbooks testify to planned trips to the mountains and document his inspiration for compositional ideas gleaned from nature. His belief that nature and art were totally interlinked belonged, as Anne Shreffler points out, 'to the organicist thinking of his age [...] his passions for mountain climbing and gardening were much more than hobbies; his love for nature was indissolubly connected to his aesthetic world.'[18] In a letter to Berg on 1 August 1919 he writes:

> Ich war am Hochschwab. Es war herrlich: weil mir das nicht Sport ist, nicht Vergnügen, sondern ganz was anderes: Suchen von Höchstem, Auffinden von Korrespondenzen in der Natur für alles das, was mir vorbildlich ist, was ich gerne in mir haben möchte...Nicht die schöne Landschaft, die schönen Blumen im üblichen romantischen Sinne bewegen mich. Mein Motiv: der tiefe, unergründliche, unausschöpfbare Sinn in allen diesen, besonders diesen Äußerungen der Natur. Alle Natur ist mir wert, aber die, welche sich dort 'oben'

---

[15] ibid., p.328.
[16] Anton Webern, *Der Weg zur neuen Musik*, ed. Willi Reich, (Vienna: Universal Edition, 1960), p.14. 'Goethe – what did he like? Zelter! Schubert sends him the "Erl-King" – he doesn't even look at it.' Anton Webern, *The Path to the New Music*, trans. Leo Black (Vienna: Universal Edition 1975), p.13.
[17] His second daughter, Maria recalls that Webern's first stop in the morning was in the garden to check the flowers. Quoted in 'Aus einem Gespräch mit Weberns Tochter Maria Halbich-Webern', in *Anton Webern 1883-1983: Eine Festschrift zum hundertsten Geburtstag*, ed. Ernst Hilmar (Vienna: Universal Edition, 1982), p.96.
[18] Anne C. Shreffler, 'Anton Webern', in *Schoenberg, Berg and Webern: A Companion to the Second Viennese School*, ed. Bryan Simms (Westport Connecticut: Greenwood Press, 1999), p.294. See also Georg Wübbolt, 'Weberns Goethe-Rezeption: Ein Beitrag zum Thema Natur und Kunst', in *Opus Anton Webern*, ed. Dieter Rexroth (Berlin: Quadriga Verlag, 1983), pp.103-107.

äußert, am wertesten [...]Diese Realität enthält alle Wunder. Forschen, Beobachten in der realen Natur ist mir höchste Metaphysik, Theosophie.[19]

Berg sent Webern a copy of Goethe's *Farbenlehre* in the Spring of 1929. In September 1929 Webern wrote to Berg declaring effusively that it was 'the most sublime book of all time'.[20] This copy is in the Paul Sacher Stiftung in Basel and the underlined passages indicate that Webern appears to have mainly restricted his interest to the introduction.[21] This 36-page introduction, written by the editor Gunther Ipsen in the 1926 Leipzig Insel-Verlag edition, contained a collection of Goethe quotes taken mostly from the *Italienische Reise* and *Maximen und Reflexionen*. In Webern's copy only two of the quotes are from the *Farbenlehre* itself whereas the other twenty-six are from this introduction.[22] Webern, in turn, sent Hildegard Jone handwritten extracts and her estate contains a nine-page manuscript entitled 'Passages copied by Anton Webern from Goethe's Farbenlehre'. As one might expect, these correspond almost exactly to the passages marked by Webern in his own copy. Moldenhauer suggests that Webern found in Jone's poems 'the realization of Goethe's *Farbenlehre*, the fusion of all the philosophical tenets in which he had always believed. The serenity and spirituality of her verses, their gently pulsating rhythms, glowing colours and all-pervading nature worship made them singularly suited to his own sensibility'.[23] But Webern was not trying to transfer to music Goethe's theories of complementarities between colour and sound or the relationship between light and dark and the polarities of black and white, and Angelika Abel's detailed attempt to do so in relation to the Piano Variations op.27 (i.e. 'klingen/nicht klingen') has been strongly criticized by Barbara Zuber.[24] Rather he uses Goethe's writings to underline his own aesthetic and poetic convictions. In one of his private lectures in February 1933 he states that:

---

[19] Published in *Die Reihe* 2, see Eimert, pp.23-24. 'I have been to the Hochschwab. It was glorious, because this is not sport for me, not amusement, but something quite different: it is a search for the highest, a discovery of correspondences in nature for everything that serves me as a model, a model for all that I would like to have within myself [...] It is not the beautiful landscape, the beautiful flowers in the usual romantic sense that move me. My objective is the deep, unfathomable, inexhaustible meaning in everything, especially in these manifestations of nature. All nature is dear to me, but that which expresses itself "up there" is dearest of all [...] This physical reality contains all the miracles. Studying, observing amidst real nature is for me the highest metaphysics, theosophy.' Trans. Moldenhauer, p.231.

[20] Letter to Berg, 28 September 1929. ibid., p.328. The following year he wrote again saying, 'Ich muß sie immer bei mir haben und wenigstens von außen anschauen können', 3 March, 1930, cited in Essl, p.17. 'I must always have it with me so that I can at least look at it.'

[21] Essl, p.17.

[22] Essl includes these passages in an appendix. ibid., pp.225-32.

[23] Moldenhauer, p.427.

[24] Abel, p.81, and Zuber, p.307.

> Goethe sieht die Kunst an als Produktion der allgemeinen Natur in der besonderen Form menschlicher Natur. Das heißt, daß zwischen Naturprodukt und Kunstprodukt kein wesentlicher Gegensatz herrscht, sondern daß es dasselbe ist, daß das, was wir als Kunstwerk ansehen und so nennen, im Grunde nichts anderes ist als ein Produkt der allgemeinen Natur [..] Der Mensch ist nur das Gefäß, in das gegossen ist, was die 'allgemeine Natur' ausdrücken will…Und das gibt uns eigentlich den Aspekt, daß die Dinge, von denen in der Kunst im allgemeinen die Rede ist, mit denen sie zu tun hat, nichts 'Ästhetisches' sind, sondern daß es sich da um Naturgesetze handelt, daß alle Betrachtungen über Musik nur im diesem Sinne erfolgen können.²⁵

In an earlier lecture in 1932 explaining thematic unity he drew parallels with Goethe's *Urpflanze* stating that, 'Die Würzel ist eigentlich nichts anderes als der Stengel, der Stengel nichts anderes als das Blatt, das Blatt wiederum nicht anderes als die Blüte: Variationen desselben Gedankens'.²⁶ For Webern the tone-row was clearly analogous with the Urplanze and implied all manner of structural potential. Ernst Krenek wrote in his commentary to the Sketches that Webern 'found Goethe's idea that all organic life originated from one germinal nucleus to be a notion related to the basic concept of the twelve-tone technique.'²⁷ In a way it is a synthesis of Goethe's organic theories and Schoenbergian Grundgestalt. Put starkly: Urplanze = Reihe. In a letter to Willi Reich in 1941 he quotes from Goethe's *Urpflanze*, 'Dasselbe Gesetz wird sich auf alles übrige Lebendige anwenden lassen' and adds, 'Ist das nicht im tiefsten der Sinn unseres Reihengesetzes?'²⁸ While exploring the hypothesis that the Variations for Orchestra op.30 attempt (ultimately unsuccessfully) to express an engagement with Goethe's philosophical ideas, Arnold Whittall muses that Webern 'given the clarity with which [he] proclaimed the Goethean analogy [could well have, like Strauss, given his op.30] 'the explicitly Goethean title of Metamorphosen'.²⁹

---

²⁵ Reich, pp.10-11. 'Goethe sees art as a product of nature in general, taking the particular form human nature. That is to say, that there is no essential contrast between a product of nature and a product of art, but that it is all the same, that what we regard as and call a work of art is basically nothing but a product of nature in general [...] Man is only the vessel into which is poured what "nature in general" wants to express…This leads us to the view that the things treated by art in general with which art has to do, are not "aesthetic", but that it is a matter of natural laws, that all discussions of music can only take place along these lines.' Trans. Black, pp.10-11.

²⁶ Reich, p.56. 'The root is in fact no different from the stalk, the stalk no different from the leaf, and the leaf no different from the flower; variations of the same idea'. Trans. Black, p.53.

²⁷ *Anton von Webern: Sketches (1926-1945)*. Commentary by Ernst Krenek. Quoted in Moldenhauer, p.319.

²⁸ 'The same law will be found to apply to all other living matter!' Reich, p.69. 'Isn't that the meaning of our law of the row, at its deepest?' Trans. Black, p.63.

²⁹ Arnold Whittall, 'Music-discourse-dialogue: Webern's Variations, op.30', in *Webern Studies*, ed. Kathryn Bailey (Cambridge: Cambridge University Press, 1996), p.265.

And now to his main Goethe settings which I will deal with chronologically, 'Blumengruß' (1903), 'Gleich und Gleich' (1917) and 'Zwei Lieder' (1926):

Table 8.1 Goethe, 'Blumengruß'

Der Strauß, den ich gepflükket,	The bouquet that I have picked,
grüsse dich vieltausendmal!	may it greet you many thousand times!
Ich habe mich oft gebükket,	I have often bent down,
ach, wohl eintausendmal,	ah, well over a thousand times.
und ihn ans Herz gedrükket,	And pressed it to my heart,
vielhunderttausendmal![30]	many hundred thousand times!

'Blumengruß', [M21][31] one of the so-called 'Eight Early Songs' written in Klagenfurt, Vienna and at the Pregelhof between 1901 and 1903, was first performed in 1962 in Seattle by Esther LaBerge accompanied by Rudolph Ganz, and an edition prepared by Ganz was subsequently published by Carl Fischer, New York, in 1965. 'Blumengruß' had been set by many others including Zelter and Wolf, and it can be assumed that Webern probably knew Wolf's setting of 1888. Webern's early songs are, in Jim Samson's words, 'heavily indebted in their general conception to German Romantic Lieder, and in particular to the songs of Brahms'[32] with James Beale suggesting that 'Blumengruß' 'might have been written by a composer as remote from Webern's circle as Gabriel Fauré'.[33] This naive song begins by spending four bars settling on the tonic in bar 5 with the piano accompaniment in bars 6 to 9 sustaining the descending C-B-A mirroring the vocal line (this related back to the ascending A-B-C in the soprano of bars 4/5). The piano climbs with the voice from bar 10 to climax passionately on 'vielhunderttausendmal' (bar 12), before fading out in a gentle six-bar piano postlude.[34]

---

[30] Translation, author's own. There is also an attractive (unaccredited) rhyming translation in a 12/8 setting by Otto Goldschmidt in his four songs op.23: 'The flowers I here am sending, greet thee ten thousand times. To pluck them was I bending, ah, full a thousand times. And kisses on them spending, oh scores of thousand times.'

[31] Here and later I use the 'M-numbers' which Moldenhauer used to catalogue Webern's opus and non-opus pieces and fragments, Moldenhauer, pp.697-750.

[32] Jim Samson, *Music in Transition* (London: Dent, 1977), p.126.

[33] James Beale, 'Webern's Musical Estate', in *Anton von Webern Perspectives*, ed. Demar Irvine (Seattle & London: University of Washington Press, 1966), p.18.

[34] See Kolneder, p.20.

Example 8.1: Webern, 'Blumengruß'

Edward Cone, writing in 1972 about what he calls Webern's apprenticeship, was justly harsh: 'The earlier songs, as one might expect, are at worst awkward and at best derivative [owing] much of their awkwardness to insufficient assimilation of the late Romantic styles from which they naturally derive.'[35] Enough, therefore, of 'Blumengruß'. I have written elsewhere about the problems associated with the over-performance of Webern's juvenilia to the neglect of his op.1-31.[36]

---

[35] Edward T. Cone, 'Webern's Apprenticeship', in *MQ* 53, no.1 (1967), p.268. Cone continues: 'They contain a few self-consciously simple passages that attempt to evoke either a religious or a folk-like atmosphere, but for the most part, their harmonic technique is an inept combination of Wagnerian and impressionistic methods [resulting in] a lack of harmonic direction ... The youthful composer seemed to think that a dramatic interpretation of a text, held together musically by a few repeated motifs and momentarily arresting chord progressions, could create a song.'

[36] Gareth Cox, *Anton Weberns Studienzeit: Seine Entwicklung im Lichte der Sätze und Fragmente für Klavier* (Frankfurt: Peter Lang, 1991), pp.153-60. The frequent performances of his 'pre-opus' *Im*

Table 8.2 Goethe, 'Gleich und Gleich'

Ein Blumenglöckchen vom Boden hervor	A flowerbell blossomed early,
War früh gesprosset in lieblichem Flor;	from the ground in lovely bloom;
Da kam ein Bienchen und naschte fein:	There came a little bee and sucked:
Die müssen wohl beide für einander sein.	They must have been made for each other.[37]

All four songs of op.12 are set to texts by four different authors, a folksong text, Li-Tai-Po (from Hans Bethges 'Chinesische Flöte'), Strindberg, and Goethe. They were first published by UE in 1925, although no.1, 'Der Tag ist vergangen', had appeared in *Musikblätter des Anbruch* in May 1922. Like many of his vocal collections, these four songs should perhaps not be considered as a cycle as such given their dissimilarity. Another reason is found in Webern's letter to Willi Reich in October 1939, where he proposed that op.12 nos. 1 and 4 could be partnered with op.3 nos. 1 and 5 as well as two from op.4 for a concert in Basel.[38] On the other hand, Berg wrote to Webern in 1925 congratulating him and praising the collection as a whole.[39]

Op.12, no.4, 'Gleich und Gleich' ('Like and Like') is a setting of one of Goethe's later 'nature-philosophical' poems.[40] It is dated 31 March 1917 and was completed in Vienna. According to Webern's diary, the first complete performance was in January 1927 but he also notes that in October 1926 an unnamed Dutch singer performed no.4.[41] It is the first work that Webern wrote after spending almost two years in the Austrian army (from February 1915 to December 1916). During the war years he only wrote nine

---

Sommerwind for orchestra (1904) and *Langsamer Satz* for String Quartet of 1905 are particularly glaring examples of this.

[37] Translated notes to *Webern: Complete Works* (Boulez) CD SM3K 45845, p.121, unaccredited but presumably by Susan Bradshaw.

[38] Moldenhauer, p.523.

[39] Berg, 'Die Zusammenziehung zu einem Ganzen! [...] Und gar erst die Musik! Ja, es erscheint mir, als sähe ich Dich auf ganz neue Weise [...] Das letzte z.B.: eine solche Anmut. Man kann ruhig sagen: die findet sich sonst in der ganzen Musikliteratur nicht wieder – : so ein Lied von Dir ist für mich geradezu ein Freudenspender, ein Spender einer mein ganzes Sein überstrahlenden Freude. Wie wenn an trüben Tagen plötzlich die Sonne hervorbricht und man gar nicht weiß, warum man plötzlich so froh wird. *Die Reihe* 2, see Eimert, p.24. 'It seems to me as if I see you in an entirely new light [...] The last, for example: such charm is to be found nowhere else in all music. This kind of song by you is a veritable dispenser of joy for me, a distributor of delight that radiates through my entire being. It is as if on gloomy days the sun breaks suddenly through, and one does not know at all why one is suddenly happy.' Trans. Moldenhauer, p.265.

[40] See also Hellmut Kühn, 'Gleich und Gleich? Zum Konzept des Opus Anton Webern', in: Rexroth, pp.13-17.

[41] Moldenhauer, p.265.

pieces (all songs) setting what Anne Shreffler has described as 'bewilderingly diverse [texts] [...] the four poems of op.12 alone span centuries and nations'.[42] 'Gleich und Gleich' is tightly constructed and begins with a statement of the complete twelve-note aggregate in bars 1 to 3. In a lecture fifteen years later in 1932, Webern explained this opening by recalling that, 'Das Gesetz war uns damals nicht bewußt, aber es war uns längst gefühlt'.[43] Within this aggregate it would not be unreasonable to propose that both the horizontal octad 8-21 and its complement, the tetrachord 4-21 were surely 'made for each other' (as are the interlocking minor thirds in the final sonority). Julian Johnson's suggestion that 'Goethe's bee and flower 'must have been made for each other' is more than a naïve poetic conceit. It is a concise statement of what Kant called 'the formal purposiveness' of nature, the idea that nature is designed for human understanding.'[44] Forte points out (rather uncharacteristically) that while the bee swoops up and down, the bluebell (represented by a tetrachord) 'just sits there being nibbled upon'[45] (see bars 1 to 3 and 20 to 21 in example 8.2). He also contrives by segmentation to identify certain interlocking octatonic passages, but is on more secure ground when he notes the complete octatonic collection bars 8 to 28 (although it excludes the final c#) in the piano interlude in bars 15 to 16.[46] The rhyming words in the first verse, 'hervor' and 'Flor' (bars 6/7 and 11), are unified by the use of ic4 in both cases, whereas in the second verse, 'fein' and 'sein' (bars 14 and 20), both employ falling major sevenths or ic1s.[47] Further unity is achieved by the proliferation of similar trichordal interval classes and the ubiquitous semitonal ic1s.[48] Shreffler notes that 'the short lines, strophic construction, and nursery-rhyme character belie the subtle wit that informs the underlying sexual metaphor',[49] but all analytical considerations aside, it is, as Forte points out, 'a song with a humorous text [...] unique in Webern's oeuvre'.[50]

---

[42] Shreffler (1999), p.274.
[43] Reich, p.55. 'at that time we were not conscious of the law, but had been sensing it for a long time'. Trans. Black, p.51.
[44] Julian Johnson, *Webern and the Transformation of Nature* (Cambridge: Cambridge University Press, 1999), p.136.
[45] Allen Forte, *The Atonal Music of Anton Webern* (New Haven: Yale University Press, 1998), p.274.
[46] ibid., p.277
[47] See Dorothea Beckmann, Sprache und Musik im Vokalwerk Anton Weberns: Die Konstruktion des Ausdrucks (Regensburg: Gustav Bosse, 1970), pp.172-73.
[48] See Edward Murray, *New Approaches to the Analysis of Webern*, Ph.D diss., Yale University, 1979, pp.78-80.
[49] Shreffler (1999), p.275.
[50] Forte, p.273.

Example 8.2: Webern, 'Gleich und Gleich', op.12, no.4

©1925 by Universal Edition
renewed copyright 1953 by Anton Webern's Erben

Anne Shreffler records that in the period between 1915 and 1922 there are about 130 pages of sketches and drafts of song settings.[51] These pages include two attempted settings from 1917-1918 of the Goethe poems, 'Gegenwart' and 'Cirrus'. For 'Gegenwart' ('Alles kündigt dich an') [M220] from Goethe's *Lieder*, there are 38 bars (in pencil) extant. The draft is marked '1917, Wien, Auhofstrasse' and is scored for baritone and piano. Webern sketched a setting for the first two (three-line) stanza and one line from the third verse. Moldenhauer reports that 'the piano accompaniment, largely chordal, is well worked out. Here, as generally, detailed dynamic directions show that Webern's earliest vision of a work already included the last nuance of shading'.[52] 'Cirrus' ('Doch immer höher steigt der edle Drang') [M235] from *Gott und Welt* ('Howards Ehrengedächtnis' cycle) was sketched in Mödling in 1918. There are four pencil sketches

---

[51] Anne C. Shreffler, *Webern and the Lyric Impulse: Songs and Fragments on Poems of Georg Trakl* (Oxford: Clarendon Press, 1994), p.12.
[52] Moldenhauer, p.276. See also Shreffler (1994), op.cit., pp.60-61.

of six to thirteen bars length in short score for voice and orchestra. He returned to the same text again in the early summer of 1930 in Mödling when he attempted a twelve-tone setting.[53]

Table 8.3 Two Songs from Goethe's Chinesisch-Deutsche Jahres- und Tageszeiten, op.19

I
Weiß wie Lilien, reine Kerzen,
Sternen gleich, bescheidner Beugung,
Leuchtet aus dem Mittelherzen,
Rot gesäumt, die Glut der Neigung.

So frühzeitige Narzissen
Blühen reihenweis im Garten.
Mögen wohl die guten wissen,
Wen sie so spaliert erwarten.

II
Ziehn die Schafe von der Wiese,
Liegt sie da, ein reines Grün;
Aber bald zum Paradiese
Wird sie bunt geblümt erblühn.

Hoffnung breitet lichte Schleier
Nebelhaft vor unsern Blick:
Wunscherfüllung, Sonnenfeier,
Wolkenteilung bring' uns Glück!

White, like lilies, pure candles
Star-like, with modest mien
Shines from the core of the heart
Red-hemmed, the glow of affection.

Thus the early narcissus
blooms in rows in the garden.
Let's hope the dear ones know
for whom they stand so expectantly at attention.

When the sheep have left the meadow
It lies there a pure green;
But soon it will bloom
Into a colourfully-flowered paradise.

Hope spreads light veils
Mist-like before our glance:
Wish-fulfilment, sun-feast,
May parting clouds bring us luck![54]

In 1926, the same year as Krenek's enormously successful *Jonny spielt auf* and Hindemith's Cardillac, Webern conducted Mahler's Eighth Symphony at the International Society for Contemporary Music Festival in Zürich. More significantly for his future vocal output, however, it was the year that he met the poet Hildegard Jone, and the texts which he chose for his Two Songs op.19 from Goethe's Chinesisch-deutsche Jahres- und Tageszeiten represent the very last setting of any poet other than Jone, whose poetry he was to set exclusively from 1933 onwards. Webern began this

---

[53] Listed as M306, dated 29 June-9 July 1930 and located in Sketchbook 3.
[54] Trans. Bradshaw, p.143.

composition around Christmas 1925 and his sketchbooks show that he worked on the two songs (mentioning them in letters to Schoenberg and Berg) up until July of 1926.[55] He dedicated the songs to his close friend David Josef Bach and in 1928 they were published by Universal Edition both in full score and in a piano reduction. There is, however, no record of a performance during his lifetime.

Webern had not composed for mixed choir since the *a cappella* op.2, 'Entflieht auf leichten Kähnen' of 1908[56] and they were probably inspired by Schoenberg's *Vier Stücke für gemischten Chor* of 1925. Regarding the overall form, Moldenhauer points out that these two songs introduced a series of two-movement compositions (up to the Concerto op.24) where 'in each case, the composer originally envisioned a third movement, only to reach the conclusion that the principle of unity through variety had been amply fulfilled by the two finished movements.'[57] Although his sketches show that op.19 was probably going to consist of three movements originally, Johnson suggests that there is 'some evidence to suggest that the concerns of the abandoned movement were in each case taken up in some way by the next piece.'[58] Webern uses piano for most of his *Lieder* accompaniments up until op.13, then a combination of instruments (with no piano) to op.18 and then reverts to piano accompaniment for the later Jone settings. In these *Two Songs* op.19 for mixed choir Webern's exact title is significant: 'Zwei Lieder für gemischten Chor *mit Begleitung* [my italics] von Celesta, Gitarre, Geige, Klarinette und Bassklarinette' where the accompanying ensemble occupies a secondary yet independent role. It is divided into two groups of (a) violin, clarinet and bass clarinet and (b) celesta and guitar, whereby the first group often doubles the material of the vocal parts (the soprano line in the first song is mainly accompanied by ATB).

Kathryn Bailey has made extensive studies of the topography of Webern's twelve-note rows and their sketches. She points out that op.19 was the first work for which he constructed row tables and for which he established the use of designated colours to indicate certain rows.[59] It is also the first work where he bases both movements on the same row (each of the songs of op.18 are built on different rows) and the first in which he uses a transposition (at the tritone) of the row.

---

[55] Drafts are present in Sketchbooks 1 & 2 and the final date is Mödling 8 July 1926. Webern originally indicated that, 'the work might be performed by a quartet of solo voices in place of a full chorus' but later crossed this out. Moldenhauer, p.319.

[56] In Freiburg in 1991 the Anton Webern Chor performed all five choral works in the order op.29, 2, 26, 19, 31 and then again after the interval, in retrograde, op.31, 19, 26, 2, 29. The programme booklet for this concert included a short essay on Webern and Goethe by Manfred Schradi, 'Farbe und Ton: Zu Weberns "Goetheanismus" ', pp.23-25.

[57] Moldenhauer, p.319.

[58] Johnson, p.177.

[59] Kathryn Bailey, 'Webern's row tables', in Bailey (1996), pp.180-81. See also Bailey, *The Twelve-note Music of Anton Webern* (Cambridge: Cambridge University Press, 1991), pp.36-38.

Example 8.3: Webern, Twelve-Note Row, op.19

Example 8.3 shows that the row is partitioned by Webern in the table into tetrachords (see also the ATB parts in bars 7 to 11 in example 8.4) and has no sequential origin. The two songs differ somewhat in texture, the first being more homophonic, the second more polyphonic. Noller suggests that it is significant that the first six notes of the row's retrograde appear melodically in the soprano line in bars 20 to 21 on the word 'reihenweis' as the row is otherwise distributed vertically.[60] The text of the first song is progressively shortened by lines 4 + 2 + 1 (and the final one subdivided again). The rapid repetitions of the same note in the accompaniment (see bar 13, for example where single notes 'vibrate') make the surface come alive for Johnson who suggests that this textural background creates a 'paradisial space [which] is entirely in keeping with the imagery presented by the texts':

> The green meadow about to burst into bloom with myriad flowers (op.19, no.2) is an image of the immanence of heaven, just as the early-flowering white narcissus (op.19, no.1) is an image of the immanent grace of the Virgin Mary [...] It seems as if the immediate consequence of Webern's adoption of serialism was a loss of anxiety. Assured perhaps through serial technique of the formal rigour and inner coherence of his music, Webern allowed himself to bring back colouristic elements, 'purified' as they were now of any motivic redundancy. That these two aspects of Webern's style are reunited in these works is not unrelated to the return of nature imagery through Goethe's texts. Natural images and religious symbols mix freely here as a maternal nature and a Marian imagery become equally the symbol for the immanence of the kingdom of heaven. [61]

---

[60] Joachim Noller, 'Das dodekaphone Volkslied', in: Metzger, p.147.
[61] Johnson, pp.163-64.

Example 8.4: Webern, 'Weiß wie Lilien', op.19, no.1, bars 1-15

Three other sketches on Goethe texts exist from this period: 'Auf Bergen, in der reinsten Höhe' for mixed chorus a cappella [M288] from Goethe's *Gott, Gemüt und Welt* was written in Mödling and dated 'Autumn 1926'. In Sketchbook 2 there are two pages of sketches which follow 'Ziehn die Schafe' and it must be assumed that Webern was going to add a third chorus onto op.19, particularly as its row is identical with the other two choruses. This incomplete sketch is scored for mixed choir without instruments. Moldenhauer notes that the text 'Auf Bergen, in der reinsten Höhe, tief rötlich blau ist Himmelsnähe' 'evoked in Webern, the mountaineer and nature philosopher, so deep a response that he wrote the word 'Motto' at the head of his musical realization'.[62] He had quoted these words a year earlier in 1920 in a letter to Berg. Towards the end of the decade, Webern also sketched five pages in all of ideas for 'Nun weiss man erst, was Rosenknospe sei'[63] for voice and piano, again from Goethe's Chinesisch-deutsche Jahres- und Tageszeiten cycle, and 'Der Spiegel sagt mir: ich bin schön!' for four-part women's chorus from the *West-östlicher Divan* cycle.[64]

I conclude with Moldenhauer's words regarding 'Auf Bergen' which was

> one of sixteen couplets written by Goethe at Weimar around 1810, in an apparent attempt to give poetic expression to the tenets expounded in his *Farbenlehre*. For Webern, as for Goethe, the wedding of nature's beauty to scientific principles was the magic key to the essence of art, and his quest for that elusive amalgam was perpetual.[65]

This quest led him from Goethe to the texts of Hildegard Jone whose poetry he set exclusively for the rest of his life. So did Goethe serve as a catalyst for Webern? Well yes, he read Goethe widely if selectively; yes, he appears to have consciously chosen Goethe for two of his important vocal compositions at times of stylistic shifts in his career; and yes, Goethe's nature-philosophical writings were tremendously significant for him, not only personally and spiritually, but also as a retrospective legitimation for his serial technique.

---

[62] Moldenhauer, p.318.
[63] Dated Mödling, 7 March, 1929 and listed as M303.
[64] Dated Mödling, 7-[14] July 1930 and listed as M307. Both M303 and M307 are located in Sketchbook 3.
[65] Moldenhauer, p.318.

D: Musical and Philosophical Reflections of *Wilhelm Meisters Lehrjahre*

9 | 'Thealogy': gods, goddesses and *Wilhelm Meisters Lehrjahre* in Goethe's religious development
Nicholas Boyle

Goethe described himself as a 'heathen'.[1] Though born a Lutheran, he last took his church's sacrament at the age of twenty-one, he chose to blight his social life at the Weimar court for sixteen years by living with his mistress and his illegitimate son rather than legalize his arrangements by going through what he regarded as the hypocrisy of an ecclesiastical ceremony, he avoided attendance at church functions whenever he could, and particularly in the 1790s his unpublished, and even occasionally his published, writings contain some savagely satirical remarks about Christians, Christianity, and Christ. His very first publishing successes brought him ecclesiastical censure and censorship and throughout his life his critics charged him with blasphemy and immorality. Yet in later years, if Varnhagen von Ense is to be believed, he described himself as more Christian than his critics: he enjoyed the company of Jews, contributed to the support of the first Catholic chapel in Jena, and upbraided Herder for not being sufficiently orthodox in his sermons;[2] his writings of all periods contain sympathetic depictions of the beliefs and practices of Protestant and Catholic Christians, Muslims

---

[1] See for example *WA* I, 23, p.302, I, 32, p.491, and especially the letters to Herder, 15 March 1790, and to Jacobi, 7 March 1808 (the latter countering the powerful influence of the visit of Zacharias Werner; see the conversation with Riemer on 27 March 1808: *Goethes Leben von Tag zu Tag: Eine dokumentarische Chronik*, ed. Robert Steiger (Zurich: Artemis, 1982-) 5, p.178) in: *Goethes Briefe*, Hamburger Ausgabe, ed. Karl Robert Mandelkow (Hamburg: Wegener, 1962) (henceforth *HABr*) 2, p.123; 3, p.66.

[2] *Goethes Gespräche* ed. F. von Biedermann and W. Herwig (Zurich: Artemis, 1965-84) 2, p.575 (No.3285); Nicholas Boyle, *Goethe. The Poet and the Age. Volume II. Revolution and Renunciation* (Oxford: Clarendon, 2003), pp.263 and 284; *HABr* 1, p.424.

and even Zoroastrians; and a recent volume on Goethe and Religion, a valuable collection edited by Paul Kerry,[3] includes speculation on how far he can be described as a closet Catholic or a crypto-Mormon. More important still, I think, is T. J. Reed's remark about what is 'religion in the broadest sense', a remark quoted by Kerry in his Introduction:

> Meditation and self-questioning about one's inner life and relation to the shaping forces of existence – spirituality, in short – do not end when orthodox faith ends. This continuity is as much what is meant by 'secularization' as is any rejection of orthodox faith.

That Goethe was a heathen does not mean that he did not have a religious development. Heathens have a religion too. Questions such as what it is to be, or to be subject to an obligation, whether life has a direction or can be evaluated, questions about loss and gain, about the autonomy or dependency of the self, do not go away because the formulations of them, or the answers to them, provided by particular cultural traditions are thought to have lost their hold.

Goethe's thoughts, feelings, and attitudes in relation to ultimate questions went through several distinct phases. These phases have been relatively little studied, but a crucial turning-point is, I think, represented by his novel *Wilhelm Meisters Lehrjahre* (*Wilhelm Meister's Years of Apprenticeship*), on which he worked intensively in the years 1794 to 1796. I shall deal here firstly with some of Goethe's religious ideas in the years before his work on *Wilhelm Meister's Years of Apprenticeship*, concentrating on poems known through their musical settings, especially by Schubert, and then with the novel itself, which has proved a particularly rich source of inspiration for composers. In conclusion I shall mention a variation on these themes to be found in *Faust II*.

Goethe's brush with Pietist – as we would now say, evangelical – Christianity in the years 1768-1769 coincided with a period when his health was critically poor and his survival at times in doubt. The association of Christianity with sickness and death remained a feature of his writings ever afterwards. By 1770, when he was twenty-one, the Christian episode was over, his health was rapidly improving, and at the university of Strasbourg, where he resumed the legal studies that the crisis had interrupted, he soon had a reputation as a wealthy, horse-riding tearaway, with advanced views on everything from theology to landscape. The next three years brought his first adult love affairs, with moments both of ecstasy and of guilt and loss, a revolution in his literary taste, and the first explosive manifestations of his genius in poems and plays that were as yet unpublished. The colossal self-confidence with which he transformed the language of prose and verse in these years, without as yet the support of a reading public – though there was a growing circle of those who knew something of what he was doing, and

---

[3] *Goethe and Religion* (*Literature and Belief* 20.2), ed. Paul E. Kerry (Provo: Brigham Young, 2000). Reed's remark: p.xvii.

admired it – had a metaphysical or theological counterpart. Goethe saw himself as a favoured young man living his exceptional life under the eyes of higher powers, sometimes companionable and admiring, sometimes discreetly or manifestly helpful, sometimes aloof and envious, as if threatened by the independence of his own quasi-divine creativity, sometimes an impotent and obsolete but self-important establishment. This last role is on the whole reserved for representations, under a thin disguise, of the Christian deity; the names under which Goethe speaks of, or to, the metaphysical audience interacting with his life are those of the Greek pantheon; and collectively he knows them as 'the gods'. Like a character in Homer he knows them as personalities who may make obvious or concealed interventions, who may speak to him under the appearance of other human beings, who take a benevolent or hostile interest in his doings, and whose power over him, though not absolute, is to be reckoned with seriously. Cronos – no doubt, whatever the lexicographers say, as a god of time – is his postilion, 'Schwager', a word which also means 'brother-in-law' and in student parlance of Goethe's time was the equivalent of 'mate', and Cronos, in the ode addressed to him,[4] leads the genius at a rattling pace, on a bone-shaking path, down to Hades where the great figures of the past, divine or semi-divine, stand up to honour his arrival. In the rhapsody 'Wandrers Sturmlied' (*HA* 1, pp.33-36) Dionysus and Jupiter, as the god of storms and foul weather, are his patrons and the sources of the wild energy coursing in his verse as in that of Pindar, while Apollo, the sunshine god, is potentially envious and needs to be won over, or intimidated, by a demonstration that the poet can if necessary do without him. Jupiter/Zeus has a much more ungrateful role in the outstanding ode 'Prometheus' (*HA* 1, pp.44-46), which had the capacity to cause so much scandal that Goethe did not publish it himself: the father of the Greek gods here clearly stands for the God of Christian monotheism, and perhaps even more specifically of the Pietism from which Goethe had quickly freed himself, the object of the ceaseless prayers of the weak and the infantile, who none the less is incapable of doing anything to help his worshippers. The Prometheus of this poem treats this feeble figure with contempt – all Prometheus has achieved has been his own work and he will not be cowed by stage-thunder into attributing it to any power but his own heart. Unable – and no doubt unwilling – to disavow this radical anti-Christian polemic once it had been made public by F. H. Jacobi in 1785, Goethe sought to conceal its true nature by printing it, in all collected editions of his poetry, alongside a poem written at a different time and in a different mood, with no thought of a relation to it – 'Ganymed' (*HA* 1, pp.46-47). 'Ganymed' shares with 'Prometheus' a reference to Jove, but this Jove is a God unknown to the Pietists, an 'all-loving father', it is true, but one who is approached

---

[4] *Goethes Werke*, Hamburger Ausgabe, ed. Erich Trunz (Munich: Beck, 1988) (henceforth *HA*) 1, pp.47-48.

through the natural world, the transports of spring, a flowering landscape, the intoxication of high places and a love that does not deny its homoerotic component.

There is no point in seeking some system or method behind Goethe's mythological references in his poetry of the 1770s, his so-called 'Storm and Stress' period, for it is clear that the deployment of the myth is always subordinate to the needs of the poetic and psychological moment. But that does not mean that there is not a consistent theology at work in the poetry. The theology of which the – essentially literary – allusions to Greek myths are the occasional and metaphorical expression was formulated with increasing clarity as Goethe's own affairs moved into crisis, as he experienced the pain of an unhappy engagement, eventually broken off, and as it became clear to him that he could not stay and flourish, as the moving spirit in German literature that he had now become, in the Frankfurt that had nurtured him, but where he was the prisoner of a provincially minded society of merchants and bankers, and where he would permanently be under the eye of his father. Should he set off on a grand tour to Italy? Should he accept an invitation to visit the new young Duke of Weimar and stay for an indefinite period? Goethe clearly felt the significance of this moment of decision, felt its relation to the foundations of who he was and what he had to do, felt its religious significance – and he concluded the poem 'Seefahrt' (*HA* 1, pp.49-50), an explanation of his decision to opt for Weimar, with the firm statement that 'foundering or landing' he 'put his trust in his gods'. Whatever the mythology, the belief it expressed was a belief that his life was watched over by unknown, or half-known, powers, in whose hands, at least to some extent, lay the course of events.

The belief, however, was about to change. With the beginning of his intense and painfully platonic relationship with a married lady-in-waiting at the Weimar court, Charlotte von Stein, and with the death of his sister, Cornelia, a year younger than himself and his only surviving sibling, Goethe's relations with the powers that ruled his life took on an altogether more serious and at times a tragic tone. On a splendid moonlit night, just after he had received the news of Cornelia's death, an unrhymed, almost prosaic, quatrain came to Goethe, that he then included in a letter to Countess Stolberg, whom he never met, but to whom he confided some of his most intimate thoughts:

Alles geben die Götter, die unendlichen,
Ihren Lieblingen ganz,
Alle Freuden, die unendlichen,
Alle Schmerzen, die unendlichen, ganz.[5]

---

[5] *HA* 1, p.142. I have however given the text in the more familiar form in which it originally appeared in editions of Goethe's works (see e.g. *HA*, first (1949) edition, 1, p.142). 'The gods, the endless ones, give everything to their darlings in full; all joys, the endless ones, all pains, the endless ones, in full'.

The insistent repetition of 'die unendlichen', 'the endless ones', enacts the presence in our finite world, in which pain and joy are mixed, of a transcendent meaning on which we are dependent, and the reference to the darlings of the gods is as bittersweet in its hubris as the world of which the poem speaks. For the darlings of the gods are those who are chosen to experience not only the joy of the world but also its pain, 'to the full'. These four lines seem powerfully to have impressed the young Hölderlin. E.C. Mason, in his study of the relation between Goethe and Hölderlin, traced so many and so profound associations between them and Hölderlin's phraseology in his poems that he felt sure Hölderlin must have known them, but he was at a loss to explain how, since he believed they had first been published in 1839.[6] Only after Mason's death did it become known that they had appeared sixty years previously in a German literary periodical shortly after they were sent to Countess Stolberg. If we take into account the extraordinary power and authority that Goethe's early verse had for the next generation of poets, and that in it, as we have seen, 'the gods' are a ubiquitous presence as the vehicle of an alternative, non-Christian, theology, then this quatrain, which summarizes a decade of Goethe's experience of the divine, can perhaps be seen as the channel through which Goethe contributed to the concepts both of 'the gods' and of 'the poet' which are the intellectual foundations of all Hölderlin's mature work.

Once Goethe was in Weimar, the confident manner in which his earlier poems dealt with 'the gods', sometimes boisterous and familiar, sometimes ecstatic and contemplative, seemed less appropriate and the theological vein in his poetry became more reflective and tentative, more resigned and at times even bitter. The years of adjustment to Weimar court-life were not easy for a middle-class parvenu who did not know the ropes[7] and was excluded from higher-profile social events because he lacked a title. In his moments of greatest doubt and uncertainty Goethe turned to his gods seeking guidance and reassurance that he was after all on the right path. In December 1777 he suddenly disappeared from Weimar and in vile weather trekked through the Harz Mountains to the Brocken, reputedly the haunt of witches, and a place of mysterious significance to the local population. If he could climb this, the highest mountain of North Germany, in the snow, as no one had done for a generation, he would regard himself as having received a sign from his gods that in Weimar he was on the right path and should continue in it. Miraculously, as it seemed, the weather did indeed improve enough for him to reach the summit and enjoy a moment of sunlight above the world.[8] The anxieties of his quest, and his triumph in its crowning moment, are recorded step by step in the poem 'Harzreise im Winter' (HA 1, pp.50-52), whose

---

[6] E. C. Mason, *Hölderlin and Goethe*, ed P.H. Gaskill, *Britische und Irische Studien zur deutschen Sprache und Literatur* 3 (Bern: Herbert Lang, 1975), p.42.
[7] See the autobiographical poem 'Ilmenau' (1783), HA 1, pp.107-12, especially ll. 112-19.
[8] *HABr* 1, p.247.

prophetic or augural character was first recognized by Albrecht Schöne[9] (and which of course furnished the text for Brahms's *Alto Rhapsody*). The poem culminates in a celebration of the Brocken's 'snow-hung brow' which the poet's experience has transformed from a place of fear into an 'altar of sweetest thanks'. 'You know how symbolical my existence is' Goethe wrote to Frau von Stein,[10] telling her of his success – life, poetry, and theological meaning were for him inseparably intertwined.

The principle first recognized by Schöne can be extended to a number of episodes in Goethe's first decade in Weimar, not all of them however accompanied by the inspiration for a poem such as rewarded his first visit to the Harz. In 1779 on a tour to South Germany and Switzerland which he had undertaken with Duke Carl August as a deliberate survey of the events and places associated with his Storm and Stress past, Goethe arranged for another mountaineering expedition, this time through the snows of the Furka pass up to the Gotthard pass, which he regarded as the centre of the Alps. The Gotthard had a special significance for Goethe as the frontier of Italy from which he had already turned back once in 1775, and he now turned from it again to go back to Weimar to take up a much heavier burden of official duties than he had previously shouldered. This significant moment was also marked by a literary monument, though in prose this time, not verse, his *Briefe aus der Schweiz*,[11] but the 'symbolical' role of the journey had already been recognized in a poem about the Staubbach and Reichenbach waterfalls, 'Gesang der Geister über den Wassern' (*HA* 1, p.143). That poem already suggests that Goethe's thoughts about the gods are taking a fatalistic turn: the gods as personal beings are not mentioned in it but instead the superhuman power that affects human lives is called fate, 'das Schicksal', which blows us about as the wind blows the spray of the waterfall. And indeed, despite the positive augury represented by the climb to the Gotthard pass, the next few years, which saw Goethe's deepest involvement in the administration of the duchy, including a spell as the chancellor of its embarrassed exchequer, were a period of increasing doubt and poetic frustration. He wrote less and less verse, what he wrote became more colourless, and he forced himself to keep himself in existence as a writer by completing every year one book of a rambling picaresque novel, *Wilhelm Meisters theatralische Sendung* (*Wilhelm Meister's Theatrical Mission*). Goethe had once thought he had a poetic mission, perhaps even a theatrical one, but that now seemed questionable to him. He had published nothing since 1776, partly from choice but mainly because he had finished nothing that he thought worthy of publication. *Wilhelm Meister's Theatrical Mission* was not finished either, but we may be sure that it was no part of Goethe's plan for the novel that Wilhelm's ambition to transform Germany, or at least its cultural life, by the foundation of a national theatre

---

[9] A. Schöne, 'Auguralsymbolik', *GJh* 96 (1979), pp.22-53.
[10] *HABr* 1, p.246.
[11] Later published as *Briefe aus der Schweiz. Zweite Abtheilung*, *WA* I, 19, pp.221-306.

would have been fulfilled. Thanks to the practical requirements of his involvement in the duchy's affairs, particularly the silver mine at Ilmenau and the university of Jena, Goethe had been interesting himself in natural science and he eventually came to think that his literary period might be over and that he would in future be devoting himself to the sciences. Had he then been given his literary gifts only in order that he might suffer the torment of feeling them gradually strangled? Had he sacrificed so much, for example, the moral innocence of an ordinary middle-class family life back in Frankfurt with Lili Schönemann, for the pursuit of a chimera in Weimar? The bitterness of such a thought spilled over into a brief and utterly tragic poem which in 1783 he put into the mouth of a character in his novel, the Harpist, though it may have been written earlier, and independently of *Wilhelm Meister*:

Wer nie sein Brot mit Tränen aß,
Wer nie die kummervollen Nächte
Auf seinem Bette weinend saß,
Der kennt euch nicht, ihr himmlischen Mächte.

Ihr führt ins Leben uns hinein,
Ihr laßt den Armen schuldig werden,
Dann überlaßt ihr ihn der Pein,
Denn alle Schuld rächt sich auf Erden.[12]

Goethe had given a dramatic representation of a figure tormented by this antitheology, by this belief in predatory deities, to whom we are as flies to boys, for sport, in the character of Orestes in his prose drama *Iphigenie auf Tauris* written in 1779.[13] Orestes, in this play, was healed of his belief that he was pursued by spirits of vengeance, the Furies, by the influence of the Charlotte von Stein-like figure of his sister Iphigenia who had faith that the gods were benevolent beings seeking the long term good of humanity and the healing of the wounds humanity inflicted on itself. That faith was coming under increasing strain for Goethe particularly after the year 1782 which saw not only his reaching the top of Weimar's administrative tree and his raising to the nobility as 'von Goethe', but also - and perhaps crucially - the death of his father after a long dementia. It was as if his arrival in adulthood, as a man of his own making, had deprived him of the irresponsible and unpredictable creativity of a protracted adolescence and he was now forced to shake off the habits of thinking and writing that had so far provided him with an identity. After 1783 he wrote few lyrical poems – songlike verses suitable for

---

[12] HA 7, p.136. 'He who has never eaten his bread with tears, who has never spent nights of sorrow sitting weeping on his bed, does not know you, o you heavenly powers. You lead us into life, you make the wretch become guilty, then you leave him to his torment, for all guilt is avenged on earth'.

[13] WA I, 39, pp.321-404.

musical settings – for many years, and entirely ceased writing the free-verse hymns or odes that since 'Wandrers Sturmlied', or even before, had been the principal vehicle for his more reflective and theological writing.

The last such hymn, entitled 'Das Göttliche' ('Divinity') (*HA* 1, pp.147-49) indicates that a profound change is on the way. The gods in this poem are projections – perhaps not yet mere projections, but projections nonetheless – from human moral qualities. Only through human moral choice, through human acts of goodness and productive help, can we form a concept of those transcendent beings who are, perfectly, what we aspire, and normally fail, to be. That was perhaps the inspiration, or the rationalization, for Goethe's devotion to his life of self-sacrifice in the Weimar civil service and in his chaste relationship with Frau von Stein. But the duchy was unreformable, the Duke had his own agenda, and neither Goethe nor Frau von Stein was getting any younger: Goethe had good reason for thinking that the gods had let him down. He resolved to make one last desperate bid to restore meaning and purpose to his life. He signed a contract to bring out a collected edition of his works, including his unfinished and imperfect pieces, which would serve either as a monument to a period of his life that was now over, or as a spur to finish off what he could and to start again. And he decided to seek relief from his servitude as an official, the stimulus of a new climate, new people and new experiences of art, architecture and landscape, and probably also the sexual fulfilment that had evaded him in Weimar, by at least partially carrying out the plan for a Grand Tour that his father had long ago seen as the climax of his son's education. He decided to undertake another symbolic journey, in the hope that at its end he would find some new and decisive divine revelation: in September 1786 he set out for the most symbolic goal of all, the capital of the ancient and modern world, Rome.

The revelation however did not come – not, at any rate, in the form which Goethe expected, or hoped for. 'Rome disappoints me much', wrote A. H. Clough[14] three quarters of a century later, and Goethe's experience at first was much the same. Rome was too ruinous and too priest-ridden, the capital of a church, not of the world, and he took advantage of the Duke's indefinite prolongation of his leave to go on to Naples and Sicily. In the landscape and flora of the coastal regions of Southern Italy, and in their remarkably well-preserved monuments from the Greek colonial period, Goethe finally caught a breath of the classical atmosphere he had been seeking and on his return to Rome was able to make it for a year into a place where his hopes and wishes could temporarily all seem fulfilled. He surrounded himself with artists, kept away from political grandees, and hired a Roman widow to experiment in manhood at last. In two respects though his time in Italy was not the success he had looked for: firstly, he wrote little, and little of it was good – the best things, his travel diary and the versification of

---

[14] A. H. Clough, 'Amours de Voyage', I, i, in: *Poems* (London: Macmillan, 1895), p.269.

Iphigenie auf Tauris, were the fruit of his journey to Rome, not of his stay in Rome itself; and secondly, the crowning symbolic act, having eluded him on his first arrival in the Eternal City, obstinately refused to materialize later on. In Sicily he made a pilgrimage to Enna, reputedly the entrance to the underworld, where Proserpine, for Goethe the image of his dead sister, had been abducted by Pluto. So insignificant did the visit prove to be, however, that Goethe subsequently did his best to conceal his motives in undertaking it.[15] The oracles, it seemed, had fallen silent.

In January 1777, even before Goethe's first expedition to the Harz to sound out the gods about his fate, he had written to Lavater, the enthusiastic clergyman who wanted nothing so much as to convert him, but whom at first he admired for the sincerity of his charity and his intellectual openness:

> Dein Durst nach Crist[us] hat mich gejammert. Du bist übler dran als wir Heiden uns erscheinen doch in der Noth unsre Götter.[16]

Ten years later it seemed to Goethe that divine manifestations were no longer to be hoped for, and his feelings for Christians – and for Lavater in particular – moved from pity to contempt and angry hostility. The years after his return from Italy were in their own way even more difficult than those immediately preceding it. True, he now had a mistress, Christiane Vulpius, whom he soon regarded as his wife, even though he refused to seek the Church's blessing on their union, and he had a son. But no other child survived from Christiane's five pregnancies to enlarge his family as he hoped, and the death or stillbirth of his children was one of Goethe's most private and painful tragedies. Moreover, the ménage was unacceptable at the Weimar Court and the inevitable breach with Frau von Stein added personal anguish to the social isolation. Goethe had no reason to feel kindly towards institutional Christianity and now, as an adult and Enlightened man, sexually content and with a scientific attitude to Nature, he felt not only that Christianity had no intellectual foundation, but that he no longer needed the emotional support of a theological alternative to it. In 1787 when he was in Rome Herder had sent him his newly published volume called *Gott. Einige Gespräche* (*God. Some Conversations*). Reminded of the gift in 1788 he commented smiling, 'Then I was given God, and this year I don't believe in one'. 'Disagreeable things must be going through his mind', commented Herder's wife[17] and the disagreeable thoughts soon proved to have literary consequences.

---

[15] Nicholas Boyle, 'Faust, Helen, and Proserpine: Reflections on Some Goethe Drawings', *Publications of the English Goethe Society*, 63 (1993), pp.64-96.

[16] *HABr* 1, p.231. 'Your thirst for Christ makes me sorry for you. You're in a worse state than us heathens: at least our gods appear to us when we are in need.'

[17] *Goethe. Begegnungen und Gespräche*, ed. E. and R. Grumach (Berlin: De Gruyter, 1965-) iii, p.228.

In the December of 1793 Goethe, shaken to the core by the loss of another child, resolved to devote himself in the new year to a literary project that could absorb his mind and emotions. 'I think it will turn out to be my old novel', he wrote to a friend.[18] *Wilhelm Meister* had never been included in Goethe's plans for his collected edition – perhaps it was too large a task for completion in the time available; perhaps he always intended it as the material for a second phase in his writing career. But for two and a half years from the start of 1794 he worked steadily on a revision of the six books of *Wilhelm Meister's Theatrical Mission*, which he cut down to four and a half, and on the composition of another three and a half books to complete the novel. (Most remarkably, after the first year the writing proceeded simultaneously with the publication, so that Goethe had no opportunity to revise the earlier books in the light of any changes to his intentions for the later ones.) The result was *Wilhelm Meister's Years of Apprenticeship* (*HA* 7), the first of Goethe's works to be written in close collaboration with Schiller, with whom his friendship (though not his acquaintance) began in the summer of 1794. Schiller was a more dogmatic atheist than Goethe[19] but he was also much more committed to the Kantian system of ethical theology, and Goethe's revised and redirected novel shows clear signs of its origins in the high summer of German Kantianism.

For two years after his return from Italy Goethe worked intensively on completing his collected edition: this work was highly productive, if essentially retrospective, and it was accompanied by a new burst of poetry inspired by Christiane Vulpius, admittedly in the highly artificial and ironical form of the *Roman Elegies*. But once the work on the edition was over Goethe found himself looking into a void, and for three or four years of what he later called a 'realistical' [i.e. materialist] 'tendency' his writing lost direction, original poetry ceased completely, and no new large-scale project was launched. 'I [...] destroyed all sentimentality within me and so suffered damage to the closely related ethical and mental sphere', he wrote.[20] However these were the years in which Germany at large was going through an intellectual revolution in parallel to the political revolution taking place in France. New ethical issues and a new ethical consciousness were coming to preoccupy the younger generation as the Kantian philosophical movement started to gather momentum. Kant's refoundation of moral principles in the self-understanding of the autonomous moral agent had an even broader and deeper effect in Germany than his refoundation of scientific knowledge in the subjective necessities of thought. Goethe could not stand aloof from these developments and did not wish to – the new energies might after all revitalize and redirect his own writing, even if they tended to reinterpret and so to re-establish theology, rather than to complete its abolition.

---

[18] *HABr* 2, p.174.
[19] Boyle, *Goethe II*, p.161.
[20] *WA* I, 33, p.363.

The story of Wilhelm Meister, in the form in which it first reached the German public, is the story of a young man's emancipation from belief in 'the gods' – from the belief, that is, that his life is being shaped by the guiding hand of a higher power than himself. Wilhelm initially calls this power 'Fate', or 'Destiny' (Schicksal), a term much used by Goethe also in his letters during the period of his belief in 'the gods'. In a philosophical conversation with a stranger not further identified to us, Wilhelm remarks at the end of Book 1 that he honours 'the Destiny that knows how to initiate what is best for me and best for everyone' (HA 7, p.71) and provokes a diatribe against the very word. By confusing the boundaries between what in our lives is inevitable, and what in them is mere chance, and so obscuring the different roles that our reason has to play in dealing with these two very different categories of experience, the concept of 'Destiny' – the stranger says – allows us to loiter aimlessly through life and to call the result 'by the name of divine guidance'. Wilhelm needs to recognize, the stranger goes on, that 'Everyone has his good fortune in his own hands, as the artist has the raw material that he intends to transform into a figure'.

But like all arts this one has to be learnt, and in the course of the next three books Wilhelm shows little sign of learning it. Chance and his own moods seem to get the better of him in determining his involvement with the theatre and his wanderings through eighteenth-century Germany, until his faith in his guiding star very nearly costs him his life. However, after an ambush which leaves him seriously wounded and his fellow-actors plundered, Wilhelm, lying on his sickbed, begins to think seriously about the shape of his career so far. He is particularly concerned by the place in his life of the striking horsewoman in male clothing, the Amazon, as he calls her, who arrived in time to rescue him. She has now disappeared, but Wilhelm has become obsessed with her image, which seems to him to be related to 'all the dreams of his youth' – his feelings for her seem to have been anticipated by his childhood fascination with Tasso's heroine Chlorinda, who disguised herself as a man in order to fight, or with the princess Stratonice, the object of her stepson Antiochus's incestuous love:

> 'Sollten nicht', sagte er manchmal im stillen zu sich selbst, 'uns in der Jugend wie im Schlafe die Bilder zukünftiger Schicksale umschweben und unserm unbefangenen Auge ahnungsvoll sichtbar werden? Sollten die Keime dessen, was uns begegnen wird, nicht schon von der Hand des Schicksals ausgestreut, sollte nicht ein Vorgenuß der Früchte, die wir einst zu brechen hoffen, möglich sein?'[21]

---

[21] HA 7, p.235. ' "Might it not be", he sometimes said to himself in secret, "that in our youth as in our sleep the images of our future fates surround us and are visibly prefigured to our innocent eye? Might it not be that the seeds of what is to occur to us are already sown by the hand of Fate, might not a foretaste be possible of the fruits we one day hope to pluck?" '

Wilhelm has begun to discover the secret of the construction of his own life, which is at the same time the secret of the construction of Goethe's novel – namely that it is built up on the principle of motivic repetition.[22] There are patterns laid down in it from the earliest days he can remember, from even earlier perhaps, and these recur throughout his life, ever more insistently, ever more clearly. Two of these structuring patterns are mentioned explicitly by Wilhelm in this moment of insight – a third which is not mentioned is of course the various forms of the theatre – firstly, the image of the woman in man's clothing, the androgyne, and secondly, the image of a love that transgresses socially established boundaries. The motif of the androgynous woman will prove to be of particular importance, for it is this motif which links the puppets of Tancred and Chlorinda in Wilhelm's childhood with the image that opens the whole novel, that of his lover, the actress Mariana, dressed in soldier's uniform, and then with the figure who has above all appealed to artists and musicians after Goethe, the figure of Mignon. The female Mignon dresses as a boy, sings some of Goethe's finest poems, and seems to be associated with the freedom and unbiddability of Romantic art, but her hermaphrodite character also links her, not only with the fair Amazon who first reveals the principle of structural interconnection, but with the figure in Books 7 and 8 who might seem to be Mignon's antithesis. Theresa, the countrywoman who stomps about in boots and trousers, who is completely impervious to sentiment and the arts of fiction, is also briefly described as an 'Amazon'. The motif of socially transgressive love, already sounded in the liaison between Wilhelm, the son of a respectable merchant, and Mariana the actress, runs through the whole of the novel, culminating in the clutch of marriages at the end of Book 8, every one of which, as the first critics of the novel noted,[23] is a *mésalliance*, and in the awful warning that is the counter-example, the story of the incestuous love between the Harpist and his sister, from whose unnatural union the doomed Mignon was born.

However, when Wilhelm begins to suspect this underlying unifying principle in his experience he still makes the mistake of attributing it to the operation of Fate or Destiny. He still has to learn how much it is his own work, the work of a creative imagination that he is misapplying by confining it to the unprofitable world of the theatre. That lesson becomes clearer to us than it does to Wilhelm in the aesthetic discussions that take up much of the rest of Book 4 as Wilhelm approaches what he thinks of as his supreme goal – a production of *Hamlet* in which he will play the lead. Wilhelm shows himself able to apply to a text the shaping hand that he is as yet unable to apply to his own life, and if he recognizes that the difference between a drama and a novel is that a drama deals with Fate while a novel deals with chance, he fails to recognize that he has

---

[22] U. Mölk, *Goethe und das literarische Motiv*, Bursfelder Universitätsreden 11 (Göttingen, 1992).
[23] *Der Briefwechsel zwischen Schiller und Goethe* ed. S. Seidel (Munich: Beck, 1984) 1, p.191.

hitherto been living his life as a drama when it is really a novel. The turning point in Wilhelm's development comes precisely halfway through the novel, at the beginning of Book 5, and it is, as it was for Goethe, the death of his father. At first the significance of this event is not recognized, but Wilhelm is confronted with it at the climax of his theatrical career when he hears the words, 'I am thy father's spirit', and half believes them: the boundary between play and reality, on which his theatrical frivolities have been predicated, breaks down. He gives the performance of his life, because he is playing himself, but thereby demonstrates his lack of a true actor's vocation.

Held together in the past only by Wilhelm's determination to reach this one point, the troupe fragments and the theatre sets itself new, less demanding, and more lucrative tasks. Wilhelm, already drifting away from it, begins at last to formulate the lesson which is now becoming clear to us as readers. Wilhelm, like us, reads, in Book 6, the life-story of a woman, known only as 'the Beautiful Soul', who concentrates as entirely on her inner development as he on wandering through the outer world, but who learns, as he learns, to discern truth through the erroneous images that at first preoccupy her, and so to tell her own story to herself as a story of recurrent leitmotifs. Wilhelm summarizes the wisdom that this autobiography contains in terms that apply also to his own life: it is not in the interventions or intentions of some external power, whether the gods, or Fate, or Christ, that the meaning and value of our life lie, but in the interpretation and estimate that we put on it ourselves. That, evidently, is a change in moral consciousness that a Kantian generation could at once appreciate, though it was already implicit in Goethe's thinking at the time he wrote the poem 'Divinity'. Wilhelm, however, goes further, though he is still pursuing a strictly Kantian line of thought; we cannot, he says, give a meaning to our life without assuming that that meaning is grounded somewhere outside us:

> Ein heiterer Tag ist wie ein grauer, wenn wir ihn ungerührt ansehen, [says Wilhelm at the start of Book 7 as he rides away from the theatre under a magnificent rainbow] und was kann uns rühren, als die stille Hoffnung, daß die angeborne Neigung unsers Herzens nicht ohne Gegenstand bleiben werde?[24]

The balance of power in Wilhelm's life has suddenly shifted – from his destiny to the inclination of his heart – but he recognizes that the inclination of his heart still requires completion by some external goal or purpose. The death of his father has released Wilhelm into responsibility for his own actions, but it remains a responsibility to a standard outside himself. Like the Beautiful Soul, and like Kant, Wilhelm finds in moral and aesthetic experience the confirmation that faith and hope has, as the Beautiful Soul puts it, 'a real object':

---

[24] *HA* 7, p.421. 'A fine day is like a grey one if we look at it unmoved, and what can move us but the quiet hope that the innate inclination of our heart will not remain without an object?'

Uns rührt die Erzählung jeder guten Tat, uns rührt das Anschauen jedes harmonischen Gegenstandes; wir fühlen dabei, daß wir nicht ganz in der Fremde sind, wir wähnen einer Heimat näher zu sein, nach der unser Bestes, Innerstes ungeduldig hinstrebt.[25]

The question which the last two books of the novel have to answer, then, is: what is this external goal, where does the home lie towards which Wilhelm's heart is striving, what is the object of his innate inclination? Plainly the answer to that question, given by the structure of all Wilhelm's previous experience, is 'the fair Amazon'. But since the structural significance of the fair Amazon in Wilhelm's life can no longer be assumed to be the consequence of some decision or hidden plan of an external Destiny, but is rather a significance bestowed by the innate inclination of Wilhelm's heart, to give that answer is only to beg the further question: but who or what is the fair Amazon as a 'real object'? Towards what is Wilhelm striving by pursuing this androgynous figure through her many manifestations? To the question in this form Books 7 and 8 of the *Lehrjahre* give two different successive answers.

The answer given by Book 7 involves only a partial emancipation of Wilhelm from the idea of Destiny that has so far dogged him. In the place of a mysterious, transcendent, unaccountable guiding hand, in the place of the gods who persecute the Harpist as they once persecuted Orestes, there is briefly put the wholly transparent and comprehensible guiding hand of human society, of a human society, the Society of the Tower, as it is called. The Society of the Tower is a kind of Masonic group of the reasonable, the benevolent, and the humane, who guide each other to a rational goal and enable their members to look back on their own development and see in it in retrospect a clear and logical pattern, however confused it may have appeared at the time. This society, into which Wilhelm is initiated at the end of Book 7, claims to have been guiding and influencing him through secret emissaries since his youth, and his story, as the Society of the Tower understands it, has been written down, like the stories of all its members, on a scroll, which he is shown, bearing the title 'Wilhelm Meister's Years of Apprenticeship' (*HA* 7, p.497). It is the novel of Wilhelm's life which he should have taken it upon himself to write – not the drama he thought he was involved in as the pawn of Destiny. There is certainly something admirable about the Society of the Tower: it sees human beings as reasonable and as free, as capable of development and as best left to develop for themselves, if necessary through error, in the confidence that they will tend naturally to move upwards towards the light. It sees human beings also as essentially social and sociable and it acts as a structure for the mutual support even of

---

[25] *HA* 7, p.421. 'We are moved by the narration of any good deed, we are moved by the contemplation of any harmonious thing; we feel then that we are not altogether in a strange land, we imagine ourselves nearer to a home towards which our best and inmost being is impatiently striving.'

those who do not know each other personally. But it cannot provide Wilhelm with the right answer to the question: who is the fair Amazon? It points him to the wrong person entirely, to Theresa, who loves in Wilhelm only what he is, not what he is to become (*HA* 7, pp.530-32), and who is the ideal practical companion, but not the Ideal itself.

Only in Book 8 does Wilhelm meet the Ideal itself, the Ideal as a real object, the fair Amazon in her full reality, and that reality proves a mysterious thing indeed. It takes Wilhelm beyond his life as a novel that it is incumbent on him to write and takes him into the life that is his and his only, not shaped for anyone else, but shaped for the fulfilment of his own entelechy, of the purpose for which he was born and towards which he must move for as long as he is alive. It therefore bears the name Natalia. It is the home towards which all moral and aesthetic experience directs him, the meaning and significance of his life not as something that the gods have kept concealed from him even as they have taken responsibility for guiding him towards it, but the meaning and significance of his life as that which is implied by his own complete responsibility for himself and his own self-orientation towards the good – which is for Kant the only compelling evidence for the existence not of the gods, but of God.[26] Natalia, therefore, to whom Wilhelm is betrothed in the last lines of the novel, is God, God, at any rate, for him, and a Kantian God at that. She is the Ideal, the Idea that is regulative of all Wilhelm's experience, that derives from his own inmost rationality, but that imprints on all his experience the mark and reminder of the androgynous perfection for which his experience is made, and she is the Idea thought of as real – what Kant calls the Ideal. Kant also says, in his treatise on religion, that the historical instantiation of the Ideal may properly be thought of as the Son – or presumably the Daughter – of God.[27]

Wilhelm Meister at the end of his apprenticeship is therefore on the point of marriage to a female Christ. Goethe's return to the conceptual repertoire of the religion he abandoned at the age of twenty-one is nothing if not heterodox. Having once made the breakthrough into subversive reinterpretation he seems to have enjoyed its potential for mischief and I should like in conclusion to point to another well-known example, from a much later work, of Goethe's enjoyment of what we may surely call thealogical speculation.

Faust Part Two, Goethe said, was a collection of very serious jokes[28] and Albrecht Schöne has shown how one of the jokes Goethe seriously intended, though he did not in the end carry it out in its entirety, was to conclude the play with the salvation not just

---

[26] I. Kant, *Kritik der Urteilskraft*, §§86-91, in: *Werke* ed. W. Weischedel (Frankfurt: Insel, 1957) 5, pp.567-606.
[27] Kant, *Die Religion innerhalb der Grenzen der bloßen Vernunft* II. i. a, *Werke* 4, pp.712-14.
[28] Letter to Wilhelm von Humboldt, 17 March 1832, *HA* 3, p.468.

of Faust, but of the Devil and the entire contents of Hell.[29] Schöne does not, however, note the thealogical joke in the last two of the play's over 12,000 lines. 'Das Ewig-Weibliche Zieht uns hinan' – 'The ever-womanly Draws us onwards' – are among Goethe's best-known words, but their significance, I suspect, is usually overlooked. Probably they are assumed to refer to some erotic lure held by Romantics to be characteristic of women. Not a bit of it, I say. They are another case of Goethe's tweaking the sensibilities of the orthodox. 'Are there no men in heaven, then?'[30] an irritated male critic is reputed to have expostulated on reading the last scene, and thereby fell into the trap Goethe had set for him. *Faust*, as I have argued elsewhere,[31] has two conclusions – an earthly and a heavenly. Faust's earthly end is in meaningless delusion – the moment of his death is worthless and empty, says the Devil, and once all the perturbation of spirit that has been his life is over it might as well never have been at all. Indeed uninterrupted nothingness would for Mephistopheles be preferable to the vexations of memory – 'Ich liebte mir dafür das Ewig-Leere'. 'The eternally empty' is the last word pronounced on Faust's life in what we might call the realistic, the terrestrial, section of the drama. But that realistic section is encased within a metaphysical frame which puts an Idealist gloss on the story and which provided Mahler, of course, with the text set in the second movement of his Eighth Symphony. The full nature of the gloss and of the re-reading it requires need not concern us here – all we need notice is that the invocation of 'Das Ewig-Weibliche' is the response that the metaphysical framework makes to Mephistopheles' taunt of 'Das Ewig-Leere'. 'Das Ewig-Weibliche' is the source of the redemption and love that fills out the Mephistophelean emptiness. It swamps Mephistopheles in a flood of love represented by rose-petals that to him are indistinguishable from the fires of Hell, it threatens to redeem him too, though with a great effort he diverts this power of love into the channels of the unnatural, and through the intercessory prayer of the penitent women it is effectual for the redemption of Faust.

Despite the appearance of a wholesale adoption of Catholic imagery and allusions to Dante, however, Goethe deliberately introduces some discords that alert his audience to the presence of another conceptual scheme that is making use of the religious vocabulary for its own metaphorical purposes. The other scheme is a later variant of the Kantian idealism that subtends *Wilhelm Meister's Years of Apprenticeship* and the first

---

[29] A. Schöne, *Fausts Himmelfahrt. Zur letzten Szene der Tragödie*, Themen 56 (Munich: Carl Friedrich von Siemens Stiftung, 1994).
[30] Schöne, *Himmelfahrt*, p.14.
[31] Nicholas Boyle, ' "Du ahnungsloser Engel, du!": some current views of Goethe's *Faust*', *German Life and Letters* 36 (1982-3), pp.116-47. See also my *Sacred and Secular Scriptures. A Catholic Approach to Literature* (University of Notre Dame, 2004), pp.171-86.

discord that alerts us to its presence is the use of the title 'Göttin', 'goddess', in an address to the Virgin Mary – an impossible title in a Catholic context, but entirely natural as part of the Kantian adaptation in the *Years of Apprenticeship* of Goethe's earlier thoughts about the gods. If the Virgin Mary, like Natalia, is a metaphor for the ultimate Ideal she may with equal propriety be called either God or Goddess. And if she is called 'Goddess' we may then notice the discordant quality of the title 'Das Ewig-Weibliche' too, for it is certainly not an orthodox attribute of the divine. But it is not an orthodox Catholic world in which Faust is saved, even though it is an orthodox and not only Catholic sentiment to think of God as drawing all the redeemed permanently onwards and upwards into an ever deeper vision of the Divine mystery. In the heaven to which the last lines of *Faust II* allude, however, not only are there no men, but God Herself is, eternally, a woman.[32]

---

[32] For the sake of brevity I have here omitted most of the second half of the story. After *Wilhelm Meisters Lehrjahre*, Goethe's thinking about the Divine was largely (though not entirely) dominated by the concept of (feminine) Nature. The roots of this concept lay in his earliest adulthood and excluding it from this paper meant also excluding a significant element in his theology even before 1796. It was rightly pointed out in the discussion that the argument presented here needs to be complemented by consideration of the Spinozan (or apparently Spinozan) vein in Goethe's scientific and religious thought.

10 | Schumann's *Requiem für Mignon* and the Concept of Music as Literature
Julian Horton

I

One of the most fascinating aspects of musical reception history is the issue of how critical perceptions of a composer change and propagate. Sometimes, the reversals characterizing this process can be extreme; one thinks, for example, of the case of J.S. Bach, whose relative parochialism in the eighteenth century was transformed, in the nineteenth century, into absolute canonical centrality.[1] More often, such reversals tend to involve the critical reorientation of the image of, or cultural weight accorded to, a composer's work. So, for example, the pervasive nineteenth-century view of Chopin as a rhapsodically inclined and essentially feminine composer ceded increasingly in the twentieth century to the identification of rigorous formalism, due in no small measure to the efforts of Heinrich Schenker.[2] Shifts in reception history can also involve changes in the way value judgements are distributed across a composer's career. Thus Mendelssohn, whose fame in the early nineteenth century rested on mature large-scale works such as

---

[1] On this matter, see for example Gerhard Herz, *Essays on J. S. Bach* (Michigan 1985), pp.19-50 and 67-109.

[2] On the trajectory of Chopin reception, see for example John Rink, 'Chopin's Ballades and the Dialectic: Analysis in Historical Perspective', *Music Analysis*, 13 (1994), pp.99-115. For a consideration of Chopin as 'feminine' composer, see Jeffrey Kallberg, 'Small Fairy Voices: Sex, History and Meaning in Chopin', in: John Rink and Jim Samson, eds, *Chopin Studies* 2 (Cambridge 1994), pp.50-71. On Schenker's reception of Chopin, see Ian Bent, 'Heinrich Schenker, Chopin and Domenico Scarlatti', *Music Analysis* 5 (1986), pp.131-49.

Elijah, St Paul and the Second Symphony, was reinvented for the twentieth century as a child prodigy who lapsed, in maturity, into refined but often superficial classicism.³

Viewed in these terms, Schumann's case is especially interesting. His reputation was made, during his lifetime, by the public compositions of the 1840s: the symphonies and above all the dramatic works. When Eduard Hanslick remarked of the oratorio *Das Paradies und die Peri* that 'Master Florestan is getting a bit older', he voiced, albeit flippantly, a general perception that Schumann had found a balance between gravity, innovation and popularity that his youthful works lacked.⁴ One hundred years later, this perception had been comprehensively reversed. Following on from Donald Frances Tovey's conviction that Schumann was essentially an epigrammatic composer who fell prey to tautology when confronted with large-scale Beethovenian forms, the past century has focused almost exclusively on the piano music of the 1830s and the song cycles of 1840.⁵ The symphonies have persisted in the concert hall, but have endured a barrage of critical invective.⁶ And, notwithstanding some recent revivals, the dramatic and choral works – chiefly *Das Paradies und die Peri*, the *Szenen aus Goethes Faust*, the opera *Genoveva, Manfred* and the *Requiem für Mignon* – have fallen into almost total obscurity.

Critical trajectories of this kind raise some difficult questions. Primarily, they broach a conflict between relativism and objectivity that is hard to resolve. In brief: is the value of Schumann's music nothing more than the sum of the phases of its reception history, or are there objective grounds for reappraisal arising from its inherent properties? To be sure, such trends frequently reflect broader movements in the history of ideas. The

---

³ A cogent overview of the course of Mendelssohn reception is provided in Leon Botstein, 'The Aesthetics of Assimilation and Affirmation: Reconstructing the Career of Felix Mendelssohn', in R. Larry Todd, ed., *Mendelssohn and His World* (Princeton 1991), pp.5-42. See also R. Larry Todd, 'Mendelssohn, Felix', in *NG* 16 (London 2001), pp.389-424 and more recently *Mendelssohn: A Life in Music* (Oxford 2003).
⁴ Quoted in John Daverio, *Robert Schumann: Herald of a New Poetic Age* (Oxford 1997), p.268.
⁵ 'Schumann cannot develop an idea, he can only make sequences on it. He cannot even state an idea that is capable of development: the main theme of his finale [of the First Symphony] shows that he does not know the difference between a symphonic theme and a lyric arabesque'. See 'Schumann: Symphony in B flat Major, no.1, op.38', in: *Essays in Musical Analysis, II: Symphonies (II), Variations and Orchestral Polyphony* (Oxford 1935), pp.45-52, this quotation p.46.
⁶ Tovey's opinions are reproduced by Julius Harrison and Mosco Carner amongst many others; see Harrison, 'Robert Schumann', in: Robert Simpson, ed., *The Symphony, vol.1: Haydn to Dvorák* (Harmondsworth 1966), pp.246-61 and Carner, 'The Orchestral Music', in: Gerald Abraham, ed., *Schumann: A Symposium* (London 1952), pp.176-244 and especially p.180. A version of these criticisms even prevails in Carl Dahlhaus' work: 'by substituting the motivic unity of the character piece for that of the Beethoven symphony [Schumann] became embroiled in contradictions between lyricism and monumentality [...] that led not so much to a productive dialectic as to mutual paralysis of its various components'. See *NCM* trans. J. Bradford Robinson (Berkeley 1989), p.160.

positive reception of Schumann's public works in the nineteenth century was tied to a widespread preoccupation with the necessity of following Beethoven; as Anthony Newcomb famously pointed out, the favourable contemporary reception of the Second Symphony drew heavily upon a collective perception of the narrative patterns established by Beethoven.[7] Similarly, preferences for the early piano works emerged in tandem with the modes of formalist thought that came to dominate compositional and music-analytical attitudes from the 1920s onwards. From this perspective, modifications of critical stance are simply functions of the vicissitudes of cultural history, and the immanent value of Schumann's music becomes at best inaccessible, at worst irrelevant. On the other hand, the idea that the musicological judgements we make have no foundations in works of music is hard to digest. There is a real danger that such attitudes will perpetuate a condition of musicological false-consciousness, as a result of which we consign whole regions of a composer's output to the dustbin of history because our critical and analytical faculties cannot see beyond the governing orthodoxy. This tendency cannot be resisted by passively accepting the primacy of epistemic change.

These considerations press heavily upon any attempt to evaluate Schumann's *Requiem für Mignon*. Although the most substantial of Schumann's single-movement works for voices and orchestra, and by some estimations the most successful, it has disappeared almost entirely from the concert repertoire.[8] The considerable secondary literature has tended to treat the *Requiem* as a minor adjunct to the larger dramatic and vocal works, themselves widely regarded as poor relations of the songs and early piano cycles. Thus far, extended analytical or contextual research into the work remains to be undertaken.[9] Grounds for substantial value judgement, arising either from detailed analysis or from assessment of the piece's literary or aesthetic motivations, are in short supply. The principal motivation of this paper, if not to embark on a wholesale explosion of critical orthodoxy, is at least to investigate how analysis might contribute to its reorientation in the case of the *Requiem*. And this, in turn, might furnish tentative responses to the broad questions of reception history posed above.

---

[7] See Anthony Newcomb, 'Once more between Absolute and Programme Music: Schumann's Second Symphony', *NCM* 7 (1983-4), pp.233-50.

[8] See, for example, Daverio, *Robert Schumann*, p.436.

[9] To my knowledge, there is currently no extended analysis of the *Requiem für Mignon* (Daverio's brief engagement is considered below). Studies of the *Faust* music are more plentiful: see for example Donald Mintz, 'Schumann as Interpreter of Goethe's *Faust*', *JAMS* 14 (1961), pp.235-56, Eric Sams, 'Schumann and Faust', *MT* 113 (1972), pp.543-46, Gisela Probst, *Robert Schumanns Oratorien* (Wiesbaden 1975), especially pp.116-34, Gerd Nauhaus, *Robert Schumann: Szenen aus Goethes Faust* (Zwickau 1981) and also Daverio, *Robert Schumann*, pp.364-87.

II

To place the work, first of all, in context: the *Requiem für Mignon* was completed in 1849, and comprises a setting for soloists, chorus and orchestra of the funeral rites for Mignon taken from the eighth book of Wilhelm Meisters Lehrjahre. It complements two other Goethe projects that occupied Schumann around this time. It is linked most closely to the composition of the Lieder on texts from Wilhelm Meister composed in mid-1849, with which it was published under the collective title *Lieder, Gesänge und Requiem für Mignon* as Schumann's op.98. More broadly, these works form a companion to the most protracted Goethe project of the late 1840s, the *Szenen aus Goethes Faust*, which was conceived in 1844 but not completed until 1853, and (as a postscript) to the overture *Hermann und Dorothea*, which, however, never lead to an operatic project on the same subject. Widening the field of vision further, these pieces evince a preoccupation with composition for voices and orchestra that begins with the oratorio *Das Paradies und die Peri* of 1843, encompassing also *Genoveva* (1848), *Manfred* (also 1848), *Der Rose Pilgerfahrt* (1851), the various choral-orchestral ballades of the late 1840s and early 1850s, and ultimately the Mass and Requiem of 1852-53.

English-language commentary on this repertoire has in the past varied between apology and outright condemnation. Gerald Abraham and Joan Chissell attempted reappraisals of *Faust* that often damned with faint praise, while Alan Walker contrived to write an entire book about Schumann without considering the dramatic and choral music at all.[10] John Horton's view of *Das Paradies und die Peri* is by-and-large representative:

> [Schumann's] melodic and harmonic riches are lavished equally on narrative, descriptive and reflective passages, so that the total effect [...] is cloying and monotonous [...] It is unlikely *Paradise and the Peri* will ever return to the choral society repertory, but it should be given at least an occasional 'token' performance.[11]

John Daverio has recently offered a more complex response to the critical dilemmas posed by these works. For him, the distinction habitually made between the early epigrammatic style and Schumann's later, more consciously post-Beethovenian ambitions conceals an underlying thread, which remained essentially invariant between the *Papillons* of 1832 and the various Goethe projects of the 1840s. This, as he describes it, is the concept of 'music as literature':

---

[10] Gerald Abraham 'The Dramatic Music', in: *Schumann: A Symposium*, pp.260-82, Joan Chissell, *Schumann* (London 1948), pp.169-74, Alan Walker, *Schumann* (London 1976).

[11] John Horton, 'The Choral Works', in: *Schumann: A Symposium*, pp.283-99, this quotation pp.286-87.

> [T]he model for Schumann's creative work is less a perfectly rounded whole [...] than a constellation of fragments. But regulating the fragments and imparting them coherence is a single thought: the notion that music should be imbued with the same intellectual substance as literature. Schumann developed this conviction while he was still a teenager; he held it until the end of his career.[12]

Thus the early piano cycles, conceived under the influence of the novels of Jean Paul and E.T.A. Hoffmann amongst others, sought a musical analogue of developments in Romantic literature and aesthetics, embodied above all in the notion of the system of fragments.[13] Daverio perceives the dramatic and choral music of the 1840s as the logical maturation of this idea: as a progression from the application of a literary model to the genres of the piano miniature to the fully worked out notion of the 'literary opera', a conception that blurs the distinction between theatre and concert hall, and therefore embraces not only the opera *Genoveva*, but also *Das Paradies und die Peri*, *Manfred*, *Faust* and, in its own way, the *Requiem für Mignon*. Despite the exchange of genres, the common denominator here remains the mediation of music and literature. The piano works from *Papillons* to the *Faschingsschwank aus Wien* invest absolute musical forms with a literary substance; the dramatic works invest quasi-literary genres with absolute or symphonic musical substance.

This view is not only biographically but also historically advantageous. The convergence of music and literature was a major trope in nineteenth-century music; the estimation of Schumann's achievement frequently involved recognition of the closeness of this relationship in his case. Thus Franz Liszt, writing in 1855, observed that, 'as a man, [Schumann] felt the need to tie authorship and music together; as a musician, the need to tie the history of music more closely to that of poetry and literature'.[14] Liszt understood the *Requiem für Mignon* to have taken this project into new territory, and described the results with purple prose:

> The *Requiem für Mignon* performed the rare service of enriching the consummate creation of a master with a new idea, a fortunately successful stroke. This last lament, this thousandfold sigh repeated above a grave covering so much suffering and beauty, so much yearning and misfortune, is like the final chord of an earthly lot full of painful dissonance.[15]

---

[12] See Daverio, *Robert Schumann*, p.19.
[13] See Daverio, *Robert Schumann*, pp.55-104 and also *Nineteenth-Century Music and German Romantic Ideology* (New York 1993), pp.1-88.
[14] See Franz Liszt, 'Robert Schumann', *Neue Zeitschrift für Musik*, 42 (1855), trans. in R. Larry Todd, ed., *Schumann and His World* (Princeton 1994), pp.338-61, this quotation p.348.
[15] ibid., p.350.

Adolf Schubring later amplified these ideas, perceiving in Schumann nothing less than the dawn of a new musical epoch. This came to fruition above all in the dramatic compositions:

> As important as Schumann is in his lyric works, so fragrant with romantic magic, he is at his greatest in his epic works – not the effete religious epic but the modern, romantic one, which has found its proper form in the romance, ballade, legend, novella, novel and *Märchen*.[16]

Schubring cited *Das Paradies und die Peri*, *Manfred*, *Faust* and *Der Rose Pilgerfahrt* in this respect, and, anticipating Daverio, equated the smaller compositions to these 'epic' works on precisely the grounds that they also constitute analogues of contemporary literary forms. In short, Daverio's invocation of 'music as literature' as a revisionist tool accesses a phenomenon that was readily apparent to Schumann's contemporaries.

The practical consequence of this is a radical reorientation of Schumann's oeuvre. The piano works of the 1830s now constitute preparatory essays for a project that bore fruit in the 1840s, as Schumann successively worked his way through the post-Beethovenian genres: Lied, symphony, chamber music, oratorio, concerto, opera. This process culminated in the composition of works for voices and orchestra, which, by virtue of their literary ambitions, thwart easy generic classification: *Manfred*, which has operatic pretensions, but which the composer described as a 'dramatic poem' (*dramatisches Gedicht*); *Faust*, a dramatic oratorio in structure, which draws liberally on the genres of contemporary opera (Daverio calls it a 'musical novel'); *Der Rose Pilgerfahrt*, a sequence of orchestral songs labelled as *Märchen*, and the *Requiem für Mignon*, which mingles sacred and secular influences in the context of an extended orchestral partsong. Above all, this model reinvests Schumann's career with a teleology that twentieth-century reception largely rejected. We no longer perceive an early flowering, followed by a protracted decline in which the mismatch of ambition and ability becomes increasingly clear, but rather the progress of a single concept, which was refracted through, and consequently changed, a succession of genres.

III

In considering the *Requiem für Mignon*, the key question, therefore, is: how is this concept revealed in the musical material? To what extent, in other words, are Schumann's melopoetic intentions analytically tangible? In practical terms, this becomes a matter of establishing the way in which Goethe's text conditions the work's structure and material processes.

---

[16] See Adolf Schubring, 'The Present Musical Epoch and Robert Schumann's Position in Musical History', *Neue Zeitschrift für Musik* 54 (1861), trans. in *Schumann and His World*, pp.362-72, this quotation p.371.

Daverio isolates two main issues in this regard: the relationship of the work to the *Faust* music, and its engagement with the concept of *Bildung*, as the central theme of the novel. The connection with *Faust* is revealed both in material parallels, and in the similarity of the works' conclusions, which both convey redemption: 'Mignon, like Gretchen and Faust, finds redemption only in the hereafter'.[17] The second issue – the centrality of *Bildung* – turns on Schumann's setting of the words 'In euch lebe die bildende Kraft' ('In you lives the formative power'), which is isolated tonally and gesturally and involves a sudden shift towards an unadorned chorale. For Daverio, the turn to a sacred topic lends religious gravity to an essentially humanistic idea, and thus locates this passage as the work's effective structural core.[18]

Although these issues are undoubtedly important to the piece – the idea of *Bildung*, in particular, was a major component of Schumann's aesthetic sensibilities – they are not, in my view, structurally fundamental, but are rather supported by a more basic property of the text, which Schumann exploits with great subtlety. This is its dialogical character: the juxtaposition of the mourning children and the 'invisible choruses', by whom they are exhorted to rise from their introspection and rejoin the world. This feature not only controls the relationship between text and form, it also conditions tonal and thematic strategy, together with crucial aspects of the work's large-scale voice leading.

Schumann divides the text into six numbered sections, as indicated in table 10.1 (see overleaf).[19] He departs from the chronology of Goethe's text in a number of respects. First, the number structure does not always correspond to Goethe's division of labour. Most strikingly, the third of Goethe's designated choral paragraphs straddles the divide between sections three and four: 'Schaut mit den Augen des Geistes hinan!' forms the climactic point of section three; 'in euch lebe die bildende Kraft' opens section four. Second, Schumann sometimes allots individual paragraphs to individual sections, as for example in sections two and six, and sometimes constructs sections from multiple paragraphs, as in section three, which comprises paragraphs three, four and the first line of five, and in section four, which sets the remainder of paragraph five and paragraph six. Third, Schumann frequently augments Goethe's dialogue by interlacing elements of the texts of both chorus and children. In section two, the children's paragraph commencing 'Ach! die Flügel heben sie nicht!' ('Alas, the wings do not raise her up!') is repeatedly punctuated by segments of the chorus' previous paragraph. In section four, the technique is used more extensively: the children's material is distended by choral interjections, which become increasingly insistent. Specifically, Schumann detaches a single choral sentence, 'Schaut mit den Augen des Geistes hinan!' ('look up with the eyes of the spirit'), and compresses it to produce the lapidary 'Schaut hinan!' ('look up'). The

---

[17] See Robert Schumann, p.437.
[18] ibid., p.438.
[19] I am grateful to Lorraine Byrne for her help in translating Goethe's text.

dialogue culminates, at the close of the section, with the chorus overwhelming the children, pulling them into the communal assertion of a perfect cadence. In this way, section four represents the consummation of a process of contraction, whereby the alternation of chorus and children becomes more rapid, until they finally sing simultaneously. After this point, the dramatic antithesis recedes. The next entry of the children, from bar 252, affirms their intention to turn away from mourning and towards life; the last time they and the chorus sing in close dialogue, bars 267 to 275, it is to the same words, 'und der Schlaf uns erquickt' ('and sleep refreshes us'). All these techniques work towards the same end: the construction of a musical form, based around the dramatization of Goethe's dialogue.

Table 10.1 Schumann *Requiem für Mignon*, Distribution of Text

Schumann/translation	Goethe
[The assembled company all took their seats; and two invisible choruses asked in gentle strains]	[Die Gesellschaft setzte sich, und zwei unsichtbare Chöre fingen mit holdem Gesang an zu fragen:]
No.1 Chorus Whom do you bring to our silent company?	Wen bringt ihr uns zur stillen Gesellschaft?
Soprano 1, 2; Alto 1, 2 A tired playmate we bring to you; Here let her stay and rest, Until joyful siblings in Heaven Shall wake her once more!	Die vier Kinder antworteten mit lieblicher Stimme: Einen müden Gespielen bringen wir euch; laßt ihr unter euch ruh'n, bis das Jauchzen himmlischer Geschwister ihn der einst wieder aufweckt!
Chorus Child so young, in our circle, be welcome! Be welcome in sorrow! May neither boy nor girl follow you! May only old age proceed eagerly Calmly to this silent hall and may the dear child rest in solemn company!	**Chor** Erstling der Jugend in unserem Kreise, sei willkommen! Mit Trauer willkommen! Dir folge kein Knabe, kein Mädchen nach! Nur das Alter nahe sich willig und gelassen der stillen Halle, und in ernster Gesellschaft ruhe das liebe Kind!
No.2 Soprano 1, alto 1 Oh! How reluctantly we brought her here! Here she must stay! Let us stay too, Let us weep by her coffin!	**Knaben** Ach! wie ungern brachten wir ihn her! Ach! und er soll hier bleiben! Laßt uns euch bleiben, laßt uns weinen an seinem Sarge!
No.3 Chorus Look at the powerful wings! See the light, unspotted robe! See the golden band gleaming in her hair! See the beauty and grace of her repose	**Chor** Seht die mächtigen Flügel doch an! Seht das leichte, reine Gewand! Wie blinkt die gold'ne Binde vom Haupt! Seht die schöne, würdige Ruh'!

Look at the powerful wings!
See the beauty and grace of her repose!
See the light, unspotted robe!
Look at the powerful wings!

Soprano 1 solo
The wings do not raise her up;

Knaben
Ach! Die Flügel heben sie nicht;

Chorus See the light, unspotted robe!

Soprano 2 solo
They flap in play no more;

Im leichten Spiele flattert es nicht mehr;

Chorus Look,

Soprano 2 solo No more!

Chorus
See the golden band gleaming in her hair!

Soprano 1,2 soli
When we crowned her head with roses
Her gaze was sweet and friendly to us.

Als wir mit Rosen kränzten ihr Haupt,
blickte sie hold und freundlich nach uns.

Chorus See the beauty of her repose!

Soprano 1,2 soli
Her gaze was sweet and friendly to us.

Chorus Look at the wings!

Soprano 1 solo
Oh! The wings do not raise her up!

Chorus See the mighty wings!

Soprano 2 solo
Oh! The wings do not raise her up!

Chorus
Look beyond with the eyes of the spirit!

Chor
Schaut mit den Augen des Geistes hinan!

No.4
Chorus
May there dwell in you the power to transport that
which is finest, loveliest in life, up beyond the stars.

In euch lebe die bildende Kraft, die das Schönste,
das Höchste hinauf, über die Sterne das Leben trägt

Soprano 1,2 soli; alto 1 solo
On earth she is lost to us now,

Chorus Look up!

Soprano 1,2 soli; alto 1 solo
She walks in the gardens no more,

Chorus Look up!

Soprano 1, 2 soli; alto 1 solo
On earth she is lost to us now,

Chorus Look up with the eyes of the spirit!

Soprano 1,2 soli
On earth she is lost to us now,
She goes to the garden no more.

Chorus Look up!

Soprano 1,2 soli
She gathers flowers of the meadow no more.

Chorus Look up!

Soprano 2 solo
Let us weep!

Chorus Look up!

Alto 1 solo
We leave her here!

Chorus Look up!

Soprano 1,2 soli
Let us weep, we leave her here!

Chorus
Look up with the eyes of the spirit!

Soprano 1,2 soli (simultaneously)
Let us weep and stay with her!

Knaben
Aber ach! Wir vermissen sie hier,

In der Gärten wandelt sie nicht,

Sammelt der Wiese Blumen nicht mehr.

Laßt uns weinen,

Wir lassen sie hier!

Laßt uns weinen und bei ihr bleiben!

Soprano 1,2 soli
Let us weep and stay with her!
Chorus (simultaneously) Look up!

No.5
Bass solo
Children, return to life!
Your tears shall be dried in the freshness of the air
that plays around the meandering water.
Retreat from the night! Daylight, joy and continuity
are the fate of the living!

Soprano 1,2 soli; alto 1,2 soli
We rise and return to life again!
May the day give us labour and joy,
Until evening brings repose,

Soprano 1 solo And sleep gives refreshment

Chorus (soprano only)
And sleep gives refreshment,

Soprano 1 solo And sleep gives refreshment,

Chorus (soprano 1,2; alto 1)
And sleep gives refreshment,

No.6
Chorus
Children, hurry back to life!
And may love dressed in the pure robes of beauty
meet you with its divine gaze
And the crown of immortality!
Children, hurry back to life!
And may love dressed in the pure robes of beauty
meet you with its divine gaze
And the crown of immortality! Children,
hurry back to life! And may love dressed in the
pure robes of beauty meet you with its divine gaze,

Soprano 1,2 soli We rise and return to life!

Chorus (simultaneously)
And the crown of immortality.

Chorus Children, hurry back to life, hurry!

Chor
Kinder, kehret ins Leben zurück!
Eure Tränen trockne die frische Luft, die um das
schlängelnde Wasser spielt.
Entflieht der Nacht!
Tag und Lust und Dauer ist der Lebendigen Los.

Knaben
Auf! Wir kehren ins Leben zurück!
Gebe der Tag uns Arbeit und Lust,
bis der Abend uns Ruhe bringt,

Und der Schlaf uns erquickt.

Chor
Kinder! Eilet ins Leben hinan!
In der Schönheit reinem Gewande
begegne euch die Liebe mit himmlischem Blick
und dem Kranz der Unsterblichkeit!

The tonal design of the *Requiem* engages a theoretical problem that has a direct bearing on how we understand this process. The fact that the work begins in C minor and ends in F major prompts the question: is this a monotonal structure in the conventional Schenkerian sense, which starts over the dominant minor, or does Schumann develop a directional strategy employing two possible and successive tonics, C and F?[20] Examples 10.1 and 10.2 show these two readings in graphic form.

Example 10.1 compels us to understand all the material as far as bar 125 as a prolongation of V. Since there is no sense in which C minor functions cadentially as a dominant to F, we have to invoke a second Schenkerian category, that of *Mischung*, or modal mixture, in order to make the reading work. By these terms, the C minor opening is not really part of the fundamental structure at all, but a middleground modal alteration of the real V, which first enters at bar 52, and which is clarified just prior to the first F major section in bars 119 to 123. In example 10.2, the work is split into two successive fundamental structures: an initial, incomplete C *Ursatz*, which is subsumed into a second F major *Ursatz*, exchanging its original tonic status for a dominant function. The alternation of C minor and C major is less troublesome in this context, since there is no initial expectation of dominant identity, and we can therefore readmit the opening to the background structure.

---

[20] The issue of directional tonality has spawned a diverse literature. It originated in Dika Newlin, *Bruckner, Mahler, Schoenberg* (New York 1947) in relation to the tonal schemes of Mahler's symphonies. More recent studies include Robert Bailey, 'The Structure of the *Ring* and Its Evolution', *NCM* 1 (1977), pp 48-61, Harald Krebs, 'Alternatives to Monotonality in Early Nineteenth-Century Music', *Journal of Music Theory* 25 (1981), pp.1-16, Jim Samson, 'Chopin's Alternatives to Monotonality', in William Kinderman and Harald Krebs, eds, *The Second Practice of Nineteenth-Century Tonality* (Lincoln 1996), pp.34-44, Kevin Korsyn, 'Directional Tonality and Intertextuality: Brahms' Quintet Op.88 and Chopin's Ballade Op 38', ibid., pp.45-83.

Example 10.1 Schumann, *Requiem für Mignon* **op.98(b), Monotonal Reading**

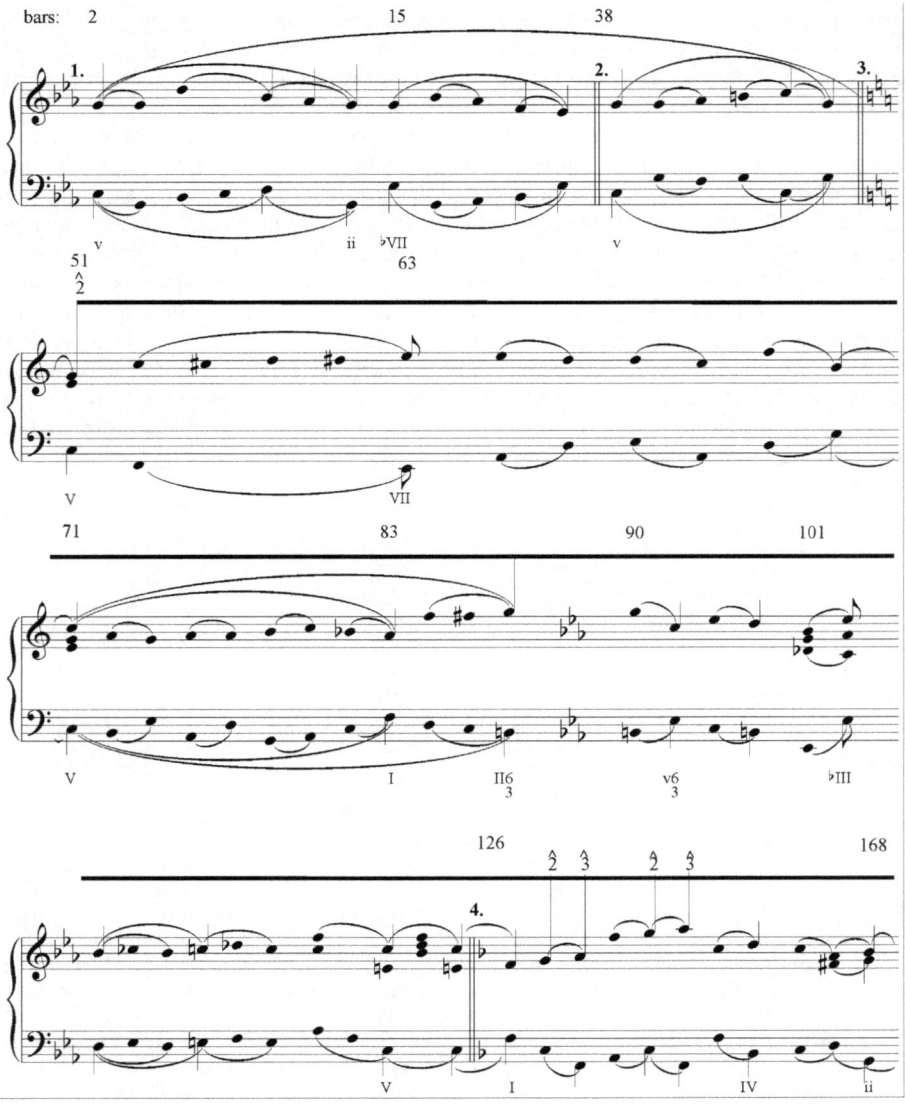

Schumann's *Requiem für Mignon*

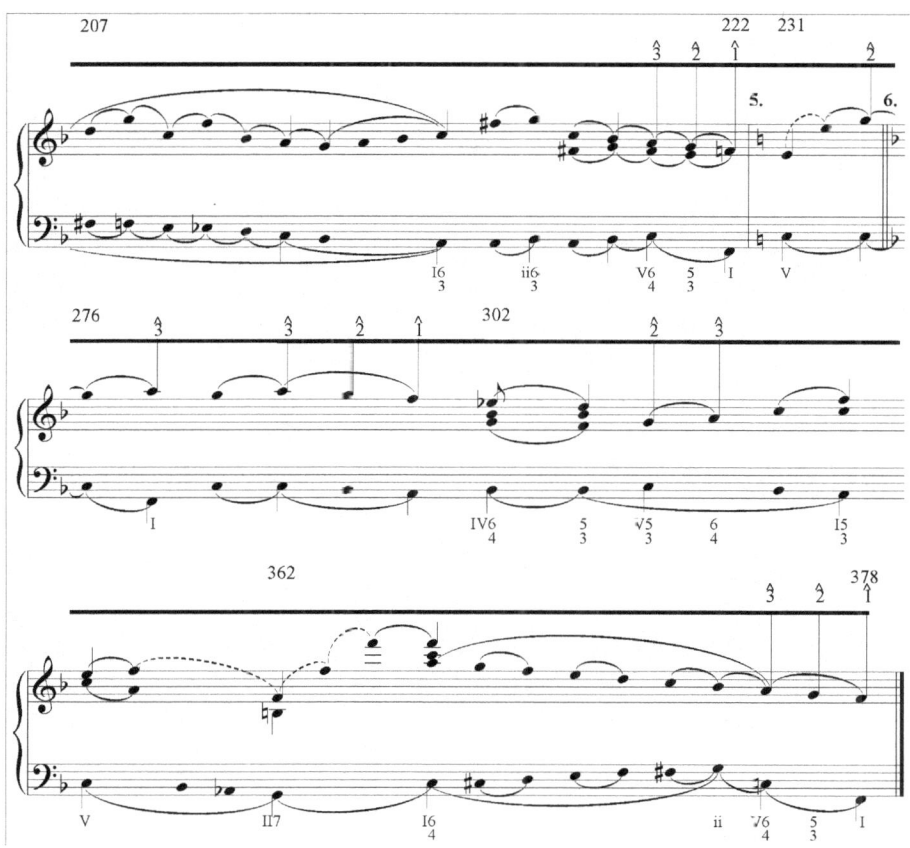

Example 10.2 Schumann, *Requiem für Mignon* **op.98(b), Directional Reading**

Schumann's *Requiem für Mignon*

Relating this controversy to the dramatization of dialogue lends credence to the directional reading. Table 10.2 summarizes the tonal scheme in relation to the text. On the largest scale, it becomes clear that the progression from C minor to F major precisely articulates the text's trajectory from mourning to overcoming: the categorical establishment of F as tonic is reserved for the final chorus and the setting of 'Kinder! eilet ins Leben hinan'. Moreover, the process of negotiation through which the children are revitalized is underpinned by a subtle and ongoing negotiation of tonal priority, involving the continuous reorientation around one of the two tonal poles. The chorus, in short, convey a tonal, as well as a textual, teleology, whereas the children are, until the closing stages, tonally, as well as emotionally, retrospective. The first intimation of this comes at the start of section three, bar 51, where the initial attempt of the chorus to comfort the children, commencing with the words 'seht die mächtigen Flügel doch an' ('see the powerful wings'), is marked by a shift from C minor to C major. The change is more than a simple matter of word painting by modal mixture: rather, this is the first point at which the dominant potential of C, as a major rather than a minor triad, is activated.

At each subsequent stage of the process, the chorus' pleadings push increasingly towards the tonicization of F, while the children insistently pull the music back towards the orbit of C minor. Thus, C minor is reasserted at bar 90 with the words 'Ach! die Flügel heben sie nicht', and the ensuing dialogue culminates, in bars 113 to 125, with a preparation of F major in the chorus pitted against the *Knaben* insinuating F minor. The chorale setting of 'In euch lebe die bildende Kraft' at bar 126 then clearly tonicizes F major; however the section is not tonally closed, modulating to B flat major by bar 165, after which the children enter in G minor, again returning the music to a relation of C minor. The end of section four brings the tonal, as well as the textual, dialogue to a point of summation: the children's inclination towards G minor is twice subsumed into the cadential motion of the chorus towards F. Tonally, as well as dramatically, the bass solo commencing section five has a cathartic function. Its tentative tonicization of C major is confirmed, at bar 252, by the children, with the words 'Auf! wir kehren ins Leben zurück!' There is a twofold unravelling of tonal process here. First, the opposition of chorus and children disappears: they are now tonally in agreement, thereafter cooperating in the dominant preparation of F as the *Schlußchor* approaches. Second, at bar 252 the children participate for the first time in dispelling C minor, and in so-doing, in reinterpreting C as part of the F major *Ursatz*.

Table 10.2 Schumann, *Requiem für Mignon*, Text and Outline of Key Scheme

Text	Keys	Bars
No. 1 Chorus		
Whom do you bring to our silent company?	C minor	1
Soprano 1, 2; Alto 1, 2		
A tired playmate we bring to you;	G minor	7
Here let her stay and rest,		
Until joyful siblings in Heaven		
Shall wake her once more!	G minor	14
Chorus		
Child so young, in our circle, be welcome!	E flat major	15
Be welcome in sorrow!		
May neither boy nor girl follow you!		
May only old age proceed eagerly,		
Calmly to this silent hall,		
And may the dear child rest in solemn company!	E flat major	37
No.2 Soprano 1, alto 1		
Oh! How reluctantly we brought her here!	C minor	38
Here she must stay!		
Let us stay too,		
Let us weep by her coffin!		
No.3 Chorus		
Look at the powerful wings!	C major	51
See the light pure robe!		
See the golden band gleaming in her hair:	(E major)	63
See the beauty and grace of her repose!		
Look at the powerful wings!	C major	71
See the beauty and grace of her repose!		
See the light, unspotted robe!		
See the powerful wings!		
Soprano 1 solo		
Oh! The wings do not raise her up;	C minor	90
Chorus		
See the light, unspotted robe!		
Soprano 2 solo Her robe no longer dances in easy play;		
Chorus See!		

Soprano 2 solo No longer!		
Chorus See the golden band gleaming in her hair!		97
Soprano 1, 2 soli When we crowned her head with roses Her gaze was sweet and friendly to us.	(A flat major)	
Chorus See the beauty of her repose!		
Soprano 1, 2 soli Her gaze was sweet and friendly to us.		
Chorus Yet look at the wings!	C as V of F major	111
Soprano 1 solo Oh! The wings do not raise her up!		
Chorus Look at the powerful wings!		
Soprano 2 solo Oh! The wings do not raise her up!		
Chorus Look up with the eyes of the spirit!	C as V of F major	119
No.4 Chorus May there dwell in you the power to transport That which is finest, loveliest in life, up beyond the stars	F major B flat major	126 165
Soprano 1, 2 soli; alto 1 solo On earth she is lost to us now	G minor	166
Chorus Look up!		
Soprano 1,2 soli; alto 1 solo She walks in the gardens no more		
Chorus Look up!		
Soprano 1,2 soli; alto 1 solo On earth she is lost to us now		
Chorus With the eyes of the spirit!	F major re-asserted	179
Soprano 1,2 soli On earth she is lost to us now, She walks in the gardens no more		

Chorus Look up!

Soprano 1,2 soli
She gathers flowers of the meadow no more.

Chorus Look up!

Soprano 2 solo Let us weep!

Chorus Look up!

Alto 1 solo We leave her here!

Chorus Look up!

Soprano 1, 2 soli
Let us weep! We leave her here!

Chorus Look up with the eyes of the spirit!	F major established	207-14
Soprano 1, 2 soli (simultaneously) Let us weep and stay with her!	(G minor)	
Soprano 1, 2 soli Let us weep and stay with her!		
Chorus (simultaneously) Look up!	F major	219-30
No.5 Bass solo Children, return to life! Your tears shall be dried in the freshness of the air Which plays around the meandering water. Retreat from the night!	C major	251
Daylight, joy and continuity are the fate of the living.	G major	251
Soprano 1,2 soli; alto 1,2 soli We rise and return to life again!	C major	252
May the day shall give us labour and joy, Until the evening brings repose,	(E minor)	264-65
Soprano 1 solo And sleep gives refreshment		
Chorus (soprano only) And sleep gives refreshment		

Soprano 1 solo And sleep gives refreshment		
Chorus (soprano 1,2; alto 1) And sleep gives refreshment	C as V of F major	271-75
No. 6 Chorus Children, hurry back to life! And may love dressed in pure robes of beauty Meet you with its divine gaze	F major	276
And the crown of immortality! Children! hurry back to life! And may love dressed in pure robes of beauty Meet you with its divine gaze And the crown of immortality! Children, hasten back to life And may love dressed in pure robes of beauty Meet you with its divine gaze.	E flat major: (reminiscence of C/c complex)	302
Soprano 1, 2 soli We rise and return to life again!		
Chorus (simultaneously) And the crown of immortality.		
Chorus Children, hurry back to life! Up!	F major	378-94

The conventional Schenkerian reading fails to capture this process. Its insistence on a universal governing tonic ignores the competition between tonal polarities that is absolutely central to Schumann's articulation of the text. If, however, we understand the structure as a dialogue between two possible tonics, then this relationship becomes apparent. The ambiguity of function that mediates the opposition – the uncertainty as to whether C is I or V, or conversely whether F is I or IV – acts as a simple but structurally potent means of generating musical form from an analogy between tonal conflict and textual dialogue. Example 10.3 clarifies this, overlaying key elements of the text onto the reading proposed in example 10.2. Pursuing the reductive approach in this way also uncovers compelling connections between text setting and long-range linear progressions. Note, for example, that the *Kopfton* degree 3 of the F major fundamental line is reached in bar 132 with the word 'Kraft', and that this is later taken up and resolved via degree 2 onto degree 1, in the same register, at two crucial moments: the end of section four, where the chorus' 'Schaut hinan' subsumes the children's 'laßt uns weinen und bei ihr bleiben'; and in the final cadence of the piece. The message of *Bildung* is therefore closely bound up with the inception and fulfilment of an F major *Urlinie*; Schumann reserves its explicit formulation for junctures at which the text most clearly expresses this goal.

This structure is augmented by some striking medium-range strategies, which example 10.3 brings sharply into relief. In bars 63 to 66, for example, the chorus' words 'wie blinkt die gold'ne Binde vom Haupt' ('See the golden band gleaming in her hair') are underscored by a modulation to E major. In the subsequent C minor passage beginning at bar 90, Schumann balances this with a digression to A flat, setting the children's words 'Als wir mit Rosen kränzten ihr Haupt' ('When we crowned her head with roses') in bars 101 to 104. The tonal plan of section three thus opposes the upper third C-E with the lower third C-A flat. The mediant rise in the major signifies the chorus' optimism, the sub-mediant fall in the minor the children's nostalgia, but both respond to complementary images in the text ('golden band [...] on her head'; 'crowned her head with roses'). No less remarkable is the passing reference to E flat major at the first statement of the word 'Unsterblichkeit' ('immortality') in the *Schlußchor* at bar 302. This is the last residue of the C minor *Ursatz*, now embedded within a secure prolongation of F major, as a neighbour-note formation around B flat. The tonal metaphor is clear: C minor as tonic signifies mourning; the relative major of C, within a prolongation of F, signifies immortality.

Example 10.3 Schumann, *Requiem für Mignon* op.98(b), Directional Reading with Text Overlaid

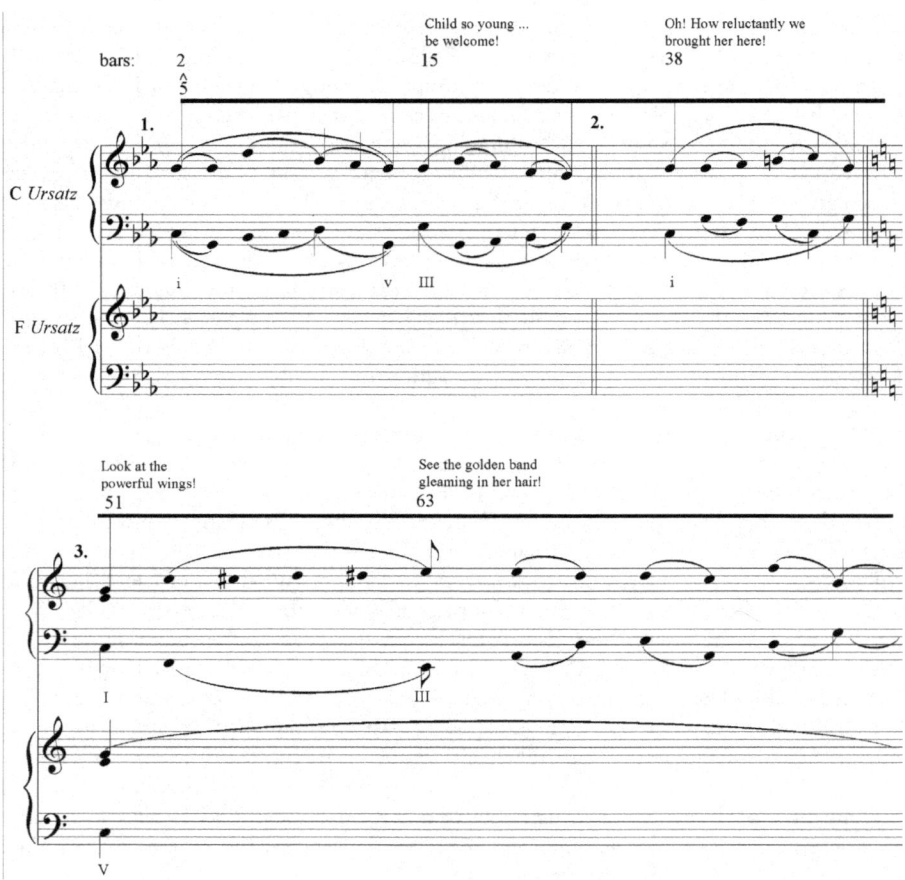

Schumann's *Requiem für Mignon*

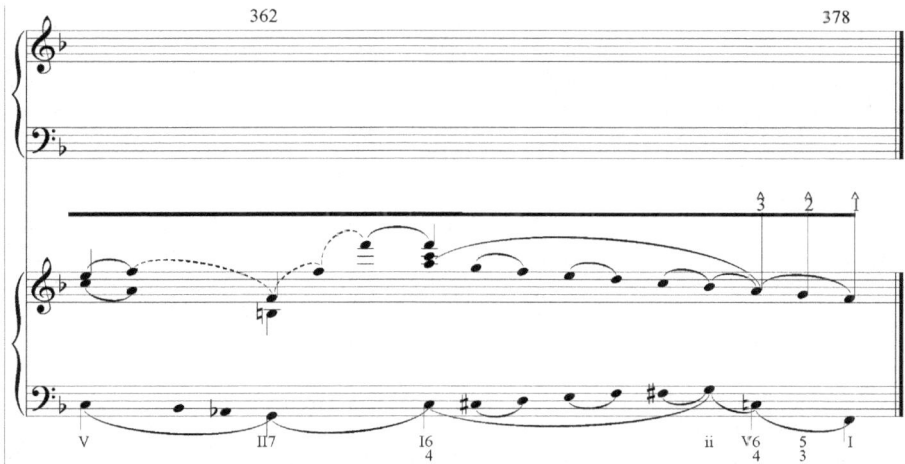

The *Requiem* also discloses a number of thematic relationships, which contribute to the dramatization of dialogue. Example 10.4 traces some of the work's significant thematic connections, together with the text they express. Several strands of thematic narrative are evident. The figure labelled 'a' in example 10.4 generates a series of variants that articulate the unfolding dialogue. It forms, for instance, the kernel of the motive introduced in section four with the words 'die, das Schönste', which is the immediate continuation of 'In euch lebe die bildende Kraft'. Subsequent deployment of this motive reflects the negotiation between children and chorus. In bars 215 to 222 the theme is taken up by the *Knaben*, in G minor, with the words 'Laßt uns weinen'. The thematic response to this comes in the bass solo at the start of section five: the motive, now in C major, forms the starting point for the setting of 'Kinder, kehret ins leben zurück', and a final minor variant in the orchestra in bars 239 to 240 is answered by the bass with the words 'Entflieht der Nacht'. The dramatic function of this theme turns on its tonal context: it is presented in a major key when associated with the chorus, and in a minor key when associated with the children. It is significant, therefore, that the children's final entry in the piece – the reassertion of the words 'Auf! wir kehren ins Leben zurück' in bars 355 to 359 – comprises an inversion of the idea, now clearly emphasizing F major. The reconciliation of chorus and children in the *Schlußchor* provokes a change in the children's approach to this material, reflected both in the inversion of interval contour and in the reconciliation of its tonal context with that of the chorus.

Motive 'a', moreover, undergoes a series of transformations prior to its incarnation in section four, which also have a bearing on how we understand the relationship between text and structure. It informs, for example, the material setting 'Seht die mächtigen

Flügel doch an' at bar 51. In fact, the whole of this phrase turns out to be a variant of the inversion of the theme established in section four, as example 10.4 shows, in which 'a' is embedded. And since this figure is in itself an elaboration of 'a' as it occurs in section one, we can posit a thematic narrative spanning the entire work, which begins at 'Erstling der Jugend' in section one, and ends with the children's concluding entry on 'Auf! wir kehren ins Leben zurück' in the *Schlußchor*. Schumann, in other words, deploys a thematic strategy as a means of reinforcing crucial textual connections. Motive 'a' begins its life as a choral expression of consolation, at the words 'Jugend', 'mit Trauer', 'dir folge' and 'kein Knabe'. It then becomes affiliated, at 'Seht die mächtigen Flügel doch an', with the chorus' message of transcendence, a function given further emphasis by its role at the start of section four. The transformation of this variant into 'Auf! wir kehren ins Leben zurück' in section six makes a direct link between the two dialogic poles of the text: once the children accept the message imputed by the chorus, they can also accept its associated thematic material.

This brief analysis by no means exhausts the work's structural and textual relationships. Suggestive thematic parallels can also be traced between the opening, 'Wen bringt ihr uns zur stillen Gesellschaft', and the children's 'Ach! die Flügel heben sie nicht' at bar 90, and between the subsidiary material setting 'Seht die mächtigen Flügel doch an' in E major in bars 63 to 64 and underpinning 'Kinder! eilet ins leben hinan' leading into the perfect cadence at the end of the *Schlußchor*, bars 371 to 378. And this is to say nothing of the way the musical realization of dialogue relates to the text's numerous more specific binary oppositions: life/death, light/dark, above/below, heaven/earth, and so forth.

It does, however, reveal enough to compel a qualification of Daverio's view of the piece. It is not only, as Nicholas Boyle has pointed out, that the role of *Bildung* in *Wilhelm Meister* may not be as central as has been frequently assumed; this notion may have informed Schumann's reading of Goethe, even if it was not pervasive for Goethe himself.[21] The main point of contention resides in the way the text generates musical structure. If the *Requiem* truly embodies the concept of music as literature, then this is not simply a matter of giving cosmetic musical expression to literary meaning; it requires a wholesale absorption of textual structure into musical form, not only in the sense of overall architecture, but also in the material processes by means of which that architecture is sustained. In the *Requiem*, the key to this is an understanding of the dramatization of dialogue, both in terms of how its central opposition is maintained, and of how it is resolved, in quasi-dialectical fashion, at the end.

---

[21] '[I]t is doubtful whether [...] Goethe's novel can properly be called a *Bildungsroman*: it is, like everything of worth that Goethe wrote, both too personal and too philosophical to be caught in the terminology of genres and movements and cultural history.' See Nicholas Boyle, *Goethe: The Poet and the Age*, 2 (Oxford 2000), p.411.

Example 10.4 Schumann, *Requiem für Mignon* op.98(b), Thematic Relationships

IV

What, finally, are the consequences of this analysis for the general reappraisal of Schumann's oeuvre? Primarily, it seems clear that the conviction, quoting Daverio again, 'that music should be imbued with the same intellectual substance as literature' is keenly at work in this piece. Schumann's response to the text goes far beyond allowing its literal progress to dictate the form, or the simple selection of material appropriate to the sense of the words. Rather, essential structural features of Goethe's text generate analogous musical processes informing every level of the music's structure. On the largest scale, the progression from mourning to awakening finds a parallel in the concept of the progressive tonal scheme. The middleground negotiation of functional priority that this strategy engenders is then manipulated as a tonal metaphor for the process of persuasion that drives the overall narrative trajectory. This is furthermore overlaid with a web of thematic relationships, which do not act leitmotivically, as melodic signs corresponding to aspects of the text, but instead participate in a continuous process of transformation that altogether reflects the text's narrative. Many other factors are also involved, which have not been considered here. The distribution of topics and figures feeds into the articulation of dialogue in a similar sense; the interaction of topic and tonality is particularly suggestive. The fact that Schumann begins the opening funeral march in C minor, for example, links it with baroque practice, which frequently associated that key with public mourning (the final sarabandes of Bach's Matthew and John Passions are obvious examples), as well as Mozart's masonic music.[22]

We are, as a result, entirely justified in regarding the major choral and dramatic works as a culmination of Schumann's art. The cross-fertilization of music and literature finds its most expansive expression in this music: tendencies evident in the early piano pieces and song cycles are here applied on the largest scale, and with complex results. *Das Paradies und die Peri*, *Faust* and *Genoveva* are no less sophisticated; indeed, the *Requiem* might be understood as embodying in a more condensed form techniques applied most substantially in the literary operas and oratorios. In this sense, Schumann's defining achievement is perhaps the *Szenen aus Goethes Faust*, as the largest single encapsulation of his literary ambitions.

Returning to the broader questions of reception history posed at the start, it seems clear that the historicism engendered in Daverio's view is at once vital and inadequate. No picture of Schumann's music can be complete without an understanding of its literary dimension, not only because it formed an essential part of his aesthetics, but also

---

[22] On this matter, see Rita Steblin, *A History of Key Characteristics in the Eighteenth and Early Nineteenth Centuries* (Michigan 1983). I am grateful to Amanda Glauert for pointing out the Mozartian relationship here.

because it relates the music to the early circumstances of its reception. If criticism neglects this context, then an incomplete frame of reference will inevitably result. At the same time, we cannot pursue these factors into the musical material without some kind of analytical method, and this necessitates recourse to techniques that have little to do with historical context. The most we can hope for, in other words, is historically informed analysis; an entirely relativist approach, which seeks to derive an understanding of music purely from its historical circumstances, denies music the persistent aesthetic presence it undeniable possesses, and ultimately eliminates the musical work as a legitimate musicological category. *Pace* certain recent scholarly developments (I think especially of Beate Perrey's work on *Dichterliebe*), we do not have to travel along the path of rigorously appropriating literary critical models in order to defend against this tendency in Schumann's case (and I am aware that my appeal to the dialogical structure of the *Requiem* perhaps tacitly invokes Bakhtin).[23] The subtleties of Schumann's engagement with his literary sources are readily accessible via a sensitive comparison of text, structure and material process. Substantial analyses of the major dramatic works making such a comparison remain to be undertaken, and would greatly enhance our understanding of Schumann's oeuvre in general

---

[23] See Beate Perry, *Schumann's Dichterliebe and Early Romantic Poetics* (Cambridge: CUP, 2003).

11 | Mignon's Exequies and Aesthetic Reflections of the Liturgy in Music
Adolf Nowak

In Mignon's exequies – *Wilhelm Meisters Lehrjahre*, Book VIII, Chapter Eight – art and the liturgy are brought into a relationship which can be considered paradigmatic of the nineteenth century: the liturgy was understood as an aesthetic phenomenon and was newly constructed in the context of an artistic work. Involvement in a traditional form of the liturgy was conceived as a fundamentally aesthetic cult. With it the poetic form of the liturgy claimed the same seriousness as the traditionally religious. The aesthetically fulfilled time was granted 'a sacred seriousness', which alone could give life eternity.[1] The following essay will present first an interpretation of Goethe's text from the viewpoint of an aesthetic reflection of the liturgy. Secondly it will be shown how, in settings of Mignon's exequies, the Goethean idea of a poetic liturgy is realized, or more exactly, to what extent this idea was first realized through these settings. Thirdly, it should at least become clear, in outline, how the idea of a poetic liturgy over and beyond Mignon's exequies influenced the poetic and musical creativity in the nineteenth-century.

I

Chapter Eight, Book VIII of the *Lehrjahre* is built on the liturgical model: double-choir motet and sermon; after an introductory description sung and spoken text are repeated verbatim. This model stems from the tradition of the Protestant funeral ceremony, a tradition which, from 1600 to 1800 and still in some isolated instances in the 1900s, is

---

[1] Johann Wolfgang von Goethe: *Wilhelm Meisters Lehrjahre* [referred to in further references as *Lehrjahre* with the page number] in *Hamburger Ausgabe* in 14 volumes, ed. Erich Trunz, special Munich edition [referred to as *HA* with volume and page numbers], vol.7, p.578.

well documented through the printed editions of 'funeral sermons' and burial-settings.[2] However, in the context of the novel this model was essentially changed and subjected to a firm aesthetic intention: in the face of Mignon's death the arts were called upon to transform the transitory to permanency.[3] Pictures illustrating the basic relations of life (mother and child, bride and bridgroom), recorded 'in reinen architektonischen Verhältnissen'[4], hang on the walls of the 'Saal der Vergangenheit', the hall of the past. These pictures let permanence through art be immediately experienced: ' "Nichts ist vergänglich", sagt Wilhelm, als der eine, der genießt und zuschaut.'[5] The corpse which is laid out on the sarcophagus is presented by the Abbé as a work of art: 'Treten Sie näher, meine Freunde, und sehen Sie das Wunder der Kunst und der Sorgfalt.'[6] Through the medical art of embalmment it is possible 'den Körper zu erhalten und ihn der Vergänglichkeit zu entziehen' (to preserve her body and save it from decay). And if the art of medicine 'den scheidenden Geist nicht zu fesseln vermochte',[7] then the poetic-musical funeral ceremony is erected as a lasting memorial. Of the 'schönen Gebilde der Vergangenheit', the 'beauteous image of the past', it is subsequently said: 'hier im Marmor ruht es unverzehrt', in accordance with the lasting nature of the spatial arts; 'auch in euren Herzen lebt es, wirkt es fort', in accordance with the immediacy of the temporal, namely the spoken and tonal arts.[8]

In Hegel's aesthetics periods are distinguished by their relationship to and perception of death. In Mignon's exequies conceptions of death are brought together which Hegel distinguishes as Egyptian, Greek and Christian ideas. In the Egyptian culture the inner being is established, for the first time, as the opposite to the immediacy of being. To be

---

[2] Wolfgang Reich, *Threnodiae sacrae. Beerdigungskompositionen aus gedruckten Leichenpredigten des 16. und 17. Jahrhunderts*, Das Erbe deutscher Musik, 79 (Wiesbaden, 1975).

[3] Georg Wilhelm Friedrich Hegel: *Ästhetik*, ed. by Friedrich Bassenge (Frankfurt am Main, 1967), 1, p.165: 'Was in der Natur vorübereilt, befestigt die Kunst zur Dauer'. Vom 'Saal der Vergangenheit' mit seinen Bogen und Pfeilern, Sarkophagen und Gefäßen, Einfassungen und Gemälden, heißt es, daß der Eintretende 'durch die zusammentreffende Kunst erst erfuhr, was der Mensch sei und was er sein könne' (*Lehrjahre*, p.540). 'Whatever rushes by in nature is made permanent in art. Of the "Hall of the Past" with its vaults and pillars, sarcophagi and vessels, frames and paintings, it is said that the one who enters it "discovers, through the coinciding arts, for the first time, what man is and what he can be" '.

[4] *Lehrjahre*, p.540 'in pure architectonic relationships'.

[5] ibid., pp.540 and 541. 'Nothing is ephemeral', says Wilhelm, 'but the one who enjoys and sees'.

[6] ibid., p.577. 'Draw near, my friends, and observe the wonders of art and artiface.'

[7] ibid., p.576f. 'could not stop her spirit from departing'.

[8] ibid., p.578. 'here in marble it rests, unconsumed' [...] also in your hearts it lives and works'. 'Der Saal der Vergangenheit ist mit Emporen ausgestattet, auf denen "die Chöre der Sänger verborgen stehen." ' The "Hall of the Past" is equipped with a gallery, in which "the chorus of singers stand concealed" ' (*Lehrjahre*, p.542f.).

precise, it is seen as the negation of life, as that which is dead. The dead gains the content of the living. The honour of the dead people is, according to this conception, not the burial, but the perennial preservation of the corpse. The pyramids, produced through art, are enormous crystals, which enfold an inner reality which is separated from its purely natural form. The Christian conception opposes this captivity of ossification with the process: decay and new life, destruction and reconciliation of the temporal and the infinite, a process in which 'the pain of negation' emerges as a fundamental moment.[9] Christianity has, therefore, a greater affinity to the art forms, in which the characteristics of time – transience, decay, transformation – emerge. The moment of negation, on which the resurrection theory as a negation of the negative can be based, is largely eliminated from Goethe's text. No thought of the destruction of the world ('solvet saeclum in favilla', *Dies irae*, Stanza 1) and of the remorsefulness of the heart ('cor contritum quasi cinis', *Dies irae*, Stanza 17). This filtering out of decline and guilt could first correspond to the rite accepted in the 1500s as that for the burial of dependent children. This rite is without prayers of intercession and without a mass: in addition to that, this omission is approaching the Protestant burial liturgy, in which the notion of the Last Judgement and prayers for the soul's intentions completely yielded to the proclamation of the resurrection.

The refusal to articulate this negativity has its real basis in the aesthetic reception of classical symbols of life and death. In place of the drastic portrayal of negativity embodied by the skeleton with its scythe, comes the friendly guardian spirit with inverted torch. In memory of Lessing's treatise, *Wie die Alten den Tod gebildet* (How death was portrayed by antiquity, 1769), Goethe wrote in Part Two, Book Eight of his autobiography, *Dichtung und Wahrheit*:

> Am meisten entzückte uns die Schönheit jenes Gedankens, dass die Alten den Tod als den Bruder des Schlafs anerkannt, und beide, wie es Menächmen geziemt, zum Verwechseln gleich gebildet. Hier konnten wir nun erst den Triumph des Schönen höchlich feiern.[10]

For this change from death to life we can recall the words which can be read on the marble statue in the hall of the past: 'Gedenke zu leben' in contrast to the famous

---

[9] Hegel, *Ästhetik*, vol.1, p.346f and p.503.

[10] *HA* 9, p.316f. 'We were particularly charmed by the beautiful idea that the ancients acknowledged Death as the brother of Sleep and depicted both so identically, as befits twins, that they are easily confused. Only now could we really celebrate the triumph of beauty […] and in the realm of art, relegate ugliness of every kind, which is in any case not to be driven out of the world, to the level of the laughable.'

'memento mori'.[11] In *Hermann und Dorothea* (the epic in hexameters of 1797) the Pfarrer says of the wise man and the pious man: 'Beiden wird zum Leben der Tod'.[12] The lament of the choir for Euphorion (*Faust II*, Act III, Scene 'Schattiger Hain') closes with the hint of death into life: 'Denn der Boden zeugt sie wieder', 'For the ground generates them again'; the final chorus of Mignon's exequies moves in the same direction: 'schreitet, schreitet ins Leben zurück', 'return to life'.[13]

In Mignon's exequies the transformation of death into life begins with discovery of beauty, first with the outward glance at the 'beautiful portrayal of the past', then in the inward directed gaze of the 'formative power', in accordance with the words of the choir, '[...]in euch lebe die bildende Kraft, die das Schönste, das Höchste hinauf, über die Sterne das Leben trägt'.[14] As Herder explains in *Kalligone*, the beautiful can also be called 'das Bildende', the formative. The exact same concept in art could be 'die Tendenz [...] die Menschheit in ihrem ganzen Umfange auszubilden', namely to develop all parts of the personality: senses, powers of the imagination, wit, understanding and sociability.[15] The formative force developed in and through art, enables life – in the words of the choir – to transcend the celestial bodies and their eternal order.

In contrast to Mignon's strophic verses the Abbé's accompanying ceremony is in prose cantos. It is a rhythmical speech, appearing in print as continuous text, which, however, allows for division into verses, as in the free rhythm of the *Prometheus* drama and in the free-rhythmical poem, *Harzreise im Winter*. It is rhythmical prose like that of the first edition of *Iphigenie* and *Proserpina* which were printed as prose in 1778 and then, in Goethe's *Schriften* of 1787, were arranged in free rhythm.[16]

In traditional requiems the retention of liturgical relationships over many generations is experienced as a comfort in the face of the transience of life; hence the preservation of traditional texts and settings, hence the quotation of liturgical music in new compositions, for example, the 'tonus peregrinus' in 'Te decet hymnus' in Mozart's

---

[11] *Lehrjahre*, p.540. On a splendid sarcophagus is the picture of the Uncle, in which he who has established the hall of the past holds up a scroll in such a way that one can comfortably read the words 'Gedenke zu leben', 'Remember to live'.

[12] *HA* 2, p.504. 'For both death becomes life.'

[13] See Erich Trunz's commentary, *HA* 3, p.692.

[14] *Lehrjahre*, p.575. '[...] May there dwell in you the formative power, that carries what is finest, loveliest in life, up beyond the stars.'

[15] Johann Gottfried Herder: *Kalligone* (1800) in *Sämtliche Werke*, ed. Bernhard Suphan (Berlin, 1877ff), 22, p.308. 'the tendency [...] to cultivate humanity to its full potential'.

[16] Compare Trunz in *HA* 4, p.665f. and p.668; according to Trunz, rhythmic prose is accounted for much more in the 1800s, for example, Klopstock, *Der Tod Adams* (1757), Geßner *Idyllen* (1756) and Goethe's Ossian translation in *Werther* (*HA* 6, 108, 5ff.).

Requiem or the quotation from the choral 'Herzlich tut mich verlangen nach einem sel'gen End', 'I have a heartfelt longing to reach my blissful goal', in the same position in the text of Abbé Vogler's *Requiem*, which dates from 1809. In its departure from its religious origins and in its accentuation of symbols of life and artistic value, the poetic requiem contains, nevertheless, certain links with the liturgical tradition. The relationship, mentioned above, with the rite used for the burial of dependent children – where any thoughts of judgement and prayers of intercession are omitted – is likely to be supported through the association with the resurrection of the weary playmate and also through association of the 'mächtigen Flügel', powerful wings, with Psalm 102,5: 'renovabitur ut aquilae juventus tua', 'your youth will be renewed like that of the eagle.' Above all it is the form of the antiphonal chant between boys' voices and the two choirs in a type of ritual prosody, an anchoring which is made plain in the liturgical tradition. The double-choir song in the funeral motet has been persistently cultivated.[17]

Mignon's exequies can, with regard to their liturgical character of the motets and sermons – be linked back to the tradition of funeral sermons which were published with musical inserts. In *Wilhelm Meisters Lehrjahre*, 'Bekenntnisse einer schönen Seele', the choral song is described in a way, which links it to the musical-liturgical discourse, 'Cur cantatur', according to which singing, through its *suavitas* and *dulcedo*, is more effective than the word alone; and according to which especially the melody of the Psalm indicates the presence on earth of the future eternal life: 'perpetuam dei laudem demonstrat', 'quodammodo angelis sociatur'.[18] 'Er ließ', according to Goethe, the creator of the 'Hall of the Past', 'durch das indes verstärkte und im stillen noch mehr geübte Chor uns vier- und achtstimmige Gesänge vortragen, die uns, ich darf wohl sagen, wirklich einen Vorschmack der Seligkeit gaben.'[19]

---

[17] Only to name the most famous: the Funeral Motets and the Canticum Simeonis in Heinrich Schütz *Musikalischen Exequien*, Motets from the Altbach Archive (ed. Max Schneider as vol. 1 in the series *Erbe deutscher Musik*, Leipzig 1935) and J.S.Bach's *Motets* BWV 225, 226, 228 and 229. See also in the above-named volume (footnote 2) the compositions of Sebastien Knüpfer (Nr.27), Johann Schelle (Nr. 28) and Andreas Scharmann (Nr.30, in this funeral lament the second choir is accompanied by a violin ensemble).

[18] Anders Ekenberg, *Cur cantatur? Die Funktionen des liturgischen Gesanges nach den Autoren der Karolingerzeit* (Stockholm, 1987), chapter 4B.

[19] 'Bekenntnisse einer schönen Seele', in: *Lehrjahre*, p.410. 'He had then', according to Goethe, 'four- and eight-part motets performed by the same choir, now increased in size and profiting from further practice, and this, I may well say, gave us all a foretaste of heaven.' The passage continues, 'Ich hatte bisher nur den frommen Gesang gekannt, in welchem gute Seelen oft mit heiserer Kehle, wie die Waldvöglein Gott zu loben glauben, weil sie sich selbst eine angenehme Empfindung machen; dann die eitle Musik der Konzerte, in denen man allenfalls zur Bewunderung eines Talents, selten aber auch nur zu einem vorübergehenden Vergnügen hingerissen wird. Nun vernahm ich eine Musik, aus dem tiefsten Sinne der trefflichsten

Of the closing words of the exequies song, – 'Nehmet den heiligen Ernst mit hinaus, denn der Ernst, der heilige, macht allein das Leben zur Ewigkeit' – Goethe writes:

> Diese Worte der Jünglinge, in die der unsichtbare Chor einstimmt, werden von den Anwesenden nicht mehr vernommen; aus den nunmehr wiederkehrenden Schmerzen und Betrachtungen wünschten se sich 'sehnlich [...] in jenes Element wieder zurück'.[20]

The liturgical song is experienced not so much as reinforcement of the returning sorrow and meditations, but as something in its own right, a work of art, according to its own laws, whose short period of fulfilled time, as an allegory of eternity, a 'foretaste of heaven', is striven for.[21]

---

menschlichen Naturen entsprungen, die durch bestimmte und geübte Organe in harmonischer Einheit wieder zum tiefsten, besten Sinne des Menschen sprach und ihn wirklich in diesem Augenblicke seine Gottähnlichkeit lebhaft empfinden ließ. Alles waren lateinische geistliche Gesänge, die sich wie Juwelen in dem goldenen Ringe einer gesitteten weltlichen Gesellschaft ausnahmen und mich, ohne Anforderung einer sogenannten Erbauung auf das geistigste erhoben und glücklich machten.' 'So far I had only been acquainted with hymn-singing, in which pious souls, often with hoarse throats, believe they are like birds of the forest singing praises to God, because of the pleasant feeling it gives them, or with the vanity of concert music that provokes admiration for the talents of the performer, but rarely provides even passing pleasure. But now I heard music issuing from the richest depths of noble, human hearts, through practiced organs and in perfect harmony, speaking to the very best in us and making us fully aware of our godlikeness. These were sacred all religious songs in Latin which stood out like jewels in the golden ring of this cultured, secular society. I was spiritually uplifted and made happy by them, without laying any claim to so-called spiritual edification.'

[20] *Lehrjahre*, p.578. 'Take this holy solemnity away with you, for it is sacred, it alone transforms life into eternity'[...] 'These words of the youths, in which the invisible choir joins, are no longer heard by those present. From the sorrow and contemplations they 'longed to return [...] to what they had left'.

[21] For discussion of this 'foretaste of Heaven' see Zelter's letter to Goethe, 4 May 1814. About the fulfilled moment in music: 'Fürwahr, die Musik füllt, in jenem Betracht, den Augenblick am entschiedensten, es sei nun, daß sie in dem ruhigen Geiste Ehrfurcht und Anbetung erzege oder die beweglichen Sinne zu tanzendem Jubel hervorrufe.' 'Indeed, from this point of view, music fills up the present moment more decisively than anything else, whether it awakens in the tranquil mind reverence and worship, or whether it summons the active senses to dance and celebration.' (Goethe to Zelter, 19 October 1829). 'Glücklicherweise ist dein Talent-Charakter auf den Ton, d.h. auf den Augenblick angewiesen. Da nun eine Folge von konsequenten Augenblicken immer eine Art von Ewigkeit selbst ist, so war dir gegeben, im Vorübergehenden stets beständig zu sein und also mir sowohl als Hegels Geist, insofern ich ihn verstehe, völlig genug zu tun.' 'Fortunately, your individual gift is bound up with sound, namely with the moment. Now, as a series of consecutive moments is always a kind of eternity in itself, you have been able to remain constant in the midst of what is transitory and thus to satisfy me and, in so far as I understand it, also Hegel's spirit.' (Goethe to Zelter, 11 March 1832).

II

The counterpart, in instrumental music, to the aesthetic reflection of the liturgy in poetry might be the reflection of liturgical song with purely instrumental means. The second movement, Allegretto, of Beethoven's seventh symphony (which dates from 1811-1812) is based upon a theme, which was perceived as a funeral march, and which with good reason can be seen as related to a rhythmical model of the sung litany.[22] The litany song, performed as a folk-like antiphonal prayer in the simplest formulation, suggests church music and procession; the funeral march suggests a particular instance of procession. If this symphonic movement of Beethoven's could be interpreted by Arnold Schering in relation to Mignon's exequies, that does not have to mean, as Schering claimed, that the poetry formed the model for the composition,[23] it can also mean, that in the poetry and in the composition a similar liturgy is reflected. In the overall structure of the composition the theme (bars 3-36) is followed by three variations in the style of cantus-firmus variations, then a middle section on A major, whose melody is related to that of the trio, no.13, 'Euch werde Lohn in bessern Welten' from Act Two of *Fidelio*, with which hope of a better world beyond[24] is articulated. The theme is taken up again in a further variation and fugue, whereupon the A major section is recapitulated and finally the march-theme is heard in rhythmic diminution. The cantus firmus variations may be seen as an artificial remodel of an antiphonal song, whose contrasting middle section can act as words of a living reminder, 'als wir mit Rosen kränzten ihr Haupt' and of the transcendant hope, 'Schaut mit den Augen des Geistes hinan'.

How is the aesthetic reflection of the liturgy realized in settings of the poem, which structures and content are first made possible through composition? In Schumann's *Requiem für Mignon* for choir, solo voices and orchestra, op.98b,[25] the phrase 'bildende Kraft' is set as a hymn 'Maestoso' in the middle section and is flanked by sentences, in which the youths' lament, 'Ach die Flügel erheben sie nicht', 'Aber ach, wir vermissen

---

[22] Wolfgang Osthoff, 'Zum Vorstellungsgehalt des Allegretto in Beethovens 7. Symphony', in: *Archiv für Musikwissenschaft* 34 (1977), pp.159-79.

[23] Arnold Schering, *Beethoven und die Dichtung* (Berlin, 1936), interpreted the complete seventh symphony in relation to scenes from Goethe's *Wilhelm Meisters Lehrjahre* (p.216f.), and the second movement, Allegretto, in relation to the *Requiem für Mignon*.

[24] Osthoff, *Zum Vorstellungsgehalt des Allegretto in Beethovens 7. Symphonie*, with reference to Karl Nef, *Die neuen Sinfonien Beethovens* (Leipzig, 1928), p.218.

[25] Robert Schumann, *Lieder, Gesänge und Requiem für Mignon aus Goethes 'Wilhelm Meister'*, composed in the summer of 1849, published in 1851 as op.98a: *Die Lieder Mignons, des Harfners und Philinens* for solo voice with piano accompaniment, and op.98b: *Requiem für Mignon* for choir, soloists and orchestra.

sie hier' are answered by the cries of the chorus, the call of the second chorus on one side 'Seht die mächtigen Flügel doch an', and the call of the third verse on the other hand, from which the central phrase in hymnic form is taken. The musical form created by Schumann is fundamentally different from the antiphonal song in strophic form, suggested by the form of the text. Schumann's arrangement:

1.	Choir – Soloists– Choir	
2.	Lament – two sopranos:	'Oh, how reluctantly'
3.	Choir	'Look at the powerful wings'
	Lament and choral acclamations	'Oh, the wings do not raise her up'
4	Choir: Hymn	'May there dwell in you the formative power'
	Lament and Choral acclamations	'But oh, on earth she is lost to us now'
5.	Bass solo	'Children, return to life'
	Soloists	'We rise and return to life again'
6.	Choir	

At the beginning and at the end of the work there are extensive choir and solo sections, while a close alternation of choir and soloists surrounds the hymn in the middle of the work. This alternation becomes tighter almost to the point of simultaneity, an alternation of that which was kept apart in the stanzas of the text: the lament on the one side and the appeal for hope on the other. The textual structure and the structure which is taken up into the composition, i.e. the alternation of choir and soloists, is made specific through a second structural principle, namely through the relation of the corresponding character sections to each other. The sections characterized by concentrated antiphonal singing encircle the choral movement, no.4. The bass solo, no.5, refers to the solo passage for two sopranos, no.2. The march-like character of the same group in no.5 corresponds to the funeral march of the four soloists in No.1. These central relations are, for their part, penetrated by a further principle, namely that of certain processional thrusts. These thrusts first become clear in the transition between sections; secondly in the acceleration in tempo between sections one to three: Lento maestoso, Un poco piu agitato, Vivace – and in sections four to six: Maestoso ma non troppo lento, Un poco piu allegro. Vivace; thirdly in the handling of the gestic motifs – from lament to appeal – in each of the tight antiphonally structured choral movements.[26] The combination of structural antiphonal singing, predominant relations

---

[26] For further discussion on the 'strömende Entfaltung eines Verlaufs', the 'streaming development of a course', see Friedhelm Krummacher, *Requiem für Mignon: Goethes Worte in Schumanns*

and dynamic processes shows the historical depth of a compositional reflection of the liturgy: firstly the tradition of antiphonal singing is present in the liturgy; secondly, there is the setting of (biblical) prose texts, particularly the tendency to embrace an arched centre in the exequies tradition,[27] thirdly the thematic processes which radiate from instrumental music into the symphonic mass settings.

It corresponds to the dynamic drive of the composition that, for Schumann, musical tropes achieve their meaning less through their presence than through their development. On its first repetition the leading funeral march-motif is subjected to a metrical alteration and harmonic opening to the double dominant. Its meaning does not derive from maintaining the character of a march, it shows itself to be a method of transition to further means of expression of grief: to the choral setting of the greeting (bar 15), then *stringendo* until the lament figure (bar 38: descending triplets in the violins; bar 39: emphasis and catabasis of the soprano, then repeated figures with diminished fifths.) The manner in which it is sung ('einen müden Gespielen bringen wir euch', 'a tired playmate we bring to you'), avoids the persistent march-like quality (of the distinctive anapaests) through the structural asymmetry and through the abandonment and reversal of the anapaests at the word 'himmlisch' (bar 12). In the same way the choral setting 'Erstling der Jugend' is reinforced as such by the trumpets just for two bars; its affirmation is retracted by the prose structuring of the melody. The lament in no. 2, characterized by a persistent use of the motif of the diminished fifth and by the repetition of the opening figure (bars 49 to 50 of the vocal parts, is a repeat of bars 39 to 40 intensified by the use of the diminished fifth). In the third movement the prayer motif is introduced and developed in two ways: first through a series of variations and then (from bar 90) through the contrast of these variations with the gestic lament motif from the second movement. A high point in the development of these variations is formed by the instrumental colour of trombones and harps at the words, 'seht die schöne würdige Ruh' (bar 77ff). Characteristics of the hymn on 'die bildende Kraft', 'the formative power' (no.4) – which likewise only appears, without being sustained – are the a cappella texture and the unison. The following lament, 'Aber ach! wir vermissen sie hier' is combined with a development of the call motif 'Schaut hinan'. The calls are characterized by the interval of a fourth (a-d, g-c, c-f, d-g; also c-e flat and a-c) and eventually fit into the cadential catabasis (bars 219-22): but then the last of the lament motifs 'Laßt uns weinen', (bar 215) is transformed into a summons to return to life at the beginning of the fifth movement (bar 233).

Musik' in: *George Friedrich Händel. Ein Lebensinhalt. Gedenkschrift für Bernd Baselt (1934-1993)* (Halle und Kassel, 1995), pp.261-87, esp. p.279ff.

[27] Adolf Nowak, 'Ein deutsches Requiem' in the context of tradition, in: Friedhelm Krummacher, Wolfram Steinbeck (eds), *Brahms Analysen*, Kieler Schriften für Musikwissenschaft, 28 (Kassel, 1984), pp.201-209.

Like Schumann, Anton Rubinstein set the songs as well as the exequies: *Die Gedichte und das Requiem für Mignon aus Goethes Wilhelm Meisters Lehrjahre*, op.91 (1872). In addition to the songs of the Harper, Mignon, and Philine he set: 'Ich armer Teufel, Herr Baron' (which is not ascribed to any particular character in Goethe's novel), Aurelien's Lied 'Ich hatt' ihn einzig mir erkoren' and Friedrich's Lied 'O, ihr werdet Wunder sehen', which is the first song after the requiem. The requiem was thus integrated into this series of Klavierlieder; compared to these songs it was given special weight through the solo quartet (four boys, later four male voices), mixed choir with an additional keyboard instrument: 'Physharmonica or harmonium'. The combination of harmonium and piano which is suitable for religious house music – there are pieces by César Franck, Saint-Saëns, Widor and others – also turns up in Giocchino Rossini's *Petite Messe Solennelle* for four solo voices and choir with two pianos and harmonium, ad lib., 1864, first performed in Count Pillet-Will's home.[28]

In Rubinstein's *Requiem* there can be no question of musical forms being superimposed on one another. The aesthetic reflection of the liturgy aims at extreme simplicity of the movement and in the simple idea of antiphonal singing. It may be a consequence of linking to the piano songs that Rubinstein set the prose text in a clear periodization with repeated figures.[29] In the section, 'Schaut mit den Augen des Geistes hinan', the transformation of the prose rhythm into metrical units of four bars follows less from the speech rhythm, which immediately suggests the anapaest, than from the musical gestures of appeal, in which steps of a triad and tone repetition are held in the rhythm of three in a bar, so that some syllables are forced into quaver triplets and some are forced into a full bar.

Only in the closing number of the chorus is the regular alternation of choir and soloists converted into simultaneity: the choral movements of summons and aspiration are combined with the soloists' key words. In spite of the text being distributed over several voices, the movement is altogether compact and cadential (the soloists are brought together in two parts, which partially merge into the upper voices of the chorus). A purely instrumental passage follows, in which the possibilities of the harmonium (dynamic differentiation, note repetition) and the exchange of melodies on

---

[28] In 1867 Rossini orchestrated the mass for orchestra and it was performed in this edition in 1869 in the Théâtre Italien in Paris.

[29] It corresponds to Goethe's expectation, that the composer could change a prose text into 'lied-like' settings; in *Wilhelm Meisters Wanderjahre* he says of the relationship of the musician to the rhythm of a poem: 'nach Belieben zerstört dieser [der Musiker] das gewissenhafteste Verfahren des Rhythmikers, ja verwandelt sogar Prosa in Gesang, wo dann die wunderbarsten Möglichkeiten hervortreten.' '[The musician] destroys at will the most painstakingly constructed rhythm of a work; he even transmutes prose into song, where the most wonderful possibilities then emerge [...]', *HA* 8, p.248.

the keyboard are explored. The concluding section builds an a cappella movement around the words which are sung by the four youths at the closing of the coffin, and which, in Goethe's description, are taken up by the invisible choir.

Max Bruch's *Trauerfeier für Mignon*, op.93 (1918) is written for two choirs, soloists, orchestra, and organ.[30] The double-choir setting takes Goethe's description literally: 'und zwei unsichtbare Chöre fingen mit holdem Gesang an zu fragen:"Wen bringt ihr uns zur stillen Gesellschaft?[31] Bruch even thought of a scenic performance:

> Sollte eine Bühne oder Chorvereinigung Goethes Absicht verwirklichen woollen, die "Exequien für Mignon" szenisch zu bringen, so ließe sich die Aufführung am Besten so gestalten, daß der Sarkophag mit den vier Knaben in der Mitte der Bühne steht und die beiden Chöre rechts und links verdeckt aufgestellt werden.[32]

The work is a celebration of art as religion set in a time when the belief in an advanced humanization through art and culture had lost any support. The topic of the sublime is developed in a self-surpassing way, for example 'Seht die mächtigen Flügel doch an': the fanfare motif above a plagal cadence and modulation to the mediant with metrical compression, a *crescendo* and harp arpeggios in increasingly wide-ranging musical space (piano score, page 14); or at 'Schaut mit den Augen des Geistes hinan' the instrumental gesture of the 'Sursum corda' (piano score, page 22), *fortissimo* and *pesante* until the organ entry at the central words of aestheticism: 'In euch lebe die bildende Kraft'. In the final chorus the words of the four youths are inserted: 'Nehmet den heiligen Ernst mit hinaus'. In order to allow the soloists and choir to come together, 'euch' and 'uns' are sung together in the passage: 'In der Schönheit reinem Gewande /Begegn' euch die Liebe mit himmlischem Blick'.[33] The sound of the harp plays an important role also in the lamentations, which thus appear in a transfiguring light.

---

[30] Between Rubinstein's and Max Bruch's settings two more should be mentioned: Theodor Streicher, *Mignons Exequien* for mixed choir, children's choir and orchestra, 1907, and Karl Beyle, *Mignons Beisetzung* for mixed choir, boys voices and large orchestra, op.11, 1909.

[31] HA 7, p.574. 'Take this holy solemnity away with you, for it is sacred, it alone transforms life into eternity.'

[32] Max Bruch's *Trauerfeier für Mignon*, op.93. 'If a stage or choral company realize Goethe's intention of a scenic performance of the 'Exequien für Mignon', it would be best if the four boys with the sarcophagus stand in the middle of the stage and the two choirs are hidden to the right and left.'

[33] 'Look at the powerful wings.' 'Look up with the eyes of the spirit.' 'May there dwell in you the formative power.' 'Take this holy solemnity with you.' 'And may love dressed in pure robes of beauty meet you with its divine gaze.'

III

The text of Mignon's exequies has led to developments of musical-historical interest not only through its various settings – among which the setting by Hans Gál, op.26 (1923) must be mentioned – but also through its idea of a non-liturgical, poetic funeral service. The text is fundamental to the aesthetic reflection of the liturgy, as it is also in its other manifestations, for example in *Faust* and in *Faust* settings, and is an early and important witness to the development of a tradition of the poetic requiem. To the settings of the Requiem mass in the Roman Catholic church, the Latin Requiem, and to the Protestant tradition of funeral music, which is based upon hymns and biblical texts, is added the poetic requiem, which is not geared to the church funeral ceremony but is composed on newly created texts and draws upon these various traditions.

In 1814, two years after the above-mentioned seventh symphony, Beethoven wrote the *Elegischen Gesang*, op.118 as a memorial to the early death of the wife of his friend Baron von Pasqualati. The text (author unknown) runs as follows:

Sanft wie du lebtest	Gently as you lived
Hast du vollendet	You passed away
Zu heilig für den Schmerz.	Too holy for pain
Kein Auge wein'	Let no eye shed a tear at the
ob des himmlischen Geistes Heimkehr.	Homecoming of the heavenly spirit.
Sanft wie du lebtest,	Gently as you lived
hast du vollendet.	You passed away

Also here it is not a question of redemption (from guilt, evil, sin) in the manner of Christian teaching, but of completion, 'maturing' in the sense of the Abbé's speech, 'Nach bestimmten Gesetzen treten wir ins Leben ein, die Tage sind gezählt, die uns zum Anblicke des Lichts reif machen, aber für die Lebensdauer ist kein Gesetz.'[34] The 'heavenly spirit' and his 'homecoming' corresponds to the 'himmlischen Geschwister', siblings in heaven, in Goethe's exequies text, the defence against crying corresponds to the drying of tears in the fresh air (*Lehrjahre*, p.575). The maturing relates to the mode of life itself: 'Diese zärtliche Neigung, diese lebhafte Dankbarkeit schien die Flamme zu sein, die das Öl ihres Lebens aufzehrte.'[35] As Mignon's exequies are not to be thought of

---

[34] *Lehrjahre*, p.576. 'Fixed laws govern our entry into life, the days that prepare us to face the light of day are numbered; but there is no law regarding length of life.'

[35] ibid. 'This tender affection and her intense gratitude seemed to be the flame that consumed the oil of her life.' See also the doctor in Chapter Three: 'Die sonderbare Natur des guten Kindes [...] besteht beinah nur aus einer tiefen Sehnsucht; das Verlangen, ihr Vaterland wiederzusehen, uund das Verlangen nach Ihnen, mein Freund, ist, möchte ich fast sagen, das einzige Irdische an ihr; beides greift nur in eine unendliche Ferne, beide Gegenstände liegen unerreichbar vor diesem

in a church, but in the hall of a castle, which is established as the 'Hall of the Past', so too the *Elegische Gesang* is to be thought of as religious house music and was first performed in the baron's home (probably on 5 August 1814). The musical forces – four voices and string quartet – are a distant reminder of the double choirs of the burial motets. Motet style is evident in the prose diction, which modifies the metrical uniformity; in the motivic imitation of the instrumental introduction and the inner vocal part (bars 33ff.) as well as in the choral episodes. That such an extract should lead to a diminished seventh and is then discontinued at that point is explained from the fact that Beethoven, in line with the idealism of the text, accentuates that which idealism would like to remove: the pain (bar 32).[36]

There is a historical connection between Mignon's exequies and Brahms's *German Requiem*. Brahms was choirmaster for the Viennese Singakademie's 1863/64 performance of Schumann's *Requiem für Mignon*. Schumann had made a note of the title 'Deutsches Requiem' in his sketchbook. As is generally known, Brahms had emphatically said to Joachim how much his Requiem was composed in memory of Schumann. That the trio theme of the second movement 'So seid nun geduldig' is reminiscent of the choral number, 'Schlaf nun und ruhe in Träumen voll Duft', in Schumann's *Das Paradies und die Peri* supports this interpretation.[37] Brahms's work, through its textual patterns, belongs to the Protestant tradition of funeral music which is based upon biblical texts and hymn verses. The bible had a different rating with Brahms than with Schütz, Bach and Handel, who had followed the sense of the words in the church liturgy. In the 1900s the bible was independent of ecclesiastical and theological claims to interpretation. It was admired as profound literature by philosophers, writers and musicians, and – as is well known – by Schopenhauer and Wagner. Brahms also shared this view, when he spoke, in relation to the biblical books, of his 'ehrwürdigen Dichtern', his venerable poets, and intentionally omitted biblical passages which were officially highlighted by the church. Reinthaler had written to him that 'für das christliche Bewusstsein der Punkt, um den sich alles dreht, nämlich der Erlösungstod des Herrn', is missing [...]'. And Brahms answered that he 'mit allem Wissen und Willen

---

einzigen Gemüt.' 'The strange personality of the dear child [...] consists almost entirely of a deep yearning: the longing to see her motherland again, and a longing, my friend, for you – these, I may say, are the only earthly things about her, and in both cases she is reaching into the infinite distance; both goals are inaccessible to this singular nature.'

[36] Adolf Nowak, 'Beethoven, 'Elegischer Gesang' for four voices and string quartet, op.118 in Albrecht Riethmüller, Carl Dahlhaus, Alexander L. Ringer (ed.), *Beethoven. Interpretationen seiner Werke*, II (Laaber, 1994), pp.202-205.

[37] Klaus Blum, *Hundert Jahre Ein deutsches Requiem von Johannes Brahms* (Tutzing, 1971), pp.26 and 95f.

Stellen wie Evang. Joh .Kap.3 Vers 16 entbehrte'.[38] Related to this understanding of the bible as literature is the view expressed by the Protestant theologian, Hugo Wilhelm Paul Kleinert of the Berlin University, about the modernity of this work: it is modern 'in dem Überwiegen des reflexiv-lyrischen Elementes, in den bezaubernden Klangwirkungen der Instrumentation'.[39]

Aesthetic reflections of the liturgy play a central role in *Faust* and in settings from *Faust*. In the cathedral scene verses are cited from the Requiem sequence. These verses, in their lapidary rhythms, stand in stark contrast to the energetic language of the Evil Spirit on one hand, and Gretchen on the other. There is a tight relationship of content between the words of the Evil Spirit and the words of the sequence, so that through their influence Gretchen relates even the vision of the Last Judgement to her own situation, which she experiences as one of guilt. Aesthetic reflection on the liturgy does not lead to a distancing here, but to an actualization which strikes home.

Schumann greatly esteemed Cherubini's *Requiem in C Minor* (1816), and wanted to perform it at an (officially opposed) Chopin-Commemoration in Dresden in 1849. With the regularly scanned, fanfare-like opening motif, Schumann appears to refer to Cherubini's *Requiem* when composing the dome scene. Into the metrical regularity of the 'Dies irae' verse the Evil Spirit interjects exclamations which give sharp focus to its content. The swift conclusion of the first choral strophe is a cry of pain 'Dies irae' reduced to a dissonance on the second; between it and the powerful cadential strides 'Judex ergo cum sedebit' the metrically and harmonically dissolved voice of Gretchen can be heard. The Evil Spirit makes use of the sustained speech tones of the words 'Quid sum miser tunc dicturus' for a forceful rendition of the words, 'Ihr Antlitz wenden Verklärte von dir ab'.

In the first scene Faust is saved from death, in the form of a poisonous cup, through the Easter bells and the choir of believers. Erich Trunz writes:

> Die Chöre nehmen in ihren langsamen schreitenden Kurzversen und preisenden Adjektiven etwas von Rhythmus und Sprache der mittellateinischen Hymnik ins Deutsche herüber, ähnlich wie später in den Versen bei Fausts Grablegung.[40]

---

[38] ibid., p.35. 'for the Christian consciousness, the point around which everything rotates, namely the redemption through the death of the Lord', is missing [...]'. And Brahms answered that he 'knowingly and willingly [...] did without verses like that of John the Evangelist, Chapter 3, verse 16'.

[39] ibid., p.126. 'in the prevalence of the reflexive lyrical element, in the magical sound effects of the instrumentation.'

[40] *HA* 3, p.525. 'In their slow striding short verses and praising adjectives the chorus take over something from the rhythm and speech of middle-Latin hymns in German, akin to the verses at Faust's burial later on.'

Especially in the chorus of angels in the two last scenes from Part Two of *Faust* there is a certain emulation of the Latin church hymns with regard to the metrical form. Gustav Mahler appears to have felt this connection to liturgical song. He reports his long-felt desire to compose music for the Hermit's scene and for the 'Mater gloriosa' ending suddenly recurred when he read the hymn, 'Veni creator Spiritus':

> Und wie mit einem Schlage steht das Ganze vor mir, nicht nur das erste Thema sondern der ganze erste Satz und als Antwort darauf konnte ich gar nichts schöneres finden als die Goetheschen Worte in der Anachoretenszene. [41]

Goethe also particularly valued this Whitsun hymn.[42]

In the aesthetic reflection of the liturgy in Mahler's 8th Symphony the theme, 'Accende lumen sensibus', on which the fugue is based in the first movement, is brought into the coda by an isolated group of trumpets and trombones. The highlighting of this theme corresponds to the recurring words in the Whitsun liturgy about the enlightenment of the believers and the kindling of the fire of love according to the text 'tongues of fire', which descended on the disciples (Acts of the Apostles, Chapter 2). This theme penetrates deep into the second movement of the *Faust* setting. It is heard as the pizzicato on the cellos and basses in the introduction, it breaks out in a new guise at the words of the Pater profundus on the power of love; in a further variant it becomes, with the choir of angels and with the hymn of Doctor Marianus, the sound space for the Mater gloriosa and becomes one with Gretchen's prayer. Also the conclusion, marked 'hymnlike' by Mahler, is to be seen as a variation of this theme. The variations of the musical motif 'Accende' are the compositional answer to the spirit of transformation, which is prayed for in the Latin hymn, and which can be seen in the transformation of Faust.

Among the poems which can be labelled as 'poetic requiems' Friedrich Hebbel's 'Requiem' be mentioned. As a reflection of the liturgy it is far removed from Mignon's exequies. Mignon's exequies have aimed at the artistic reinforcement of the relationship to the one who has died young and the return of the mourners back into life; in Hebbel's *Requiem* total separation of the dead from all relation to life is envisaged ('where there is no longer life, but only struggle of the unleashed powers') and the

---

[41] 'And with one fell swoop, the whole composition stood before me, not only the first theme but the whole of the first movement, and as an answer I could find nothing more beautiful than the Goethean words in the Hermit's scene.' The Mahler quotation cited here is from Karl-Josef Müller, *Mahler. Leben – Werke – Dokumente* (Mainz and Munich, 1988), p.328.

[42]. Goethe on the hymn: 'Der herrliche Kirchengesang, Veni creator spiritus, ist eigentlich ein Appell ans Genie; deswegen er auch geist- und kraftreiche Menschen gewaltig anspricht' (*Maximen und Reflexionen*, HA 12, p.472). 'The glorious hymn, 'Veni creator spiritus', is actually an appeal to genius; therefore it speaks tremendously to spiritual and strong people.'

liturgy is turned into an incantation against this menacing divide. The three 'Soul, don't forget', correspond to the repeated 'Dona eis requiem' of the Requiem mass. It is not God who is invoked, but the human soul. The imperative is not meant for prayer ('for the souls, whose memory we solemnize today', Requiem mass) but for remembrance itself, from which the continuation of life depends. This is 'fading life', not eternal life that is a prey to the 'Storm at night' (the struggle of the unleashed forces), or that is a prey to the day of wrath (dies irae). After the death of the poet, Peter Cornelius composed the *Requiem* for six-part mixed choir. Siegmund von Hausegger set it for eight-part mixed choir and organ, Hugo Kauder for alto solo and double choir.[43] In his setting for alto (or baritone), mixed choir and orchestra, op.144b, Max Reger had the imperative at the end 'vergiß sie nicht, die Toten', 'do not forget the deceased) sung by the choir, and freely counterpointed by the solo voice, to the melody of 'O Haupt, voll Blut und Wunden'. In this context we are reminded of the recent verse 'Wenn ich einmal soll scheiden' or of the same melody which is used for the song 'Herzlich tut mich verlangen nach einem sel'gen End'. If Reger, certainly contrary to Hebbel's intention, goes back to hymns close to the tradition of the Protestant Requiem, he is attempting to regain from Hebbel's poem something of the religious hope from which it has been separated by the poet.

The great work of aesthetic reflection and reshaping of the liturgy is *Parsifal*. The disclosure of the Grail in Act One is conceived as a Eucharistic celebration, whose holy solemnity becomes clear precisely in the contrasting effects it has on the Knights of the Grail on one hand and on Amfortas on the other. What is found in the cathedral scene in *Faust*, the confrontation of the trespassing individual with the authority expressed in the liturgy, can here be turned into a dramaturgical principle, because the sinning individual is not granted less weight than the bearer of the liturgical office. The musical-technical side of this dramaturgical principle is the confrontation of chromatic and diatonic: Amfortas's outburst follows the a cappella choir of the youths ('Der Glaube lebt [...]') and Titural's words, whose lapidary cadence is altered by the imperilment of the Grail. At the disclosure of the Grail the words of Christ's enthronement are performed (choral-like) in unison by the youths, whose melody is eloquently repeated by the oboes and trumpets; at the communal meal, the communion, antiphons of the boys, youths and knights ring out, crowned by a canonical a cappella phrase of the Grail theme sung by all. In Act Three several liturgical acts are brought together: the anointing as bestowal of the 'royal priesthood' (1, Pt 2: 9), Kundry's baptism and finally the meeting of two processions in the hall of the Holy Grail: on the one hand the official escort for Titurel, on the other hand the advent ritual for the Grail and for Amfortas. The antiphonal song of both processions forms the memorial ceremony for

---

[43] For further settings see Adolf Stübing, *Friedrich Hebbel in der Musik* (Berlin, 1913), pp.280-303.

Titural. These exequies, in Gurnemanz's words, 'the requiem of my dear Lord', evince in their textual form a certain parallelism to Mignon's exequies.[44] The processional song with Amfortas's 'Wen berget ihr im düst'ren Schrein' corresponds to the choir's 'Wen bringt ihr uns zur stillen Gesellschaft'; the processional song with Titurel's corpse, 'Es birgt den Helden der Trauerschrein' corresponds to the youths' response in the exequies: 'Einen müden Gespielen'. The underlying structural line in the antiphons is artfully recast through chromatic turns in the voice and correspondingly complicated harmonic relationships. This chromaticization of what is by its nature artless melody is suggested by the context, which lets us perceive the procession with the Grail and Amfortas, together with Titurel, as a last journey. In the setting of the first procession a quasi-ostinato striding figure (b minor) goes over into the Grail motif (F flat major = D major), whereby the impression of a shift from b minor to A major occcurs (which goes through G flat minor which is established as f sharp minor). In the second procession, introduced by the bell motif, the first line modulates from B flat minor to B minor. The motifs from the first movement can already be heard, while the second movement concludes its line. These motifs then form a true ostinato, which leads to extraordinarily dissonant sounds. Correspondingly, the second procession deals with the bell motif, which now carries the warning for the guardian of the Grail.

The radiations we have presented of an impressive scene in Goethe's *Wilhelm Meisters Lehrjahre* certainly belong to no unified context. Perhaps they confirm, precisely in their individuality, how an aesthetic reflection of the liturgy was able to influence and define the composer's consciousness. Ernst Krenek remarked of Goethe's meaning for the musicians:

> Gewiß hat der Musiker des neunzehnten Jahrhunderts fachliche Belehrung wie professionelle Begeisterung aus dem Schaffen eines Beethoven und Schubert empfangen; aber den Horizont, in den er sein Tun plazierte, die Bezogenheit, in der er es selbst reflektierend zu erblicken suchte, die Deutung seines künstlerischen Verhaltens mochte er, wenn ihn Verlangen danach ankam, viel eher aus Goethe gewinnen..[45]

---

[44] In the discussion of the paper (Frankfurt/Main, 1999) Dr Kienzle has pointed out the relationship between Wagner's text and Goethe's.

[45] Ernst Krenek, 'Erinnerung an Karl Kraus (1936)', in: *'Zur Sprache gebracht'. Essays über Musik* (München, 1958), p.230f. 'Certainly the nineteenth-century musician had gained technical instruction and professional enthusiasm from the works of Beethoven and Schubert; but the horizon in which he placed his activity, the context in which, when he reflected on it, he tried to see it, the understanding of his artistic stance, he would, if the desire for it arose in him, much sooner take from Goethe.'

Mignon und der Harfner
Song-cycle for soprano, baritone and piano

Poems: Johann Wolfgang von Goethe
Music: Seóirse Bodley

Commissioned for the performance at the conference,
'Goethe: Musical Poet, Musical Catalyst',
First Performance: 27 March 2004
Department of Music,
National University of Ireland, Maynooth

The Blind Impress of Modernity: Exile and Modernist Aesthetics in Goethe's Mignon and the Harper
Lorraine Byrne

The subject of exile is perennially topical. Through the media we hear almost daily reports of the experiences of refugees, immigrants or exiles, and the situations in Northern Ireland and Israel provide a constant reminder of the contingency of the terms 'homeland' or 'native soil'. On the other hand, the topic has a lengthy historical and mythical dimension: the exile of Adam and Eve from the Garden of Eden, the wanderings of Odysseus and Orpheus, the labyrinthine disorientation in Goethe's protagonists all speak to a fundamental sense of loss, of displacement and a desire to regain a paradisiacal sense of unity and wholeness whether spiritual or secular.

The essence of exile is separation from, and loss of, what the speaker of a Germanic language identifies as 'home' – that is, a perceived integrity of time, place, people and circumstances, which convey a sense of identity through belonging. This type of homelessness, as a loss of a sense of place, is not just geographic but also moral and cultural. In *Wilhelm Meisters Lehrjahre* Goethe portrays exile as a temporal rather than a spatial condition, and shows how our deepest senses of what constitutes 'home' can contain some elements so at odds with conventional morality. Exile is portrayed as one of the saddest of fates. Whether, like the Harper, the exile is isolated through social transgressions or is nostalgic like Mignon, who experiences the most unnerving form of exile: *exile in the home* – when that which should be the safest, most intimate, becomes alien and restless – Goethe suggests how an exile is inconsolable, forever shadowed by an absence of stability. Through Mignon, Goethe shows how exile involves dislocation on several levels. There is physical dislocation, cultural exile and the linguistic exile of functioning in another language. In the *Theatralische Sendung*, Mignon's pronominal switches between the first and the third person reflect the heroine's alienated perspective, and in the *Lehrjahre* Goethe shows the difficulty Mignon experiences in negotiating an identity for herself. The allusions to split subjectivity and to flexible self-definitions all speak to the stuff of post-modernity where displacement and self-fracturing create new possibilities for the marginal or dispossessed. Mignon presents us with a double sense of exile: exile from a lost youth and from a lost culture, which reveals a series of other borders that are metaphysical in nature, and asks questions about identity and meaning that are characteristic of late twentieth-century culture.

Goethe's Harper is a complicated amalgam which took centuries to emerge, and is coloured by Virgil's and Ovid's portrayal of Orpheus. Virgil insists, at some length, not only on the singer's ability to move man and beast, but on the pathos of the forlorn hero's wanderings in the harsh winter landscape of a nature turned hostile. Goethe does not quite follow Virgil, in that he makes no mention of nature's reflection of Orpheus' despair. The Harper's life in exile as one season succeeds another, as opposed to Virgil's seven months and Ovid's three years. Goethe's references to the Harper consist of a pyrotechnical display of musical doctrine, still partly obscure, possibly based on Macrobius, but explicitly meant to illustrate and exemplify the Pythagorean notion of the harmony of the spheres, as well as the Platonic and Neoplatonic concept of Anima Mundi. Goethe's Harper demonstrates the poet's interest in the doctrinal and philosophical implications of the myth, as well as its purely narrative aspect. In Goethe's Harper his 'backward glance' is fixed and he is trapped in a fallen time (a fall of hope rather than a fall into despair) and he desires that which is neither present nor possible within himself. He longs for self-escape from an inner truth he feels unable to cope with and he craves what Sperata's death makes impossible – banished from hope – a veritable 'hell'. Goethe's image of the Harper trapped in an ill-lit prison is metaphorical for what Auden later described as being in 'the cell of himself'.[1] In other episodes in the novel he dons a pilgrim's mantle, wandering, with no place at which to arrive, driven by a sense of dislocation, or dissonance. This juxtaposition of images is expressive of the Harper's displacement and despair. Spiritual and personal exile curses the Harper's soul. He is fractured by guilt and his suffering becomes a sort of expiation, as he seeks solace from his own uncomfortable existential condition. The typically modern obsession with the philosophical problem of freedom in relation to responsibility is raised in the Harper. In these poems of exile the concept of metaphysical border crossings is explored. The Harper crosses borders and in so doing, he breaks borders of thought and experiences self-estrangement, with its dual potential for revelation and violation. What we have in the Harper is metaphysical exile – exile from the self in which boundaries of identity are transgressed, yet meaning is disclosed. The real cause of exile is both revealed and shown to be imaginary.

---

[1] W. H. Auden, 'In Memory of W. B. Yeats', *Another Time* (London: Faber & Faber, 1940), p.108, II,1, p.27.

The American philosopher Richard Rorty has argued that the experience of modernity derives from 'chance', 'mere contingency', in contrast to the 'necessity, essential, telic, constitutive' impress optimizing the social coherence of classical Greek culture and the neo-classic Enlightenment.[2] If classical philosophy is governed by necessity and wholeness, then the fallen condition of modernity can be described as a 'blind impress', in which the 'fragmented' self is cursed with imperfect and limited vision. There are two precise ways in which Goethe's modern perspective is different from Romanticism. The Harper's first 'blind impress' represents a post-Darwinian awareness that there is no universal design, as distinct from the Romantic belief in intrinsic natural order and, second, the term suggests that the modern individual is unable to see outside his or her narrow perspective, whereas Romantic thinkers emphasized the primacy of emotional openness and pathos. The 'blind impress' of Goethe's Harper united the vision of the poet as prophet with 'imperfect vision' and extreme tenuity of modern perception.

---

[2] Richard Rorty, *Contingency, Irony and Solidarity* (Cambridge: Cambridge University Press, 1989), p.26.

Figure 12.1 Franz Ludwig Catel, 'Mignon dressed as an Angel', Ink Drawing (1799)

Mignon und der Harfner
Song-cycle for soprano, baritone and piano
Poems: Johann Wolfgang von Goethe
Music: Seóirse Bodley

I   An die Türen will ich schleichen (Harfner)
II   Heiß mich nicht reden (Mignon)
III   Wer nie sein Brot mit Tränen aß (Harfner)
IV   Kennst du das Land? (Mignon)
V   Wer sich der Einsamkeit ergibt (Harfner)
VI   So laßt mich scheinen bis ich werde (Mignon)
VII   Nur wer die Sehnsucht kennt (Mignon und der Harfner)

An die Türen

An die Türen will ich schleichen	I will steal up to people's doors
Still und sittsam will ich stehn,	I will stand quietly and respectably,
Fromme Hand wird Nahrung reichen,	Charitable hands will offer me food,
Und ich werde weitergehn.	And I will wander on.
Jeder wird sich glücklich scheinen,	Every one will consider himself fortunate
Wenn mein Bild vor ihm erscheint,	When my image appears before him,
Eine Träne wird er weinen,	He will shed a tear,
Und ich weiß nicht, was er weint.	And I do not know why he weeps.

Heiß mich nicht reden

Heiß mich nicht reden, heiß mich schweigen,
Denn mein Geheimnis ist mir Pflicht;
Ich möchte dir mein ganzes Innre zeigen,
Allein das Schicksal will es nicht.

Ein jeder sucht im Arm des Freundes Ruh',
Dort kann die Brust in Klagen sich ergießen;
Allein ein Schwur drückt mir die Lippen zu,
Und nur ein Gott vermag sie aufzuschließen.

Wer nie sein Brot mit Tränen aß

Wer nie sein Brot mit Tränen aß,
Wer nie die kummervollen Nächte
Auf seinem Bette weinend saß,
Der kennt euch nicht,
ihr himmlischen Mächte.

Ihr führt ins Leben uns hinein,
Ihr laßt den Armen schuldig werden,
Dann überlaßt ihr ihn der Pein;
Denn alle Schuld rächt sich auf Erden.

Bid me not speak, bid me be silent,
For it is my duty to keep my secret.
I would like to show you my whole heart,
But my destiny does not allow it.

Every man seeks repose in the arms of a friend
Where he can pour out his heart in lamentation;
But a solemn oath seals my lips,
And only a god can open them.

He who has never eaten his bread mixed with tears,
He who has never through nights of anguish,
Sat weeping on his bed,
Such a man does not know you,
you heavenly Powers.

You lead us into life,
You make a poor wretch guilty,
Then deliver him over to suffering;
For all guilt is atoned on earth.

Kennst du das Land

Kennst du das Land, wo die Zitronen blühn,	Do you know the land where the lemon trees blossom
Im dunkeln Laub die Goldorangen glühn,	Where the golden oranges glow in the dark foliage.
Ein sanfter Wind vom blauen Himmel weht,	A soft rain falls from the blue sky,
Die Myrte still und hoch der Lorbeer steht,	The myrtle stands silent and the laurel is tall?
Kennst du es wohl?	Do you know it perhaps?
Dahin! Dahin	It is there, there
Möcht' ich mit dir, o mein Geliebter, ziehn!	that I would like to go with you, my beloved.
Kennst du das Haus, auf Säulen ruht sein Dach	Do you know the house? Its roof rests on columns,
Es glänzt der Saal, es schimmert das Gemach,	The hall gleams, the room glistens,
Und Marmorbilder stehn und sehn mich an:	And the marble statues stand and gaze at me:
Was hat man dir, du armes Kind, getan?	'What have they done to you, poor child?'
Kennst du es wohl?	Do you know it perhaps?
Dahin! Dahin	It is there, there
Möcht' ich mit dir, o mein Beschützer, ziehn!	that I would like to go with you, my protector.
Kennst du den Berg und seinen Wolkensteg?	Do you know the mountain and its cloudy path?
Das Maultier sucht im Nebel seinen Weg,	The mule seeks its way through the mists;
In Höhlen wohnt der Drachen alte Brut,	In caves the ancient brood of dragons dwell;
Es stürzt der Fels und über ihn die Flut:	The crag falls sheer and the cataract tumbles over it;
Kennst du ihn wohl?	Do you know it perhaps?
Dahin! Dahin	It is there, there
Geht unser Weg; o Vater, laß uns ziehn!	our way leads. Oh, father, let us go!

Wer sich der Einsamkeit ergibt

Wer sich der Einsamkeit ergibt,
Ach! der ist bald allein;
Ein jeder lebt, ein jeder liebt
Und läßt ihn seiner Pein.

Ja! laßt mich meiner Qual!
Und kann ich nur einmal
Recht einsam sein,
Dann bin ich nicht allein.

Es schleicht ein Liebender lauschend sacht,
Ob seine Freundin allein?
So überschleicht bei Tag und Nacht
Mich Einsamen die Pein,
Mich Einsamen die Qual.
Ach werd ich erst einmal
Einsam im Grabe sein,
Da läßt sie mich allein!

He who devotes himself to solitude
Alas, is soon alone.
Everybody lives, everybody loves,
And leaves him to his sorrow.

Yes! Leave me to my torment,
And if I once succeed
In finding real solitude
Then I will not be alone.

A lover creeps up softly & stands listening to
find out whether his sweetheart is alone.
And so, day and night
Sorrow and suffering steal stealthily upon me
In all my solitude,
But when I finally attain
Solitude in the grave,
There it will leave me alone.

So laßt mich scheinen

So laßt mich scheinen, bis ich werde,
Zieht mir das weiße Kleid nicht aus!
Ich eile von der schönen Erde
Hinab in jenes feste Haus.

Dort ruh' ich eine kleine Stille,
Dann öffnet sich der frische Blick,
Ich lasse dann die reine Hülle,
Den Gürtel und den Kranz zurück.

Und jene himmlischen Gestalten
Sie fragen nicht nach Mann und Weib,
Und keine Kleider, keine Falten
Umgeben den verklärten Leib.
Zwar lebt' ich ohne Sorg' und Mühe,
Doch fühlt' ich tiefen Schmerz genung;
Vor Kummer altert' ich zu frühe;
Macht mich auf ewig wieder jung!

So let me appear as I am till I am transformed:
Do not strip me of this white robe!
I hasten from the joys of earth
Down to that house so fast and firm.

There will I rest in peace a while,
Then I shall see with new eyes,
Then I will cast aside my pure chrysalis.
Leaving both wreath and garment behind

For all those glorious heavenly figures,
Will not ask whether I am man or woman,
No garments long or draperies fine
Will envelop my body, now transformed.
I lived indeed untouched by care.
And yet I felt my share of deep sorrow.
Suffering has made me old too soon,
Now make me young forever more!

Nur wer die Sehnsucht kennt

Nur wer die Sehnsucht kennt,	Only those who know what longing is
Weiß, was ich leide!	Can know what I suffer!
Allein und abgetrennt	Alone and cut off
Von aller Freude,	From all joy,
Seh ich ans Firmament	I keep gazing over yonder
Nach jener Seite.	Into heaven's demesne.
Ach! der mich liebt und kennt,	Alas! He who loves me and knows me
Ist in der Weite.	Is far away.
Es schwindet mir, es brennt	I feel giddy,
Mein Eingeweide.	I am on fire inside.
Nur wer die Sehnsucht kennt,	Only those who know what longing is
Weiß, was ich leide!	Can know what I suffer!

Translations: Lorraine Byrne

Composer's Note

Accidentals apply to the note they prefix for the rest of the bar at the same pitch only: they do not apply to other octaves.
Vorzeichen beziehen sich auf die Noten, neben denen sie jeweils gedruckt sind, als auch auf die Noten derselben Tonhöhe des gleichen Taktes, aber nicht auf die gleiche Note in anderen Oktaven.

In 'Kennst du das Land' Takt 233 heißt das Vortragszeichen 'stonily': steinhart.

In 'Nur wer die Sehnsucht kennt', Takt 408, heißt die Anweisung, 'ruminatively, like an echo of Mignon's thoughts': nachdenklich, wie ein Echo von Mignons Gedanken.

Figure 12.1 Franz Ludwig Catel, 'The Harper in his Cell', Ink Drawing (1799)

1. An die Türen will ich schleichen

© 2004 Seoirse Bodley

Mignon und der Harfner'

2. Heiß mich nicht reden

3. Wer nie sein Brot mit Tränen aß

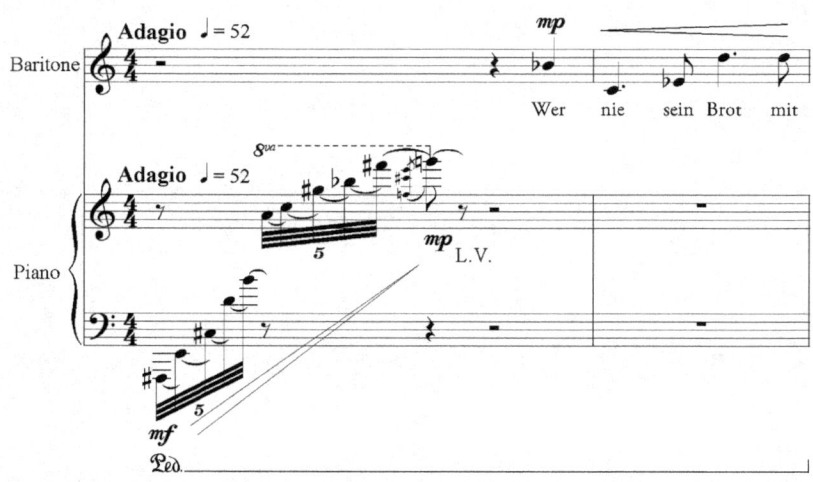

© 2004 Seoirse Bodley

4. Kennst du das Land?

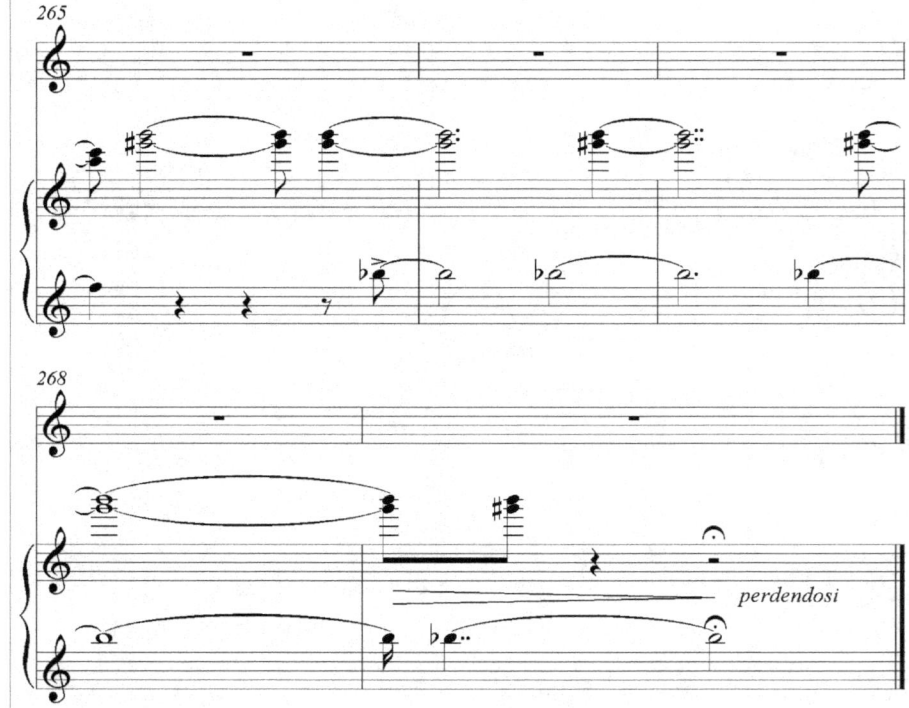

5. Wer sich der Einsamkeit ergibt

6. So laßt mich scheinen, bis ich werde

© 2004 Seoirse Bodley

'Mignon und der Harfner'

7. Nur wer die Sehnsucht kennt

© 2004 Seoirse Bodley

'Mignon und der Harfner'

Appendix 1 | Conference Programme

An International Symposium

Goethe: Musical Poet. Musical Catalyst

Friday 26 March 2004
8.45am   Registration
9.00am   Official Opening and Welcome
             Prof. Gerard Gillen (Head of Department of Music, NUI Maynooth)

Goethe and Music

Chair: Dr Barra Boydell (Department Of Music, NUI Maynooth)

9.10am   Prof. Otto Biba (*Gesellschaft der Musikfreunde*, Vienna): 'The Presence of Goethe's Work in the Viennese, Austrian, Hapsburg Music Scene in the late 18th and early 19th century.'

Eberl:	'Meeresstille und Glückliche Fahrt'
Krufft:	'Lied aus Wilhelm Meisters Lehrjahren'
	'Trost in Thränen'
Czerny:	'Das Geheimnis'
	'Des Mädchens Klage'
	'Der Erlkönig'
Dietrichstein:	'An die Entfernte'
	'Nähe des Geliebten'
	'Wandrers Nachtlied'
Tomášek:	'Mignons Sehnsucht'

Una McMahon (mezzo), Mairead Buicke & Anna Devin (sopranos)
Dearbhla Collins (piano)

10.00am   Prof. Jan Smaczny (School of Music, The Queen's University of Belfast): 'Goethe and the Czechs.'

Tomášek:	'Heidenröslein', op.53
	'Mignons Sehnsucht', op.54, no.1
	'Die Bekehrte', op.54, no.3
	'Frühzeitiger Frühling', op.54, no.4
	'Erlkönig', op.59, no.1

Una McMahon (mezzo) & Dearbhla Collins (piano)

11.00am Coffee.

11.15am Dr Lorraine Byrne (Department of Music, NUI Maynooth): 'The Goethe-Zelter Letters: Musical Implications.'
    Zelter: 'Wandrers Nachtlied'
           'Rastlose Liebe'

  Una McMahon (mezzo), Anna Devin (soprano), Dearbhla Collins (piano)

The Music of Felix Mendelssohn-Bartholdy College Chapel

12.15pm Recital: Prof. Gerard Gillen (organ).
    Nachspiel in D (1831)
    Prelude in c (1841)
    Fugue in C (1839)
    Sonata in A, op.65 no.3
    Sonata in B Flat, op.65 no.4

1.15pm Lunch (Pugin Hall).

Goethe, *Wilhelm Meisters Lehrjahre*

Chair: Prof. Moray McGowan (Head of Department of Germanic Studies, Trinity College Dublin)

2.30pm **Keynote Address: Prof. Nicholas Boyle** (Department of German, University of Cambridge): ' "Thealogy": Gods, Goddesses, and *Wilhelm Meisters Lehrjahre* in Goethe's Religious Development.'

Goethe's Mignon

Chair: Prof. Harry White (Head of Department of Music, University College Dublin)
4.00pm 'The Wondrous Child: Mignon's Story.' Dramatic Reading by Peter Jankowsky.

5.15pm Buffet Supper (Pugin Hall).

Schumann's *Requiem für Mignon*

St Mary's Church of Ireland, Maynooth

6.15pm Dr Julian Horton (Department of Music, University College Dublin): 'Schumann's *Requiem für Mignon* and the Concept of Music as Literature.'

Schumann: 'Requiem für Mignon' from Goethe's *Wilhelm Meisters Lehrjahre* (op.98b)

  I   Soloist and Choir: 'Wen bringt ihr uns zur stillen Gesellschaft'
  II Soloists (Soprano I and Alto I): 'Ach wie ungern brachten wir ihn her'
  III Soloists and Choir: 'Seht die mächtigen Flügel doch an'
  IV Soloists and Choir: 'In euch lebe die bildende Kraft'
  V   Soloists and Choir: 'Kinder, kehret in's Leben züruck'
  VI Soloists and Choir: 'Kinder! eilet in's Leben hinan'

North South Performers:

Queen's Consort & Maynooth Chamber Choir

Helen Kearns (soprano),
Toni Walsh (soprano),
Niamh O' Hanlon (alto),
Cliodhna McDonogh (alto),
John Malloy (baritone),
Accompanied by Frances Kelleher.
Conducted by Colman Pearce.

7.30 pm Coffee.

Mignon und der Harfner

Bewerunge Room, Department of Music, Maynooth

8.00pm   Seóirse Bodley: Mignon und der Harfner
         (First performance, commissioned for the conference.)

        I   'An die Türen' (Harper)
        II   'Heiß mich nicht reden' (Mignon)
        III   'Wer nie sein Brot' (Harper)
        IV   'Kennst du das Land?' (Mignon)
        V   'Wer sich der Einsamkeit ergibt' (Harper)
        VI   'So laßt mich scheinen' (Mignon)
        VII 'Nur wer die Sehnsucht kennt' (Mignon and the Harper)

        Kathleen Tynan (soprano),
        Sam McElroy (baritone),
        Dearbhla Collins (piano).

Short pre-concert talk by the composer at 8.00pm.

9.00pm   Wine Reception.

Saturday 27 March 2004

Goethe and Music

Chair: Prof. Gerard Gillen (Head of Department of Music, NUI Maynooth)

9.00am Dr Gareth Cox (Head of Mary Immaculate College, University of Limerick): ' "Blumengruss und Blumenglöckchen": Goethe's Influence on Anton Webern.'

>   Webern: 'Blumengruss'
>   'Gleich und Gleich'
>   Mairead Buicke (soprano)
>   Dearbhla Collins (piano)

10.15am Briony Williams (Royal Academy of Music, London): 'Maker, Mother, Muse: Bettine von Arnim, Goethe and the Boundaries of Creativity.'

>   Bettine von Arnim: 'An Luna'
>   'Ach neige du Schmerzenreiche'
>
>   Una McMahon (mezzo) & Anna Devin (soprano)
>   Dearbhla Collins (piano)

11.00am Coffee.

Goethe and Beethoven I

Chair: Prof. Nicholas Boyle (Department of German, University of Cambridge)

11.15am Prof. Moray McGowan (Head of Department of Germanic Studies, Trinity College Dublin): '*Fidelio* and *Faust* in the German *Wende* of 1989/90.'

12.15pm Lunch.

1.15pm Recital: Schubert: Quartet for Flute, Guitar, Viola and Cello (D96)
John Feeley (guitar), William Dowdell (flute), William Butt (cello) and John Lynch (viola). Schubert: 15 Original Dances for Flute or Violin and Guitar (D365) (Bill Dowdell and John Feeley).

Goethe and Beethoven II

Chair: Prof. Jan Smaczny (School of Music, The Queen's University of Belfast)

2.15pm   Dr Amanda Glauert (Royal Academy of Music, London): 'Ich denke dein': Beethoven's Retelling of Goethe's Poetry.
        Beethoven   'Kennst du das Land', op.75, no.1
        Reichardt   'Ich denke dein'
        Beethoven/ Erk-Boehme   'Ich denke dein'
        Beethoven   Six Variations on 'Ich denke dein', woo74

        Colette Boushell (soprano)
        Frances Kelleher (piano)
        Adele Commins (piano)

3.15pm   Dr Claus Canisius (Badisches Konservatorium, Karlsruhe): Göthe and Beethowen: Men of Genius between Distance and Affinity.
        Beethoven   'Marmotte' op.52, no.7
                                            'Mailied', op.52, no.4

        Colette Boushell (soprano)
        Frances Kelleher (piano)

4.30pm   Wine Reception.

Cadenza for a Conference

5.15pm   Dr Alison Hood (Music Department, NUI Maynooth): piano
        Beethoven, Bagatelles, op.119, nos.1, 3 & 4

5.20pm   Cadenza for a Conference.
        Micheal O' Siadhail: 'Hopscotch': A Meditation on Boundaries

7.30pm   Conference Dinner in the Glenroyal Hotel, Maynooth.

Appendix 2 | Goethe and the Guitar

The Guitar in the *Goethezeit*
Derek McCulloch

As fate was to have it, the rapid rise in popularity in the German-speaking area of the 'Spanish' or 'Italian' six-stringed guitar in the outgoing years of the 18th and the first few decades of the 19th century had its origin in familiar Goethe territory: the Court of Saxe-Weimar under its talented duchess, Anna Amalia (1739-1807). Here Goethe lived and worked, travels apart, for half a century, the earlier years spent under her formidable patronage. Ironically Goethe does not appear to have enjoyed the popularity *in situ* that was evident elsewhere. Court composer Ernst Wilhelm Wolf in his *51 Lieder der besten deutschen Dichter* of 1784 and, before him, municipal organist Adam Eylenstein in his *Lieder von beliebten Dichtern Teutschlands* of 1782 both pointedly omitted any single poem by Anna Amalia's poet laureate. Significantly, too, it was not Wolf who had set Goethe's Singspiel *Erwin und Elmire* to music in 1776, but the Duchess herself. Her beautifully constructed setting of 'Das Veilchen', with its colourful orchestration and melodic charm, make it still worthy of concert performance, even in the piano reduction published by Friedländer nearly a century ago.[1] Groomed at one stage to become the bride of George III, Anna Amalia is certainly the most musically talented queen that Great Britain never had.[2]

---

[1] Amalia/Goethe, *Erwin und Elmire*, ed. Max Friedländer (Leipzig, 1921).
[2] See Derek McCulloch: 'Royal Composers. The composing monarchs that Britain nearly had', in: *MT*, 122, pp.525-29, August 1982.

Appendix 2

As Wilhelm Tappert[3] first pointed out over one hundred years ago, it was at Anna Amalia's behest that in 1788 an Italian guitar in her possession was presented to the Jena *luthier* Jakob Ernst Otto for the purpose of making a similar instrument for 'Herr Einsiedel', presumably a lutenist in the court band. Otto describes the prodigious success of the new instrument, which rapidly ousted the familiar French instrument of five strings:

> [...] in the space of 15 years I had more orders than I could carry out. [...] the guitar quickly won admirers everywhere, since for anyone keen on and good at singing, it provides the pleasantest and easiest accompaniment and furthermore is easily carried about. Everywhere one saw guitars in the hands of the most respected ladies and gentlemen.[4]

The instrument caught on far beyond the provincial court in Weimar, with customers in Dresden, Leipzig and Berlin, and large numbers made by builders 'in such places as Vienna, Neukirchen and Tirol'.

Armed with financial support from the Leverhulme Trust and the British Academy, the present writer set out in 2000 to explore German song c1800, and the composers' text preferences. Soon a premier division of poets emerged, some familiar still, some less so: Bürger, Claudius, Hagedorn, Hölty, Kosegarten, Matthison and the Count of Stolberg. To these names were soon to be added those of Schiller and Goethe, who emerge as among the most frequently set poets, though the texts, especially in the case of Schiller, were not necessarily those that have survived in popular anthologies of their works.

What also soon became apparent was the number of songs set to music using the guitar as the accompanying instrument. In cognizance of this perhaps surprising fact and of the prolific number of Goethe and Schiller settings, the present writer, as proprietor of the chamber music ensemble *Café Mozart*, subsequently produced a CD under the catchpenny title of *Goethe & the Guitar*.[5] The CD comprises mostly Goethe texts (18 tracks), one ascription to Goethe – a translation of a Rousseau poem – one French text on the death of Werther ('plomb fatal'!) and four Schiller tracks. Primarily they have guitar accompaniments, though six use a square piano, and six have an optional additional flute.[6]

---

[3] Wilhelm Tappert, 'Zur Geschichte der Guitarre', *Monatshefte für Musikgeschichte*, XIV/5 (1802), pp.77-92.
[4] Jakob Ernst Otto: *Über den Bau der Bogen-Instrumente und über die Arbeiten der vorzüglichsten Instrumente* (Jena, 1828), pp. 94-97.
[5] *Goethe and the Guitar: Songs and Ballads c1800. Café Mozart* on period instruments, DanubiaDiscs CM 002, 24 tracks, 68'47".
[6] All Goethe/Schiller settings discussed in this article are recorded on this CD.

Song collections from c1790 to c1810 deploying the guitar as accompanying instruments fall into three categories:

1. Piano accompaniments arranged by the composer or a contemporary for guitar
2. Accompaniments conceived *ab initio* for the guitar
3. Songs to be accompanied by piano *and* guitar

Inevitably the bulk of songs were written at this time to be performed with a piano accompaniment. Songs extolling the virtue of the piano are by no means rare. Carl in one of his *6 Lieder nach Gerstenbergk* exemplifies the sentiment of the piano's propensity to move the listener: 'Jetzt klaget Sehnen nur in diesen Saiten'.[7] Similar characteristics were also ascribed to the guitar – invariably referred to in the texts as the *Laute* (lute), 'guitar' being reserved merely for the information on the title page of a collection. Thus we have 'An die Laute' in settings by the guitar specialists Friedrich Methfessel and August Harder, as well as a keyboard setting by Johann Friedrich Reichardt, one of Goethe's favourite composers, who also has a song 'An meine Laute' to his credit. Karl Siegmund Freiherr von Seckendorf composed a 'Gespräch mit der Laute' (Conversation with the lute). The above Eberwein, in 'Rückkehr', No. 1 of allegedly *Sechs Lieder* (though the source has only five!) informs us that, 'Der erste Ton der Laute mich gelehrt, / wie süß, wie süß zur Heimat hin zu kehren'.[8]

While the title page of the Eberwein's collection informs us that two of them are intended for guitar accompaniment – presumably including this one, most songs in praise of the 'lute' are actually piano songs. This is, of course, also true of Schubert's setting of 'An die Laute', though we are told that Schubert on his travels often initially drafted the accompaniments on the guitar.[9] Alas, no such original drafts have survived. Goethe's friend and music mentor Carl Friedrich Zelter likewise has a piano song addressed to the lute, the opening line of 'Ständchen' beginning 'Zu meiner Laute Liebesklag' (To the amorous lament of my lute). Of all the settings in praise of an instrument the most intriguing must surely be 'An die Harmonika' by Friedrich Franz Hurka[10]. Meanwhile, to intensify the poetic connotations of the 'lute', while exploiting the popularity of the six-stringed guitar, German makers began producing a hybrid

---

[7] Bayerische Staatsbibliothek München, 4 Mus.pr.39812. 'Plaintive longing is heard now only in these strings.'
[8] Above library, Mus.pr.887. 'The first note from the lute taught me how sweet it is to return to one's own country.'
[9] In 1821, in his first publication of Schubert Lieder, Diabelli chose to issue four of his songs in guitar versions. The simultaneous printing of select Schubert songs with both guitar and piano accompaniment became a pattern as Schubert became respected as a composer of Lieder.
[10] *Sämmtliche Lieder von Friedrich Franz Hurka*, (Regensburg: Thurn & Taxis-Bibliothek, 1800), 9/27.

instrument such as is still to be seen occasionally in music shops today: a guitar built in the shape of the round-bellied lute of bygone times.

Of the many collections of songs that began life as piano songs, but ended up with the accompaniments arranged for guitar, mention might be made here of *VI Lieder von Betzwarzofsky* (Antonín Frantisek Bečvařovský), which were published in 1799 as *Gesänge beym Klavier* but reissued in 1802 with 'an accompaniment for the Spanish guitar realised by Bernhard Joseph Mäurer'[11]. The third of these songs is an exquisite setting of Goethe's 'Nähe des Geliebten' ('Ich denke dein'). Schiller's soliloquy by Mary Queen of Scots, stirringly set by his Swabian compatriot Rudolf Zumsteeg, was published as an individual item with an accompaniment arranged for guitar and flute by Anton Methfessel, while the touching Farewell of Joan of Arc was arranged for voice and guitar by Leopold Carl Reinicke.

The majority of the settings of poems by Goethe and Schiller with guitar accompaniments are by fairly (or even totally) obscure composers. The best-known are the above mentioned Zumsteeg and Zelter. Many – such as Ludwig Berger – were well-respected figures in their time. Berger's *Vier Gedichte von Goethe und Schiller* (in fact all four are by Goethe!) are specifically 'set to music for piano or guitar',[12] with both accompaniments given in the score. Berger was a notable protagonist of the guitar, dubbing it 'the poor man's pianoforte'. No 3 is a wonderful strophic setting of 'Der Musensohn'.

Likewise the specialist guitar composers such as Harder and the Methfessel brothers were greater respected figures in their time than their non-inclusion in New Grove[13] might indicate. But other virtually unknown composers prove to be absolute winners, such as Johann Heinrich Gottlieb Streitwolf, with Goethe's 'Schäfers Klagelied' and his arrangement of Grosheim's setting of Schiller's 'Mädchen aus der Fremde'. A notable feature of his accompaniments is the manner in which the basic version given for the first stanza gives way to accompaniments of increasing technical difficulty in the subsequent stanzas. He and Johann Chr. Jusdorf skilfully deploy an optional flute part, the latter to good effect in Goethe's 'Der Fischer'. While some information on these composers is to be found in Philip Bone's invaluable publication[14], on some of the composers who have set Goethe poems to the guitar no reliable information can be found. Among these, one stands out: F. Stein, with a sublime setting of Goethe's 'Nachtgesang' from his opus 1, *Zehn Lieder mit Begleitung der Guitarre*[15].

---

[11] Bayerische Staatsbibliothek München, Mus. pr. 2344.
[12] Goethe-Museum Düsseldorf, Katalog der Musikalien 137.
[13] *New Grove Dictionary of Music and Musicians* (London: Macmillan, 2001).
[14] Philip Bone: *The Guitar and Mandolin* (London, 1914, enlarged repr. 1954).
[15] Goethe-Museum Düsseldorf, Katalog der Musikalien 1393.

We have heard how these Goethe and Schiller settings were to be accompanied either by piano, or by an arrangement of the original accompaniment for the guitar, or even published with alternative accompaniments for either instrument. There is yet one further variant: the deployment of guitar and pianoforte together. Telling examples of this scoring may be found in the unknown J. G. Quandt's setting of 'Der König in Thule' and Traugott Maximilian Eberwein's rollicking setting of one of Goethe's most frequently set texts, the drinking song, 'Mich ergreift, ich weiß nicht wie'.[16] But nowhere is the simultaneous deployment of plucked instrument and pianoforte more charmingly deployed than in Zelter's tinkling account of Goethe's humorous dialogue 'Ich wollt' ich wär' ein Fisch', scored for two voices with zither and pianoforte. Surprisingly the combination of harp and piano, which would have reflected the likely contents of affluent bourgeois and noble households familiar to Goethe, hardly appears. One exception is the *Lieder der Liebe und der Einsamkeit*[17] (Songs of Love and Solitude) by Goethe's associate Reichardt, which are designated *zur Harfe und zum Clavier zu singen* (to be sung to the harp and piano). This is probably intended as an 'and/or' indication. The improvisation of a second accompaniment based on the one given will surely have been self-evident practice in informal *Hausmusik* at the time.

As the 19th century wore on the music critics became increasingly scathing about the guitar and those who wrote for it. In discussing the composer Theodor Gaude, Schilling in *Das Musikalische Europa* (1842) tells us that 'unfortunately he chose the guitar, achieving on that not exactly admirable instrument extraordinary dexterity'. In similar vein Eduard Bernsdorf in *Neues Universal-Lexikon der Tonkunst* (1857) informs us that Gaude was prevented by illness from going to St Petersburg, and that 'sadly certain circumstances (teaching) pushed that dead and limited instrument, the guitar, into his hand'.

Rudest of all is the article in *Erstes Toiletten-Geschenk. Ein Jahrbuch für Damen* (First Toilet Gift. An Annual for Ladies: Leipzig, 1805):

> The delight in achieving fast results seduces us to learn an instrument that can never be other than imperfect, and inevitably soon ruins the music for those listening. Let the guitar keep its place. It is just fine where no other accompaniment is available.

In Britain, Samuel Arnold (1740-1802) in his song 'When I play'd on my Spanish Guittar' viewed the instrument more favourably, namely as an invaluable aid to seduction:

> When I was a lover in Cadiz / I played on my Spanish Guittar
> Which so tickled the ears of the Ladies / who to hear me would flock from afar
> With my o tira, tira, tira / while I simpered and ogled, the Ladies

---

[16] op.cit., catalogue nos. 629 & 255 resp.
[17] op.cit, two collections 1798 & 1804 (961/962).

Who to hear me would flock from afar, as I played on my Spanish Guittar. [18]

These are sentiments that also found resonance in Goethe's witty setting of 'Der Rattenfänger', set as a guitar song by Friedrich Methfessel:

[...] Und wären Mädchen noch so spröde, und wären Weiber noch so blöde,
wird allen doch so liebebang, bei Saitenspiel und bei Gesang.[19]

Here then the dilemma. Can so apparently morally dubious and musically deficient an instrument prove to be an appropriate medium for the texts of a great poet? One can only urge prejudices to be put aside, and judgement to be made by open minds and ears.

---

[18] Arnold's version is also for keyboard accompaniment, with an arrangement for guitar by Zaniboni.
[19] *Kleine Romanzen und Lieder für die Gitarre*, op.6. (Goethe-Museum Düsseldorf, 803). 'For though they once were coy and virgin, both young and old need no more urging; / All jelly-kneed to him they cling, when to his lute they hear him sing.'

358 Goethe: Musical Poet, Musical Catalyst

Schubert/Goethe, 'Heidenröslein', arr. John Feeley

Zeiten des Jahres

Schubert/Goethe, 'Meeresstille', arr. John Feeley

Appendix 2

Appendix 2

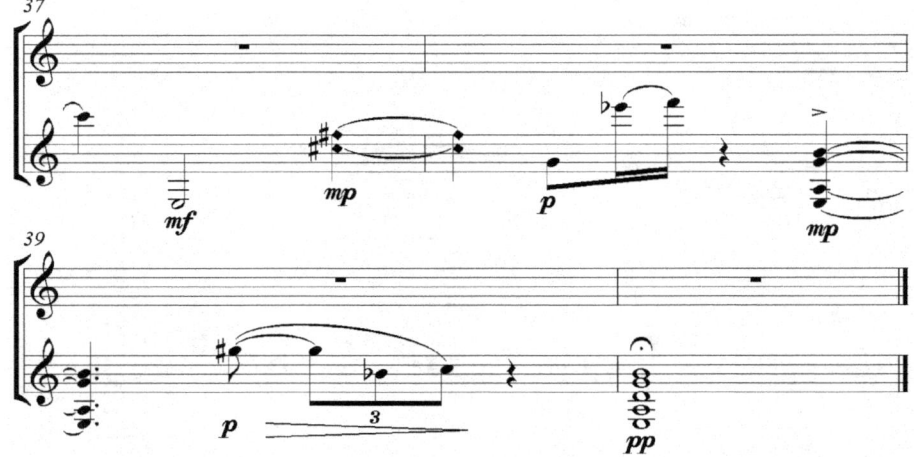

This piece was composed for the launch of the Proceedings, Goethe: Musical Poet, Musical Catalyst, at the Abbey Theatre, Dublin, 25 November 2004. Performers: Lynda Lee (soprano) and John Feeley (guitar).

Index

Abel, Angelika, 203, 206
Abraham, Gerald, 243, 245
Adler, Guido, 204
aestheticism, 282
Ahbe, Thomas, 127
Akademie der Künste, Berlin, 60
Amfortas, 287
androgynous, 236, 238
Anna Amalia (1739-1807)
    'Das Veilchen', 347
Antiochus, 235
Applegate, Celia, 129
Armin, Achim von, 187, 190f., 193
Arnim, Bettina von, 81f., 100f., 185-97, 202
    'Ach neige, du Schmerzenreiche', 198
    'An Luna', 193-95, 197
    'Lied des Hemdchens', 187
    Clemens Brentanos Frühlingskranz, 187
    Goethes Briefwechsel mit einem Kinde, 135, 187
Arnold, Samuel (1740-1802), 83, 207, 278, 352
    'When I play'd on my Spanish Guittar', 351
Auden, W.H., 291

Bach, Carl Philip Emanuel (1714-1788), 62
Bach, David Josef, 216
Bach, Johann Sebastian (1685-1750), 43-46, 60, 62, 169, 242, 270, 276, 284
    Das Wohltemperierte Clavier, 84
    St Matthew Passion, 62
Bailey, Kathryn, 207, 216
Bailey, Robert, 253
Bakhtin, Mikhail (1895-1975), 271
ballad, 82, 103, 110
Barak, Helmut, 7
Bartnig, Hella, 136
Baucis, 149
Bauer, Anton, 40
Bauer, Elisabeth Eleonore, 130
Bayerdörfer, Hans-Peter, 140
Bayerische Staatsbibliothek, Munich, 349, 350
Beale, James, 208
Beautiful Soul, 237

Beecke, Ignaz Franz (1733-1803)
    Claudine von Villa Bella, 39
Beethoven, Ludwig van (1770-1827), 3, 17, 21f., 27, 40, 43, 45, 48, 61f., 66-75, 81-136, 163f., 168, 170, 185, 204, 243f., 278, 284, 288
    'An die ferne Geliebte', 85
    'An die Freude', 81
    'Andenken', 118
    'Mailied', 21
    'Gesang der Mönche', 81
    'Ich denke dein', 3, 119
    'Kennst du das Land', 82, 101f., 107
    'Komm süßer Schlaf', 92
    'Mailied', 22, 74, 76
    'Marmotte', 69
    'Meeresstille und Glückliche Fahrt', 21
    'Mignon', 87, 101
    'Adelaide', 111
    Christus am Ölberge, 60
    Egmont, 3, 40, 88-91, 96
    Fidelio, 87, 122, 126, 130
    Elegischer Gesang, 283
    Fifth Symphony, 45
    Liederheft, 72, 31
    Missa Solemnis, 101
    Sechs Variationen
    Lied mit Veränderungen, WoO 74, 122f.
Begas, Karl, 42
Belgum, Kirsten, 141
Benda, 63
Benda, Jiří Antonín (1722-1795)
    Ariadne, 160
Bent, Ian, 242
Berg, Alban (1885-1933), 205f., 211, 216, 222, 296
Berger, Ludwig (1777-1839), 350
    Vier Gedichte von Goethe und Schiller, 350
Berghahn, Klaus, 147
Berghofer, Wolfgang, 136
Berlin Lieder School (Berliner Liederschule), 26, 72, 75
Berlioz, Hector (1830-1869), 49, 168

Bernd, Josef, 280
Bernsdorf, Eduard
   Neues Universal-Lexikon der Tonkunst, 351
Biba, Otto, 3 f., 7, 39
Bible, 49
Biedermann, F. von, 225
'Bildung', 97, 248, 263, 268
Blackall, Eric A., 102
Bloch, Ernst, 130
Blum, Klaus, 284
Blumenthal, Liselotte, 87, 89
Blümml, Emil Karl, 7
Bodley, Seóirse, 2, 289f., 294ff.
Bohemian folksong, 167
Böhm, Horst, 129, 136
Bone, Philip, 350
Botstein, Leon, 243
Boyle, Nicholas, 3, 166, 225, 233 f., 240, 268
Brahms, Johannes (1833-1897), 208, 280, 284f.
   Alto Rhapsody, 230
   German Requiem, 284
   Beherzigung, 204
   Quintet Op.88, 253
Brandenburg, Sieghard, 22, 139
Brecht, Bertolt (1898-1956), 142
   Der gute Mensch von Sezuan, 153
Breitkopf und Härtel, 90
Britten, Benjamin (1913-1976)
   'Um Mitternacht', 1
Brocken Mountain, 229 f.
Bruch, Max (1838-1920)
   Trauerfeier für Mignon, op.93, 3, 282
Brun, Friederike (1765-1835)
   'Ich denke dein', 110-14
Brunsvik, Therese, 120
Buquoy, Count, 168
Bürger, Christa, 192
Bürger, Gottfried August (1747-94), 348
Busch, Regina, 204
Busoni, Ferrucio (1866-1924)
   Entwurf einer neuen Ästhetik der Tonkunst, 83f.
Byrne, Lorraine, 3, 41, 49, 248, 290, 298

Café Mozart, 348
Calico, Joy Haslam, 129

Canisius, Claus, 3, 69
Capriccio, 169
Carl August, Duke of Saxe-Weimar-Eisenach, 230
Carl Fischer, Music Publishers, 208
Carl Friedrich (1758-1832)
   'Rastlose Liebe', *53*
Carner, Mosco, 243
Čelakovský, František Ladislav, 167
Challier, Ernst
   Grosser Lieder-Katalog. Ein alphabetisch geordnetes Verzeichniss sämmtlicher Einstimmiger Lieder mit Begleitung des Pianoforte, 1
Chamisso, Adelbert von (1781-1838), 160
Chissel, Joan, 245
Chladni, Ernst (1756-1827), 46
Chlorinda, 235
Chopin, Frédéric François (1810-1849), 242, 253, 285
Christ, 3, 147, 225, 233, 237, 239, 287
Christian, 3, 225-29, 233, 273f., 283, 285
Cicero, Marcus Tullius, 87, 97
Cimarosa, Domenico (1749-1801), 40
Claudius, Matthias (1740-1815), 348
Clough, A.H., 232
collegium musicum vocale, 60
Comte, Ferdinand, 186
Cone, Edward T., 210
Contemporary Music Festival, Zürich, 215
Cooper, Barry, 101
Corelli, Archangelo (1653-1713), 63
Couperin, François (1668-1733), 62
Court of Saxe-Weimar, 347
Cox, Gareth, 3,203
Cronos, 227
Czech National Museum, 163
Czech National Theatre, 159
Czechoslovakia, 142
Czerny, Carl (1791-1857), 27, 81, 87
   'Der Erlkönig', 28
   'Des Mädchens Klage', 27
   'Das Geheimnis', 27

D'Agoult, Marie (1805-1876), 193
Dahlhaus, Carl (1928-1989), 243, 284

Danhauser, Joseph, 98
Darwin, Charles (1809-1882), 292
das Bildende, 275
'das Ewig-Leere', 147, 152, 240
'Das Ewig-Weibliche (the Eternal Feminine)', 240f.
Daverio, John, 243-248, 268, 270
DeLong, Kenneth, 168
Dennis, David B., 130
Destiny. See fate
Deutscher Liederhort, 120
Deutsches Allgemeines Sonntagsblatt, 154
Deutsches Theater, Berlin 151
Deym, Josephine, 120, 125
Diabelli, Anton, 27
Diana, 192
Diderot, Denis (1713-1784)
    Neveu de Rameau, 46
Die Reihe, 204, 206, 211
Dieckmann, Christoph, 130
Dieckmann, Friedrich, 127, 135, 138
Dietrichstein, 18, 20-23
Diffenbach, Birgit, 192
Dionysus, 227
Dithyramb, 169
Divine, 241
Divinity, 232, 237
Dohnanyi, Klaus von, 138 f.
Drechsler, Joseph (1782-1852)
    Claudine von Villa Bella, 39
Dresen, Adolf, 142
Dreyschock, Alexander (1818-1869), 169
Dürhammer, Ilija, 9
Dusseck, Johann Ladislaus (1760-1812), 43
Dvořák, 159, 166-169
    Armida, 164

Eberl, Anton (1765-1807) 17, 21, 22, 27
    'Songs with piano accompaniment', op.23
    'Nähe des Geliebten'
    'Der Fischer'
    'An die Entfernte', 17
    'Meeresstille, Glückliche Fahrt', 10
Eberl, Anton (1765-1807) 17
Eberwein, Carl (1786-1831), 349

'Rückkehr', 349
6 Lieder nach Gerstenbergk, 349
Eberwein, Traugott Maximilian (1775-1831), 351
Eckermann, Johann Peter (1792-1854), 46, 82, 204
Eclogue, 169
Eden, 290
Egyptian culture, 273
Eichenauer, Richard, 130
Eichendorff, Joseph Freiherr von (1788-1857), 160
Eichhorn, Andreas, 45
Eimert, Herbert, 204, 206, 211
Einstein, Alfred, 9
Eisler, Riane, 188
Ekenberg, Anders, 276
Empfindsamkeit, 204
Endymion, 193 f.
Engel 140, 143-154
Engel Wolfgang, 140
Enlightenment, 144, 292
Erben, Karel Jaromír, 167
    A Garland of National Tales, 167
    Water Goblin (Vodník), 167
Erk-Böhme
    Deutscher Liederhort, 120
Essl, Karlheinz, 203, 206
Esterházy, Prince, 8
Euphorion, 275
Exile, 290
Eylenstein, Adam
    Lieder von beliebten Dichtern Teutschlands, 347

Farrelly, Daniel J., 140
fate, 235
Fauré Gabriel Urbain (1845-1924), 208
Fibich, Zdeněk (1850-1900), 4, 159f., 164
    Jarní paprs, 160
    'Kennst du das Land', 160
    'Über allen Gipfeln ist Ruh', 160
    Hippodamie, 160
Fischenich, Bartholomäus, 81
Flöricke, Karl, 63
Forkel, Johann Nicolaus (1749-1818), 169

Forte, 212
Franck, César Auguste Jean Guillaume Hubert (1822-1890), 281
Frankfurt, 26, 45, 82 f., 127, 128-30, 135 f., 141, 210, 228, 231, 239, 273, 288
freedom, 84, 91, 93, 127, 131, 134, 138 f., 141 f., 146 f., 151, 191, 236, 291
French Revolution, 131, 136, 153
Frieberth, Karl (1736-1816), 8 f.
Friedländer, Max, 9, 26, 110, 193, 347
Fulbrook, Mary, 135

Gablik, Suzi, 202
Gadamer, Hans-Georg (1900-2002), 88
Gall, Franz Joseph, 97
Ganz, Rudolph, 208
Garlandia, Johannes Gallicus de (ca.1270-1320), 86
Gaskill, P.H., 229
Gaude, Theodor, 351
Geißler, 137
George III, 347
Gesellschaft der Musikfreunde, 8f., 17, 20, 23, 26 f., 167
Gickelhahn, 50 f.
Glauert, Amanda, 3, 100, 270
Gleim, Johann Wilhelm Ludwig (1719-1803), 8
Gluck, Christoph Willibald (1714-1787)
    Iphigénie en Tauride, 60
god, 2, 44, 227, 232-39, 241, 277, 287, 295
Goethe, Christiane (née Vulpius) (1765-1816), 96, 233f.
Goethe, Cornelia (1750-1777), 228
Goethe, Johann Wolfgang von (1749-1832), *passim*
    'An den Mond', 2
    'An die Entfernte', 17, 22, 53
    'An Mignon', 26 An Schwager Kronos, 2
    'An Schwager Kronos', 2
    'Bekenntnisse einer schönen Seele', 231, 276
    'Blumengruß', 203, 208
    Briefe aus der Schweiz, 230
    'Cirrus', 214f.
    Clavigo, 160
    'Das Göttliche', 231

'Das Gastmahl', 47
'Das Geheimnis', 27
Das Jahrmarktsfest zu Plundersweilen, 69
'Des Mädchens Klage', 27
'Das Veilchen', 8, 347
'Der Erlkönig', 27, 167, 170, 205
'Der Fischer', 17, 165f., 350
'Der Rattenfänger', 26, 352
Der Triumph der Empfindsamkeit, 204
Dichtung und Wahrheit, 75, 82
'Die Bothen', 22
Die Leiden des jungen Werthers, 7, 8, 69, 72f., 88, 91, 186, 348
'Die Spinnerin', 2
Die vereitelten Ränke, 40
Egmont, 40, 87-92
Erwin und Elmire, 8, 40
Faust I, 143f.
Faust II, 142, 151, 241
'Ganymed', 2, 227
'Gleich und Gleich', 211
'Glückliche Fahrt', 17, 22, 204
Gott und Welt, 215
'Harzreise im Winter', 26, 230
'Heidenröslein', 26, 170, 187
Hermann und Dorothea, 245, 275
Iphigenie auf Tauris, 233
Italienische Reise, 97
'Jägers Abendlied', 26
Jery und Bätely, 40
'Johanna Sebus', 50
'Kennst du das Land', 22, 82f., 101-103, 107, 160
'Lied des Mephistopheles', 26
'Lotte auf Werthers Grab', 8
'Mailied', 21, 72
'Marmotte', 69, 72
'Meeresstille', 17
'Nähe des Geliebten', 110, 294
Proserpina, 275
'Seefahrt', 228
'Trost in Thränen', 26
'Um Mitternacht', 1
'Wandrers Sturmlied', 227, 231
'Wechsel-Lied zum Tanze', 26

Zur Farbenlehre, 4, 205, 206, 222
Görne, Dieter, 145
Götting, Franz, 82
Gounod, Charles-François, 164
   Faust, 161
Grail, 287
Graun, Carl Heinrich (1703-1756)
   Der Tod Jesu, 60
Grillparzer, Franz (1791-1872), 61, 102
Grimm, Jakob (1785-1863) 185
Grimm, Reinhold, 141, 147
Grimm, Wilhelm (1786-1859), 185
Grosheim, Georg Christoph (1764-1841), 350
Grosser Lieder-Katalog. Ein alphabetisch geordnetes Verzeichniss sämmtlicher Einstimmiger Lieder mit Begleitung des Pianoforte, 1
Großer Redoutensaal, Vienna, 22
Grotewohl, Otto, 141
Gründgens, Gustav, 140, 144, 149
Gruppe der 20, 129
Gugitz, Gustav, 7
Günderode, Caroline von (1780-1806), 192
Gysi, Klaus, 129

Hagedorn, Friedrich von (1798-1754), 348
Hamlet, 143, 151, 236
Handel, Georg Friedrich (1685-1759), 43, 49, 60, 64, 284
   Messiah, 48, 64
   Samson, 49
   Tamerlan, 154
Hänig, Frank, 145
Hanslick, Eduard (1825-1904), 168f., 243
Harder, August, 350
   'An meine Laute', 349
harmony of the spheres, 291
Harnisch, Henriette, 144, 147
Harnisch, Jutta, 145
Harper, 2, 42, 50, 107, 187, 281, 290-92, 299
Harpist, 231, 236, 238
Harrach, Jan, 166
Harrison, Julius, 243
Harz Mountains, 229f., 233
Hassler, Hans Leo (1564-1612), 60

Haydn, Joseph (1732-1809), 8, 39, 43, 61f., 75, 168, 243
   Creation, 60
   Seasons, 60
Hebbel, Friedrich (1813-1863), 286f.
   Requiem, 287
Hegel, Georg Wilhelm Friedrich (1770-1831), 97, 273f., 277
Heidegger, Martin (1889-1976), 88
Heilein, Peter, 132
Heiligenstadt, 91f
Hein, Ludwig, 42
Heine, Heinrich (1795-1856), 1, 160
Heinz, Wolfgang, 142
Herder, Caroline (née Flachsland), 233
Herder, Johann Gottfried (1744-1803), 166f., 225, 275
   Gott. Einige Gespräche, 233
   Kalligone, 275
Hermand, Jost, 141, 147
hermaphrodite, 236
Herwig, W, 225
Herz, Gerhard, 242
Herzfeld, Marianne von, 125
Hiller, Ferdinand von (1811-1885), 62, 99
Hiller, Johann Adam (1728-1804), 69
Hindemith, Paul (1895-1963)
   Cardillac, 215
Hofburgtheater, 7, 39, 40
Hoffmann, E.T.A. (1776-1822), 83, 90, 246
Hofmann, Michael, 127
Hohmann, Christoph, 149
Hölderlin, Johann Christian Friedrich (1770-1843), 229
Hölty, Ludwig Christoph Heinrich (1748-1776), 348
Homer, 227
Honecker, Erich, 128, 136, 151, 154
Hopp, Julius
   Doctor Faust and his little home-made hat, 164
Horace, 99
Horton, John, 243
Horton, Julian, 242
Hössli, Philip, 191, 193
Hostinský, Otakar, 164

hubris, 229
Humboldt, Wilhelm von (1767-1835), 65, 97, 239
Hummel, Johann Nepomuk (1778-1837), 48, 61, 99
Humplik, Josef, 204
Hurka, 349
   'An die Harmonika', 349

Ideal, 191, 239-41
Ilmenau, 50f., 229, 231
Ipsen, Gunther, 206
Irvine, Demar, 208

Jacobi, Fritz H., 225, 227
Jaeger, Michael, 153
Jean Paul, 246
Jeitteles, Alois Brünn (1794-1858), 84, 111
   An die ferne Geliebte, 84
Joachim, Joseph (1831-1907), 101, 217, 284
John the Evangelist, 285
Johnson, Julian, 212, 216f.
Jommelli, Niccolò (1714-1774), 41
Jone, Hildegard, 204, 206, 215f., 222
Jungius, Joachim (1587-1657), 60
Jupiter, 227
Jusdorf, Johann Chr., 350

Kallberg, Jeffrey, 242
Kant, 234, 237, 240
Kant, Immanuel (1724-1804), 88, 212, 234, 237, 239
Kärnten, 205
Kärntnertortheater, 39f.
Kayser, Philipp Christoph (1755-1823), 64
Kerry, Paul E., 226
Kienlen, Johann Christoph (1783-1829), 26, 40
   'An Mignon', 26
   'Der Rattenfänger', 26
   'Heidenröslein', 26
   'Lied des Mephistopheles aus Faust', 26
   'Ritter Curts Brautfahrt', 26
   'Trost in Thränen', 26
   'Wechsel-Lied zum Tanze', 26
   'Wer kauft Liebesgötter', 26

Scherz, List und Rache, 40
Kienzle, Ulrike, 288
Kinderman, William, 253
Kirst-Gundersen, Karoline, 141
Klagenfurt, 208
Klein, Franz, 98
Kleinert, Hugo Wilhelm Paul, 285
Klingemann, August Ernst, 40
Klopstock, Friedrich Gottlob (1724-1803), 275
Klunker, Heinz, 154
Kolar, Josef Jiří, 161, 163f.
Kolneder, Walter, 203, 208
Konrad, Ulrich, 9
Konwitschny, Peter, 154
Körner, Karl Theodor (1791-1813), 2
Korsyn, Kevin, 253
Kosegarten, Ludwig Theobul (1757-1818), 348
Krebs, Harald, 253
Krenek, Ernst (1900-1991), 207, 288
   Der Triumph der Empfindsamkeit, 204
   Jonny spielt auf, 215
Krenz, Egon, 136
Kreutzer, Conradin (1780-1849)
   Jery und Bätely, 40
Krufft, Nikolaus Freiherr von (1779-1818), 23, 24, 27
   'Kennst du das Land', 22
   'Trost in Thränen', 22
Kuberski, Angela, 126
Kühn, Ulrich, 140, 211
Kussi, Peter, 166

La Roche, Georg Michael
   Briefe über das Mönchswesen, 189
La Roche, Maximiliane von (1756-93), 186
La Roche, Sophie von (née Gutermann) (1731-1807), 160
   Die Geschichte des Fräuleine von Sternheim, 186
Laelius, 87
Landshoff, Ludwig, 103
Lavater, Johann Caspar (1741-1801), 97, 233
Leiße, Kerstin, 134
Lemke, Ann Willison, 185, 187, 190f., 194, 201
Lenau, Nikolaus (1802-1850), 160
Leonardo da Vinci

Last Supper, 45
Lessing, Gotthold Ephraim (1729-1781), 89
  Wie die Alten den Tod gebildet, 274
Levesque, Paul, 141
Libussa, 168
Lindpaintner, Peter Josef von (1791-1856), 163f.
Liszt, Franz (1811-1866), 193, 246
Li-Tai-Po, 211
Lobkowitz, Joseph Franz Maximilian Fürst von (1772-1816), 39
Loewe, Johann Carl Gottfried (1796-1869), 49, 170
Loft, A, 168

Magirius, Heinz, 136
Mahl, Bernd, 141
Mahler, Gustav (1860-1911), 9, 204, 215, 240, 253, 286
  Symphony no.8 in E flat Major, 253
Marshall, Kimberley, 186
Martin, Russell, 99
Masaryk, Tomás, 166
Mason, Eudo C., 144, 229
Mattenklott, Gert, 190
Mattheson, Johann (1681-1764)
  Der Vollkommene Kapellmeister, 46
Matthisson, Friedrich von (1761-1831), 112, 118
  'Adelaide', 110, 111
  'Ich denke dein', 112, 114
Mäurer, Bernard Josef, 350
Mayeda, Akio, 84
Mendelssohn, Felix (1809-1847), 43-45, 48f., 62f., 243
  Concerto in A Minor for piano and string orchestra, 62
  Die wandernden Komödiarten, 62
  Der Onkel aus Boston oder Die beiden Neffen, 62
  Die Hochzeit des Camacho, 62
  Double Piano Concerto in A flat Major, 62
  Elijah, 242
  Erste Walpurgisnacht, 204
  Gloria in E flat Major, 62
  Magnificat in D Major, 62

Octet in E flat Major, op.20, 62
Performance of Bach's St Matthew Passion, 44
Piano Quartet in C Minor, op.1, 62
St Paul, 242
Mephistopheles, 26, 140-47, 149, 152-54, 161, 163, 240
metamorphosis, 88
metaphysics, 44, 206
Methfessel, Friedrich, 350
  'An die Laute', 349
  'Der Rattenfänger', 352
Metscher, Thomas, 147
Metzner, Günter
  Heine in der Musik, 1
Meyer, Ernst Friedrich (1791-1838), 46
Meyerbeer, Giacomo (1791-1864), 49
Mielitz, Christine, 127-38, 154f.
Mignon, 2f., 26, 41f., 82-87, 101-104, 107, 160, 170, 236, 242-48, 254, 256, 259, 264, 269-294, 298
Milder-Hauptmann, Pauline Anna (1785-1838), 60
Miller, Norbert, 125
Milton, John (1608-1674), 49
Mintz, Donald, 244
Mitter, Armin, 128
modernity, 144, 153, 285, 291f.
Modrow, Hans, 128-30, 135-37
Möhrmann, Renate, 190
Moldenhauer, Hans and Rosaleen, 203f., 206-208, 211, 214, 216, 222
Mölk, U., 236
Moltke, Carl Melchior Jacob (1783-1831), 50
Monk, Egon, 142
Montuori, Alfonso, 188
moral, 231, 232, 234, 237, 239, 290
Moscheles, Ignaz (1772-1884), 61
Mosel, Ignaz von (1772-1844), 26
  'Sehnsucht. Aus dem Roman Wilhelm Meisters Lehrjahre', 26
  'Jägers Abendlied', 26
Mozart, Wolfgang Amadeus (1756-1791), 9, 17, 21, 43, 62, 169, 270
  Die Zauberflöte, 9, 60

Don Giovanni, 161, 168
Marriage of Figaro, 60
Il Seraglio, 48
Requiem, 60, 62, 275
Müller, Friedrich von, 185
Müller, Heiner (1929-1995)
  Hamletmaschine, 151
Müller-Blattau, Joseph, 72, 81, 286
Murray, Edward, 212
Muses, 186
Musikblätter des Anbruch, 211

nature, 17, 43, 46, 72, 91, 187, 203-206, 211f., 217, 222, 233, 291
Nauhaus, Gerd, 244
Neefe, Christian Gottlob (1748-1798), 69, 89
Neoplatonism, 291
Neumann, Amalie, 193
Newcomb, Anthony, 244
Newlin, Dika, 253
Nicoli, Otto, 49
Nostitz, Count, 161
Nowak, Adolf, 3, 272, 280, 284

Odysseus, 290
Oehlke, Waldemar, 185
Offenbach, Jacques (1819-1880), 162
opera, 8, 26, 39f., 45, 63, 89, 91, 127-138, 160-66, 193, 243, 246, 247
  Berlin, 60
  Dresden, 127, 132
  Prague, 159
  Vienna, 39
  Weimar, 48
Orestes, 231, 238
Orpheus, 290, 291
Ossian, 275
Osthoff, Wolfgang, 278
Otto, Jakob Ernst, 347
Ovid, 291

Pachelbel, Johann (1653-1706), 60, 62
Paganini, Niccolò (1782-1840), 61, 168
Palast der Republik, 130

Palestrina, Giovanni Perluigi da (ca. 1525-1594), 48, 60
Pasqualati, Baron von, 283
Paul Sacher Stiftung, Basel, 206
Perrey, Beate, 271
Philomel, 111
Pichler, Caroline (1769-1843), 7f.
Pietism, 226f.
Pindar (522 BC-443 BC), 81, 227
Platonism, 291
Pluto, 233
Polnauer, Josef, 204
Polzelli, Anton (1763-1855), 39
Potter, Pamela, 129
Prague Provisional Theatre, 159-166
Prometheus, 3, 227, 275
Protestantism, 3, 225, 272, 274, 283-85, 287
Pückler-Muskau, Hermann von, 101
puppet play, 161
Purser, Ronald, 188

Quandt, J.G. von
  'Der König in Thule', 351

rationalism, 144
Reed, T.J., 226
Reich, Willi, 205, 207, 211f.
Reich, Wolfgang, 273
Reichardt, Johann Friedrich (1752-1814), 20f., 26, 50, 64, 103, 105, 114, 120, 349,
  Lieder der Liebe und der Einsamkeit, 351
  'Kennst du das Land', 103, 105
  'Ich denke dein', 117
Reichenbach Waterfall, 230
Reinhardt, Hartmut, 125
religion, 3, 226, 239, 282
requiem, 3, 60, 62, 242-47, 253-56, 259, 264, 267-71, 276, 278-86
resurrection, 274, 276
Retzer, Joseph Friedrich Freiherr von, 17
Rexroth, Dieter, 205, 211
Riehn, Rainer, 203
Riemer, Friedrich Wilhelm (1774-1845), 65, 225
Ries, Ferdinand (1754-1812), 81
Rink, John, 242

Rittersberku, Jan Ritter z, 167
Rochlitz, Johann Friedrich (1769-1842), 22, 48
   Die Entwickelung des Messias, 48
romanticism, 168
Rorty, Richard, 292
Rosenlöcher, Thomas, 128
Ross, Corey, 135
Rossini, Giacchomo (1792-1868), 61, 281
   Tancredi, 60
   Wilhelm Tell, 60
   Othello, 60
   The Siege of Corinth, 60
   La Gazza Ladra, 61
   Petite Messe Solennelle, 281
Royal Academy of Religious Music, Berlin, 60
Rubinstein, Anton, 3, 281f.
   Die Gedichte und das Requiem für Mignon aus Goethes Wilhelm Meisters Lehrjahre, op.91, 281
Rückert, Friedrich (1788-1866), 160
Ruprecht, Josef Martin (1756-1800)
   Erwin und Elmire, 40

Sabina, Karel, 162
Sächsische Neueste Nachrichten, 137, 139
Sächsische Staatsoper (Semperoper) 127, 132f.
Sächsische Zeitung, 134
Sächsisches Hauptstaatsarchiv, 128
Saint-Saëns, Charles Camille (1835-1921), 281
Salieri, Antonio (1750-1825), 61
Salmen, Walter, 103
Sams, Eric, 244
Samson, Jim, 208, 242, 253
Scarlatti, Domenico (1685-1757), 62, 242
Schäffner, Christina, 136
Scheidt, Samuel (1587-1654), 62
Schenker, Heinrich, 242
Schering, Arnold, 278
Schicksal. See fate
Schikaneder, Emmanuel (1751-1812), 39f.
Schiller, Friedrich (1759-1805), 2, 81, 89, 164, 204, 234, 236, 348, 350f.
   'An die Freude', 81
   'Mädchen aus der Fremde', 350
   The Bride of Messina, 160, 164

Wallenstein, 161
Wilhelm Tell, 81, 146
Schilling, Gustav (1805-1880)
   Das Musikalische Europa, 351
Schlegel, Caroline von, 190
Schlosser, Johann Georg (1739-1799), 46
Schmidt, Hans, 121
Schneider, Max, 276
Schoenberg, Arnold (1874-1951), 83, 204f., 216, 253
   Vier Stücke für gemischten Chor, 216
Schöne, Albrecht, 230, 240
Schopenhauer, Arthur (1778-1860), 284
Schröder-Devrient, Wilhelmine (1804-1860), 61
Schubert, Franz (1797-1828), 2f., 17, 21-23, 26f., 39, 48f., 169f., 205, 226, 288, 349
   'An den Mond', 2
   'An die Laute', 349
   'An Schwager Kronos', 2
   Claudine von Villa Bella, D239, 39
   'Der Erlkönig', 170
   'Der Fischer', 17
   'Die Spinnerin', 2
   'Ganymed', 2
   'Jägers Abendlied',26
   'Rastlose Liebe', 26
   'Sehnsucht. Aus dem Roman: *Wilhelm Meisters Lehrjahre*', 26
Schubring, Adolf, 247
Schumann, Clara (née Wieck) (1819-1896), 168
Schumann, Robert (1810-1856), 242-49, 253-56, 259, 263f., 263-71, 278-85
   Das Paradies und die Peri, 243
   Der Rose Pilgerfahrt, 246
   Die Lieder Mignons, des Harfners und Philinens, 278
   Genoveva, 243, 245f.
   Lieder, Gesänge und Requiem für Mignon, 245
   Manfred, 243, 245f.
   Märchen, 247
   Papillons, 246
   Szenen aus Goethes Faust, 161, 270, 243
   Requiem für Mignon, 244, 249
Schüremann, G., 81, 87
Schütz, Heinrich (1585-1672), 62, 276, 284

Schütz, Johann Heinrich Friedrich (1779-1829), 43f.
Schwab, Heinrich W., 101, 110
Schwabe, Uwe, 127
secularization, 226
Seidel, S., 236
self-estrangement, 291
Semper, Gottfried, 127, 136
Semperoper. See Sächische Staatsoper
Seyfried, Ignaz (1776-1841), 40
Shreffler, Anne C., 205, 212, 214
Simms, Bryan, 205
Simpson, Robert, 243
Simrock Music Publishers, 81
Sing-Akademie zu Berlin, 60, 64
Singspiel, 39f., 40, 75
Smaczny, Jan, 3, 159-63
Smetana, Bedřich (1824-1884), 4, 159-61, 165f.
    'Der Fischer' (in Czech, Rybář), 165
    Doktor Faust, 160
    Judgement of Libuše, 165
    Vltava, 166
    The Bartered Bride, 161f.
    The Brandenburgers in Bohemia, 162
Society of the Tower, 238
solitude, 2, 189, 297
Sontag, Henrietta Gertrude Walpurgis (1806-1854), 60
soul, 46, 73, 88, 91f., 111, 147, 187, 274, 287, 291
Spinoza, Benedictus de (1632-1677), 241
Spohr, Louis (1784-1859), 170
    Faust, 40
    Macbeth, 60
Spontini, Gasparo Luigi Pacifico (1774-1851), composer, director of the Royal Opera 60, 61, 193, 197
    Cortes, 60f.
    La Vestale, 60f.
    Olympia, 69
Stadtbibliothek zu Berlin, 1
Staehelin, Martin, 9
Staritz, Dietrich, 129
Staubbach, 230
Steblin, Rita, 270

Steffan, Joseph Anton (1726-1797), 8
Stein, Charlotte Ernestine von (née Scharst), 125, 228, 230-33
Stein, F.
    Zehn Lieder mit Begleitung der Guitarre, 350
Steiner, Sigmund Anton (publisher), 22, 26, 203
Sternfeld, Frederick, 102, 110
Stiehler, Volker, 127
Stieler, Joseph Karl (1781-1858), 66
Stolberg, Countess, 228
Stolberg, Friedrich Leopold, Graf zu Stolberg (1750-1819), 192
'Storm and Stress'. See *Sturm und Drang*
Strauss, Johann (1825-1899), 162
Streicher, Theodor, 282
Streitwolf, Johann Heinrich (1779-1837), 350
Streller, Friedbert, 134
Stübing, Adolf, 287
Sturm und Drang, 84
Suphan, Bernhard, 275
Sušil, František, 167
Swales, Martin, 135
Switzerland, 230
Sym, C. Melvil, 125

Tancred, 236
Tappert, Wilhelm, 347
Tartini, Giuseppi (1692-1770), 63
Tasso, Torquato (1544-1595)
    Gerusalemme liberata, 88, 164, 235
Telemann, Georg Philipp (1681-1767), 62
Tennyson, Lord Alfred (1809-1892), 164
Teplitz, 69, 96, 97, 100, 101
Theater an der Wien, 40
theology, 226-31, 234, 241
Thomson, James (1700-1748)
    'Summer', 102
Tieck, Ludwig (1773-1853), 144, 192
Todd, R. Larry, 243, 246
Tomášek, 3, 101, 159, 160, 167, 168, 169, 170
    'Der Erlkönig', 178
    'Heidenröslein', 170f.
    'Mignons Sehnsucht', 175
Tovey, Donald Francis, 243
Trunz, Erich, 227, 272, 275, 285

Tyrrell, John, 162, 166

Ulbricht, Walter, 141f, 145, 151
Umlauf, Ignaz (1746-1796)
  Die Schöne Schusterin, 75
Unger, Friederike Helene (née Rothenburg), 48
Universal Edition, 204f., 216
Urich, Karin, 128, 130
Urzidil, Johannes, 160, 168

Varnhagen von Ense, Rahel (1771-1833), 190, 225
Verdi, Giuseppi (1813-1901), 162
Vienna Court Theatre, 39, 89
Viennese Singakademie, 284
Viëtor-Engländer, Deborah, 141-43
Virgil, 291
Vivaldi, Antonio (1678-1741), 62
Vogl, Michael, 26
Vogler, Georg Joseph (Abbé) (1749-1814)
  Requiem, 276
Volkstheater, 140
Volkstümlichkeit, 2
Vrchlický, Jaroslav (1853-1912), 164

Wagner, Herbert, 127
Wagner, Richard (1813-1883), 91, 128, 140, 160, 165f., 168, 204, 284
  Das Rheingold, 210
Walker, Alan, 245
Walser, Martin, 136, 137
Wayne, Philip, 141, 143
Weber, Carl Maria von (1786-1826)
  Euryanthe, 63
Weber, Carl Maria von (1786-1826), 64
Weber, Friedrich Dionys, 167
Webern, Anton (1883-1945), 4, 203-13, 222, 288
  Zur Farbenlehre, 204
Webern, Maria (Webern's daughter), 205
Weigl, Joseph (1766-1846)
  Die Schweizerfamilie, 61
Weimar Court Theatre, 39

Welleck, René, 165
Wessely, Othmar, 40
Whittall, Arnold, 207
Widor, Charles-Marie (18844-1937), 281
Wieland, Christoph Martin (1733-1813)
  Geschichte des Agathon, 8, 160
Wildgans, Friedrich, 203f.
Willemer, Marianne von, 87
Williams, Briony, 3, 185
Winkelmann, Johann Joachim (1717-1768), 48, 65
Winter, Peter von (1754-1825)
  Scherz, List und Rache, 40
Wolf, Ernst Wilhelm (1735-1792), 347
  51 Lieder der besten deutschen Dichter, 208
Wolf, Friedrich August, 49
Wolf, Hugo (1860-1903), 204
Wolle, Stefan, 128
Wranitzky, Paul (1736-1808)
  Oberon, 39
  König der Elfen, 39
Wübbolt, Georg, 205

Yeats, W.B., 291
Youens, Susan, 1

Závodský, Artur, 167
Zelter, Carl Friedrich (1758-1832), 3, 20, 26, 41-50, 60, 61-65, 97, 103, 106, 111-15, 205, 208, 277
  'An die Entfernte', 53
  'Das Gastmahl', 47
  'Gleich und Gleich', 50
  'Harper's Klage', 50
  'Johanna Sebus', 50
  'Rastlose Liebe' 53
  'Wandrers Nachtlied', 52
  Viola Concerto in E flat Major, 63
Zentrum für Theaterdokumentation, Akademie der Künste, Berlin, 132
Zeus, 193, 227
Zuber, Barbara, 203, 206
Zumsteeg, Johann Rudolf (1760-1802), 350

www.ingramcontent.com/pod-product-compliance
Lightning Source LLC
Chambersburg PA
CBHW071224230426
43668CB00011B/1293